SOCIETY FOR NEW TESTAMENT STUDIES
MONOGRAPH SERIES
General Editor: R. McL. Wilson, F.B.A.
Associate Editor: M. E. Thrall

44

THE REVIVAL OF THE GRIESBACH HYPOTHESIS

The Revival of
the Griesbach Hypothesis

An analysis and appraisal

C. M. TUCKETT
Lecturer in New Testament Studies
The University of Manchester

CAMBRIDGE UNIVERSITY PRESS
CAMBRIDGE
LONDON · NEW YORK · NEW ROCHELLE
MELBOURNE · SYDNEY

Published by the Press Syndicate of the University of Cambridge
The Pitt Building, Trumpington Street, Cambridge CB2 1RP
32 East 57th Street, New York, NY 10022, USA
296 Beaconsfield Parade, Middle Park, Melbourne 3206, Australia

© Cambridge University Press 1983

First published 1983

Printed in Great Britain by
Redwood Burn Ltd
Trowbridge, Wiltshire

Library of Congress catalogue card number: 81-6128

British Library Cataloguing in Publication Data
Tuckett, C. M.
The revival of the Griesbach hypothesis.
- (Society for New Testament studies monograph series; 44)
I. Title   II. Series
226'.304   BS 2585.2
ISBN 0-521-23803-X

CONTENTS

v

ACKNOWLEDGEMENTS

An earlier version of the present study was accepted as a Ph.D. thesis by the University of Lancaster in 1979, and the present book is an abbreviated version of that thesis. I owe an enormous debt of gratitude to my supervisor, Dr D. R. Catchpole, whose unfailing kindness and helpful criticism at every stage of my research have provided a constant source of support and encouragement. Whilst none of the shortcomings of this book is due to him, his insistence on the highest standards of logical rigour in any form of argument has provided me with an ideal to which I can aspire but rarely attain. I would also like to thank the Governing Body of Queens' College, Cambridge, for electing me into a Bye-Fellowship in the middle of my period of study, enabling me to give more time to the research necessary for this book. Although I have often disagreed with him, I would like to thank Professor Farmer: he has been generous with his time on a number of occasions in discussing his views with me, and he has also kindly made available to me a number of his unpublished papers. The Reverend Robert Morgan provided the initial stimulus which enabled me to start thinking about starting post-graduate research and his constant encouragement has proved invaluable. The editors of the Monograph series, Professor Wilson and Dr Thrall, made very helpful suggestions for preparing my original thesis for publication and I am very grateful to them. Finally, I must thank my wife, but for whose encouragement and patience this book would never have been begun, continued or ended.

C. M. Tuckett
Manchester
December, 1979

NOTE ON ABBREVIATIONS

The following abbreviations have been employed in the book:

GH	Griesbach hypothesis
2DH	Two-document hypothesis
MattR	Matthean redaction
MkR	Markan redaction
LkR	Lukan redaction
ET	English translation
LXX	Septuagint
MT	Massoretic Text

A set of figures in the form 5 - 2 - 3, referring to a Greek word, indicates that the word occurs 5 times in Matthew, 2 times in Mark, 3 times in Luke. A set of figures in the form 5 - 2 - 3 + 4 indicates that the word also occurs 4 times in Acts.

A full list of abbreviations of journals etc. appears at the end of the book with the Notes and Bibliography. Articles and books are referred to in the notes with only an abbreviated reference. Full references for each work cited are to be found in the Bibliography.

INTRODUCTION

The subject of this book is the contemporary revival of the Griesbach hypothesis, i.e. the hypothesis that, of the three synoptic gospels, Matthew was written first, Luke was written second in dependence on Matthew, and finally Mark was written using both Matthew and Luke. This old hypothesis about the relative order of the gospels has been revived recently by a number of scholars, notably by W. R. Farmer. Farmer's main contribution to the debate has been the publication of his book *The Synoptic Problem* in 1964, and since then he has indicated his continuing belief in the Griesbach hypothesis in a number of other articles. Other studies have brought forward additional arguments which might support the Griesbach hypothesis from a number of different angles: these include the works of G. W. Buchanan, O. L. Cope, D. L. Dungan, T. R. W. Longstaff, B. Orchard and H. H. Stoldt. (See the bibliography for details.) Farmer's work has aroused a new interest in the Synoptic Problem, and doubts have been raised about how firmly the traditional solution, i.e. the two-document hypothesis, is based. By the 'two-document hypothesis' is meant the theory that Mark was written first and was a common source for Matthew and Luke, and that the latter two gospels also made independent use of common source material, usually abbreviated as 'Q'. This hypothesis was developed during the middle of the nineteenth century, and since then has received widespread acceptance. Moreover, it has been the basic assumption behind much recent redaction criticism, and hence doubts about its validity must call into question the value of a great deal of such work. Attempts to question the traditional solution to the Synoptic Problem are thus extremely important and have very far-reaching implications.

This study attempts to analyse some of the current debate about the Griesbach hypothesis and the implied criticism of the two-document hypothesis. In his original book, Farmer devoted a considerable amount of space to an examination of the history of the study of the Synoptic Problem, and so some aspects of that history are examined briefly in Part I. In the rest of this study, the gospel texts are examined to see if the Griesbach hypothesis can be adequately supported there. In Part II, various general considerations are treated, including the arguments of supporters of the Griesbach hypothesis. In Part III, some individual pericopes are analysed in detail to see which source hypothesis can best explain the detailed wording of the texts.

PART I SOME ASPECTS OF THE HISTORY
OF THE STUDY OF THE SYNOPTIC PROBLEM

All the proponents of the Griesbach hypothesis (GH) in its contemporary revival are well aware that they are advocating nothing new. The hypothesis itself was first put forward in 1764 by Henry Owen,[1] but its present name derives from its adoption by J. J. Griesbach at the end of the eighteenth century.[2] However, during the second half of the nineteenth century, it was generally discounted in favour of the theory of Markan priority, and since then it was only rarely advocated until 1964. The major part of W. R. Farmer's book, *The Synoptic Problem*, is devoted to analysing some of the history of the study of the Synoptic Problem over the last two hundred years, looking in particular at the way in which the GH was gradually rejected, and the two-document hypothesis (2DH) adopted, by nearly all scholars. The implication drawn is that an analysis of the history of research may offer some justification for reviving the GH and reconsidering its merits in the modern discussion.[3]

One of the results of Farmer's historical survey is the claim that extra-scientific factors were at work in the establishment of the 2DH, and in this respect the recent work of H. H. Stoldt has come to similar conclusions.[4] The most significant developments occurred initially in Germany in the early part of the nineteenth century, where there was a growing consensus, following the work of Sieffert, that Matthew's gospel was written after the eye-witness period.[5] Thus, if Matthew was the first gospel to be written (as the GH maintained) then none of the synoptic gospels was an eye-witness account. Hence, if the historicity of the fourth gospel was questioned, there was no reliable point of contact with the historical foundations of Christianity.[6] Next, the GH was adopted by Strauss, Baur and other members of the so-called 'Tübingen school', and was used by them to develop their theories which resulted in radical scepticism about the historical reliability of the gospels. The demise of the Tübingen school was then an important factor in the general loss of support for the GH. Farmer writes: 'The real enemy was the Tübingen school and only incidentally the Griesbach hypothesis, which Baur had accepted. But there can be no doubt that the Griesbach hypothesis lost "popular" support with the collapse of the Tübingen school.'[7]

The GH was generally replaced by the 2DH, and Farmer claims that the latter satisfied a theological need: for it established a basis for the historicity of at least the Markan narrative in the face of both the generally accepted view that Matthew was written after the eye-witness period and also the overall scepticism of the Tübingen school. Farmer refers to Weisse's work of 1838 (where what was essentially the 2DH was first proposed) as 'a constructive attempt to enable Christianity to lay claim to eye-witness accounts through Mark and the *Logia*'.[8] Similarly, for Holtzmann and his readers, the priority of Matthew was never considered as a serious option, simply because it was written after the eye-witness period and 'therefore was not suitable to be used as a primary source in the quest of the historical Jesus'.[9]

The implication is that the GH has never received a fair hearing, indeed that it was summarily rejected because it could provide no eye-witness account of the gospel events, and because of its association with the radical scepticism of the Tübingen school. Further, its main rival, the 2DH, also gained in popularity at its expense because the ideas of the two proposed basic sources, Mark and Q, appeared to provide 'historical' support for the prevailing dogmatic ideas of the time.[10] Farmer never gives any details in his writings about any arguments which were brought against the GH during this earlier period.[11] Insofar as he claims that his historical survey is 'to help the reader understand that this view [i.e. the GH] was abandoned in favor of another that was less satisfactory, for reasons which scholars would not now justify'[12], this implies that either no criticisms of the GH existed (apart from the question of historical reliability and the eye-witness nature of the material), or, if they did, they were not worth recording in any historical survey which aimed to show, at least in part, why the GH was abandoned.

In fact a study of the history of the debate in this period does not support Farmer's claims.[13] First, there was clearly no integral, necessary connection between the GH and the theories of the Tübingen school. Although the GH was adopted by Strauss, Schwegler and Baur,[14] other members of the school could work with different source hypotheses, without altering the basic presuppositions that all three gospels were relatively late documents, theologically motivated and not necessarily eye-witness accounts of the events they describe. Thus, Hilgenfeld consistently held to the Augustinian hypothesis;[15] Ritschl was converted to Markan priority in 1851;[16] Köstlin postulated the existence of an early Petrine version of Mark used by Matthew, even if our Mark was still the last to be written;[17] finally Volkmar adopted Markan priority in his work of 1857.[18]

Then secondly, there is no evidence that either the adoption of the GH by Strauss or Baur, or the desire to rescue the eye-witness nature of at least some of the tradition, had any influence at all in the general rejection of the GH and the adoption of Markan priority. The GH had never been universally accepted even before the work of Sieffert and Strauss. C. G. Storr had already argued against the GH, and indeed had argued for the priority of Mark, as early as 1786.[19] No concern about historicity in general, or the theories of the Tübingen school in particular, is discernible in Lachmann's article of 1835 which sought to show the originality of the Markan order.[20] Nor is there evidence for such a concern in the works of Wilke and Weisse in 1838, advocating Markan priority.[21] It is quite clear that Wilke had formed his views at least twelve years earlier, i.e. well before the appearance of Strauss' work.[22] Further, he was totally unconcerned about the question of historical reliability or the eye-witness nature of the tradition: he believed that Mark was the earliest gospel, but it was *not* the work of an eye-witness and indeed its presentation was determined more by general principles than by historical accuracy.[23] Weisse, too, believed that Mark's gospel was not an eye-witness account, and he thought that the vivid details of Mark's presentation were historically worthless.[24] Further, his explicit concern to refute Strauss had nothing to do with the GH: it was solely to do with Strauss' adoption of the 'tradition hypothesis', i.e. the theory that there had been a long period of oral tradition which had reached fixed written form only in the mid-second century.[25]

The situation is no different in the case of the two later leading proponents of the 2DH, Holtzmann and B. Weiss. Holtzmann followed Weisse in asserting the non-eye-witness character of Mark,[26] and Weiss also conceded the secondary nature of Mark, for the latter was, according to his theory, preceded by a primitive 'Ur-Matthew'.[27] The treatment by Holtzmann and Weiss of the adoption of the GH by the Tübingen school is also significant. It is clear that both scholars were aware that the GH had a history of its own, and that it had been adopted by others quite independently of the Tübingen school. Hence both scholars took care to present detailed arguments against the GH as proposed by Griesbach, De Wette, Bleek and others, and to separate them from those they used against the use of the hypothesis by Baur and others in the Tübingen school.[28]

Thus real arguments were brought against the GH during this period, and these were believed to be sufficiently cogent to warrant the rejection of the hypothesis, quite independently of the latter's adoption by the

Tübingen school and of the question of the eye-witness nature of the tradition. Many of these arguments were essentially that Mark's alleged procedure, according to the GH, seemed to have no inner consistency and no obvious motivation. Mark was alleged to have conflated his sources on some occasions with very great care (e.g. Mk. i. 32), and yet at other times he failed to do so.[29] Similarly, Griesbach had thought that Mark's order and choice of material could be explained by Mark's switching between his two sources, and had claimed that good reasons could be given for the precise changes involved.[30] However, Weiss showed that these reasons were unsatisfactory and did not adequately explain Mark's alleged procedure in detail.[31] None of these arguments is mentioned by Farmer and, insofar as part of the aim of his historical survey is to show how and why the GH was abandoned (as well as why the 2DH was accepted), this constitutes a gap in his presentation. Simply to return to the GH, partly on the grounds that the hypothesis was unfairly rejected in the past, is therefore not possible.

The rest of Farmer's historical survey concerns the increasing acceptance of the 2DH, especially in England. In particular, he seeks to show that all defences of the hypothesis were ultimately dependent on the argument from order, but that gradually the terms of reference of the argument were disastrously changed.[32] This appealed to the lack of agreement in order between Matthew and Luke against Mark, and deduced from this the originality of the Markan order. At first the argument was used assuming the existence of a common *Grundschrift* lying behind all three gospels, and on these terms the argument has some validity. However, the difference between Mark and the assumed *Grundschrift* gradually disappeared and the two were identified, and at this point the argument becomes logically fallacious.[33] The dominant role implicitly played by the argument from order in the establishment of the 2DH means that the theory is built on a logically impossible foundation.

A detailed discussion of the history of the debate will not be given here, since it is perhaps more relevant to a study of the 2DH than of the GH.[34] Nevertheless, two brief points need to be mentioned. First, there are at least two quite distinct arguments from order and these should not be confused. There is the argument which appeals to the lack of agreement between Matthew and Luke against Mark. But there is also an argument which appeals to the disagreements in order, and claims that good reasons can be found for the changing of Mark's order by Matthew and Luke, but not vice versa. It is this argument which was used by Lachmann and many others after him.[35] This argument is, of course, not dependent for its validity on the existence of a common *Grundschrift*, and hence does not become fallacious when Mark is identified with the assumed *Grund-schrift*.[36] Secondly, the argument which does appeal to the lack of agreement between Matthew and Luke against Mark is a fallacy only in its logic. The conclusion of the argument (i.e. Markan priority) is not inconsistent with the premiss: the fallacy lies only in the assumption that this is the only conclusion possible.[37] Thus this argument from order would still have some validity if other hypotheses, equally consistent with the facts, were rejected on other grounds. The argument might not be logically probative, but it could still have value if supported by other considerations. And indeed this is the way in which the argument has been used by advocates of Markan priority: for example, Abbott and Woods both recognised that the GH was a logically possible explanation of the facts and they offered quite independent reasons for rejecting it.[38]

The relevance of some of these considerations will be seen later when the arguments themselves are examined. Nevertheless, it is also worth noting that study of the history of research can have only limited value in seeking to solve the Synoptic Problem today. Arguments used in the past cannot necessarily be simply repeated without alteration. Presuppositions change, and what might have been an acceptable argument in the past is no longer so today. For example, one of Griesbach's strongest arguments against Markan priority was based on the unquestioned assumption that the author of the first gospel was the apostle Matthew: hence it was inconceivable that he should be dependent on the work of someone who was not an eye-witness.[39] Such an argument worked within acceptable presuppositions in the eighteenth century, but would probably find few defenders today. Further, a demonstration that some particular defence of, say, the 2DH is weak can neither disprove the validity of the hypothesis itself,[40] nor in itself establish the validity of any other source hypothesis. Study of the history of research may help one to recognise where the strengths and weaknesses of different hypotheses have been felt to lie, but one must in the end examine the text itself to see which is the best explanation of the source question. Such is the aim of the rest of this book.

1 CRITERIA

Before examining the text itself, some methodological questions must be considered. In particular, there is the problem of what criteria one can legitimately use to decide about literary priority. Very often the evidence is ambiguous and open to more than one interpretation. For example, in the case of Mark's 'duplicate expressions', where Mark has A+B and where Matthew had A and Luke has B, one can explain this in diametrically opposite ways: either Mark has conflated Matthew and Luke, or both Matthew and Luke have independently abbreviated Mark's apparent redundancy. Each theory explains the facts in one particular example. One requires, therefore, some more wide-ranging criteria for deciding between different possible explanations in any one case.

In this respect, the study of the Synoptic Problem is very similar to the study of the historical Jesus in its attempt to decide what is authentic in the gospel tradition. Both fields of study are concerned with seeking to distinguish between early material and later adaptations. The areas of study differ: historical Jesus research is concerned with the period from Jesus up to that of the earliest gospel, whereas study of the Synoptic Problem is concerned with the period from the earliest synoptic gospel to the latest. Nevertheless, the fundamental similarity in aim means that many of the methodological insights gained in one area can usefully be applied in the other. In the study of the historical Jesus, a great deal of work has been done in analysing and refining the various criteria which can usefully be employed.[1] In fact, analogous criteria can be, and often have been, applied to the study of the Synoptic Problem. The parallelism between the two areas of study means that criticisms of the criteria in one area can, in some cases, be transferred to the other area.

Farmer himself gave four criteria, or 'canons of criticism', for use in the study of the Synoptic Problem, to add to the six from the work of Burton.[2] Farmer proposed that (1) traditions which do not reflect a Jewish or Palestinian provenance are secondary to those which do; (2) a more specific tradition is secondary to a less specific one; (3) forms of a tradition with explanatory redactional glosses are secondary to those without; (4) a feature which is clearly redactional in one gospel is secondary to a parallel tradition which lacks this; and further, as a corollary, where a tradition in one gospel retains a feature which is clearly redactional in a parallel text, then the former is secondary. This section of Farmer's work has been acclaimed by Fuller as one of the most important parts of the book: he writes that Farmer 'established invaluable direction indicators which must now be used in all synoptic work, regardless of what solution we favour'.[3] Nevertheless, not all these criteria are above criticism. In the second edition of *The Synoptic Problem*, Farmer himself withdrew the second criterion, concerning 'more specific' traditions, in the light of the work of E. P. Sanders.[4] His third criterion, referring to explanatory redactional glosses, is also questionable and it may not always give a clear-cut line of chronological development. It may be that some explanations, felt to be necessary for the audience of an earlier gospel, were considered superfluous for the audience of a later writer. Explanatory redactional glosses may thus say more about the different intended audiences of the gospel writers than about their relative dates.

Similar criticisms can be made of Farmer's first criterion, referring to the 'Jewishness' of a tradition. For example, the note in Mk. vii. 3f. is almost certainly a redactional gloss, explaining Jewish customs for a non-Jewish audience, and this is lacking in Matthew. However, it would be wrong to conclude from this alone that Mark's version is secondary to Matthew's.[5] It probably implies only that Matthew's audience was better acquainted with Judaism than Mark's. An appeal to Matthew's 'Jewishness' in this respect does not substantiate the claim that it was precisely Matthew's version to which Mark added his explanatory gloss. To assume that the whole gospel tradition underwent a simple, unilinear development from a Jewish to a non-Jewish provenance imposes too rigid a scheme on the historical, geographical and cultural influences which are now known to have been at work. The widespread interpenetration of Jewish and Hellenistic ideas, both inside and outside Palestine in the first century A.D., precludes any neat theory of a move by the church from a Palestinian, 'Jewish' milieu to a non-Palestinian, 'Hellenistic' one.[6] Besides, the Christian church continued to exist on Palestinian soil in close contact with Judaism for some time. One may not assume, therefore, that all later writers were non-Jewish, or, conversely, that all non-Jewish Christian writers must be later than Jewish ones. There is thus no *a priori* reason why any particular tradition could not have been 're-Judaised', or why explanatory glosses, originally added for Gentile readers, could not have been excised by an evangelist writing for a community well acquainted with Judaism.[7] This criterion of the 'Jewishness' of a tradition is very similar to the criterion of 'Aramaisms' in the quest for the historical Jesus. However, exactly parallel criticisms have been made there: an Aramaism in the tradition need show only an origin in an Aramaic-speaking community, rather than in Jesus' own words.[8] So then, in the study of the Synoptic Problem also, 'Jewishness' and 'glosses' can only be used with care to decide on the question of literary priority.

Farmer's fourth criterion, about redactional elements in one gospel appearing in a parallel tradition, is perhaps the most useful. In itself it is not new, as it was used prominently in the debates of the Tübingen school. For example, it was the basic presupposition in Zeller's linguistic arguments for the GH,[9] and Ritschl was appealing essentially to this criterion in arguing for the priority of Mark.[10] Fuller suggests that this legacy from the Tübingen school may be a 'criterion of permanent value' if only because, unlike so many other arguments used, this one is not reversible.[11] In many respects it is analogous to the criterion of 'dissimilarity' in historical Jesus research: where there is a parallel between a gospel saying and an idea in either Judaism or the early church, one suspects that the latter might be the source of the former. So too, in the Synoptic Problem, if a dominant Markan motif appears in a Lukan parallel, one deduces that Luke's text is dependent on Mark. This is certainly a very valuable criterion in view of its irreversibility. It is also, however, not without its difficulties, as the analogy to the dissimilarity criterion shows. In the study of the historical Jesus, the criterion allows what is dissimilar to Judaism and the early church to be counted as authentic material. But it has often been pointed out that we do not know enough about either Judaism or the early church to be able to say with confidence what could, or could not, come from these sources.[12] Thus, exactly analogously, it is not always clear that we can establish what are the tendencies (theological, linguistic or whatever) of each evangelist. So often, opinions about these depend on a prior solution to the Synoptic Problem, and many of the standard works on the stylistic and theological characteristics of Matthew and Luke presuppose the 2DH. For example, Cadbury's classic work on Lukan style is explicitly based on the 2DH,[13] and different source hypotheses may lead to very different results about what is redactional.[14] So too, Mark's theology according to the GH will presumably be rather different from that based on the assumption of Markan priority: for it will have to account for the deliberate omission of a large amount of material directly available to the evangelist in his sources. The assumption of the GH might thus imply something new about Mark's redactional aims. Nevertheless, Farmer's fourth criterion can be employed provided it is used with care.

Thus, theories about the linguistic preferences of each evangelist may need to be determined more on the basis of the total number of uses of any given word or phrase than on a direct comparison of parallel texts, which presupposes a particular solution to the Synoptic Problem.[15] Similarly, characteristic theological ideas may have to be based on the overall evidence of each gospel as a whole, rather than on the changes which one evangelist may have made to his alleged source.

Exclusive use of the dissimilarity criterion in the study of the historical Jesus can lead to a distorted picture of Jesus. Partly in order to correct this, a criterion of 'coherence' has been proposed as a way of expanding the stock of authentic material which the dissimilarity criterion can establish.[16] Now something very similar to this has been used implicitly in the past in study of the Synoptic Problem. Moreover, an analogous criterion may be capable of overcoming some of the ambiguity, and the dangers of circularity, in arguments based on individual texts. Applied to the study of the historical Jesus, the criterion demands that the authentic material should cohere with itself, and with the known cultural background of the time of Jesus, to form a reasonably self-consistent picture, as well as cohering with what can be established as authentic by other criteria, e.g. dissimilarity. The criterion here is not without its difficulties. On the one hand, if the later church invented sayings of Jesus, it would presumably be unlikely to have invented ones which did not, to a certain extent, fit in with the other genuine material.[17] On the other hand, one could point to a good novel, which is 'coherent' but totally fictitious.[18] Nevertheless, not all these criticisms apply in the study of the Synoptic Problem if this criterion is used to consider the redactional activity of each evangelist, rather than the content of the material, as follows.

Any source hypothesis can in fact be proposed. There is no logical law which excludes any theory of synoptic interrelationships with the degree of finality which would be attained if it could be shown that such an hypothesis led to a self-contradiction of the kind $0 = 1$. One can, therefore, postulate any hypothesis and then make a list, in a purely mechanical way, of the changes which the later writer must have made to his source(s). For example, if Luke were prior, Mark second, and Matthew a conflation of both, then one could go through a synopsis showing that Mark must have omitted this from Luke, added that, changed this, retained that, etc.; then Matthew must have taken this from Luke, that from Mark, ignored Luke here, preferred Mark there, etc. What is then required, if the hypothesis is to be made credible, is a presentation of the reasons why the later writers made the changes they are alleged to have done. The application of a 'criterion of coherence' would then demand that these reasons form a reasonably coherent whole: they must be rational, consistent with each other and also consistent with the facts as they are. With this in mind, the gospel texts can be examined at a number of different levels: one can consider small grammatical changes, the changes of words and phrases with wider theological implications, and the changes involving the choice and ordering of whole pericopes. Any proposed source hypothesis must then give a reasonably coherent and self-consistent set of reasons why these changes occurred in the way that the hypothesis claims if the theory is to be seriously considered. The extent to which an hypothesis gives a coherent, consistent picture of the total redactional activity of each evangelist will then be a measure of its viability.[19]

This criterion is, of course, open to objections. There is, for example, the fact that one is not (and indeed cannot be) testing a source hypothesis directly, but only at the 'secondary' level of looking at the reasons behind the changes allegedly made. Thus it may be that the GH is right about what the actual interrelationships between the gospels were, but that its advocates are wrong in the redactional motives they attribute to Luke and Mark. Merely to show the latter to be unsatisfactory does not of itself prove the prior theory of literary relationships to be wrong. On the other hand, Turner's remarks about a coherent novel, referred to above, apply equally well here: to show that one series of alleged changes is consistent and coherent indicates that they could have happened in this way, but not that they necessarily did so.

In fact this criterion has been used implicitly very frequently in the past, as scholars have appealed to the coherence or otherwise of some alleged redactional activity. Negatively, it was used by Wilke, Lachmann, and Weiss against the GH: Wilke and Lachmann pointed to the general lack of consistency or coherence in Mark's alleged procedure in dealing with his two sources, and Weiss criticised Griesbach's detailed reasons for Mark's switching between his sources in precisely the way Griesbach claimed.[20] So too, Woods' argument against the GH, and Streeter's against the Augustinian hypothesis, applied what was essentially this criterion at the level of the overall choice of material: both claimed that there seemed to be no coherent reason why Mark should have omitted so much.[21]

When the criterion is used positively, its greatest danger is its circularity. Lachmann's original argument from order used essentially this criterion in a positive way: he claimed that the changes made by Matthew and Luke to Mark's order could be seen to be meaningful and coherent (and also, of course, that the opposite changes could not). Stoldt, referring to Holtzmann's use of this form of the argument from order, writes: 'Der einzige, der hier die Reihenfolge des Markus als die ursprüngliche voraussetzt, ist

Holtzmann. Er begeht dabei eine geradezu klassische Petitio principii: die Behauptung, die erst noch bewiesen werden soll, wird bereits als bewiesen vorausgesetzt und von ihm als Beweismittel herangezogen.'[22] This is one of the major criticisms levelled by Stoldt against advocates of the 2DH, viz. they assume their solution and then seek to make it convincing by attributing the changes made to the redactional activity of the later writer. This method of 'proof' he calls 'der psychologische Reflexionsbeweis' and asks: 'Was wissen wir denn nun objectiv über die Motive und die gedanklichen Erwägungen der Evangelisten, von denen sie bei der Konzeption ihrer Werke bewegt und getrieben worden sind?'[23] Later, he concludes this section of his book by saying: 'Der ganze psychologische Reflexionsbeweis stellt eine riesengrosse Petitio principii dar.'[24]

At the purely formal level this is probably justified: to assume the Markan order as original, and then to produce reasons for Matthew's/Luke's alleged deviations from it, is to argue in a circle. Nevertheless, some such form of argument is inevitable. For if all three gospels are directly related to each other, then, at the purely formal level, no abstract considerations can prove that dependence lies one way and not the other: given two parallel versions, A and B, one cannot tell whether B is derived from A, or A from B, without first looking at the contents of A and B and seeing which change is the more likely. One will then necessarily be involved in an appeal to the redactional motives which might underlie the supposed change. Further, these motives may be deduced, at least in part, from other changes which the evangelist in question may have made to his alleged sources, i.e. they may presuppose a solution to the Synoptic Problem.[25] However, if one is primarily testing the self-consistency of a proposed solution to the Synoptic Problem, such a procedure is still valid. The argument may be partly circular, but the main point at issue is whether the redactional activity postulated by the hypothesis in question is reasonably coherent and consistent: thus in order to determine the precise nature of this alleged redactional activity, the source hypothesis must first be assumed.[26] A corollary of this is that in any critical evaluation of the 2DH with this criterion in mind, it can still be justifiable to use some of the standard works on the characteristics of each evangelist which in themselves presuppose the 2DH. For if one is testing only the self-consistency of the 2DH, then the results of such studies can still be used to see if a coherent pattern for the redactional activity of the secondary writer(s) emerges. One must, however, take care not to assume that all such characteristics derived in this way necessarily have absolute validity and that they can be applied without more ado in testing the consistency of another hypothesis.

Advocates of the 2DH are not alone in using this potentially circular form of argument. Griesbach's own argument from order made implicit appeal to the same criterion and was equally circular: he proposed a source theory and then sought to give reasons why Mark might have proceeded in the way the theory demanded. So too, many of the arguments adduced by those who would revive the GH today make implicit appeal to a criterion of coherence. Farmer himself explicitly shuns the method of approaching the problem from scratch, and opts for the course of 'writing about the problem from his own point of view'.[27] In part, therefore, he is appealing to the coherence of the overall picture which the GH will give. Orchard's work on the relationship between Matthew and Luke is similarly orien-tated, as he seeks to show that the Lukan order can be seen as part of a perfectly coherent redactional plan, based on Matthew's order of events alone.[28] Longstaff's work on conflation seeks to show that the Markan text is quite consistent with the theory that it is a conflation of Matthew and Luke, in that it appears to exhibit the same characteristics as other known examples of conflation.[29] Dungan's work on finding a convincing *Sitz im Leben* for Mark seeks to show that Mark's text could be the result of a process of seeking to remove contradictions from sources, a desire which can be seen to exist elsewhere in the ancient world.[30] In all these, there is an implicit appeal to the criterion of coherence. All these works attempt to show that the GH's source theory can be used to produce patterns of redactional activity by Luke and Mark on their alleged sources which are coherent, consistent with the facts, and also consistent with such parallels in contemporary literature as can be adduced.

It is here that the GH can be tested critically to see if it offers a better, or more consistent, coherent explanation of the redactional activity involved than, say, the 2DH. What is required is to consider various aspects of the texts, and to see how they might be explained by any one hypothesis, in particular the GH. This can be done with small grammatical details, with problems of a possible *Sitz im Leben*, with the phenomenon of the ordering of whole pericopes, and with theological motifs. To do this is the aim of the rest of this part of the present study, before I turn to a detailed analysis of a number of individual pericopes in Part III.

2 MARK'S DUPLICATE EXPRESSIONS

The first phenomenon to be considered here is that of Mark's 'duplicate expressions'. Although the results of the analysis will be largely inconclusive, they will nevertheless have some importance, since some have argued that the phenomenon is not easily explicable on the 2DH, whereas it does receive an easy explanation on the GH. However, it must first be made clear precisely what is being discussed.

The phenomenon of pleonasm in Mark has long been recognised as a feature of Mark's style,[1] although this is usually investigated on the initial assumption of Markan priority. With the contemporary revival of the GH, the possibility is raised that the duplicate expressions are the result of Mark's conflating his sources. However, the two issues, of whether Mark's text is pleonastic, and whether it can be viewed as the result of conflating sources, should not be confused. The possibility of conflation arises where Mark has an expression A + B, where Matthew has A and Luke has B. The possibility of pleonasm arises where Mark has A + B, and where A and B are virtually synonymous. What requires investigation is how far these two areas overlap, i.e. how far examples of Mark's pleonastic text could be explained as a result of Mark's conflating two sources, Matthew and Luke. (This, however, does not preclude the possibility of there being non-pleonastic examples of apparent conflation, i.e. cases where Matthew has A, Luke has B, Mark has A + B, but where A and B are not synonymous.)

The phenomenon of the apparently conflated text of Mark has certainly been used in arguments in the past. Some proponents of the GH saw in such examples support for the theory that Mark was conflating Matthew and Luke. Writing about Mk. i. 32 (probably the most famous example), Bleek said: 'It is improbable that an independent writer would have used two such expressions side by side to designate the eventide, had he not been led thereto by finding them elsewhere.'[2] De Wette too gave a list of thirty-nine examples which, he thought, supported the theory that Mark was conflating Matthew and Luke: Mark 'hat öfters einen Text, der aus dem der beiden Andern zusammengewebt zu sein scheint',[3] but only some of these can count as examples of pleonasm. Schwarz repeated De Wette's list,[4] and Bleek too referred to what he considered to be the six most striking examples, saying that more could be found in De Wette's work.[5] In fact five of Bleek's list could also be classed as pleonasms (i. 32 and 42; iv. 15; xi. 1; xii. 14, the other being i. 34). On the other hand, Wilke and Holtzmann pointed to places where Mark had not taken the opportunity to produce a pleonastic text by combining two synonymous phrases from his alleged sources.[6] This must count as some evidence against the GH, since one would expect Mark to use his sources in such a way that the resulting version was stylistically Markan, and the statistics alone suggest that pleonasm is a feature of Mark's style. Thus for most advocates of the 2DH, the phenomenon was due to independent abbreviation by Matthew and Luke.[7]

The treatment of Mark's pleonasms by modern writers sympathetic to the GH is not very extensive. Farmer himself does not make it clear how significant he thinks the phenomenon is. In referring to Stanton's somewhat tortuous suggestion that some of Mark's pleonasms might be due to a later editor making additions to an original non-pleonastic Ur-Marcus under the influence of one of the other two gospels, Farmer writes: 'According to the Griesbach hypothesis the Evangelist Mark, rather than some later editor, was held responsible for the same pleonastic text, but through the more normal (i.e., well known) process of combining or conflating two closely related texts.'[8] Elsewhere, Farmer discusses Abbott's famous phrase about Mark's alleged conflation according to the GH as being a '*tour de force* even for a skilful literary forger of these days'. He refers to Abbott's suggestion that Mark is not a skilful writer and asks: 'How is that to be determined? The best evidence would be the pleonasms with which Mark's text is replete.'[9] He then goes on to say that, if in fact Mark did conflate Matthew and Luke, then his apparent cumbersomeness and lack of skill should be viewed in the light of this fact. Farmer's introduction of the phenomenon of Mark's pleonasms here seems to suggest again that these are most satisfactorily explained as a result of conflating sources. Similarly, the double reference to the wilderness in Mk. i. 12f. 'is taken by the adherents of the Griesbach hypothesis as a sign that the text of Mark has been conflated from Matthew and Luke'.[10] However, later in his book, Farmer discusses Mk. i. 32 in some detail and says that 'such duplicate expressions do not by themselves constitute evidence for or against Marcan priority'.[11]

Other writers have suggested that the phenomenon of Mark's pleonastic text can be explained by the GH as being due to conflation, whereas the 2DH requires too much coincidence to be reasonable. Orchard says that the phenomenon 'is easily and naturally explained as the result of Mark conflating both Matthew and Luke'.[12] Dungan goes further and claims the 2DH gives an unreasonable explanation:

> As for Mark's well-known pleonastic style, could this not be the natural result of an author combining two sources? – especially because, as Streeter himself declares, it seems most remarkable to view it the other way, where, as if guided by the left hand and right hand of the Holy Spirit, Matthew independently selects precisely one half of a Markan pleonasm, and Luke the other, time after time.[13]

Sanders too refers to this and takes up the section of Hawkins' work which dealt with the duplicate expressions.[14] Hawkins had claimed that many of the examples in Mark could not be explained as due to conflation, since, for example, sometimes Matthew and Luke have the same half of Mark's dual phrase. Sanders comments: 'The difficulty with Hawkins' explanation is the frequency with which Matthew and Luke independently would have had to decide to select one half of a Markan double phrase and would have, by happenstance, selected different halves.'[15] In all these remarks, there is the implicit assumption that the phenomenon of Mark's pleonasms is explicable as the result of his conflating Matthew and Luke. Such an explanation, it is implied, would fit a large number of examples, so large in fact that the reverse changes (i.e. independent abbreviation of Mark by Matthew and Luke) imply an unreasonably high measure of coincidence in the number of times Matthew and Luke have each somehow chosen a different half of Mark's double phrase. This appears to have been never thoroughly tested, and the required investigation is the aim of this chapter.

The main problem in such an investigation is to find reliable evidence which is also comprehensive. Isolated examples in themselves prove nothing, and part of the criticism of the 2DH (noted above) appeals to the frequency of the phenomenon in question. Hawkins gives a list of duplicate expressions in Mark, but he limits consideration to cases where 'one or both of the other synoptists use one part or its equivalent'.[16] From his list, Hawkins rejects the possibility that these duplicate expressions are due to Mark's conflating Matthew and Luke, since, as often as not, the two halves of the expression in question are not neatly divided with one half in Matthew, one half in Luke: rather, these expressions are probably a Markan stylistic peculiarity. Undoubtedly, Hawkins' methodology is correct. One must look at all the duplicate expressions with their synoptic parallels, and see if the examples which could be explained as conflation of Matthew and Luke form a statistically significant proportion of the whole. For if Matthew and Luke are independently reducing some of Mark's redundancy, one would be surprised if they did not do so by omitting different halves of a duplicate expression at least a few times. One needs, therefore, as complete a list as possible of Markan pleonasms with their synoptic parallels.

Often such a list is made from the point of view of one or other of the other gospels to show how this feature of Mark's style is avoided by Matthew and/or Luke.[17] However, such lists will not include those examples (if any) where the duplicate expression appears unaltered in both the parallel versions, nor those where it has no parallel in either version. (For a consideration of the GH, these will be important negatively, in that they will be further examples which cannot be explained as due to conflation.) A massive list is given by Neirynck,[18] but it is not at all certain how many of his examples should be counted here. He seeks to show, by the sheer weight of evidence, that 'duality' is a feature of Mark's style. Yet this duality covers many more cases than the so-called 'duplicate expressions', where one phrase simply repeats another in different words but with little discernible additional meaning. Included in his lists are examples of 'grammatical usage',[19] which concern the repetition of prepositions, or cognate nouns, or the repetition of a noun instead of a pronoun. But in all these cases it is hardly likely, and never suggested, that such redundancy is due to the conflation of sources (i.e. that in παράγων παρά in i. 16, παράγων comes from one source, παρά from another). Another group of categories involves 'correspondence within one pericope',[20] and again conflation is extremely unlikely as an explanation. It is within the remaining group, constituting 'duplicate expressions and double statements', that one finds the required examples.[21] Yet even here, not all Neirynck's examples are really applicable in a study of Mark's pleonasms. Cases of Aramaic words followed by Greek translations (his category no. 14) are pleonasms only in the most formal sense. Thus attention here has been limited to the categories numbered 10–13 by Neirynck: double temporal statements (no. 10), a general expression followed by a more specific one (no. 11), repetitions of a motif in narrative and discourse (no. 12), and synonymous expressions (no. 13).[22] Neirynck himself implies that these may form a significant subgroup of categories as he compares these with the lists of Weiss, Holtzmann, Hawkins, Allen and Cadbury of cases of Mark's duplicate expressions.[23] But again not all his examples are acceptable in this context. For example, under the wide-ranging rubric 'general and special' is included Mk. i. 32 (which is a good example of pleonasm) and Mk. i. 5, 9 ('all came to be baptised . . . Jesus came') which, though formally the same, is not really a case of verbal redundancy (since both halves are essential to the story). In the section of 'synonyms' it is dubious whether i. 4 ('repent/for

the forgiveness of sins') or i. 24 ('Jesus of Nazareth/the holy one of God')
can be regarded as examples of verbal redundancy. Thus not all of
Neirynck's examples have been included for consideration. Only cases
where it does appear that there is a certain measure of verbal redundancy
have been counted. Inevitably, there is an element of subjectivity here, but
still the use of Neirynck's lists enables one to supplement the shorter lists
of Hawkins, Schmid and others, and to try to obtain a more comprehensive list of examples of the phenomenon in Mark. With these provisos in
mind, the following results emerged from an analysis of the examples
listed by Neirynck in comparison with their synoptic parallels.

Of 213 of Mark's duplicate expressions:
Matthew has one half, Luke the other half 17 times[24]
Matthew has one half, Luke has both halves 11 times[25]
Matthew has one half, Luke has no parallel 46 times[26]
Luke has one half, Matthew has both halves 17 times[27]
Luke has one half, Matthew has no parallel 25 times[28]
Both omit the same half 39 times[29]
Both have Mark's duplicate expression 6 times[30]
Matthew has both halves, Luke has no parallel 14 times [31]
Luke has both halves, Matthew has no parallel 1 time[32]
Matthew and Luke both have no parallel 37 times[33]

(In the cases of 'no parallel', it is immaterial whether there is no parallel to
the phrase alone or to the whole context. In either case, Matthew/Luke
cannot be the source of either half of Mark's duplicate expression.)

From these results, the following conclusions emerge. First, on any
source hypothesis, duality is a feature of Mark's style, in that Matthew and
Luke have significantly fewer cases. Of the 213 cases considered, Matthew
has some parallel in 150 cases, and has a duplicate expression in 37 of
them (25%); Luke has a parallel in 116 cases and has a duplicate expression
in 18 of them (16%). On the theory of Markan priority, there is nothing
surprising here: Mark is fond of dual expressions, and Matthew and Luke
regularly omit some of his redundancy. Moreover, the number of times
they do this by omitting different halves of the dual expression is not
significantly high, despite the claims of Sanders and Dungan. Matthew
omits one half of Mark's dual expression 113 times while Luke does so
98 times, but of these there are only 56 instances where they both do so.
Of these 56, 17 are instances where the two halves of the expression are
split between Matthew and Luke, whereas in the other 39 they omit the
same half. Indeed, if Matthew and Luke are independently redacting Mark

by cutting out some of his verbal redundancy, the number 17 is lower than expected. The expected number would be half the total, i.e. 28.

For the GH, there is nothing to disprove the theory, but equally nothing to support it. Mark's pleonastic style can only be explained by his conflating his two sources in 17 out of 213 cases. He could have taken over a dual expression from one of his sources in 49 cases. But in the remaining 147, he must have created the duplicate expression himself, either by adding a redundant second half to a phrase from one of his sources, or by creating both halves himself. Thus the vast majority of instances of Mark's pleonasms must, on either hypothesis, be due to Mark's own style. By the criterion of coherence, neither hypothesis is shown to be preferable, although the GH must explain why Mark does not conflate his sources more often, especially when he is presented with the opportunity in his sources.[34] However, when Farmer writes 'According to the Griesbach hypothesis the Evangelist Mark . . . was held responsible for the same pleonastic text, but through the more normal . . . process of combining or conflating two closely related texts',[35] the fact is that in many cases, those two texts cannot have been Matthew and Luke. Thus the phenomenon of Mark's duplicate expressions gives no positive support to the GH.

3 THE HISTORIC PRESENT

The second point at which the criterion of coherence can productively be applied is in a consideration of the use of the historic present in the gospels. The problem of whether this particular idiom reflects Aramaic or Latin influence is immaterial for the limited purposes in mind here. (Farmer's other attempts to show that various features of Mark's Greek have affinities with later, second-century, apocryphal gospels, notably the *Acta Pilati*, are really beside the point.[1] It is impossible to argue anything positive about Mark's date on the basis of these grammatical or verbal affinities. Such peculiarities, if they are indeed Latinisms, are much more likely to reflect Mark's own style or background than any relation to Matthew and Luke.[2] Nor, indeed, need Latin influence reflect a non-Palestinian provenance. Latin influence must have been present in Palestine since the occupation of the country by Roman troops. On the other hand, a Latin provenance for Mark does not preclude an early date of writing for Mark, since there was clearly an established Christian community in Rome itself by the early 50s if not before.)[3] Nevertheless, whether the use of the historic present is an Aramaism or a Latinism, it is still a phenomenon which exists and which is used in varying amounts by each of the three synoptists.

Farmer appeals to what is essentially the criterion of coherence in his argument that the 2DH gives a basically inconsistent picture of what Matthew and Luke must have done with Mark's usage. He also says that the possibility that the usage is a Latinism, rather than an Aramaism, renders it unlikely that Matthew and Luke would cut out this feature of Mark's Greek, since they were writing for audiences on whom the influence of Latin had long been felt.[4] This, however, really proves nothing: although it is clear that Matthew and Luke were both capable of using Latin loan-words and Latin constructions, this does not preclude the possibility that they may have wanted to avoid this particular Latinism (if such it be). Certainly the figures for the total number of usages of the historic present – Matthew 78, Luke–Acts 17, Mark 151 (excluding occurrences in parables) – show that they did not use this particular construction very much. Farmer thinks it unlikely that Matthew would have 'corrected' Mark's 'more colloquial Greek' (Streeter's phrase) since Matthew uses the same 'colloquial' expression fifty times elsewhere.[5] (He restricts attention to the use of the one verb λέγω). Ten of these fifty examples could be explained on the 2DH as due to dependence on Mark, but this is not possible for the other forty instances. If Matthew is correcting Mark's idiomatic Greek, why does he introduce the same idiom forty times elsewhere? Further, Luke's procedure is hard to understand if he is using Mark as a source. Farmer observes that there are thirteen instances of the historic present in Acts, and six times in his gospel Luke has copied this usage from his special source material. Thus, in view of Luke's readiness on occasion to use the historic present, there is no reason why he should have scrupulously avoided it whenever he found it in Mark. In fact he must have taken over one instance from Mark (Mk. v. 35/Lk. viii. 49), and Farmer concludes: 'There is no ground for Streeter to expect his readers to imagine that Luke would borrow the historic present from Mark in this one instance, and then accidentally coincide with Matthew in twenty instances in rejecting this usage and in correcting Mark's "colloquial" Greek.'[6] (He is restricting attention to the twenty cases where Matthew and Luke agree in having εἶπεν for Mark's λέγει). On the other hand, the phenomenon receives a simple explanation on the GH: '(1) Matthew wrote "he said" in these twenty cases, having freely used the historic present elsewhere; (2) Luke followed Matthew in these instances, since he often copied a source carefully. . . ; (3) Mark substituted the historic present in all twenty cases.'[7]

However, in all this Farmer limits attention to the twenty cases where Matthew and Luke have εἶπεν for Mark's λέγει, together with consideration of Matthew's use of λέγω. But this does not do justice to the total phenomenon of the use of the historic present by each of the evangelists. Clearly, the bare statistics of total number of usages in each gospel show that the idiom is one of Mark's favourites; equally clearly the idiom is not favoured by Luke. However, although Luke generally does not use it, the fact that it is not entirely absent is not surprising. Hawkins lists the number of occurrences of the idiom in the books of the LXX, and whilst it is clearly favoured in some books (notably 1 Kingdoms), it does still occur a few times in books where it is clearly not favoured.[8] Thus the fact that Luke generally avoids the historic present does not preclude the occasional occurrence. Indeed, Farmer's objection to the 2DH, that it does not explain Luke's scrupulous avoidance of the idiom in Mark whilst using it elsewhere, applies equally to the relationship between Luke and

Matthew. If, as the GH asserts, Luke is dependent on Matthew, then Luke must have avoided even more carefully every single one of Matthew's 78 usages of the historic present whilst still using it elsewhere. (There is now not even one exception, since Lk. viii. 49 has no parallel in Matthew, as is the case for all the Lukan uses of the idiom.) Thus, if Luke's procedure on 2DH causes difficulties, so too does his procedure on the GH.

If one takes into account the lengths of the gospels, one gets a better perspective on the relative use of the idiom. In terms of the number of occurrences per page (of the Greek BFBS text) Matthew has 0.80 usages per page, Mark 2.36, Luke 0.10. Whilst then the usage is favoured by Mark, and generally avoided by Luke, it appears to be a matter of indifference to Matthew. There is not a large number of occurrences, but equally he is quite prepared to use it. However, it is by no means clear that the GH can explain the total phenomenon of the usage better than the 2DH. If one looks at Matthew's 78 usages, and compares them with Mark's version, the result is somewhat surprising if Mark is using Matthew. In 27 cases Mark has no parallel to Matthew's verb,[9] and in 21 cases Mark also uses the same historic present.[10] However, of the remaining 30, at most 11 could be explained as places where Mark is using Luke rather than Matthew.[11] Of the remaining 19, according to Farmer's own judgement, Mark is using Matthew as his main source, and yet in 7 cases he must have changed Matthew's use of the historic present to another verb in the past tense,[12] and in 12 cases he must have simply changed the same verb into the past tense.[13] Thus, on the GH, Mark appears to be completely inconsistent: as a writer who clearly has a strong predilection for using the historic present, he has apparently deliberately changed it almost as often as he has retained it (19 cases compared with 21) when presented with it in his alleged source. He thus avoids half of Matthew's usages, and yet introduces the idiom 129 other times on his own initiative.

On the theory of Markan priority, on the other hand, a more coherent picture emerges. Mark likes the idiom and uses it 151 times. Luke dislikes it and so almost always avoids it (though not entirely, as viii. 49 shows). Matthew appears to be indifferent to the idiom. Of Mark's 151 uses, 44 have no parallel at all in Matthew.[14] Of the rest, Matthew simply changes the verb into a past tense 49 times,[15] retains the historic present 21 times,[16] changes the verb to a participle 24 times,[17] and uses a different verb in the past tense 13 times.[18] Thus Matthew has a slight tendency to avoid the historic present, but he is not totally opposed to the use of the idiom. He does indeed introduce it 30 times into Markan verses which do not use it, but this must be seen in the context of the 500 or so other verses where he does not do so. Matthew's slight inconsistency on the 2DH (in sometimes altering Mark's historic present, but at other times adding some instances of the idiom in Markan contexts) is less significant than Mark's on the GH, if only because the idiom is a clear favourite of Mark's, but not particularly one of Matthew's. Thus it is very surprising if Mark does not take over a use of the historic present in his source; Matthew's apparent procedure of both adding and subtracting historic presents in Mark is more plausible, given his relative indifference to using the idiom.

This tiny piece of evidence suggests that the theory of Markan priority gives a more coherent and self-consistent picture of what must have been the redactional activity of the secondary evangelists than does the GH. Indeed unlike the case of the duplicate expressions, it points to a phenomenon which is better explained by the theory of Markan priority than by the GH, rather than simply giving a neutral result. In view of the extremely unimportant nature of the phenomenon (no vast theological import belongs to the use of λέγει as opposed to εἶπεν), this makes it all the more difficult to see why, as the GH implies, Mark has often avoided in his sources the use of an idiom which he usually favours. Thus considerations of coherence count substantially against the GH here.

4 THE ORDER AND CHOICE OF THE MATERIAL

Another point where the coherence criterion has been applied in the past, explicitly or implicitly, is the phenomenon of the ordering and the choice of the material in the later gospels. Although the two issues can be considered separately, they are sometimes treated simultaneously. For example, as was seen earlier, Griesbach himself believed that his hypothesis could explain the order of events in Mark's gospel on the basis of Mark's having followed the order of each of his sources in turn. However, Griesbach also believed that it was important to explain precisely why Mark left one source, and why he picked up the other, at just the points which the theory implied. Thus his argument, which sought in part to explain the Markan order, became also an explanation of Mark's choice of the material. Griesbach's argument then depends, at least in part, on the plausibility of the reasons he ascribes to Mark, and the extent to which they explain the facts. Weiss' arguments against Griesbach were essentially that they either did not fit the facts, or that they did not form a self-consistent set of explanations.[1] On the other hand, appeals to coherence have been made by those arguing on the basis of both order and choice of material for Markan priority. Lachmann's own argument from order was based on this criterion, as were Woods' objections to the Griesbach hypothesis and Streeter's to the Augustinian hypothesis, both referring to the choice of material.[2] Although these two issues, of order and choice, have often been considered together, and indeed will be here, one should note that they are not identical, and it is with the problem of order that I shall start.

I

The history of the study of the Synoptic Problem shows that there were, and still are, at least two quite separate arguments based on order. One is Lachmann's own, and depends on the plausibility of the reasons given for Matthew's and Luke's changes to Mark's order. The second argument appeals to the lack of agreement between Matthew and Luke against Mark, and infers that Mark's order must be the more original. This second argument has been shown by Butler to be fallacious, in the sense that the logic is faulty if it is assumed that Markan priority is the only source hypothesis possible. The 'Lachmann fallacy' only arises when this formal argument is deemed to be logically probative, for Butler's analysis showed that there were a number of hypotheses which were possible.[3] This means that the argument is equally fallacious if it is assumed that any one of these possibilities is the only one consistent with the facts. The relevance of this to the contemporary revival of the GH will be seen shortly.

Farmer makes it clear in one of his later articles that one consideration which gives the GH a decisive advantage over other hypotheses concerns the phenomenon of order. He refers to the 'rediscovery of its [the hypothesis'] central and essential strength – viz. that it offers a credible explanation for the order of the episodes in the synoptic gospels',[4] and later he writes: 'The great merit of the Griesbach hypothesis was and remains that it offers a credible explanation for the phenomenon of order – lacking in the alternative accounts.'[5] Other arguments for Markan priority based on the phenomenon of order are rejected by Farmer. In particular he rejects the argument based on the lack of agreement between Matthew and Luke against Mark as 'inconclusive', referring to the work of Butler. He also rejects Lachmann's own argument, that the changes made by Matthew and Luke to Mark's order are easily explicable. However, his objections are not to do with any of the reasons given for the alleged changes; rather, he says that the whole argument 'involves . . . a methodological oversimplification. It seems simple enough to explain what seems easy to explain. But in this case the relationship between all three, where the differences in order are more complex, remains unexplained.'[6] Farmer seems to be saying that a two-fold relationship is easier to explain, but what we have in the gospels is a three-fold relationship which requires a single explanation to explain it all. This in itself makes a prior assumption, viz., that there is a three-fold literary relationship to be explained at all. *If* the third gospel to be written depends on both the others, then this requires an explanation of the order of that gospel in relation to both its predecessors simultaneously, but it is precisely this assumption which is denied by the 2DH. Farmer's reasons for asserting that there is such a three-fold relationship are not clear. Elsewhere he says that such a relationship is demanded by the fact that there are agreements between any two of the gospels against the third, and that one should not appeal to other unknown sources before exhausting the possibility that all three gospels are directly related.[7] This, however, simply means that the theory of independent use of Mark by Matthew and Luke is excluded *a priori*; Farmer's terms of reference have simplified the situation no less than Lachmann did by concentrating on explaining the differences which were easy to explain. It may well be that the complex phenomenon of a three-fold relationship between Matthew, Mark and Luke is purely an invention of modern makers of synopses and has no basis in historical reality. Excluding this possibility *a priori* is itself a methodological oversimplification.

The argument which Farmer believes does give support to the GH

> is based on the observation that whenever the order of Mark is not the same as that of Matthew, it follows the order of Luke, i.e. that Mark has no independent chronology. Griesbach held that this is best explained if Mark is third and is dependent for his order on Matthew and Luke . . . Griesbach's point may be simply put this way: all that is needed to understand the order of events in Mark is that given in Matthew and Luke (excepting the single case of his ordering of the cleansing of the temple). This seems explicable only by a conscious effort of Mark to follow the order of Matthew and Luke.[8]

However, when this is reduced to its logical essentials, this phenomenon is simply the fact that there are no agreements between Matthew and Luke against Mark: sometimes all three agree, sometimes Matthew and Mark agree, sometimes Mark and Luke, but Mark is never the odd one out. In Farmer's words, Mark 'has no independent chronology'. (The only alternative, that all three are different, never occurs, but this only shows that there is some close relationship involved.) Now if Farmer thinks that this phenomenon, by itself, shows the validity of the GH, as against the 2DH (cf. 'only' above, and 'lacking in the alternative accounts' in the quotation on p. 27), then he is guilty of committing the Lachmann fallacy in a slightly different form. For Farmer is drawing the conclusion from these facts that one and only one hypothesis, in this case the GH, explains the phenomenon satisfactorily. In fact, the evidence is inconclusive, and the 2DH can, formally, explain the facts just as well as the GH.

Farmer does offer some arguments which seek to exclude the 2DH as giving a viable explanation of the phenomenon. He says that Matthew and Luke 'would have had to conspire with one another or find some other way to contrive this chronological neutering of Mark'.[9] This was developed earlier in his book, where Farmer argued that Matthew's and Luke's deviations from Mark should have coincided more often if they were independently changing Mark: 'Since both frequently desert Mark . . . and since neither knows what the other is doing, why do not their desertions of Mark coincide more frequently?'[10] However, the 'frequent' number of desertions is an overstatement. Referring to this claim of Farmer's Neirynck writes:

Emphasis on the alternating support seems to imply that agreements and disagreements with the relative order of Mark are treated as comparable quantities. In fact the disagreement against Mark is the exception and the absence of concurrence between Matthew and Luke is less surprising than the somewhat misleading formulation 'whenever the other departs' may suggest.[11]

Morgenthaler's judgement is 'In Wirklichkeit stellt sich nun heraus, dass Mt und Lk fast nie von der Mk-Folge abweichen', and indeed, prior to the passion, Morgenthaler allows only Lk. vi. 17-19; viii. 19-21 as examples of Luke's changing the Markan order.[12] So too Jameson writes about the differences in order as follows:

(1) Matthew and Mark, after the dislocations of order in the early chapters, agree throughout the rest of their course, and (2) Luke, when he is following Mark, scarcely ever deserts his order at all except towards the close. It is evidently very unlikely, under these conditions, that variations in order in (1) and (2) should coincide.[13]

Thus the implicit appeal to the coherence criterion by Farmer and others (to show negatively that the 2DH does not give a coherent explanation of the facts) fails to convince, since it overestimates the degree to which Matthew and Luke individually deviate from Mark.

Farmer's detailed analysis of the way in which Mark must have followed the order of each of his sources in turn is formally a repetition of Griesbach's. Now Griesbach himself coupled this with reasons for Mark's switching between his sources at precisely the points he did, and such reasons make the attempt to explain Mark's choice, as well as the order, of material. Since in fact the formal argument from order, appealing to the lack of agreement against Mark, is logically inconclusive, some such attempt to explain Mark's detailed reasons for his decision to follow his sources alternately in precisely the way he is alleged to have done is required by any advocate of the GH. In the light of Weiss' criticisms of Griesbach's reasons, this is all the more necessary; yet very few advocates of the GH have given this question adequate consideration.

Farmer himself has given only limited space to the problem of the choice of material. Writing about the phenomenon of order, he says: 'The striking fact that Matthew and Luke rarely (or almost never) agree in order against Mark is simply explained on the Griesbach hypothesis by Mark's redactional tendency to adhere to the order to which Matthew and Luke bear concurrent testimony.'[14] However, it is not clear how far this is to be taken as implying anything positive about Mark's redactional aims. If it is implied that Mark's aim was to include the material where Matthew and Luke agreed in order, then this is clearly belied by the facts: the Baptist's preaching and the Temptation stories both occur in Matthew and Luke at the same relative place, but Mark does not use this 'concurrent testimony' of his sources.[15] In his chapter dealing with Mark's redaction of the material, Farmer gives few reasons for how Mark might have chosen his material. He says that the Sermon on the Mount, and the Sermon on the Plain in Luke, marked two 'clearly distinguishable and quite comparable literary transitions in his sources',[16] and this is why Mark switched at precisely these points. However, it is by no means clear why the transitions are any clearer here than at the seams between other pericopes (e.g. Matt. iv. 17 or Lk. v. 16). Elsewhere Farmer says that 'Matthew's Sermon on the Mount and its Lucan parallels presented almost insuperable redactional problems for satisfactory conflation',[17] and he refers to the different forms of the Beatitudes; but the Beatitudes are not so different in form, and other parts of the two sermons are verbally extremely close (e.g. Matt. vii. 3–5/Lk. vi. 41f.), so a simple appeal to the difficulty of conflating will not really explain the omission of the Sermon on the Mount.

In a later article, Farmer has laid more stress on the affinities of Mark with the Petrine speeches in Acts as giving a more adequate explanation of the choice of material in Mark, especially the omissions from Matthew and Luke.[18] For example, the speech in Ac. i. 22 speaks of the ministry of Jesus 'beginning with the baptism of John', and this corresponds with Mark's beginning with John's ministry, thus omitting the birth stories. So, too, there is no reference to Jesus as a teacher in the Petrine speeches, and correspondingly Mark omits much of the sayings material in Matthew and Luke. This enables Farmer to say about the omission of the Sermon on the Mount: 'Since Mark has no long discourses, *ipso facto* he has no Sermon on the Mount, as that by definition is a long discourse.'[19] Nevertheless, this theory can explain the choice of material in Mark only in the most general terms. The argument based on Mark's dislike of long teaching discourses, whether stated apodictically as by Griesbach, or whether deduced from the Petrine speeches as by Farmer, is still open to the objections of Weiss, that this does not account for all the changes in detail. Further, it is simply not true that 'Mark has no long discourses'. He does have some teaching material, which in chapters iv and xiii is arranged in a long discourse. An alleged dislike of long discourses cannot of itself, therefore, explain why Mark has chosen to have some long discourses of teaching, but not others. Further, the lack of mention of Jesus' teaching in the Petrine speeches does not explain the well-known stress in Mark on Jesus as a 'teacher'.[20] Farmer also appeals to the omission by Mark of 'a great

deal of what in Matthew or Luke was peculiarly Jewish and Palestinian',
since he was probably writing for Gentiles, possibly far from Palestine.[21]
This is, however, not substantiated in detail. There are certainly some parts
of Matthew which are peculiarly Jewish (e.g. some of the woes in chapter
xxiii, or the particularism in x. 5). Nevertheless, there is plenty of material
in Mark which is scarcely separable from its Jewish context, e.g. the stories
about the Sabbath (ii. 23 - iii. 6),the food laws (vii. 1-23) and the debate
on divorce (x. 1-10).

The result of this section is that Farmer's argument for the validity of
the GH based on the ordering of material in Mark needs a great deal more
demonstration if it is to be made convincing. In particular a detailed
account of the reasons behind Mark's omissions is still required. A simple
appeal to the phenomenon of lack of agreement in order between Matthew
and Luke against Mark cannot of itself prove the validity of the GH without the proof's becoming fallacious. The GH does offer an explanation of
the facts at one level, in that it can point to the way that Mark must have
followed his two sources alternately. But this observation needs to be
supplemented with a coherent set of reasons for Mark's having proceeded
in the way he is alleged to have done. Griesbach's reasons were shown to
be unsatisfactory by Weiss, and so far they have not adequately been
either revised or replaced by any of those who would revive the GH today.

II

So far, in this discussion of the order and choice of material, attention has
been focussed on the gospel of Mark. However, the GH also asserts that
there is a direct literary relationship between Matthew and Luke, and this
claim has not received the same degree of consideration in the modern
debate. In his original book, Farmer admitted that 'in the history of the
Synoptic Problem the redactional process followed by Luke in his use of
Matthew seems never to have been effectively set forth by the adherents
of the Griesbach hypothesis'.[22] In a later article, Farmer claims that explanations of why Luke might have changed Mark's order prove nothing
about Markan priority, since at the points where Mark and Luke differ,
Mark agrees with Matthew. Thus such explanations would serve just as well
to explain why Luke had changed Matthew's order.[23]

This is, of course, true as far as it goes. But it leaves unmentioned the
fact that there are various other differences between Matthew and Luke
which must also be explained by the GH, viz. all the places where Mark
and Luke agree and where Matthew is the odd one out. There are many
modern scholars who are sceptical of the existence of Q, and who assert
Lukan dependence on Matthew, but who still hold to Markan priority;

thus they would maintain that Luke used Matthew in the 'double tradition' passages, but that in the 'triple tradition' Luke used Mark, and the differences between Matthew and the other two are due to Matthew's changes. However, on the GH, no such distinction between double tradition and triple tradition passages exists:[24] the latter are just those parts which Mark happened to copy later, and Luke is held to be dependent on Matthew alone for all the tradition. Thus the Lukan wording and structure in the whole tradition must be explained from Matthew. This adds an extra difficulty to the task of any advocate of the GH; for it is well-known that Matthew's order in the first half of his gospel is very different from that of Luke and Mark. On the theory of Markan priority, this is usually explained as being due to Matthew's collecting of disparate elements from his various sources to form the teaching discourses in chapters v-vii, x and xiii and a cycle of miracle stories in chapters viii-ix.[25] Luke's order is then simply a reproduction of Mark's. Part of the case for Markan priority depends on the plausibility of these reasons for Matthew's changes, appealing to the coherence and reasonableness of the alleged procedure. It is, however, theoretically possible that the changes were made in the reverse direction, and very often this possibility is dismissed summarily by advocates of the 2DH. For example, Kümmel asserts categorically: 'The opposite position – that Mark has altered the sequence of Matthew or Luke – offers no clarification in any of the cases mentioned.'[26] (In cases where Mark and Luke agree in order against Matthew, any claim about the impossibility or otherwise of Mark's changing Matthew's order applies equally well to Luke's alteration of Matthew.)

Now such arguments are at best dangerous. The claim that no reason can be discerned does not mean that reasons did not exist; moreover, it becomes incumbent on any critic to look at any claims that such reasons did exist. A case has recently been made for explaining Luke's redactional procedure on the GH by Orchard in his book *Matthew, Luke & Mark*. This has been praised by Farmer as one of the significant modern developments giving support to the GH, and he claims that 'Orchard is able to offer a credible explanation for Luke's literary method.'[27] In view of the claim by many advocates of Markan priority that Matthew's and Luke's changes from Mark are explicable but the opposite changes are not, a claim that the opposite changes from Matthew are explicable (whether made by Luke or Mark) deserves careful attention.

Orchard confines attention to the choice and order of the material, rather than looking at the detailed wording within any one pericope. He claims that it is in the ordering and structure of the gospel that the final redactor's hand is most clearly to be seen.[28] Further, if the structures of two gospels are similar, and the differences in structure can be seen to be part of an intelligent divergence by one editor, then this implies that this editor is dependent on the other gospel.[29] Thus Orchard starts by claiming that there is a great similarity of structure and arrangement between Matthew and Luke. He sets down the various sections in a table and claims that this shows a 'massive agreement'.[30] However, the sections chosen are so large that they hide many smaller differences within each one. Also, the avoidance of any consideration of the detailed content of each section leads to some of the evidence being over-valued. For example, part of the common pattern is that both Matthew and Luke start with birth stories, and finish with the passion story and resurrection narrative. But besides ignoring the great differences in content between the two gospels, this agreement in positioning is scarcely surprising since it is dictated by the contents themselves: e.g. birth stories can only come at the beginning. It is the material in between which is distinctive, and where a common overall structure would be more significant, but it is here that such a common structure is far more difficult to find. Orchard recognises that there are differences in order but believes that he can account for them; nevertheless, however successful he may be in this, one must recognise that there has been considerable displacement one way or the other. On the 2DH, the common order is explained as mostly that of Mark (with some consider-able alteration by Matthew in the first part of his gospel). On the GH, the agreement in absolute order covers mostly the material which Mark decides later to include (possibly precisely because it is in a common order). However, this does not extend to more than about half the total extent of the gospel tradition. Yet Orchard still maintains that Matthew and Luke share a common underlying structure.

Orchard says that the six Matthean teaching discourses, which form the basis around which Matthew constructs his gospel, are still clearly visible in Luke's structure.[31] Yet even so, Orchard has to admit that Luke has interchanged the Parables Discourse and the Mission Charge.[32] This is said to put the Parables Discourse 'in a more logical (and probably more chronological) setting',[33] but what logic or chronology is meant is not stated. Also it becomes more doubtful how far Luke still 'respects the framework he has borrowed (even when he changes a main element in it)':[34] if he has altered it, he has presumably not entirely respected it. Further, it is not at all obvious that the Lukan parallels to the six Matthean discourses form the basic framework for Luke's structure. (This is required if they are to be evidence of a common underlying framework in Luke as well as Matthew.) Although they form a clear feature in Matthew, the Lukan parallels are often comparatively meagre in content (cf. the remains of

Matt. xxiii in Lk. xx. 45–47, or of Matt. xviii in Lk. ix. 46–48). It is true that vestiges of each Matthean discourse appear in Luke, but it is not the case that these form the basis of Luke's structure. There is some agreement in absolute order, but this covers only about half the material, and it is thus wrong to deduce that there is a common basic agreement in structure between the whole of each gospel.

Similarly, Orchard's attempt to show a basic underlying unity of structure in some of the smaller sections is unconvincing. He deals with the section in Matt. iv–xiii and claims that, despite some rearrangements, there are a number of 'fixed points'.[35] He cites the first preaching tour, the Gathering of the Crowds, the Great Sermon, the Centurion's Slave, the Sending of the Twelve, the Missionary Discourse, and Herod's interest in Jesus. But all these are very variable in their size and relative importance in the structure of each gospel. The Gathering of the Crowds and the Great Sermon are not really separable, nor are the Sending of the Twelve and the Missionary Discourse; further, Herod's interest in Jesus is a very minor feature. All that Orchard seems to be saying is that these pericopes are the ones which retain their relative sequence in both gospels, whilst there has been considerable rearrangement in the rest of the material (which in quantity amounts to more than half the total). But these 'fixed points' do not function as the pillars around which the gospels are built (certainly not for Luke, cf. the very short version of the Mission Charge in ix. 1–6).

Orchard deals in some detail with the differences in order, as well as the similarities, and this forms the main part of his argument that Luke's order can be seen as an intelligent re-editing of Matthew's gospel. The success of his thesis depends largely on the plausibility of the reasons he gives, since simply listing the changes made can prove nothing. First, he says that it was one of Luke's general rules to change the context of a pericope when he used a different, but parallel, tradition. This then explains the different positions of the genealogies, the call of Peter, the rejection at Nazareth and the story of the Great Commandment. For example, he says that the new position of the Nazareth scene 'avoids a clash with the different story told in Mt 13: 53ff.'[36] but quite how far this gives a real reason for Luke's changes is not clear. Certainly such a procedure may avoid an immediate clash, but the real difference lies in the different content of the two versions, and this is only partially (if at all) avoided by a change in order.

Secondly, Orchard says that one of Luke's aims was to fill out the first preaching tour, alluded to in Matt. iv. 23/Lk. iv. 44, by drawing on material from elsewhere in Matt. viii, ix and xii.[37] This is a valid explanation in general terms, but it is by no means clear that the details of Luke's choice are satisfactorily explained. Orchard claims that the first miracle story in Matthew after the Sermon (Matt. viii. 1-4) becomes the first miracle story of Luke's tour (Lk. v. 12-16). He also says that Luke remains true to Matthew's intention by showing Jesus' first miracle on the tour to be directed to a representative of his own people, and by showing Jesus' explicit re-affirmation of the demands of the Law in telling the healed leper to go to the priests (cf. in Matthew the miracle follows the Sermon which is introduced by Matt. v. 17).[38] However, in Luke, it is not the command to go to the priests which is the climax of the story, but rather the widespread fame which Jesus enjoyed as a result of the cure.[39] Moreover, the section which follows shows Jesus to be in conflict with the Jewish authorities because of his apparent readiness to sit lightly to the Law. Further, the miracle is not the first one in Luke (unlike in Matthew) since it is preceded by the cure of Peter's mother-in-law and the general healings recorded in Lk. iv. 38-41. Thus, although Luke may have transferred the story of the leper from Matthew's position and put it here, the reasons cannot be what Orchard claims they are.

In fact the stories of Peter's mother-in-law and the general healings are also problematical. On the GH, they must have been moved from their position in Matt. viii. 14-17 to an earlier one. Orchard says that

> Luke's motive for transfer would seem to be chronological; for he separates these two items from the other miracle stories he transfers, cf. Lk 5: 12 – 6:11, because they describe events which occurred at the place from which Jesus began the Preaching Tour that led to the Great Sermon, i.e. at Peter's house.[40]

This however would be more convincing if there were anything in Luke's alleged source to suggest that the Preaching Tour did start at Peter's house. But there is no mention of this in Matt. iv. 23. The idea comes only from within the pericope itself, and Orchard's theory does not explain why this change should be necessary. Moreover, a start at Peter's house does not explain why the block of general healing in Matt. viii. 16f. also needs to be moved. Other stories transferred to this section include the sabbath stories of Matt. xii. 1-14. Orchard says that this change is made in such a way that the healing of the leper and these two stories become the first and last events in Luke's tour, just as they are the first and last events in Matthew in the series between the Sermon and the saying about the suffering servant.[41] But it is not clear that Matthew or Luke ever saw such a series as significant, and the idea that the saying in Matt. xii. 15f. constitutes a definite break in Matthew's structure, and marks the end of a series of events starting in chapter viii, contradicts the theory that it is the teaching discourses which form the main pillars of Matthew's structure. (Thus the

series of events starting at viii. 1 should end at ix. 34, not xii. 14.) Moreover, since the two series in Matthew and Luke are very different, one
cannot see why Luke, wanting to complete one cycle of stories, should
feel compelled (or even want) to choose something in Matthew which
completes a different cycle.

It is also hard to see what has governed Luke's choice of material to fill
out Jesus' first preaching tour in Galilee. If Orchard is right in identifying
Luke's aim in this way, then the occasion must be the tour alluded to in
Matt. iv. 23, and this speaks of Jesus' 'preaching, teaching and healing all
disease and sickness'. But the net result in Luke is a collection of stories of
which only one is a pure miracle story (the leper), the rest being controversy stories whose main theme is the confrontation of Jesus with the
Jewish authorities. Such a narrowing of interest is not implied in Matt. iv.
23; nor is it apparent in Luke's parallel at this point which speaks of Jesus
simply 'preaching' (iv. 44), and there is no hint here that Luke saw the
activity of Jesus as any more specialised than Matthew did. If Luke had
wanted more general material, dealing with Jesus' teaching and healing, it
would have been available to him in Matt. viii. 18–22 (teaching); viii. 28–34;
ix. 28–31 (healings). Now it may well be that the collection of these five
controversy stories is purposeful, whether by Luke or by his source. On
the theory of Markan priority, this collecting is Markan or pre-Markan, and
certainly it fits better in Mark as a foreshadowing of the passion which so
dominates Mark's gospel. However, there is no other evidence that this is
LkR (as the GH must assume), either in the way Luke must have redacted
the summary in iv. 44, or in any overall emphasis in the gospel as a whole.

The remaining changes of order within this first section of the gospel
are just as problematical. The transfer of the names of the Twelve, from
the commissioning (Matt. x. 2–4) to Lk. vi. 14–16, is noted but not
explained by Orchard, and the same is true of the transfer of the note
about Jesus' family to a position after the Parables Discourse.[42] Luke is
said to have left the story of the centurion's slave where it is in relation to
the Great Sermon as the first miracle to follow it: 'For Luke had noted its
suitability for this purpose, namely to stand as the first beneficent act of
Jesus towards a Gentile, a sign of the grace and healing now being made
available in equal measure to the Gentiles.'[43] However, it is not clear how
this is related to anything in the Sermon, nor how this could be deduced
from the position (rather than the content) of the story itself. The new
position of the unit about the messengers of John (Matt. xi/Lk. vii) is said
to be 'the right place chronologically speaking. For it was the great fame
of Jesus which came to its climax at the Great Sermon that reached John
and caused him to send his envoys to question Jesus.'[44] This, however, is

pure conjecture. Matthew says that it was 'the works of Christ' which led John to send his message, and not the teaching activity of Jesus, nor the Sermon in particular. Luke does not alter this significantly so as to imply that he thought otherwise. He refers to John's hearing 'all these things', and the immediate antecedent is the two miracles in vii. 1–17, not any teaching activity. There is thus no warrant in either Matthew or Luke for a theory that John's question was prompted by the fame attracted by Jesus as the result of the Great Sermon; also there is no hint that this is a Lukan idea (which might have established the possibility of the change in order being due to LkR). Thus reasons of 'chronology' do not satisfactorily explain Luke's change of Matthew's order here.

Many of the reasons given by Orchard for the changes which Luke is alleged to have made to Matthew's order are therefore seen to be unsatisfactory and unconvincing when examined in detail. The assumed source theory must therefore remain unproven, or other more convincing reasons found for the changes involved, if the GH is to be made plausible.

One feature of Luke's gospel which requires explanation is the central section in Lk. ix. 51–xviii. 14. Orchard's claim is that this is a Lukan creation designed to include in one large unit material scattered throughout Matthew's teaching discourses.[45] Thus he says that Luke left a parallel to 'the first part of each Matthean Discourse' in its original place in the main structure, and transferred the rest of the material which he wanted to retain from each discourse to his central section.[46] However, such a neat division of each Matthean discourse is not so clear when examined. 'Lk. vi. 20–22 = Matt. v. 2–11' is partly true, though Luke must have chosen only verses 3, 4, 6 and 11 from Matt. v; further, Orchard does not explain why, in this discourse, so much more is left as part of a Sermon and not transferred to the central section. 'Lk. ix. 1–6 = Matt. x. 1–15' is something of an oversimplification of the relationships involved here: Lk. ix. 1–6, if derived from Matthew, takes verses 1, 7, 9, 10, 12a, 11b and 14 from Matthew, whilst reserving the rest for chapter x. 'Lk. ix. 46–48 = Matt. xviii. 1–2 and 4–5' ignores the fact that Matthew's verse 4 is not in Luke, and Luke's verse 48 considerably expands Matthew's verse 5. 'Lk. xx. 45–47 = Matt. xxiii. 1–6' is wrong: verse 46 in Luke is parallel in part to verse 6 in Matthew (even though it forms a doublet with Lk. xi. 43), but verse 47 in Luke has no parallel in Matthew, and Matthew's verses 2–5 (the first part of the discourse) have no parallel in Luke. Thus Luke has not simply taken the 'first part' of each discourse and moved the rest to his central section: the interrelationships are more complex.

Orchard's other claim about the central section, that it is a Lukan creation designed to collect together a lot of teaching material, is in itself unexceptional. But Orchard seeks to go a stage further by trying to show that it is Matthew who provides the basis for this new collection. He believes that, despite the fact that 'the sequence of material transferred to the Central Section bears no direct relation at all to its sequence in Matthew',[47] there is still a method discernible in that Luke 'is seen to move steadily forward time after time through the material he intended to retain until he had exhausted it'.[48] He illustrates this by reference to the material in the central section which Luke is said to have taken from the Great Sermon. Thus, Luke goes through picking out material on prayer (Matt. vi. 9-13; vii. 7-11/Lk. xi. 1-4, 9-13), then he goes back and starts again on the subject of inner cleanliness (Matt. v. 15; vi. 22f./Lk. xi. 33 and 34-36), then detachment (Matt. vi. 25-34/Lk. xii. 22-32), then he returns for the item on treasure in heaven (Matt. vi. 19-21/Lk. xii. 33f.). Thus Orchard sees a systematic procedure on Luke's part, working through each discourse, picking out the relevant sections on any one theme in their Matthean order, and then starting again with a different theme. Orchard thus implies that the order within the central section bears a recognisable resemblance to the order in Matthew within each discourse. This is partly simply a reversal of the argument of Taylor, who showed that there is a basic similarity in order between all the 'Q' material in Luke and the same material in the Matthean discourses when the latter are considered separately.[49] Within each discourse, according to Taylor, Matthew went through Q putting down in order what he wanted. This is intelligible since the discourses do have a certain thematic unity.

However, what is lacking in Orchard's theory is the necessary thematic unity which would make Luke's procedure intelligible. Both Taylor and Orchard appeal to the agreement in relative order of some of the sayings, but the thematic links, which are said by Orchard to govern the order in which Luke chose his material from Matthew, have now no relation to the actual contexts of the sayings in Luke. Thus sayings on a theme are allegedly picked out by Luke from Matthew, and their relative order is retained, but they are also now widely separated from each other. For example, in Matt. xiii, Orchard says 'we find him [Luke] taking up the following pieces of Mt 13 in the order in which they are found in Matthew, the theme being participation in the Kingdom, i.e. Mt 13: 16-17 = Lk 10: 23-24; Mt 13: 31-33 = Lk 13: 18-21.'[50] But the alleged thematic unity, i.e. the theme which led Luke to take precisely these parts from Matthew, does not now correspond to any actual contextual unity of the various parts as they now stand in Luke. The relative order is maintained, but the two parts of Matt. xiii are now separated by three chapters in Luke. Similarly, Luke's choice of the material in Matt. x can be seen theoretically as a steady moving forward, picking up verses 34-36, 37-38, 39 in Lk. xii. 51-52; xiv. 26-27; xvii. 33 respectively.[51] But the thematic unity (on sacrifices necessary in discipleship) is no longer a contextual unity in Luke. In fact the opposite changes are much more comprehensible if Luke preserves (or is) Matthew's source: Matthew takes these sayings from his source, and puts them together whilst preserving their relative order, and there is a clear theme linking them. The opposite process would involve Luke's going through Matthew, picking out the relevant parts he wants to retain on any one theme, retaining these sayings in their relative order, but also simultaneously widely separating them into different contexts. Further, the process involves Luke's carrying out this procedure, of working through each section of Matthew, nine times (i.e. in each Matthean section) simultaneously. Nor do Orchard's suggestions on Luke's thematic choice correspond to his proposed schematisation of the actual thematic division of the central section.[52] For example, the verses on the sacrificial nature of discipleship are split between the sections of teaching on vigilance, the kingdom, and the eschatological coming of Christ. If there is a common relative order between the sayings in Luke and each Matthean discourse in turn, then it is rather easier to see Matthew's ordering as secondary, since in Matthew the thematic unity is also a contextual one. On the 2DH, Matthew extracts from Q the material he wants, and keeps the relative order of his source. On the GH, Luke extracts what he wants from each Matthean discourse, and preserves some of the relative order from within each discourse; but the alleged themes, which lead him to make this ordered selection, do not correspond with any actual links in the present text of Luke.

Orchard's theory also leads to other difficulties. The idea that Luke goes back and again starts combing each discourse has to be applied too frequently for comfort. For if, each time round, Luke, as he steadily moves forward through Matthew, picks up only one verse or logion, the net result is that Luke will be going backwards, not forwards. Moreover, it is precisely the forward movement which is essential to Orchard's thesis that it is Matthew's order which is presupposed. To show that Luke's arrangement is simply coherent, and different from Matthew's, shows nothing. A correlation between the two orders must involve a correlation between the forward movements of both gospels. However, in Matt. x, Luke 'goes back' to verses 26-30 after verse 40, then back to verses 19f., before going on to verses 34-39. In Lk. xi/Matt. xxiii, Luke must have picked up Matthew's verses in the order 25f., 23, 6f., 27, 4, 29f., 34-36, 13, i.e. four backward steps as opposed to three forward ones. He also includes here a doublet to one of the verses of Matt. xxiii which he will later leave behind at the point in the overall structure where Mt. xxiii occurs (Lk. xi. 43; xx. 46/Matt. xxiii. 6), and this despite the fact that many of Luke's omissions are said to be due to Luke's wish to avoid doublets.[53] Luke may have wished to schematise the woes into one series for the Pharisees and one for the lawyers (this is the most obvious division of Luke's structure here), but he has certainly not picked out the woes he is going to apply to the Pharisees and given them in their Matthean order (in fact they are in precisely the reverse of the Matthean order), nor is this the case with the woes against the lawyers (where the last one is not in its Matthean order).

The conclusion of this section must be that Orchard's explanations of Luke's redactional procedure on the GH are not convincing. The overall similarity in structure between the two gospels is not so great as to compel assent to the claim that there is a direct relationship between Matthew and Luke; indeed, the fact that agreement in structure covers about half the gospel tradition suggests that Matthew and Luke are directly or indirectly related here in a different way from in the rest of the tradition, and it is precisely this which the 2DH explains in terms of dependence on the Markan structure. The explanations of Luke's procedure in filling out the first preaching tour, and creating his central section, are satisfactory in general terms, but the further detailed explanations given by Orchard are not convincing and do not explain the facts. Moreover, in considering the order of the central section, Taylor's argument is more convincing than Orchard's, and hence mutual dependence by Matthew and Luke on a common source (or even Matthean dependence on Luke) is a better explanation of these facts than is the theory of the GH. Insofar as Orchard's work attempts to make the direct use of Matthew by Luke a plausible hypothesis, it fails in its details. This does not of itself prove the GH wrong. However, by the criterion of coherence, one demands that the redactional changes involved form a coherent set, and this study of Orchard's book suggests that this has not yet been shown in the case of the theory that Luke's gospel is directly dependent for its order and structure on Matthew.

5   CONFLATED TEXTS

In the previous chapter, it was seen that the fact that Mark's order is supported either by Matthew, or by Luke, has been used in discussions of the Synoptic Problem. Advocates of the GH have claimed that the phenomenon is easily explicable only if Mark followed each of his sources alternately. The question of the same phenomenon of alternating agreement has been raised by Longstaff,[1] looking at the detailed wording within each pericope rather than at the ordering of the material. Longstaff takes up the critical remarks made about the GH by Abbott, Beare and others,[2] viz. that it is impossible to conceive of any writer conflating his sources in the way Mark must have done if the GH is correct. With these remarks in mind, Longstaff examines various examples of authors who are known to have conflated sources, to see what in fact conflators did with their sources. Thus he examines Tatian's composition of the Diatessaron, together with two mediaeval chroniclers, Benedict of Peterborough (who used a life of Becket by John of Salisbury and an anonymous document known as the *Passio Sancti Thomae*) and Roger of Hovedon (who used Benedict's chronicle and also made independent use of the *Passio*). From these Longstaff seeks to derive a number of 'literary characteristics which result from conflation',[3] and which might then provide a measure of objectivity in deciding whether Mark's gospel is a conflated document. He then proceeds to analyse six pericopes in Mark, and concludes (i) that there is a pattern of alternating agreement between Mark and the other two gospels which is very difficult to account for on the 2DH, but which is easy to explain on the GH; and (ii) that Mark's gospel exhibits many of the literary characteristics derived from known examples of conflation.[4] His work has been noted by Farmer as one of the 'modern developments' which have given added reason for the GH's receiving more favourable attention today.[5] His book therefore deserves careful analysis to see if it will give support to the GH in the way suggested.

I start with the question of the literary characteristics of a conflated text, and also an examination of the extent to which these are capable of distinguishing a conflated from a non-conflated text. (Although this is not explicitly considered by Longstaff, it is important if his results are to have any critical value in distinguishing between the possibilities of Mark's being a conflation of, or a common source for, Matthew and Luke.)

Longstaff's first characteristic is that 'a part of the content and vocabulary of each source will appear in the conflated document'.[6] However, this phenomenon only establishes that the three documents in question are in some form of literary relationship. As Longstaff himself says, it is implicit in the word 'conflation' itself, and proves nothing about whether the document concerned is posterior or prior to the other two.[7]

The second characteristic is that conflators did not follow the rule 'one source at a time' inflexibly, but that they 'carefully compared their sources', and evidence for this will usually be found. This will be seen partly in the arrangement of the material, where an author will insert a single sentence from a second source to supplement the main source.[8] This also leads to the third characteristic, which is that a careful comparison of sources will lead to 'a number of rather minute verbal agreements – often consisting of only a single word or a brief phrase – between the author and a source other than that which he had been principally following'.[9] These two characteristics (which seem barely distinguishable) are the ones most frequently appealed to by Longstaff in his later analysis of the Markan passages, and are clearly regarded by him as very important. However, it is not clear whether Longstaff has taken sufficient notice of the warning, which he himself gives,[10] about conflation's being a very varied process, with different conflators having very different aims. In the case of Tatian, it is probably a justifiable conclusion to say that his work is characterised in this way; but, on the other hand, Tatian's method is different from that of other conflators such as Benedict or Roger (or even Mark on the GH), in that in any one given pericope, Tatian's specific aim was (probably) to include every detail of his sources. Uncertainty about the nature of Tatian's original text makes dogmatism impossible, but if the Dura fragment is a good witness to the original text of the Diatessaron, then this general assessment of Tatian's method does seem to be justified. Longstaff's analysis of the fragment, which follows very closely that of Kraeling,[11] shows how the author must have gone through the gospel texts, taking words from each gospel and piecing them together with great care and fidelity to form a new narrative.

However, Longstaff's further analysis of other texts is methodologically more suspect. Although he clearly recognises both the introductory problems associated with recovering the original text of the Diatessaron, and also that the extant witnesses are better evidence for the structure than the

wording of Tatian's text,[12] he still uses the detailed wording of the Arabic
MSS in their English translation by Hill[13] to try to deduce what characterises the conflation process. The weakness of this approach is seen once one
recognises that the Arabic MSS are all unreliable, because of the way in
which they have apparently harmonised the text with the Peshitta version
of the gospels. Moreover, the Arabic MSS appear to fall into two textual
groups, and the ones used by Hill for his translation (and used in turn by
Longstaff) show far more assimilation than the MSS of the other group.[14]
With this in mind, it is precarious to argue that one instance of Tatian's
carefully comparing sources is to be seen in his version, 'The young man
said to him, All these things have I guarded' (Mt) 'from my youth' (Mk),[15]
for the whole text here simply reproduces the Peshitta version of Matt.
xix. 20. Similarly, the apparent careful conflation of the list of commandments given to the young man, whereby the transposition of the first two
commandments appears to come from Luke, and the inserted 'do not
defraud' from Mark,[16] is considerably less significant when it is observed
that the whole appears in the Peshitta version of Matthew at this point.
Higgins points out that where a reading in the Arabic agrees with the
Peshitta and the Old Syriac, this may be a genuine Tatianic reading; but as
the order of commandments given above does not occur in the Old Syriac,
this is unlikely to be genuine; it is probably a case of scribal assimilation to
the standard version of the day, rather than any example of 'careful comparison of sources'. Thus, although the Dura fragment still retains its value,
and shows how Tatian may well have interwoven his sources, it is somewhat dangerous to try to extend this with the other examples chosen by
Longstaff, and to draw any conclusions about Tatian's detailed method.

However, in the case of Tatian, such a comparison of sources is not
surprising. It is in fact demanded by his overall aim. If he was trying to
include every detail of his sources, then he must have carefully compared
his sources and been eclectic in his choice of words within any one sentence. Such a method is not that of Benedict or Roger, and such a careful
comparison of sources is much harder to substantiate in the case of these
two writers. In the case of Benedict, he does, it is true, include extra
sentences from his second source in his first, but in general these require
no 'careful comparison'. In the first extract given by Longstaff, Benedict
includes just two clauses from the *Passio*, both being relatively self-
contained units, and both giving slightly more eminence to the figure of
Thomas. (The crowds acclaim his return to Canterbury with the words
'Benedictus qui venit in nomine Domini', and Thomas is said to edify all
those around him by his manner of conversation.)[17] Longstaff also says
that Benedict freely used the account in the *Passio* of the reconciliation

between Thomas and Henry.[18] However, the only evidence of literary dependence between the two parallel accounts is the phrase 'Archiepiscopum recepit in gratiam et', which appears in the *Passio*, and also in Benedict though in a different form. Nevertheless, since 'et' is used in different ways in the two accounts (and is hardly a significant word), and since 'archiepiscopum' is inherent in the narrative anyway, the only significant verbal agreement is the phrase 'recepit in gratiam'. Since the paragraph contains over 100 words in the *Passio*, it is precarious to argue for literary dependence here when the verbal agreement is so small. The wealth of extra circumstantial detail in Benedict (about the date and place of the meeting, and also the names of those present) suggests that he is dependent on another source of information here. Elsewhere, Benedict's use of his sources is clearly either to copy verbatim,[19] or to omit large accounts,[20] or to abbreviate drastically. Longstaff's claim, that Benedict, like Tatian, has 'carefully compared his sources and drawn them together with considerable literary skill',[21] goes too far. There is certainly no example of Benedict's mixing up the wording of his two sources in a single clause, nor of his inserting odd phrases and individual words from his second source into his main one, as is the case in the Dura fragment, and as must be assumed to be the case in Mark if he is conflating Matthew and Luke.

The situation is not very different with Roger, for, in most cases, he uses his sources like Benedict, copying them out verbatim. For example, in the text quoted by Longstaff, Roger starts by copying Benedict, slightly changing 4 words in 66; then he copies the *Passio* adding one word ('sic') and changing 3 in 61.[22] Again and again, Longstaff's analysis shows that Roger frequently copies his sources almost exactly.[23] Indeed the relationship between the two chronicles of Roger and Benedict is so close that common authorship has been suggested.[24] (The chronicle of 'Benedict' is well-known to be written by someone other than Benedict, Abbot of Peterborough.) Although this now seems unlikely (since at times Roger adds details to Benedict, while at others he appears to misunderstand his source and makes historical mistakes),[25] nevertheless, the possibility of common authorship only arises partly because the two chronicles are verbally almost identical for such long stretches.

Longstaff maintains that Roger's method of conflation is a very varied one,[26] yet this is not always easy to establish. Creative re-writing is said to have occurred at the account of the reconciliation between Henry and Thomas,[27] but it is very difficult to know how much use has been made by Roger of Benedict's account. The two versions are quite different and there is hardly any verbal agreement between them. In contrast to

Benedict's long account of the reconciliation, Roger dismisses it in a sentence, having already included the account of it from the *Passio*.[28] He then gives greater precision to the place involved ('in Monte Laudato'), recounts the return of Thomas 'ad abbatiam Sanctae Columbae' and the divine warning of his impending martyrdom, none of which appears in Benedict. Thus, although Roger may have been prompted by Benedict's account to give his version of the events here, there is no evidence that Benedict is being used as the direct source for Roger's version. In view of the lack of verbal agreement, and extra information available to Roger, it is safer to assume that Roger is reproducing an independent version of the event here. (It is interesting to note that the Vitellus MS of Benedict's chronicle, which appears to supplement the original text with reference either to Roger's chronicle or to one of the latter's extra sources, felt that the accounts were so different that the text here should be expanded with words from Roger. Clearly the scribe of the Vitellus MS did not feel that the two accounts were very similar.)[29] The same is true of the accounts of Henry's being in Bur in Normandy on Christmas Day, 1170. Longstaff says that Roger is dependent on Benedict 'although he has re-written the account, modifying the language considerably'.[30] However, once again the verbal agreement is small, and Roger has extra information, viz. that Henry had the Queen and his sons with him, and Thomas excommunicated Robert de Broc; thus it is very uncertain how far Roger can be said to be dependent on Benedict. Again, it is more likely that Roger deserts Benedict's account here, whether by reference to another source, or by relying on his own personal knowledge.

Examples of a 'careful comparison of sources' are not very easy to find. Longstaff cites the passage where Roger includes three words from the *Passio* ('et exhortationis verbo') in a quotation from Benedict.[31] However, this immediately precedes a long quotation from the *Passio*, so that it may simply be a case of Roger's switching sources at this point. In the note about the arrival of the four knights at Canterbury, Longstaff claims that both sources are carefully conflated,[32] but the evidence for this is not strong. 'Quinta die Natalis Domini' is said to combine 'Quinta natalis die' (Benedict) and 'quinta dominicae nativitatis die' (*Passio*), but the extra 'Domini' is quite natural as a simple addition to Benedict without having to assume a conscious reference to the *Passio* here. Then Roger is said to have carefully compared his sources by writing 'venerunt' and 'Sathanae' with Benedict, against the *Passio's* 'veniunt' and 'Satanae', but also by agreeing with the *Passio* (against Benedict) in omitting 'praedicti'. However, these differences are very small indeed. In fact, the omission of 'praedicti' is probably occasioned by the fact that, in Benedict, it refers to the previous paragraph, and to the mention of the four knights who are commissioned by Henry for their task. However, Roger completely re-writes this paragraph, omitting this detail altogether, and so he cannot say that the four knights have been previously mentioned ('praedicti'). There is thus probably no 'careful comparison' here, but only a straight use of Benedict alone, with the addition of 'Domini', and the omission of 'praedicti' due to Roger's form of the previous paragraph. The next paragraph then starts with the names of the four knights which Roger took from Benedict, before switching at this point to the *Passio* for a long section. Thus Roger is probably simply using Benedict alone, followed by the *Passio* alone. The other place where a careful comparison is said to occur is in the account of the martyrdom itself.[33] Midway through the account, Roger appears to have switched from Benedict to the *Passio* as his source probably to include a few extra words ('offerens . . . sanctorum patrocinia implorabat'). Yet in the second half of the paragraph, Longstaff claims that Roger was still 'carefully consulting and comparing his sources as he wrote' and this can be seen in the presence of an agreement with Benedict against the *Passio* here. However this agreement is only a variant spelling 'exspiranti' (Roger and Benedict) for 'expiranti' (*Passio*), and this seems far too small a difference on which to base such a claim. It is more likely that Roger is simply copying the *Passio's* account.

Thus, in all, there is not much evidence that either Benedict or Roger carefully compared their sources and wove them together in an intricate way. Rather, they copied one source at a time, often very exactly.[34] The examples adduced by Longstaff do show that sometimes whole clauses, or at least self-contained 'thought-units', could be inserted; but there are no examples in these two writings where a single word, or a single phrase not easily detachable from its context, is incorporated from a second source into the middle of a section dependent on another main source. There is nothing comparable to the Dura fragment of Tatian, or to Mark on the GH; that hypothesis has to assume (for Mark) an almost continuous process of 'careful comparison', taking one word from here, one from there, and weaving them together. Moreover, there must have been a large number of very small changes in wording etc., which is quite different from the combination of strict copying and very free re-writing (if it is not dependence on a totally different source) which characterises the conflation process in the chronicles of Benedict and Roger. Thus, it is very doubtful whether the two 'characteristics' of conflation, which Longstaff infers from his analysis, are really justified by the evidence. The overall method of Roger and Benedict is quite different from that of Tatian, and any 'comparison of sources', if it exists at all, is on a quite different level.

The fourth characteristic of conflation Longstaff finds in 'the tendency of an author to make his transition from one source to another at a place where the two sources are in verbal agreement'.[35] However, this is of only limited value, since, as Longstaff himself says, it can only apply when the sources are in verbal agreement. Moreover, the phenomenon does not in fact occur very often. Longstaff notes a number of places where it occurs in Tatian, but the uncertainties of Tatian's original text, noted above, make any conclusions based on the minute examination of the wording of the text extremely uncertain. In Benedict, Longstaff notes only one such occurrence: 'The question "Ubi est archiepiscopus?" also appears in John of Salisbury and shortly after writing that question [i.e. from the *Passio*] Benedict of Peterborough began to copy from that source.'[36] However, a sentence in both Benedict and John intervenes before Benedict takes up John's account, so the transition is not exactly at this point. In the extract from Roger, Longstaff notes only two examples.[37] The first one, where the crowds acclaim Thomas' return with the words of the *Benedictus*, does fit the theory.[38] At the second example, which is in the corresponding place to the example from Benedict, Longstaff says that 'this similarity between his sources [in "Ubi est archiepiscopus?"] provided the occasion for Roger of Hoveden to turn again to Benedict of Peterborough'.[39] However, this ignores the fact that Roger continues copying the *Passio* for a further ten lines of text before switching to Benedict. Thus this 'characteristic of conflation' occurs so rarely that it is very doubtful if it can properly be said to 'characterise' the conflation process in general. At times it occurs, but there are numerous other examples of changes between sources at points of no verbal agreement. Further, as will be seen later, the phenomenon is not entirely unexpected on any source hypothesis. Thus the value of this criterion for determining whether any document is the result of a conflation process is very uncertain.

The fifth characteristic is that of redundancy and duplication, often thought to characterise conflation. Longstaff notes that this does not occur in Benedict or Roger, but is present in Tatian, so that it is more likely to occur 'when an author is copying everything (or nearly everything) found in his sources'.[40] But this then only highlights the difficulties associated with the diversity of aims and methods of different conflators. Longstaff himself sees this as a characteristic only of an all-inclusive type of conflation, and it can be used only in relation to Mark's gospel with great care. For one of the difficulties of the GH is in accounting for the great variety of ways in which Mark must have proceeded at different places: sometimes he appears to do a Tatian-like job in including all the details of his alleged sources (e.g. i. 32), but at other times he is content to omit many of the details of his sources. Thus, before one can appeal to the examples of duplication and redundancy in Mark as consistent with the theory that Mark is a conflated document,[41] one must explain the prior question of why Mark, in conflating Matthew and Luke, should conflate in an 'all-inclusive' way (and so include examples of redundancy and duplication) at some points in the tradition but not others.

The sixth and seventh characteristics are very closely related. They are simply that 'conflation is not a mechanical process', and that a conflated document can be either a condensation or an expansion of the sources.[42] However, it is not clear how these can function in any positive way. Certainly they are justified in that Longstaff's work has shown that conflation is a very varied process. But this only raises even more acutely the problem of how far one is justified in abstracting any features which 'characterise' conflated texts in general, or in discovering any features which would support the theory that any given document was a conflated text as against some other source theory.

It is thus very doubtful how much is shown when, for example, one points to features in Mark and says that they are characteristic of a conflated text. One can point to features which characterise Tatian's, or Roger's, or Benedict's method of conflating two sources, but the attempt to abstract from these any general characteristics is not always successful. The characteristic of 'carefully comparing sources', which I have tried to show does not occur very often (if ever) in Benedict and Roger, demonstrates that a conflator need not necessarily have followed one source at a time, although Benedict and Roger frequently do just that, as does Tatian apparently in the example quoted of Mk. iii. 1–6 and pars.[43] The phenomenon of switching sources at a point of verbal agreement occurs so rarely that it can hardly be said to 'characterise' the conflation process. So too the characteristic of the non-mechanical nature of conflation can only function negatively, to exclude statements to the effect that a conflator could not have proceeded in such and such a way. It cannot function positively in distinguishing between the possibilities of a document's being a conflation of, or a common source for, two given documents. Thus the characteristics which Longstaff derives have little critical value. None of them can function in a positive way, and none of them seems capable of setting up a criterion for deciding whether a document could *not* be a conflated text. His analysis of the Markan texts (some of which are examined in detail in Part III), shows that Mark shares some of these 'characteristics', but these are very vague and imply that the conflation process is so varied that, potentially, 'anything goes'.

There is one feature which Longstaff notes in his analysis of the Markan texts and which, he claims, gives rather more positive support to the theory that Mark is a conflation of, rather than a common source for, Matthew and Luke. This is the pattern of 'alternating agreement' between Mark and the other two gospels. Longstaff's comment after the analysis of Mk. i. 29-31 is typical: 'It is somewhat as though each [i.e. of Matthew and Luke on the 2DH] were free to re-write the Marcan account only in those details where the other had substantially preserved the content and language of that source.'[44] As seen above, the phenomenon has been used as an argument about the order of whole pericopes: Mark's order is usually supported by both Matthew and Luke, but when one deserts it the other retains it. For some, this is too much of a coincidence: if Matthew and Luke are independent, the way in which one of them leaps in to support Mark when the other does not seems too good to be true.[45]

Longstaff claims that this is a feature not only of the order of whole pericopes, but also of the detailed wording. However, greater precision is required about the exact nature of the phenomenon before conclusions can be drawn. Longstaff says (in connection with Mk. xiv. 12-16), 'The close parallel between Mark and Matthew ceases at exactly the place where the close parallel between Mark and Luke begins and resumes again at exactly the point where the parallel between Mark and Luke ends.'[46] Nevertheless, the 'close parallel' involved is not as close as this statement might imply, and the situation is not nearly as clear-cut as in the case of the order of whole pericopes. In the latter case, there is a clear, unambiguous situation: either Mark's order is supported by Matthew/Luke or it is not. However, in the case of the detailed wording, such a black and white decision is not possible and the options are not a simple choice between Matthew/Luke definitely supporting Mark's wording or not. For the verbal agreement between Mark and the other two gospels is close, but the relationship is by no means one of identity. Unlike the situation with Roger and Benedict, the secondary writers in the gospels (on whatever source hypothesis) have not copied out long sections of their sources verbatim, but must have introduced innumerable small changes of grammar and wording. Thus it is only a matter of degree as to which one of Matthew or Luke is closer to Mark in wording, and this will inevitably depend on a subjective judgement. For example, in the analysis of Mk. iii. 1-5, Longstaff claims that Mark is 'closely parallel' to Luke in verses 3-5a,[47] yet there are 10 disagreements here.[48] In verses 1-2, there are 12 disagreements between Mark and Matthew, 8 between Mark and Luke;[49] some of the latter may be more important, but this is not certain, and it is doubtful if they affect the sense of the passage as much as the difference made by the explicit question of legality in Matt. xii. 10.[50] However,

Longstaff then claims that, in Mark, verses 1 and 2 are 'closely parallel' to Matthew but 'significantly different' from Luke, whereas verses 3-5a are 'closely parallel' to Luke.[51] Against that, all one can really say is that verses 1 and 2 appear to be closer to Matthew than to Luke (if in fact this is so), and verses 3-5a are parallel to Luke (since Matthew has no parallel here). Similarly, in the section Mk. xi. 15-19, Longstaff suggests that the agreements and disagreements are much better defined than in fact they are. To say that there is a pattern of alternating agreement within verse 15,[52] (15b close to Luke, 15c close to Matthew) ignores the fact that the differences between Mark and Matthew do not suddenly vanish completely in verse 15c. Matthew does show some differences from Mark in verse 15b (Jesus is specified, Mark's participle εἰσελθών is avoided as is the use of ἤρξατο) but Matthew still shows differences in verse 15c (no repeated τούς, and a different position of κατέστρεψεν). The 'closeness' is therefore only a relative one, and all that one can really say is that Mark is closer to Matthew at one place, closer to Luke at another, but without being able to say always that the third gospel in question is significantly different.

Once this is recognised, it becomes clear that the method itself, of deciding which of the other two gospels Mark is closer to, is bound to produce the 'pattern of alternating agreement' which Longstaff finds so significant. For, if one goes through the Markan text, deciding at every word or phrase which of Matthew or Luke is closer to Mark's text, then one will get blocks which, since there are only two possibilities, can only alternate with each other. If one starts with Matthew, say, being closer to Mark, then this will continue for a period, precisely to the point where Matthew ceases to be closer and Luke becomes closer. This may be after two words, two sentences or two pericopes. Then Luke will be closer for a time, precisely to the point where Matthew is closer again. Thus one cannot but obtain blocks of Matthew closer – Luke closer – Matthew closer – Luke closer, etc. There will of course be some exceptions to this. Mark will sometimes have no parallel with either of the other two, but this does not affect the 'alternating agreement' at all. Another possibility is that all three gospels will be so close that no decision will be possible about which of the other two is closer to Mark. This will be preceded by Matthew, say, being closer, and followed by Luke being closer. (If the same gospel is closer on either side, this will not be significant, and the whole section would be adjudged as a single block of Mark's being closer to that gospel throughout.) This is the only alternative to there being a clear dividing line between 'Matthew closer' and 'Luke closer'. This will produce a situation of Matthew closer – all three close – Luke closer. If, then, one assumes that Mark is conflating Matthew and Luke, it will appear that Mark has switched sources at a point of verbal agreement between his sources, which is precisely Longstaff's fourth characteristic of conflation. However, the phenomenon in question will inevitably occur occasionally in such an analysis of the texts concerned. For it will always occur at the few points in the tradition where no decision is possible about which of Matthew or Luke is closer to Mark.

Thus the pattern of alternating agreement, and the phenomenon of an alleged conflator's occasionally switching sources at a point of verbal agreement between his sources, are both results which are pre-determined by the method itself. If the relation between Mark and one of Matthew/ Luke were one of verbal identity and the third gospel were widely divergent (as is the case in Benedict and Roger in relation to their sources), then this would indeed be a striking phenomenon. But this is not the case. The difference in closeness is quantitative rather than qualitative, and there is nothing improbable in the phenomenon on the theory of Markan priority (just as, of course, the GH provides an equally good explanation). All it involves is the fact that there are many passages where all three gospels are parallel to each other, and there are numerous small changes between all three. But at any one point, where Matthew ceases to be closer to Mark than Luke, the only possibilities are (a) that Luke is now closer, or, more rarely, (b) that all three are equally close. There is, therefore, nothing here which can distinguish between the likelihood of Mark's being a conflation of, or a common source for, the other two gospels.

Longstaff's study is thus inconclusive. Negatively, he has succeeded in showing that conflation is a very varied process, and hence the theory that Mark is a conflated document should not be dismissed *a priori* as impossible. However, the process is so varied that it seems difficult, if not impossible, to derive any 'characteristics' of conflation in general, which will then function in any useful way in the discussion, i.e. in providing any criteria for distinguishing between the various source hypotheses currently proposed. There are no characteristics which can only belong to conflated texts, and which could then serve to distinguish a conflated text from a non-conflated one. The other examples of conflation show that Mark could be a conflated text theoretically, but this is not in doubt. What is still required is some indication that the theory that Mark is a conflation of Matthew and Luke gives a more coherent and self-consistent explanation of the facts than other theories. Certainly the phenomenon of 'alternating agreement' does not do this when the methodology is examined in detail. Longstaff's work has shown that the GH must not be dismissed summarily, but it makes no headway in suggesting that it is a better solution to the Synoptic Problem than the 2DH.

6   PATRISTIC EVIDENCE

I

One of the most frequent criticisms of the GH is that it can offer no convincing *Sitz im Leben* for the production of a gospel such as Mark, given the existence of Matthew and Luke.[1] This is closely related to the problem, already partly considered, of Mark's choice of material: why should anyone have wanted to write a new gospel which omitted so much from the sources available? A fresh approach to this problem has been made by Dungan,[2] and his research has been said by Farmer to be another of the significant developments which explains the more favourable response given now to the GH.[3] Dungan seeks to find possible examples in other gospel literature of the early Christian centuries which might provide analogies to Mark's gospel on the GH, i.e. to a gospel which chooses only what is common to both its sources and adds virtually nothing new. Insofar as his work succeeds, Dungan too is implicitly appealing to the criterion of coherence, albeit in a slightly different way. For he is attempting to show that the GH gives a theory about Mark which fits in with what else is known of the history, in particular the 'gospel-making activity', of the period.

The problem of a convincing *Sitz im Leben* for Mark has been explicit or implicit in all the detailed discussions so far. Why should Mark have proceeded in the way he is alleged to have done? In one sense, this was the strongest support which the theories of the Tübingen school gave to the GH. For a place could be found for the composition of a gospel like Mark's within their preconceived idea of the development of the history of the early church. Mark represented the end-point of the development which saw the gradual reconciliation between the opposing parties in the early church. Mark, as the last gospel to be written, mediated between the extremes of Petrine Judaeo-Christianity and Pauline Gentile Christianity, as represented (at least partly) in Matthew and Luke respectively. Given the theory of this historical development, Mark could be placed within it, and thus a convincing reason could be found for its composition. However, when the prior theory of historical development was abandoned, Mark on the GH was left without any very convincing *Sitz im Leben*. A similar *Sitz im Leben* is sometimes advocated today, though without any presuppositions that the history of the early church developed in this way, or even a prior theory that there was a schism in the early church. Farmer says that Mark is 'irenic' (rather than neutral), and 'represents the growing strength of the mediating tendencies which had originated in the historical Peter and later led to the rejection of Marcion and to the rejection of all attempts to base theology on a single tradition'.[4] The Tübingen school could appeal to their theories of a great Petrine/Pauline division in the early church, and the resulting reconciliation which must have occurred. The difficulty today is to find evidence for the existence of such mediating tendencies as Farmer postulates. However, Dungan's work has sought to point to other tendencies which were present in the mid-second century.

Dungan looks at the general method implicit in the polemical attacks of many religious writers of the time, both Christian and non-Christian. On the 'Christian' side, there are Marcion's *Antitheses*, Irenaeus' *Adversus Haereses*, Tertullian, Tatian, etc., and on the non-Christian side there are Josephus, Celsus and Julian the Apostate. In all these writers Dungan finds a constant approach, whereby the opposition was blasted out of court by a violent attack which ridiculed the lack of consistency and the numerous contradictions which the opposing system allegedly involved. Also, this often included a refusal to allow the other side to resort to allegorising its own sacred writings. Rather, such writers fastened on the literal meaning alone to enable contradictions etc. to be more easily found. This, then, is the real reason for Marcion's refusal to allegorise the OT, and his method here is analogous to Celsus' attacks on Christianity, or to Irenaeus' attacks on 'heretics', or Tatian's attacks on Greek myths.[5] This implies, therefore, a widespread belief in the ancient world in the importance of showing that one's own beliefs were self-consistent and free from contradictions. Such a defence of 'orthodox' Christianity was that of Irenaeus and Tertullian, who both appealed to the essential unity of their own doctrine in contrast to the divergencies noted in the 'heretics'.[6]

It is in this light, Dungan claims, that Marcion's gospel and Tatian's Diatessaron should be viewed. Both were reactionary attempts to purge the Christian writings from any possibility of a charge of self-contradiction, although they proceeded in different ways. Tatian's method was to produce a single consistent narrative, constructed out of all four gospels; Marcion's method, on the other hand, was to prune down one already existing gospel (Luke), so that the result would be completely consistent with the letters of Paul. Both then were characterised by a desire to harmonise the tradition, and to do this by 'excising corruptions and redundancies from already existing and widely accepted . . . stories of the life of Jesus'.[7]

However, it is very uncertain whether all this can provide a convincing parallel to the gospel of Mark in relation to Matthew and Luke. Marcion's concern was with the one very specific basic inconsistency, i.e. the incompatibility of the God of the OT and the God of the NT. All his ideas centred around this, together with his conviction of the validity of his interpretation of Paul's teaching. It was not an abstract fear of inconsistency *per se*, but the main concern was with the specific doctrinal issue of the nature of God. 'The basic ground of Marcion's work was the Pauline doctrine, or part of the Pauline doctrine, which he found in parts of the major Pauline epistles.'[8] His method of pruning a gospel text was simply a result of the fact that he believed that the present Lukan text (as well as the text of some of Paul's epistles) had been interpolated by Judaisers. Marcion's criterion was not consistency for the sake of consistency, but consistent Paulinism (or at least Pauline teaching as interpreted by Marcion). The example of Tatian is possibly a better one, but against this must be measured the fact that we do not know what Tatian's motives were in compiling the Diatessaron; it may have been simply a desire to have all the traditions he wanted to include in a single scroll, or in some other continuous form, for convenience's sake. We do not know if it was the fear of a charge of inconsistency between the four gospels which led Tatian to produce his Diatessaron.

There is thus very little firm evidence that the fear of inconsistency *per se*, or of being self-contradictory, led to any gospel-making activity. The inconsistency charge is rather the language of polemic. In defence of Christianity, the argument was often not so much that the opposite position was inconsistent or self-contradictory in itself, but that it was inconsistent with the true teaching of the church which can be traced back to the earliest times. Thus, as in the case of Marcion, the criterion for Irenaeus and Tertullian was not consistency for the sake of it, but consistent apostolic Christianity, or consistency with the 'rule of faith'.[9]

It is hard to see how Mark's gospel could function, if it is to be viewed in this light, as a document aiming to remove the contradictions between Matthew and Luke. Dungan has suggested that Mark may have affinities with the Marcionites,[10] partly on the basis of Mark's contents (with very little on Jesus' Jewish background), partly on the basis of the statement of Irenaeus about the use of Mark by the Docetics (who included Marcionites).[11] However, this does not fit well with Marcion's known use of Luke rather than Mark. On this view, one would assume that Mark's gospel was intended for exclusive use. Farmer, on the other hand, claims that Mark was not writing to replace Matthew or Luke: rather, a church possessing Mark's gospel would be able to see how Matthew and Luke were basically not mutually inconsistent, and so could use both these two gospels.[12] But this is not easy to envisage in practice. If a church was worried about the discrepancies between Matthew and Luke, it is hard to see how the possession of a document, which simply ignores the discrepancies by omitting them altogether, helps in any way. Farmer says that 'Mark's Gospel complements and supplements Matthew and Luke not so much in terms of content but of function', and the function seems to be 'to enable the Church to accept both Matthew and Luke'.[13] It is here that historical parallels are lacking. Although the pluriformity of the gospel tradition in general may have been a problem, there is no evidence that disagreements between just Matthew and Luke caused difficulties in the period when Mark was written according to the GH, i.e. at least before 200 A.D. The existence of worries about the differences between Mark and one or more of the other gospels (possibly Matthew) may be indicated by the remarks of Papias, defending Mark's order;[14] Tatian's Diatessaron, and Irenaeus' insistence on the divine necessity of a four-fold gospel canon,[15] may reflect worries about the differences between all four gospels; concern about the differences between John and the other gospels may be reflected in the Muratorian Canon's insistence that John was an eye-witness of the gospel events, and in Clement's statement that John 'wrote a spiritual gospel'.[16] However, there is no clear evidence of any worries in the second century about the differences between Matthew and Luke which might be resolved by a gospel such as Mark's.[17]

How precisely Mark might be seen to remove the contradictions between Matthew and Luke is hardly ever spelt out in detail. Dungan says that it will repay further research but gives no concrete examples.[18] Farmer cites the omission of such conflicting traditions within Matthew as v. 9 with x. 34 (on peace), v. 18 with xii. 1ff. (Jesus' attitude to the law), x. 5f.with xxviii. 19 (the Gentiles). Luke, he says, is free from such contradictions within itself, but is inconsistent with Matthew; Mark then mediates between the two and is consistent with both.[19] However, although Mark may not contain some of the more extreme self-contradictions within Matthew's gospel, the alleged contradictions between Matthew and Luke are not specified in detail. Nor is it easy to see Mark as simply 'consistent with both', e.g. on the relative position of the rejection scene in Nazareth, or on the implied location of the resurrection appearances in Galilee rather than Jerusalem (if indeed this is what xvi. 7 refers to); Mark clearly sides with Matthew against Luke.

Dungan's arguments are, therefore, not convincing, and the problem of a *Sitz im Leben* for Mark on the GH remains. Dungan's alleged parallels do not prove that consistency in itself was valued; rather, what was required was that doctrine be consistent with what was believed to be right. Reduced to its essentials, this is nothing more than a rejection of what one disagrees with, almost on the grounds that one does disagree with it! Moreover, there is no evidence of any difficulties being experienced because of the discrepancies between Matthew and Luke specifically. There is inevitably the possibility of circularity here, and the whole argument can be turned backwards. For if the GH is correct, then Mark was composed in this way, and there must have been a *Sitz im Leben* for it. This may then be an indication that there was some embarrassment felt about the discrepancies between Matthew and Luke. However, it is by no means obvious that such a *Sitz im Leben* is the correct one, even if the GH is correct about the relationships between the gospels. Unless this can be shown to be more plausible on internal evidence, there must be some link with an independent phenomenon, outside the gospels themselves, to provide some justification for the theory. Dungan's reference to Marcion's abridgement of Luke is only a partial parallel, as is Tatian's Diatessaron. But neither of these involves the same process of simultaneous conflation and abbreviation which must be postulated for Mark. This really lies mid-way between the method of Marcion (abbreviating on clear doctrinal grounds) and Tatian (conflating): Fuller calls the problem of finding a suitable reason why Mark might have done this 'das Hauptproblem von Griesbach-Farmer'.[20] It is not apparent that even Dungan's second article (which is not noted in Fuller's survey) really solves this problem.

II

The evidence from the patristic period has also been brought into the debate about the GH by Farmer's own reference to the beliefs of the early fathers about the relative order in which the gospels were written. Among his sixteen 'steps', all of which contribute to the final solution without necessarily forming a connected chain of arguments, Farmer says in step 13, 'The weight of external evidence is against the hypothesis that Matthew was written after Luke', and in step 14 he says that exactly the same arguments can be repeated with 'Mark' substituted for 'Luke'; finally, in step 15, he claims: 'That Mark was written after both Matthew and Luke is in accord with the earliest and best external evidence on the question.'[21]

The first of these claims, that the theory that Matthew was written first agrees with most of the patristic evidence, is broadly speaking true. The two main orderings which list the gospels in order are Matt – Mk – Lk – Jo, and Matt – Jo – Lk – Mk, the latter being found mostly in Western witnesses. The belief that Matthew was written first is explicitly stated by Irenaeus, the Monarchian Prologues, Origen, Eusebius and Jerome.[22] It may also be supported by the Muratorian Canon (depending on whether (a) the note just before the statement about Luke refers to Mark, and (b) the order of enumeration is also meant to be a chronological one), and the witness of Clement of Alexandria is at least not inconsistent with this. (He says only that gospels with genealogies preceded those without.)

The evidence of Papias should, however, be noted here. Farmer says that 'Papias' testimony throws no light on the question of the order in which the Gospels were written'.[23] Now this is certainly true as far as direct statements are concerned, but there is the slightly strange fact that Eusebius (who is our only source for Papias' remarks) records the note about Mark before, not after, that about Matthew. Since Eusebius' own opinion is that the order of composition was Matt - Mk - Lk - Jo, one would expect him to put the statement about Matthew first. This is by no means certain. The order in which the gospels are enumerated may or may not signify that the author/compiler of the list believed that this corresponded with the chronological order of composition. For example, Irenaeus refers to each of the gospels in turn (for adducing quotations or for linking the exclusive use of each one with a particular heretical group) in the order Matt - Lk - Mk - Jo; and when he wants to make each gospel correspond to one of the four beasts, he enumerates them in the order Jo - Lk - Matt - Mk;[24] yet when he states his beliefs about their chronological order, that order is Matt - Mk - Lk - Jo.[25] So too Tertullian can enumerate the gospels in the order Matt - Jo - Lk - Mk, or Matt - Jo - Mk - Lk,[26] but it is clear from the context that no stress is being laid on the relative order of the last two. (Primarily he is claiming priority for the two 'apostolic' gospels, Matthew and John, and thereby trying to play down the importance of Luke in the face of Marcion's exclusive use of the latter.) Thus any firm deductions about the relative order of composition from a simple enumeration of the order in which they are mentioned is dangerous. Nevertheless, the very strange order of Papias, with Mark mentioned before Matthew, may possibly indicate that this was Papias' belief about the order of composition. (One of the few to notice the odd order is Dungan, who says that a good sense can be made out of both notes taken together – Matthew wrote in Aramaic, each translated into Greek, and in particular Mark translated Peter's reminiscences – *if* they are taken in the reverse order.[27] But the very strangeness of the order is precisely what is not explained here.)

Farmer also suggests that the unanimous witness of the early fathers to the priority of Matthew is all the more significant because of the peculiarly

Jewish features in Matthew, and the way that gospel reflects the interests of the earlier Jewish-Christian mission. A Gentile church would have found Luke more suited to its needs, and hence the fact that Matthew is given pride of place may reflect 'reliable historical memory in the gentile Churches as to the true chronological relationship between these two Gospels'.[28] Moreover, Farmer believes that exactly the same argument holds if 'Luke' is replaced by 'Mark'. However this is all questionable. Matthew's 'Jewish' features are no more dominant in many respects than Mark's or Luke's, and Matthew ends with a clear command of the risen Christ to the disciples to carry the Christian mission into all the world (xxviii. 19f.). It seems unlikely, therefore, that Matthew's gospel would have been unacceptable in a Gentile church and that its prime position can only be due to reliable historical memory. Other factors may also have been influential. One of these was probably the tradition which made Matthew's gospel the work of one of the twelve apostles, whilst Mark's and Luke's gospels were written by disciples of apostles. Although apostolicity *per se* does not seem to have been a decisive consideration in the early period, historical reliability clearly was: for Irenaeus the gospels earned their positions of authority by being the faithful work of eye-witnesses, or of disciples of eye-witnesses.[29] The same is probably true in the Muratorian Canon (cf. the stress on John's being an eye-witness, and Luke's account being reliable even though not a direct eye-witness account).[30] This too appears to be the reason behind the 'Western' ordering of the gospels, which placed the 'apostolic' gospels, Matthew and John, before the others. (This is Tertullian's reason for giving them pride of place. The other witnesses give no reasons, but this is as likely to be the true one as any other.) It would, moreover, be a perfectly reasonable deduction to assume that Mark and Luke were written later than Matthew, if the former two were believed to have been written after the deaths of Peter and Paul respectively. There is no reason why the apostle Matthew could not have lived on to a very old age; nevertheless, if Matthew was an apostle, and if Mark and Luke were written after the deaths of the two great apostles, it would not be unnatural to assume that Mark's and Luke's gospels belonged to a 'sub-apostolic' age, and hence were later than the 'apostolic' Matthew.

It should also be noted that arguments about the relationship between Matthew and Luke cannot simply be transferred unchanged and applied to the relationship between Matthew and Mark. If Matthew was more popular than Mark in the early church, this was probably due to its greater usefulness and comprehensiveness. The vast majority of apparent 'citations' in the very earliest period are from the sayings of Jesus,[31] and it is here that Matthew's gospel is far richer in material than Mark's.[32] Although this has no bearing on the relationship between Matthew and Luke, it would explain the comparative neglect of Mark in the early church. The conclusion of all this is that Matthew's being given pride of place may have been grounded in considerations other than reliable historical memory about the relative order in which the gospels were written.

If it is true to say that the weight of the patristic evidence strongly supports Matthean priority (excepting possibly the testimony of Papias), Farmer's other claim - 'that Mark was written after both Matthew and Luke is in accord with the earliest and best external evidence' - is a highly questionable one. The only positive evidence for this is the statement of Clement of Alexandria, to the effect that gospels with genealogies were written first.[33] Farmer also says that this gives an Alexandrian tradition about the order of the gospels, which is all the more likely to be reliable, given the tradition that Mark founded the church in Alexandria: one would expect an Alexandrian tradition to give pride of place to the gospel attributed to one of its first bishops.

However, Clement himself is hardly the 'earliest and best' external witness on the subject. He is no earlier than Irenaeus, who claims that the order is Matt - Mk - Lk, and he is probably not significantly earlier than the Muratorian Canon, which is probably to be dated around 200,[34] and which definitely puts Luke third. Clement does claim to be reproducing an earlier tradition, but how much weight should be put on this is uncertain. (Papias' note also partly reproduces earlier tradition.) Thus Clement's evidence is not necessarily the 'earliest'. Nor is it the 'best'. His other note about Mark, that it was written during Peter's lifetime,[35] is usually considered suspect (and certainly at variance with the other notices, e.g. in Irenaeus and the anti-Marcionite prologue to Mark, which say that Mark was written after Peter's death). Moreover Clement's claims, which are supposed to preserve old Alexandrian traditions, are not followed by Origen, writing only slightly later and himself a native of Alexandria: Origen himself supports the order Matt - Mk - Lk.[36] Further, the added significance which Farmer sees in the tradition linking Mark with Alexandria is considerably reduced by the fact that this tradition is attested only relatively late in the patristic period. It appears in Eusebius, Jerome, the Apostolic Constitutions, and Epiphanius.[37] But it is not mentioned by Papias, or by Irenaeus, or, more significantly, by the Alexandrians themselves, Dionysius, Clement or Origen. In fact, Clement himself is in line with the majority of early writers in linking Mark with Rome.[38] It is therefore highly questionable to claim that Clement's evidence is the 'earliest and best'. It is not the earliest, and, in view of his other statement about the date and place of composition of Mark, he can hardly be relied upon without further ado to provide the 'best' evidence. Clement's statement is very much out on a limb as far as the patristic evidence is concerned. Farmer's own earlier judgement on this evidence seems much more justifiable, when he refers to the 'almost unanimous tradition of the early church fathers, that the gospels were written in the order, Matthew, Mark, Luke and John'.[39]

If one is to adduce the external evidence at all, this would suggest an Augustinian, and not a Griesbachian, solution to the Synoptic Problem. However, the fact is that other considerations, such as historical reliability and eye-witness authorship, as well as convenience of source material to be quoted, were also important for the early fathers. This suggests that the patristic evidence should be used only with great care, and cannot be relied upon to give a completely unbiased account.

7 THE MINOR AGREEMENTS

> The agreements between Matthew and Luke against Mark constitute the greatest difficulty for proponents of the two-document theory and other related theories of the interrelationships of the Synoptic Gospels. The two-document hypothesis is dependent on the statement that Matthew and Luke do not agree together against Mark, and holders of that hypothesis are forced to explain away the existence of the actual agreements.[1]

So comments Sanders, and the embarrassment which the so-called 'minor agreements' cause for the 2DH is well-known. Streeter put forward a variety of explanations to cover various cases, and this chapter of his book has often been heavily criticised.[2] For any study of the Synoptic Problem, Streeter's arguments must be examined with care, especially in the light of the criticisms made by Farmer and others. However, the same texts must also be satisfactorily explained by another source hypothesis if that hypothesis is to command assent. Thus the problem raised by the minor agreements for the 2DH must be looked at in conjunction with the question of whether they constitute a problem on other hypotheses. In particular, one must see if the texts can be more satisfactorily explained by the GH, than by the 2DH, bearing in mind also that Streeter's treatment of the minor agreements is not the only way of explaining them on the assumption of Markan priority.

In Farmer's presentation of the GH, the minor agreements arise out of Mark's editorial method in conflating his sources. Farmer refers, with apparent approval, to Burton's statement that a writer, faced with two documents already in a literary relationship with each other, 'might conceivably depart from either or both of his sources, when they were not in agreement, but avoid departing from them in that to which they bore concurrent testimony'.[3] This appears to be Farmer's basic theory of Mark's overall aim in his conflation.[4] In the very broadest terms, it explains satisfactorily the phenomenon of the common content in the gospels. However, there is still the problem of Mark's omissions of whole pericopes: in all the 'double tradition' material (usually ascribed to Q), Matthew and Luke bear 'concurrent testimony', and yet Mark does not include this.[5] Nevertheless it remains to be seen how well this explanation deals with the detailed wording within each pericope which Mark has chosen, for whatever reason, to include.

Given this editorial method, Farmer believes that the phenomenon of the minor agreements is now readily explicable. He writes:

> It would be inhuman to expect a writer so motivated never to deviate in the slightest degree from the common text in his two sources. It is enough to expect him to depart only when so to do would not affect the sense or the intention of the text to which his sources bore concurrent testimony. This is a fair description of the great bulk of the agreements of Matthew and Luke against Mark. Generally speaking, these agreements do not seriously affect the literary purpose or theological intention of the passages concerned.[6]

Thus the minor agreements are due to Mark's making small, insignificant changes in the common text of his sources. In general terms, this is quite plausible, and it accounts for the minor nature of many of the agreements (which theories of a subsidiary use made by Luke of Matthew do not do so convincingly).[7] In this context, Farmer notes with approval Sanday's theory that the minor agreements are all due to the conscious effort of a single mind. Sanday had thought that the minor agreements might be due to the fact that Matthew and Luke had used a version of Mark slightly different from our present gospel. Moreover, this common text appeared to be the result of a methodical, systematic improvement of the original Markan text, and so Sanday proposed that it was the work of a single editor, improving Mark's rough Greek.[8] Referring to this theory, Farmer writes:

> Fifty years earlier, such painstaking results would have been widely accepted as but one more indication that Mark was indeed working together the narratives of Matthew and Luke. From the point of view shared by adherents of the Griesbach hypothesis, when Mark was conflating Matthew and Luke, his own stylistic preferences, especially when they did not affect the sense of the text, would naturally have influenced his account of the Gospel narratives in just such a way as this.[9]

> The only thing they [the minor agreements] would tend to have in common would be their inconsequential effect upon the meaning of

the narrative and possibly a certain unitary complexion emanating as they would, under these circumstances, from Mark's conscious or unconscious grammatical usage and stylistic preference freely influencing his adaptation of an essentially Matthean text.[10]

The inference from all this seems to be that the minor agreements have a certain unitary character, being all due to Mark's redaction of his sources; and further, that Sanday's theory of a single mind behind the minor agreements really gives support to the GH, if it is properly evaluated. Indeed, in the first quotation given above, Farmer appears to equate the 'single mind' with the mind of Mark. (Mark's 'stylistic preferences . . . would naturally have influenced his account . . . in just such a way as this'. The 'this' in context refers to the way the account has been affected by the single mind of the proposed corrector.) However, it is doubtful whether Sanday's theory can give any support to the GH in this way. Later, Farmer gives the true picture of what must have happened on the GH. For the fact is that the changes which the 2DH must account for are precisely the opposite to those envisaged by the GH. Sanday's theory was that all the changes from Mark were corrections and improvements, introduced by a single mind. The GH requires that a single mind, i.e. Mark's, has introduced precisely the opposite changes into the common text of Matthew and Luke. Farmer does admit later that his own theory is slightly different from Sanday's:

> Although this would be coming at the problem from a slightly different direction than that advocated by Abbott and Sanday, it would in an inverse manner do justice to the evidence they saw for regarding these minor agreements as stemming from a purposeful and unitary redactional source. That source in the first instance would be the stylistic and grammatical usage of Matthew . . . The minor agreements would reflect Matthean usage.[11]

Thus the single mind would be Matthew's and not Mark's. This is possible, but it is certainly not an immediately obvious deduction from Abbott's and Sanday's results, which were that the differences all looked like conscious improvements of Mark.

Although Sanday's theory has to work in 'inverse manner' for the GH, so that the 'single mind' is not the mind of a secondary redactor but that of the author of the original text, the alleged redaction by Mark is still the work of another single mind, and this mind must have made some rather strange changes in his sources. For Sanday, all the changes were in the direction away from Mark and were all explicable as 'improvements'; for the GH, all the reverse changes must be accounted for, and in Sanday's terms they will mostly be the exact opposite of improvements. For Farmer, they must also be explicable as mostly due to Mark's 'stylistic preferences'. Now some can be explained in this way, though it is often easier to envisage the changes happening the other way round. For Sanday, the single corrector did his work by, for example, changing Mark's historic present, by substituting the more idiomatic δέ for Mark's καί, by avoiding Mark's paratactic constructions, by substituting participles and subordinate clauses, by easing Mark's abrupt constructions with the addition of connecting words as well as by adding connecting particles.[12] On the GH, Mark must have been averse to using δέ, liked the historic present, had a love for parataxis and asyndeton, been averse to using connecting particles, and liked creating abrupt constructions. Now some of these are often said to be Markan characteristics, usually on the basis of the comparative total number of occurrences in each of the gospels.[13] For example, Mark uses καί considerably more frequently than Matthew and Luke do, and asyndeton and the historic present occur in Mark more often than elsewhere. However, it is not at all certain that this will explain the actual changes which must have occurred if the GH is correct. The phenomenon of the historic present has been treated already. On the GH, Mark must have frequently introduced the historic present into texts where Matthew and Luke do not have it. This is in itself plausible, but it does not explain Mark's overall inconsistency in not using the idiom when presented with it in one of his sources, in view of the fact that it is a clear stylistic preference of his.[14]

Further, simply to say that Sanday's theory can still be used, with his 'single mind' as that of Matthew, shows nothing about the relative merits of the GH and the theory of Markan priority. For, if the text of Matthew and Luke in the minor agreements is stylistically Matthean, this fact cannot distinguish between the possibilities of Matthew's redacting another source and Matthew's redacting Mark. If indeed it could be shown that these texts were stylistically Matthean and not Lukan, then this might support a theory of dependence of Luke on Matthew;[15] but the Matthean nature of the text cannot of itself exclude the possibility that Matthew has changed Mark. To be convincing, the GH must establish that the opposite changes have a unitary character, which is consistent with what is known of Markan redaction elsewhere. This is by no means easy to do.

The use of καί in Mark, with δέ in Matthew and Luke, would work in the way Farmer suggests, but an opposite change is very hard to explain. On any source hypothesis, such a change is awkward: Farmer himself points to Mk. ii. 6, where Mark has δέ and Matthew and Luke both have καί, as presenting 'a curious unexplained problem on Streeter's terms'.[16] However, it presents an equally curious problem on Farmer's terms. If the minor agreements are due to Mark's stylistic preferences, it is just here that we have exactly the opposite: Mark does not prefer δέ to καί, and yet, according to the GH, has introduced it here, despite the 'concurrent testimony' of his sources which both use his favourite καί. In fact, on the theory of Markan priority, MattR would account for at least Matthew's καὶ ἰδού (17 times in Matthew).[17] Moreover, if Mark is using Matthew and Luke, it is surprising that he has not used Luke's ἤρξαντο since this too is a Markan characteristic.[18] (The use of διαλογίζομαι by both Mark and Luke in this verse means that the GH must assume that Mark is explicitly referring to Luke here rather than Matthew, which makes Mark's non-use of ἤρξαντο even harder to explain.) There are similar cases of Mark's having δέ, parallel to καί in Matthew and Luke at Mk.xiv.47 and possibly ix.27.[19] In the former case, Matthew's καί is part of a καὶ ἰδού, and so could be explained as MattR of Mark (cf. above); Luke has an extra question in xxii. 49, and v. 50 is really a continuation of the same sentence: thus a δέ here, with its slight adversative sense, would be less appropriate. In Mk. ix. 27, the parallels are not close, since Mark's account is so much fuller. On the GH, Mark must have amplified his sources considerably, but in the process avoided this use of καί, beloved by him elsewhere. On the theory of Markan priority, Matthew and Luke are both abbreviating Mark considerably; they have reduced four sentences to one, and a δέ in the middle of a sentence would be less appropriate than a καί. So Markan priority can account for these texts where the GH faces great difficulties.

Another minor agreement which is difficult to explain as MkR is Mk. iv. 4 where Mark has ἐγένετο but Matthew and Luke do not. Turner points out that the omission of ἐγένετο by Luke is hard to explain if Luke is using Mark, since καὶ ἐγένετο ἐν τῷ + infinitive is a very common Lukan construction.[20] There is certainly no easy explanation of this agreement on the theory of Markan priority (unless it be due to common abbreviation of what was felt to be a redundancy),[21] but things are no easier for the GH. For the construction καὶ ἐγένετο with ἐν τῷ + infinitive, whilst common in Luke, occurs only here in Mark. Thus an addition of ἐγένετο here, which the GH must assert, is not in line with Mark's normal style. It is thus difficult to explain as MkR.

Other minor agreements are just as awkward for the GH. Streeter listed a number of cases where, he claimed, Matthew and Luke would inevitably correct Mark's incorrect version.[22] The GH must postulate a change by Mark from a correct version in both his sources to an 'incorrect' one. Thus, in Mk.vi.14, a change of Mark's incorrect reference to Herod as ὁ βασιλεύς to the correct title ὁ τετραάρχης is comprehensible; but there is no apparent reason why Mark should alter the concurrent testimony of his sources incorrectly. (It is a matter neither of style, nor of great theological import.) In viii. 31, ix. 31, x. 34, why should Mark change 'on the third day' in both his sources to 'after three days'? Why should he avoid the correct use of ἄγω or a compound in xi. 2 and 7; xv. 1 and 22 and use φέρω instead?[23] Mk. xiii. 11 shows that Mark could use ἄγω correctly. (This is redactional on the GH.) Why does Mark add μὴ ἀποστερήσῃς to his sources' list of commandments in x. 19? (The reverse change might be explained as assimilation to the wording of the Decalogue.)[24] Why should Mark omit καὶ διεστραμμένη in ix. 19, when the inclusion of it would provide a good example of duality, which is usually considered a feature of Mark's style? On the assumption of Markan priority, its inclusion by Matthew and Luke could be due to assimilation to the text of Dt. xxxii. 5. (In fact, there is uncertainty whether there really is a minor agreement here. The words are included in Mark in 𝔓45 Wf13 and some miniscules, and they are omitted in Luke by e Marcion and Old Latin.)

Other small verbal differences are difficult to envisage as Markan stylistic changes. Why should Mark omit θαυμάζω in iv. 41? It is in both his sources, and he himself uses the word four times, three of which must, on the GH, be due to MkR (Mk. v. 20; vi. 6; xv. 44) since the word does not occur in the parallels. On the other hand, Matthew uses the word 7 times, and Luke uses it 13 times in the gospel, 5 times in Acts, so that an addition by both to Mark would not be unnatural. The theory of Markan priority, therefore, involves a consistent picture of the redaction involved, whereas the GH does not. Why should Mark use the superlative πλεῖστος in iv. 1 with ὄχλος when both his sources use πολύς? Mark never uses πλεῖστος again, but he does qualify ὄχλος with πολύς six times elsewhere, five of which must be MkR on the GH (v. 21 and 24; viii. 1; ix. 14; xii. 37). On the other hand, a change of Mark's rare superlative (Matt. 2, Lk. 0) to the more usual πολύς is quite intelligible on the 2DH. A similar example occurs in Mk. iii. 7: why should Mark avoid ὄχλος in his sources (which he uses 38 times elsewhere) for πλῆθος (which he uses only twice)? This again is difficult to explain as due to Mark's 'stylistic preference'.

There are other minor agreements which are just as difficult to explain, where the Markan change must have involved more than a simply stylistic alteration. In Mk. xi. 27 Mark has no mention of Jesus 'teaching', as Matthew and Luke do. On the GH Mark must have omitted this word, in spite of the fact (a) that it occurs in both his sources, and (b) that Mark frequently stresses the fact elsewhere that Jesus was 'teaching'. This is therefore another case of Mark's apparently changing the common text of both his sources in a way which is positively un-Markan. For the 2DH, an explanation may be that in Mark, the question about authority is closely related to the recent action of Jesus in cleansing the temple, and the ταῦτα in the opponents' question refers to this;[25] moreover, the cursing of the fig-tree is also connected as a parabolic act which receives its interpretation in the cleansing.[26] Matthew and Luke both destroy this connection: Luke stresses Jesus' 'teaching daily in the temple' (xix. 47); hence a long gap is implied between the cleansing incident and the question about authority, which naturally picks up the teaching activity. Matthew too breaks the connection between the fig-tree incident and the cleansing; he has them in reverse order to Mark, and the cursing becomes a pure miracle (cf. παραχρῆμα in xxi. 19f.) which in turn acts as an illustration for the teaching which follows on the power of prayer. With this link made, the addition of διδάσκοντι in Matt. xxi. 23 is not surprising. On the theory of Markan priority this agreement can be explained as due to independent editing, whilst on the GH, the text is very difficult to explain.

A minor agreement of a different kind which causes difficulties for the GH is the presence in Mark, but not in Matthew or Luke, of the verse Mk. xi. 16 with the command of Jesus banning the carrying of vessels through the temple. This is part of one of the pericopes analysed in detail in Part III. Here it need only be noted that the verse appears to represent a point of view in relation to the temple which is quite at odds with Mark's own interpretation of the story.[27] On the GH, Mark must have introduced this extra verse despite the fact that it works against his own interpretation.

A similar case occurs in Mk. viii. 29, where Matthew and Luke both read τοῦ θεοῦ but Mark does not. On the GH, Mark must have omitted this. But there is no apparent reason for such an omission here, and indeed Matthew's text would have been highly appropriate to Mark's theological viewpoint. The use of the title 'Son of God' is, on any source hypothesis, clearly of great significance for Mark; it comes at the climactic moments of the gospel, i.e. baptism, transfiguration, the trial, the crucifixion, and (probably) in the title in i. 1.[28] With this in mind, it is, therefore, not at all easy to see why Mark should apparently want to avoid the use of the title in Peter's confession, if the opportunity to do so was indeed presented to him by Matthew.

There are thus many examples of texts, which are minor agreements on the 2DH, and which cannot be easily explained on the GH. Often, the change which Mark must have made on this hypothesis does not fit with his known style, or with his own theological viewpoint. Further, in many of the cases noted, the opposite changes by Matthew and Luke are easier to envisage. By the criterion of coherence, this suggests that the GH needs strengthening if it is to be a viable alternative to the 2DH. However, note must also be taken of Farmer's own criticisms of the attempts of others, notably Streeter, to explain these agreements assuming Markan priority.

One of the more general charges which Farmer brings against Streeter is that the latter ignored all agreements in omission as irrelevant, and only considered the positive minor agreements. He quotes Streeter as saying 'coincidence in omission proves nothing as to the source used', and in commenting on this says that 'contrary to the judgement of Streeter . . . agreements in omission should be studied, and not dismissed'.[29] However, Streeter only ignored such agreements in certain cases, viz. in texts where Mark was fuller than the parallels, though without really saying more of substance. On the assumption of Markan priority, Streeter said that Matthew and Luke frequently abbreviated Mark; thus only in such circumstances, agreements in omission are irrelevant.[30] Streeter in fact devoted some time to explaining common omissions of whole pericopes, or of something which was an indispensable part of the text (e.g. the pericope in Mk. viii. 22-26 or the note in Mk. xiv. 51).[31] He believed that agreements in omission were only irrelevant where Matthew and Luke had essentially the same story, but told it in fewer words.[32] Further, agreements in omission according to the 2DH are Markan additions on the GH, and the examples such as Mk. iv. 4 or xi. 16, noted above, show that these are not always easy to explain in this way.

Farmer's main charge against Streeter is that his procedure, of splitting up the agreements into categories and finding a different solution for each one, is methodologically unsound. This is the same charge which he brought against Hawkins, saying that 'the very idea that here motivates Hawkins is lethal to the science, not to speak of the art, of literary criticism'.[33] Farmer's claim is that, if the agreements are split up, 'there is a danger that the total concatenation of agreements in a given Synoptic passage will never be impressed upon the mind of the reader of such a discussion'.[34] This is also connected with the question of agreements in omission, in that whilst on their own they might appear to be irrelevant, they may in context be part of a whole series of minor agreements, positive and negative.

> If a particular passage exhibits a web of minor but closely related agreements of Matthew and Luke against Mark, there is the prospect that these different agreements will be divided into two or more of Streeter's different categories, thus dissipating the full impact which these same agreements would make on the mind of the reader if he were to have them all brought to his attention at the same time.[35]

As a criticism of Streeter's general methodology, this is certainly valid, and it exposes a flaw in Streeter's approach. Farrer too has criticised Streeter for just such 'atomisation',[36] and the presence of a 'web' of agreements has been used by others to support their own theories which modify the traditional 2DH, cf. Morgenthaler's revival of Simons' theory that Luke made a subsidiary use of Matthew, or Schramm's view that Luke had access to parallel versions.[37]

In some respects, the possibility of a web of agreements is allowed for in the 2DH by an appeal to an overlap between Mark and Q: in some cases Matthew and Luke seem to be so close as to imply the existence of a common source.[38] Farmer attacks Hawkins for segregating the ten passages which exhibit the greatest degree of verbal agreement as warranting such an explanation. Why should not the top five, or the top fifteen, be explained in this way?[39] There is certainly an element of subjectivity here, but this is inevitable. If Matthew and Luke were verbally identical, and had no word in common with a parallel version in Mark, one would be forced to admit the existence of independent parallel versions. If, on the other hand, they had one minor agreement (e.g. a δέ for καί) and otherwise agreed verbatim with Mark, there would be no question of literary independence. And one has to draw the line somewhere in between these two extremes. Farmer is right to criticise Hawkins' simple characterisation of these pericopes as 'discourse'; but they are nevertheless distinguishable from other passages in that Mark appears to be independent of the version common to Matthew and Luke. Some of these 'overlap' passages are considered in detail in the next chapter. But the independence of the Markan version (which must of course be established in each case) does give some justification for treating these passages as a separate category.

In other passages, the agreements between Matthew and Luke are more sporadic and perhaps easier to explain individually. Whilst a 'web' of agreements would be embarrassing for the theory of Markan priority, it is difficult to establish the existence of such a web that is (a) significant in itself, but (b) not of such large proportions as to imply the existence of two independent, parallel accounts. Thomas has sought to give examples of possible webs of agreements. He says that, very often, cases of minor agreements dismissed by Streeter individually (e.g. δέ for καί) occur near to another minor agreement, either in the same sentence or in an adjoining one.[40] Again, this is impressive in general terms, but in detail, the other minor agreement in question usually turns out to be equally insignificant.[41] It is also very uncertain whether the existence of a web of minor agreements would give any support to the GH. If the minor agreements are due to Mark's stylistic changes, a cluster of such agreements would imply that

Mark suddenly took it upon himself to introduce a large number of small changes all at once. On the GH, one might reasonably expect some Markan changes, partly stylistic, partly theological. But there is no reason why Mark should choose to alter his sources in the ways suggested in any sudden 'bursts'. Rather, one would expect the minor agreements to be distributed uniformly across the whole tradition. Thus, the existence of a web of agreements, which might cause embarrassment for the theory of Markan priority, is equally problematical for the GH.

Farmer deals with two passages where such a 'web' is alleged to exist. The first is Mk. ii. 1-12,[42] which contains a number of minor agreements.[43] Farmer lists 'Behold . . . on a bed . . . (being carried by four men) . . . he said . . . and . . . (in his spirit) . . . he said . . . (to the paralytic) . . . (and take up your bed) . . . upon the earth to forgive sins (but only the word order) . . . he went away to his own house.' (Bracketed words signify common omission.) However, in relation to the whole passage, the number of these is relatively small, and certainly considerably smaller than in other overlap passages; moreover, none of these really adds or subtracts any essential information. Farmer deals with all of them in turn, but not all his arguments convince one of the validity of the GH. On the agreement of ἰδού in Mk. ii. 3, Farmer refers to Abbott's theory that this was one of the 'corrections' of Mark, in this case giving a closer translation of the supposed Hebrew original. Farmer is right to point out the inconsistency between this explanation and the theory that the other 'improvements' are meant to make Mark's Greek more idiomatic, including the removal of various Hebraisms. But the inconsistency is in Sanday's theory of the single mind, not necessarily in the 2DH. Abbott himself showed how later Greek versions of Hebrew originals could improve the Greek whilst also giving a more literal translation. Since ἰδού never appears in narrative in Mark, and is frequently used by both Matthew (32 times) and Luke (16 in Lk, 8 in Ac), an addition by Matthew and Luke is easy to envisage.[44] An omission by Mark is possible, but one must then explain why Mark would have disliked the word so much in narrative, but still used it 8 times in direct discourse.

Farmer points to the agreement of 'on a bed' as being difficult on Streeter's terms, since it is a case where Matthew and Luke are fuller than Mark, rather than compressing him. In fact, it is a compression of what is implied in Mk. ii. 4, placed in an extra phrase in the previous verse. Farmer also points to the omission of 'carried by four men' as being a case where Mark is more specific. This, he says, shows that Mark has affinities with the later, second century, apocryphal gospels, and implies a later date for Mark than for Matthew and Luke.[45] However, in the second edition of his book, Farmer withdrew this criterion in the light of Sanders' book,[46] and so his argument here loses force. The agreements of εἶπεν for λέγει in Mk. ii. 5, 8 are examples of the historic present in Mark. The earlier discussion has shown that this phenomenon can be explained reasonably consistently on the 2DH, but not on the GH, as it would involve an inconsistent procedure on Mark's part.[47] The use of καί for δέ in Mk. ii. 6 was also noted above, as giving no support to the GH. The change in word order in 'on earth to forgive sins' in Mk. ii. 10 is noted as significant only because of the other agreements, as is the agreement in 'he went to his own house'. Streeter explained this as due to Matthew's and Luke's making clear that the man obeyed Jesus' command to the letter,[48] but Farmer brings no counter-argument against this. On the GH, one must explain why Mark avoided this five word agreement in his sources, (a) if he was aiming to reproduce the text to which they bore concurrent testimony, and (b) when inclusion of the phrase would give an example of a typically Markan 'repetition of motif'.[49] Farmer then gives what he calls 'the total extent of the agreement between Matthew and Luke' and concludes that there is *prima facie* evidence for a direct relationship between Matthew and Luke. But all the words given here, with the exception of ἰδού and καί, are in Mark as well and there is considerable further agreement between Mark and each of the others separately. Moreover, the differences between Matthew and Luke are far greater than those between Matthew and Mark, or between Luke and Mark. The absence of any significant[50] minor agreements reduces the importance of any alleged 'web'. There are some agreements, but they are not very numerous, and many of them are just as difficult (if not more so) to explain on the GH.

Farmer deals with each of Streeter's categories in turn. Many of his detailed arguments are considered elsewhere,[51] and so I now turn to his treatment of Streeter's appeal to 'textual corruption'. He considers Mk. i. 40–42, where Streeter explained three minor agreements by appealing to textual variants. (κύριε may be in Mark; an original αὐτοῦ ἥψατο αὐτοῦ as in some Western texts would explain all the other readings; εὐθέως for εὐθύς may be due to scribal and redactional personal preferences.)[52] Farmer gives Streeter's conclusions briefly without arguing against them; he appeals to some common omissions and two other positive minor agreements, and says that such a web is hard to account for in the space of three verses.[53] Moreover, Matthew and Luke agree in 18 consecutive words, so that the simplest hypothesis is that Luke used Matthew. However, the omissions in question are not very surprising (a redundant αὐτῷ twice, a ὅτι recitative, and σπλαγχνισθείς, though the original reading may have been ὀργισθείς, in which case common omission would be due to a desire to avoid attributing anger to Jesus).[54] Further, although Streeter's textual theories may not be convincing, independent editorial activity might easily account for the changes here. Matthew uses κύριε as an address to Jesus 20 times, Luke 17 times, Mark once; Matthew and Luke regularly put the object after the verb (hence the change in word order ἥψατο αὐτοῦ); the addition of ἰδού occurs frequently in Matthew and Luke; the change from Mark's historic present has already been considered; the use of εὐθέως instead of εὐθύς is also not unusual in Matthew and Luke (12 times in Matt, 6 + 9 times in Lk).[55] Moreover, as Beare points out, 14 (possibly 15) of the 18 words in which Matthew and Luke agree appear in Mark as well, so that Farmer's conclusion is not the only possible one.[56] Several of these minor agreements cause no difficulty for the GH, since they could easily be due to MkR (e.g. omitting κύριε and ἰδού, using the historic present and εὐθύς, changing the word order to αὐτοῦ ἥψατο) so the evidence here is neutral. The GH and the 2DH both explain the minor agreements here reasonably well.

Farmer also says that, by using textual variants, one could greatly increase the number of minor agreements.[57] This is certainly so, but it is also a not unexpected phenomenon. For whenever one of Matthew and Luke differed from the other, it would not be surprising if the texts of these two most frequently used gospels were assimilated to each other. Hence a minor agreement would be produced whenever the assimilated text was different from Mark. What is required, therefore, is not a blanket study of all textual variants which could produce minor agreements, but a study of what was, as far as can be determined, the original reading in each case.

The final example to be considered here is the minor agreement in Mk. xiv. 65.

Matt. 26	*Mk. 14*	*Lk. 22*
[46] τότε ἐνέπτυσαν εἰς τὸ πρόσωπον αὐτοῦ καὶ ἐκολάφισαν αὐτόν, οἱ δὲ ἐρράπισαν [68] λέγοντες· προφή-τευσον ἡμῖν, χριστέ, τίς ἐστιν ὁ παίσας σε;	[65] καὶ ἥρξαντό τινες ἐμπτύειν αὐτῷ καὶ περι-καλύπτειν αὐτοῦ τὸ πρόσ-ωπον καὶ κολαφίζειν αὐτὸν καὶ λέγειν αὐτῷ· προφήτευσον. καὶ οἱ ὑπηρέται ῥαπίσμασιν αὐτὸν ἔλαβον.	[63] καὶ οἱ ἄνδρες οἱ συνέχοντες αὐτὸν ἐνέπαιζον αὐτῷ δέροντες, [64] καὶ περικαλύψαντες αὐτὸν ἐπηρώτων λέγοντες· προφήτευσον. τίς ἐστιν ὁ παίσας σε;[65] καὶ ἔτερα πολλὰ βλασφημοῦντες ἔλεγον εἰς αὐτόν.

Streeter resorted to a theory of two-fold assimilation in the textual tradition to explain the presence of the question 'Who struck you?' in both Matthew and Luke.[58] Farmer rejects this suggestion, with its obvious weakness that the proposed original text of Matthew (without the question) has no textual support at all.[59]

The initial problem concerns the original text of Mark, i.e. whether one should read the longer text which includes the blindfolding, or the shorter one (as in D a f syrsin) which does not. Many of the arguments used in the past have presupposed Markan priority: e.g. the shorter text would explain the omission of the blindfold in Matthew, but this assumes that Mark is Matthew's source. However, careful consideration must always be given to any 'Western non-interpolation', and in this case it is supported by the Sinaitic Syriac.[60] Further, many have inferred that there is an allusion to Is. l. 6 LXX here.[61] Some have objected to this on the grounds that it is difficult to fit the blindfolding into this.[62] But this does not affect the shorter text, where the 'face' goes with the 'spitting', exactly as in Isaiah. In view of the extreme rarity of the words used,[63] a reference to Is. l, in Mark at least, seems certain, and since this is much clearer without the blindfolding, this gives some further reason, from internal considerations, for accepting the shorter text. Further support may be found in the Caesarean witnesses Θ and 565 who have a conflate reading.[64]

It is noteworthy that Luke's version contains none of the allusions to Is. l.[65] This is of itself some indication that the Lukan version is independent of the Markan one, since Luke is not generally averse to the idea of parallels between Jesus and the Servant.[66] Mark's text and Luke's are thus quite separate, and the only verbal link is in the word 'Prophesy!' But this functions differently in the two accounts. In Mark it may be a taunting jest: 'Play the prophet now!'[67] Alternatively, there may be deep irony intended, with Jesus' 'prophetic' predictions in xiv. 30, 58, 62 highlighted: Jesus is mocked as a prophet, and yet his prediction in xiv. 30 is about to be fulfilled in xiv. 66ff., and this then gives the reader more confidence in the truth of the other predictions mentioned in xiv. 58, 62.[68] Thus 'prophesy' here refers primarily to the ability to predict the future. In Luke, however, it refers to the possession of the gift of second sight. Moreover, the Lukan text presents a scene with totally different presuppositions. Jesus is asked to prove his messianic claims by showing his ability to work without seeing or hearing, and so satisfying the conditions implied in Is. xi. 3. A similar test for messianic claims was applied later to Bar Kochba (b. Sanh. 93*b*).[69] Thus the ill-treatment is purely physical, and the verbal exchanges reflect a Jewish technical procedure. Lk. xxii. 65 then misunderstands this by summarising the mockery with βλασφημοῦντες. Thus Lk. xxii. 63f. are probably from a pre-Lukan source, and Luke has added verse 65 as a conclusion.[70]

With this in mind, one can consider Farmer's explanations of this passage.[71] He says that Matthew's text is unimpeachable, presenting a clear, consistent account, with its picture of Jesus, spittle running down his face and being buffeted by blows, so distracted that he could only with difficulty identify who had struck him. But the suggestion of spittle running down the face, and Jesus' distraction, reads a certain amount into the text, and indeed, it is precisely the lack of reference to the blindfolding which makes Matthew's version so difficult.[72] Then, says Farmer, Luke makes Jesus' incapacity more explicit by adding the blindfold. (But this seems to imply that the question without the blindfold is in need of some supplement to make it intelligible, which suggests that Matthew's account is not so straightforward after all.) Luke's account gains in verisimilitude here, but loses its dramatic power (a) by omitting the reference to the spitting, and (b) by the addition of verse 65 'which is both repetitive and anticlimactic'. But verse 65 is not simply repetitive, since in Luke's version there has been no verbal mockery at all. It is a misunderstanding. The ill-treatment has been all physical, and separate from the blindfold and question. The lack of reference to the spitting, as well as a different word for the beating ($\delta \acute{\epsilon} \rho o \nu \tau \epsilon \varsigma$ not $\acute{\epsilon} \rho \rho \acute{\alpha} \pi \iota \sigma \alpha \nu$), remove all references to Is. 1, and this suggests that Luke's version is therefore not dependent on Matthew, since Luke would be expected to retain such allusions.[73] Rather, his is a totally independent account, partly misunderstood.

With regard to Mark, Farmer says that he omits the question, but this 'does not change the narrative in any obvious way'. However, Mark is shown to be secondary, since he retains Luke's secondary blindfold. But this is probably not part of Mark's original text, if one accepts the shorter reading in Mark; also Luke's blindfold has been shown to be part of an independent version, not a secondary Lukan addition. Mark then, says Farmer, conflated down to 'Prophesy!', but was undecided whether to include Matthew's 'You Christ', and/or Luke's concluding comment. Farmer says

> Mark's decision is editorially comprehensible. He conflated down to the command 'Prophesy!' then he ended the narrative in his own words. Mark had an editor's right to omit the question, 'Who struck you?' It was not absolutely necessary to the narrative. But by omitting this question Mark's text has lost the point that the men were taunting Jesus in their demand that he 'Prophesy!' Their taunt was to the effect: 'If he be the Son of God, he surely will surely be able to tell us who it is who has struck him!'[74]

However, the 'editor's right' exercised by Mark here is not in line with his overall aim, which is to include all that is common to his sources. Also, it is hard to see how 'Mark's text has lost the point' of the taunt if the question is 'not absolutely necessary to the narrative'. In fact, Mark's 'Prophesy!' functions quite differently without the question (cf. above). Thus Farmer's explanations of the text do not seem to be any more satisfactory than those of Streeter or others.

On the theory of Markan priority, the shorter Markan text would explain the omission of the blindfold in Matthew, and the theory that Matthew's question is due to textual assimilation to Luke is at least possible.[75] Streeter's explanations were very complicated, but it is difficult to see any simple solution giving an adequate account of the texts as they stand. Certainly the GH, in the form expounded by Farmer, does not succeed in explaining the texts any better.

The results of this chapter are largely negative. The arguments have shown that the GH accounts for the minor agreements no better than the 2DH, and indeed in some cases fares even worse. Many of the agreements can be explained separately on the basis of Markan priority, and some cannot be so easily explained by the GH, since all the agreements have to be due to Mark's editing. Often Mark's alleged procedure must have led him to redact his sources in unexpected or inconsistent ways. Whilst the minor agreements all present some difficulties for the 2DH, and whilst some of Streeter's own arguments were suspect (e.g. his stress on textual corruption), overall, the 2DH can often give a more coherent explanation of these agreements than can the GH.

8 THE MARK-Q OVERLAPS

One of the explanations which Streeter used to account for the minor agreements was an appeal to an overlap of sources: both Mark and Q might contain a particular section, and hence Matthew's agreements with Luke could stem from a Q source underlying them both.[1] Many have felt that this theory constitutes a weakness for the 2DH, and others have claimed that the passages in question can be explained more easily by other hypotheses. Thus Devisch says:

> Pour ceux qui défendent d'autres solutions du problème synoptique, les textes que, dans la théorie des deux sources, on appelle générale-ment 'les passages qui se recouvrent', ne font aucun problème. Ils constituent, au contraire, les exemples les plus probants pour confirmer ces autres théories.[2]

The question to be discussed here is whether in fact these passages can be explained any more easily by other hypotheses, and in particular by the GH.

For the 2DH, the theory of overlapping sources gives rise immediately to interesting problems about the relationship between Mark and Q. If these two sources give two accounts of the same pericope, the question arises as to whether there is any relationship of literary dependence between them. Dependence of Q on Mark has rarely been advocated and is usually rejected.[3] However, dependence of Mark on Q has often been advocated, either as dependence on a recension of Q slightly different from that known to Matthew and Luke,[4] or on Q *simpliciter.*[5] The majority of scholars, however, assume that Mark and Q are independent of each other.[6] (Streeter, as is well-known, changed his mind on the question.) At first sight this might appear to be only a secondary problem, as questions about possible relationships between Q and other documents should presumably only be discussed after settling the question of whether Q exists at all (a thesis which advocates of the GH claim is unnecessary to explain many of the agreements between Matthew and Luke).[7] However, the relevance of the problem is seen as soon as one observes that one's answer to the question of literary dependence determines one's theories about the wording and extent of Q.[8] For if Mark is dependent on Q, then there are three, not two, potential witnesses to Q, and Q might contain all the triple tradition as well as those parts of the tradition common to Matthew and Luke alone. Thus Q might expand to become a whole gospel. Moreover, if the wording of Q were judged to be identical with that of Matthew, then dependence of Mark on Q would be indistinguishable from dependence of Mark on Matthew. A theory of dependence of Mark on Q could therefore lead to a situation in which the hypothesis of a second source Q is redundant, and the priority of Q becomes the priority of Matthew. Thus those who advocate Matthean priority have often referred to Harnack's book on Q, *Sprüche und Reden Jesu*, which decided in almost every case that Matthew had preserved the text of Q more faithfully than Luke.[9] In fact other studies of the Q material have not supported Harnack's almost exclusive preference for Matthew's wording. (For example, Streeter thought that, in general, Luke's version was closer to the original Q wording.)[10] But these considerations do show that, under certain circumstances, the results of those who investigate the relationship between Mark and Q could be highly relevant to the consideration of the GH.

Advocates of the GH regard the theory of an overlap of sources as a desperate expedient to explain awkward passages where Mark's account contains features which appear to be secondary in comparison with Matthew or Luke. Thus Dungan says: 'The existence of Q has always been essential to the argument for Mark's priority – precisely as the loophole to invoke anytime one finds a pericope that is more primitive in Matthew and/or Luke when they are supposedly using Mark: the blessed overlap!'[11] In fact, however, an overlap of sources is usually only postulated where Mark's account appears to offer a different version from the other two, but this different version need not necessarily be secondary. Whether it is later or earlier is really a further problem. It is perfectly possible, logically, to postulate the existence of two overlapping sources before deciding on the question of which version is secondary.

It should also be noted that advocates of the GH are driven to postulate the existence of overlapping sources as well, often in passages usually ascribed to Q on the 2DH, where Luke's version appears to be unrelated to, if not more primitive than, Matthew's. For example, Farmer says that Luke had access to parallel traditions for his versions of the parables of the lost sheep, the talents/pounds, and the wedding feast, as well as for parts of the apocalyptic discourse,[12] Thus the theory of overlapping sources is not peculiar to the 2DH. Nor is it inherently unlikely. It seems quite feasible that many stories were remembered in different communitites and in differing forms. This was almost certainly the case in the account of the institution narratives at the Last Supper, the Matthean/Markan and Lukan/ Pauline traditions being independent of each other.[13]

It has also been said that there are no satisfactory criteria for determining when a Mark–Q overlap exists.[14] Streeter said that an overlap should only be postulated 'in places where the existence of obviously different versions, or of doublets very distinctly defined, provides us with objective evidence of the presence of Q',[15] and in *The Four Gospels* he did not appeal to this very frequently as an explanation of agreements between Matthew and Luke.[16] Sanders claims that Streeter did not stick to his criteria, and that they are in any case somewhat inadequate.[17] However, Sanders' own method of analysing the material and classifying the agreements is also unsatisfactory. He makes a simple count of common words, counting 'as agreements instances in which the same root appears in two or more gospels'.[18] By this, the words of John the Baptist in Mk. i. 8 and parallels (Matt: ἐγὼ μὲν ὑμᾶς βαπτίζω ἐν ὕδατι, Mk: ἐγὼ ἐβάπτισα ὑμᾶς ὕδατι, Lk: ἐγὼ μὲν ὕδατι βαπτίζω ὑμᾶς) would count as a triple agreement in four words, with a double agreement (i.e. between Matthew and Luke) in only one word μέν. This however ignores the other Matthew–Luke agreements here, i.e. in the use of the present tense not the aorist, and in placing the logion before, not after, the saying about the mightier one. Thus a simple word count such as Sanders makes does not allow for other points of agreement (e.g. in grammar and word-order). Perhaps it is wrong to lay down in advance rigid criteria and it may be better to look at the text itself, and further, to look at it from the point of view of the theory to be tested. Thus, in considering the GH, one may consider how Mark must have dealt with his sources if the GH is valid. One may then apply the criterion of coherence and ask if Mark must have redacted his sources in a way that is coherent, and consistent with his alleged procedure elsewhere.

I start with the parable of the mustard seed (Mk. iv. 30–32 and parallels). On the GH, Mark was faced with two versions of the parable in his two sources with many agreements between them. The fact that the parable is included at all presents some problems, at least indirectly. Mark must have just switched from using Luke as his main source (in iv. 21–25) to using Matthew. (Mk. iv. 21–25 has a parallel in this context only in Luke; Mk. iv. 30–32 has a parallel in this context only in Matthew. The Matthean parallels to Mk. iv 21–25, and the Lukan parallel to Mk. iv. 30–32, are in quite different contexts.) In so doing he must have omitted Matthew's parable of the tares and inserted his own parable of the seed growing secretly. Does he pick up Matthew at just this point because there is a Lukan parallel, albeit in a different context? But if so, why does Mark not include also the parable of the leaven, which follows immediately in both his sources? To explain why Mark omits some of the parables, Farmer says that Mark 'never conflated parables from Matthew, which, though found in Luke, reached Luke independently from Matthew'.[19] But this cannot apply to the parable of the leaven: the verbal agreements between Matthew and Luke here are so great as to demand some immediate literary relationship between the two versions, be it a direct dependence of one on the other or common dependence on a prior source. If, however, the existence of a Lukan parallel is not a significant factor governing Mark's selection of material from Matthew, how did Mark decide which parables of Matt. xiii to include?

Given that Mark has chosen to include this parable, the detailed wording of his version also presents problems for the GH. If one continues to postulate the basic assumption of the theory, then the following picture emerges. Having just reverted to using Matthew as his main source, Mark immediately avoids using Matthew's form of the introduction. He has a simple καὶ ἔλεγεν followed by a double question, presumably inspired by Luke. But he does not take over Luke's form of the double question. Instead, he changes it so that the verb ὁμοιόω now stands in the first half of the double question, not the second, and is prefaced by πῶς, not by the usual construction with a dative.[20] The second half of the double question now bears no relation to Luke's version, though it may be inspired by Matthew's παραβολήν (but if so the wording is different). It is possible that this double question is in fact a Markan stylistic peculiarity, the second half giving greater precision to the first half,[21] so that MkR might account for the verbal differences here on the GH; but the lack of close verbal agreement makes any theory of direct literary dependence here difficult.

After the introduction, Mark was faced with a common grammatical construction and strong verbal agreements in his sources. Yet just here, when he should, according to Farmer, be reproducing the text common to his sources,[22] Mark does precisely the opposite. Matthew and Luke both have ὁμοία ἐστίν + dative; Mark avoids this grammatically perfect construction and has instead ὡς + dative. The grammar here is odd; Swete comments: 'Two constructions seem to be combined – ὡς κόκκον [θήσομεν] and κόκκῳ [ὁμοιώσομεν].'[23] Moreover, Mark's version has left the sentence without a main verb. Matthew and Luke agree in the construction ὃν λαβὼν ἄνθρωπος; Mark avoids this by making the seed the subject of the clause, putting the verb into the passive, and using σπαρῇ (possibly under the influence of Matthew but the word is not in Luke). Next, Matthew alone has a reference to the size of the seed in a new sentence. Mark, after rewriting freely when his sources agree, takes this over verbatim; but unlike Matthew, he continues with the original clause so that, when copying Matthew's μικρότερον, he thereby creates an almost impossibly abrupt change in genders from the masculine relative pronoun ὅς (in apposition with κόκκος) to the neuter μικρότερον (agreeing presumably with an implied σπέρμα).[24] Matthew and Luke now differ in construction, and Mark follows Matthew in using ὅταν rather than a simple καί; but then, when his sources agree in using αὐξάνω, Mark instead repeats σπαρῇ and uses ἀναβαίνει. Mark has used αὐξάνω in iv. 8 in a phrase which the GH must assume is redactional (it does not appear in Matthew or Luke), so why Mark should object to the word here is not clear; even if Mark did dislike the word (iv. 8 is its only occurrence in Mark) the repetition of ὅταν σπαρῇ is still problematical: why could he not just have written ἀναβαίνει?[25] Matthew alone now has the phrase about the full-grown mustard seed being the biggest of the shrubs, which Mark takes over. As for the end-result of the seed's growth, Matthew and Luke agree that it 'becomes a tree', γίνομαι and δένδρον being common to both. Mark uses neither of these common words and talks instead of 'making great branches'. Matthew alone now has a ὥστε construction which Mark accepts. Finally Matthew and Luke agree verbatim in having an allusion to Dan. iv. 21 (Theod.) with the birds nesting in the branches; Mark avoids this and has the birds resting under the shade, probably alluding to Ezek. xvii. 23.

It is possible that some of these last changes are due to Mark's efforts to make the picture more true to life: a mustard plant is not a tree, and birds might shelter under the shadow of the leafy branches but not in the branches themselves.[26] But this will not account for all the changes. For the overall picture, if Mark is using Matthew and Luke as his sources, is that Mark has carefully and systematically avoided everything that is common to Matthew and Luke: where they agree, Mark disagrees, and where Matthew disagrees with Luke, Mark follows Matthew closely. Thus Mark appears to have taken an intense dislike to Luke (apart from the form, but not the wording, of the opening double question), and to have gone through Matthew's text, changing it where Matthew and Luke agree, but leaving it alone where they differ. Moreover, the result is, in places, grammatical chaos. This seems such an incoherent redactional procedure, and so inconsistent with Farmer's general thesis about Mark's redactional method ('not to deviate from the text to which his predecessors bore concurrent testimony') that it must place a serious question-mark against his overall theory.

There is in fact a strong case to be made for the traditional solution to the problem of literary relationships here. For there is evidence favouring the existence of two independent versions of the parable, namely the Markan one and the Lukan one. The difficulties which the GH encounters are due mainly to the fact that Mark and Luke have virtually nothing in common beyond the barest essentials necessary for telling a parable comparing the Kingdom of God to a mustard seed. Sanders' word-count gives a misleading impression when he says that Mark agrees with Luke in 14 triple-word agreements and in 6 cases with Luke alone, for by this he implies that there is a far greater similarity between Mark and Luke than is in fact the case.[27] The six special Mark–Luke agreements all occur in the introduction ($\check{\epsilon}\lambda\epsilon\gamma\epsilon\nu$, $\dot{o}\mu o\iota\dot{o}\omega$, $\tau o\hat{v}$ $\theta\epsilon o\hat{v}$, $a\dot{v}\tau\dot{\eta}\nu$, $\tau\acute{\iota}\nu\iota$). Of these, $\tau o\hat{v}$ $\theta\epsilon o\hat{v}$ only counts here because Matthew has $\beta a\sigma\iota\lambda\epsilon\acute{\iota}a$ $\tau\hat{\omega}\nu$ $o\dot{v}\rho a\nu\hat{\omega}\nu$, but the latter is easily explicable as MattR. Really, the only points of contact of any significance are the use of $\dot{o}\mu o\iota\dot{o}\omega$ and the form of the double question (where there may be some influence of Is. xl. 18).[28] But, after the introduction, Mark and Luke are totally different: Mark starts with $\dot{\omega}\varsigma$, Luke with $\dot{o}\mu o\acute{\iota}a$ $\dot{\epsilon}\sigma\tau\acute{\iota}\nu$; Mark has the seed as the subject of the relative clause, Luke has it as the object; Mark has a passive verb, Luke an active one; Mark speaks of 'sowing', Luke of 'throwing'; Mark has 'on the earth', Luke has 'in the garden'; Mark has the seed 'rising', Luke has it 'growing'; Mark speaks of the plant 'making great branches', Luke of it 'becoming a tree'; Mark has the birds resting under its shadow, Luke has them nesting in the branches; Mark's version is in the present tense, telling of an everyday occurrence, and his references to the size of the seed place the stress on the contrast between the beginning and the end of a natural process; Luke's version is in the aorist, telling of an event in the past and the contrast between the tiny mustard seed and the mighty tree stresses the extraordinary features of the story. Apart then from the form (but not the actual wording) of the introduction, there is no point of contact at all between Mark and Luke except what is necessary to tell the story at all. Sanders' claim that 'the two forms of the story do not seem clearly marked' is thus questionable, and more to the point is Hawkins' remark that 'Luke's disuse here of his customary Marcan authority was not only comparative but entire'.[29]

The great number of differences between the two versions also makes any theory of dependence of Mark on Q very difficult, especially if Luke is believed to preserve the Q version more faithfully than Matthew. Streeter, in arguing for Mark's knowledge of Q, could only point to the appended parable of the leaven and claim that Mark's single parable must be a mutilated version of Q's pair; he could point to no actual literary contacts between Mark and Q.[30] Later he realised that Mark's parable forms a pair with the parable of the seed growing secretly so that his original argument loses force.[31] Most recently, Lambrecht has tried to show that all the differences between the two versions can be explained by MkR of Q;[32] but in a case like this, where the two versions in question are so different, his method cannot distinguish between the possibilities of Mark's version being (a) MkR of Q, and (b) MkR of an independent tradition, written or oral. Nor is his detailed consideration convincing. He claims that Mark adapted the wording of the Q version to correspond with that of the parables of the sower and the seed growing secretly. $\sigma\pi\alpha\rho\hat{\eta}$ is said to come from $\sigma\pi\acute{o}\rho o\nu$ in verse 26 and $\sigma\pi\epsilon\acute{\iota}\rho\omega$ in verses 3-9 and 14-19; but still the repetition is awkward, and there seems no good reason why Mark should change the grammatical construction. (If he was so keen to use the verb, he could simply have copied Matthew, if he knew Matthew's version; or, if it is Luke who has preserved the Q version here used by Mark, he could have changed Q as Matthew did and simply written $\mathring{o}\nu$ $\lambda\alpha\beta\grave{\omega}\nu$ $\mathring{\alpha}\nu\theta\rho\omega\pi o\varsigma$ $\mathring{\epsilon}\sigma\pi\epsilon\iota\rho\epsilon\nu$.)[33] $E\pi\grave{\iota}$ $\tau\hat{\eta}\varsigma$ $\gamma\hat{\eta}\varsigma$ is said to come from verse 26, but its repetition is unexplained, as is also the change in meaning from 'ground' to 'world'. $\Pi\hat{\omega}\varsigma$ and $\delta\acute{\upsilon}\nu\alpha\mu\alpha\iota$ are said to be Markan words, but the statistics are not overwhelming ($\pi\hat{\omega}\varsigma$: 14 - 15 - 16 + 9; $\delta\acute{\upsilon}\nu\alpha\mu\alpha\iota$: 27 - 33 - 26 + 1). All they show is that Mark can use the words freely but they do not show that they are necessarily redactional. In view of the wide differences between the two accounts, any theory of direct literary dependence is difficult.

The Markan version of this parable has always presented problems with its awkward grammar and repetitions, and some have thought that Mark's version is the result of conflating two sources.[34] However, if the two sources are Matthew and Luke, this does not lead to a satisfactory explanation, as shown above. Wenham has sought to modify this slightly, by claiming that Mark used Matthew and combined this with a version similar to, but not identical with, Luke.[35] Thus, he says that Mark turned the opening phrase around in order to be more idiomatic, but then got into difficulties when he came to Matthew's relative clause, having had one already. So, 'naturally enough he resorted to a participle', but then his grammar broke down and he had to start again. (This is rather strange for an author trying initially to be more idiomatic.) There is too the problem of the repetition of $\gamma\hat{\eta}$ with its change of meaning; Wenham says that this is a favourite Markan word and that the repetition is intelligible if the editor's train of thought was interrupted; but does this explain the change in meaning? Mark then, says Wenham, used Matthew's other size reference, but this rendered impossible the source's 'becoming a tree', so Mark paraphrased. But why should what is possible for Matthew be impossible for Mark? Why too should the OT allusion be changed to Ezek. xvii?

It may well be that the size references are a later addition to an earlier form of the parable. Moreover, if the addition took place at the stage of the final redaction, this might explain the repetition of ὅταν σπαρῇ, as this kind of repetition after a redactional insertion appears to be a Markan characteristic.[36] There is thus no need to assume the existence of two pre-Markan forms of the parable. A redactional insertion into a single pre-Markan form will account for the evidence equally well. Moreover, the pre-Markan form bears very little resemblance to either Matthew or Luke. The main similarities between Matthew and Mark lie in the size references, and here it is easier to see Matthew improving Mark's grammar, than Mark making Matthew's worse.

Matthew's version in fact has links with both the other accounts. With Mark, Matthew has the size references, the use of ἔσπειρεν in xiii. 31, the ὅταν and ὥστε constructions, and the present tense γίνεται in xiii. 32 so that the parable becomes a description of a general situation and no longer of a past event.[37] With Luke, he has λαβὼν ἄνθρωπος, αὐξάνω, δένδρον, ἐν τοῖς κλάδοις αὐτοῦ, 'similarities which, though not being very distinctive in themselves, are too numerous to have occurred accidentally in this small passage'.[38] Since these verbal agreements are so great, some sort of direct literary relationship between Matthew and each of the others is demanded. If Matthew were the source of either of the other two, then one encounters all the difficulties met by the GH, for one would have to account for the fact that whichever of Mark or Luke has used Matthew as a source (or both, if the case may be) has taken from Matthew precisely what the other has omitted. Thus, if Matthew's version is not the common source of the other two versions, it must be a secondary conflation of them. This would also explain why Matthew's account changes half way through from being a description of a past event to a generalised description of the present: the former is the Lukan version, the latter is the Markan one.

The secondary nature of Matthew's version, and the fact that Matthew and Luke may be dependent on a common source, is shown too by a detailed consideration of their wordings: for, in some instances, Luke's wording is not characteristic of Luke himself, whilst Matthew's different version is characteristic of Matthew. Thus, for example, the use of ὁμοιόω and ὅμοιος here appears to be uncharacteristic of Luke. The phrase ὁμοία ἐστὶν (or ὁμοιώθη or ὁμοιωθήσεται) ἡ βασιλεία is very characteristic of Matthew, being prominent in chapter xiii.[39] In this sense it corresponds to a Semitic ל with a developed meaning of 'it is the case with the Kingdom as with . . .' Luke however uses this root only sparingly. In vi. 47, 48, 49 the adjective is used in a strict comparison (i.e. one object is compared to a similar object, here one man to another man). In vii. 31f. Luke uses the adjective and the verb, but, unlike Matthew, he uses it again for a strict comparison of like with like: Matthew says that this generation is like children (Matt. xi. 16), Luke says that the men of this generation are like children. Luke may therefore have changed his source here to avoid this developed sense of the ὁμοιο-root. The same may also be true at the only other occurrence of the root in Luke's gospel, viz. xii. 36, if it is a true parallel to Matt. xxv. 1. Matthew has characteristically τότε ὁμοιωθήσεται ἡ βασιλεία τῶν οὐρανῶν, Luke has ὑμεῖς ὅμοιοι ἀνθρώποις, i.e. a strict comparison of like with like. Thus Luke's general usage[40] throws into sharp relief the use of ὅμοιος and ὁμοιόω in the two parables here in xiii. 18, 20, both in this developed sense. This suggests that Luke is dependent on a pre-Lukan source, and that Matthew has rewritten the source in his own idiom. The same is the case in the use of ἔβαλεν in Lk. xiii. 19: it is unusual in Luke in this sense (Luke normally uses the verb in the stereo-typed phrase 'throwing into prison').[41] Matthew's ἔσπειρεν could be inspired by Mark, or by the frequency of the word elsewhere in Matt. xiii.[42] Further, κῆπος is a Lukan *hapax*. It is often noted that this reflects a non-Palestinian culture, but how this should be interpreted is not clear. Jewish law decreed that mustard should not be sown in gardens;[43] but is Luke changing a story which was originally in line with Jewish law, as many have said?[44] This depends on how far one believes that the parable is meant to be describing an everyday occurrence. Some have seen the transition from the proverbially tiny mustard seed to the mighty tree, which in OT imagery represents the power of a great kingdom (cf. Jud. ix. 19; Ezek. xvii. 22f.; xxxi. 6; Dan. iv. 9, 18), as so incongruous as to suggest that the OT references to the mighty tree must be secondary expansions.[45] However, it is more likely that the main thrust of the parable lies in the extraordinary features of the story, in the details which do not make good botanical sense.[46] It may be, therefore, that Luke's 'garden' is not a secondary change, but an integral part of the original story, the point being that the Kingdom will erupt from the most unexpected beginnings in the most unexpected places. Certainly it is unlikely that Luke would have wanted to change an original ἀγρός (9 times in Luke, 1 in Acts); on the other hand, a change by Matthew to ἀγρός if κῆπος had stood in his source is quite intelligible given Matthew's liking for the word (he uses it 16 times, and cf. the use of it in verses 24, 27, 44 of this chapter).[47] Thus again there is evidence of the existence of a pre-Lukan source with Matthew rewriting it in his own idiom.

The result of this analysis is that there is strong evidence for the 'existence of obviously different versions' (to use Streeter's terms). There is a non-Markan source here which probably extended to the parable of the leaven too (in view of the very similar introductions). Luke's source cannot be Matthew, as the GH would maintain, since Luke would have then changed Matthew's wording in a wholly uncharacteristic way. Rather, Luke's source must be a common source prior to both Matthew and Luke. If one calls this source 'Q' (without necessarily postulating what else might belong to it), one must conclude that there is here a 'Mark–Q overlap'.[48] Further, the Q form of the parable can be seen in Luke, since Luke appears to have copied his source with very little change.

Similar results emerge in other passages too. For the passages usually ascribed to both Mark and Q have certain characteristics. In many of them there are close agreements between Matthew and Luke, some between Matthew and Mark, and virtually none between Luke and Mark.[49] In other words, Matthew is in some sort of medial position with respect to the other two, having agreements with both of them whilst they rarely agree between themselves. Thus, in these passages, Matthew occupies the position usually taken by Mark. As seen above, this kind of alternating support for Mark has been used as a proof that Matthew and Luke used Mark independently; others have shown that the evidence only indicates that Mark must occupy a 'medial' position.[50] Thus in this particular small group of passages, where it is Matthew who is in the medial position, one (but not the only) possibility is that Matthew is the source of the other two. However, similar considerations of the redaction involved for Mark will show that this presents great difficulties.

To take another example, the Beelzebub controversy (Mk. iii. 20–30 and parallels) is generally regarded as another case of a Mark–Q overlap. But how must Mark have treated his sources if these sources were Matthew and Luke? Initially, Mark must have ignored the context, i.e. the occasion of an exorcism, which is in both his sources. Yet this would be despite the fact that (1) the charge of being in league with, or possessed by, Beelzebub now comes very abruptly in Mark, and (2) Mark is usually very ready to record exorcisms: indeed this is the only non-Markan exorcism in the whole gospel tradition. The charge levelled against Jesus is identical in Matthew and Luke: there is one charge in identical words (with small variations in word order). Mark rejects this 'concurrent testimony' and has instead two separate charges: Jesus is mad (he *has* Beelzebub) and/or he is using demonic power. Matthew and Luke then agree in saying that Jesus knew his opponents' thoughts, a phrase which Mark ignores although he says something similar elsewhere, so it is not clear why he should omit it here (cf. ii. 8; ix. 33f.). Mark now has the saying about Satan driving out

Satan, which occurs in Matthew but not in Luke, before he deals with the divided kingdom saying. Here Mark avoids what is common to his sources (the πᾶσα + participle construction, the use of ἐρημοῦν) and adds a saying similar to, but not identical with, Matthew's about the divided house, thereby incidentally creating a piece of perfect synthetic parallelism.[51] Mark now has the saying about the division of Satan, but in the second half, he chooses to ignore the verbatim agreement of his sources' πῶς σταθήσεται ἡ βασιλεία αὐτοῦ and he paraphrases, changing the form from a question to a statement (though with no significant change in meaning). Next, he omits the saying about the Jewish exorcists, despite the verbatim agreement in his sources, whereas in the 'strong man' saying there is no verbal agreement at all between Matthew and Luke yet Mark chooses to include it, copying Matthew closely. In the blasphemy saying he must have taken the general saying, that all sins and blasphemies are forgivable, from Matthew, and the unforgivable blasphemy against the Holy Spirit may be from Luke; but there is nothing in Mark about 'speaking a word against the Son of Man' even though this is in both his sources. Finally Mark ends with a notice which may be from Lk. xi. 18, but is not close verbally. All this again renders questionable Farmer's theory of Mark's redactional method; once again Mark seems consciously to have avoided all the parts where his sources agree, and either omitted the relevant part or rewritten it, whilst taking over verbatim one of his sources, almost always Matthew, where they disagree.[52]

Attempts have been made to explain some of these differences as being due to MkR. Crossan argues the case for a great deal of redactional activity having taken place on the assumption that Mark is using a source which is very close to, but not identical with, the Q version used by Matthew and Luke.[53] (How close is not clear, since Crossan regards differences between Mark and the parallel versions as significant for determining where Mark has redacted his source.)[54] Lambrecht argues the case for direct dependence of Mark on Q, by trying to show that all the differences between the two accounts can be explained by MkR.[55] Certainly some of the differences may be due to this. The sandwiching of the Beelzebub story between the two parts of the story of the encounter with Jesus' family, and the parallel form of the charges against Jesus by his family and by the scribes, may be due partly to MkR, possibly by Mark's adding verse 21 at the start.[56] However, none of this proves that Mark was actually using the Q version as used by Matthew and Luke, or Matthew, or Luke, as his sources. He could have used an independent source and redacted that. There are other differences which are difficult to account for as MkR of Q (as Lambrecht), or of Matthew and Luke (as Farmer). Crossan too doubts if there is direct dependence on Q, and asks why Mark should change πᾶσα βασιλεία to καὶ ἐὰν βασιλεία, or πῶς σταθήσεται to οὐ δύναται στῆναι.[57] One could add: why has Mark omitted the logion on the Jewish exorcists, and the 'he who is not with me is against me' saying? One possibility might be that Mark objected to the lack of any obvious connection here, but in fact all the versions seem to be composite. The saying on the divided kingdoms assumes that Satan's kingdom still stands, the strong man saying assumes that Satan has already been bound; Matt. xii. 27 assumes that Jesus' activity is parallel to that of Jewish exorcists, Matt. xii. 28 assumes that it is unique.[58] All this implies that it is very precarious to try to prove literary priority here by appealing to the coherence of one of the accounts, as, for example, Streeter and Butler have done in the past.[59] The most recent attempt to understand the Matthean account as a tightly knit structure is that of Cope.[60] Cope sees the whole section as a 'consistent, highly organised account which has been constructed as support for the claim that the line in the Isaiah quotation, "I will pour out my Spirit upon him", applies to Jesus'.[61] Thus the whole section depends on the quotation of Is. xlii in Matt. xii. 17-21 for its internal cohesion. However, the theory runs into great difficulties in accounting for the link between verses 27 and 28. Cope says that there is an unwritten assumption here, viz. 'the contention that Jesus is the Messiah and activity on his part done by the power of the Holy Spirit would prove it, because this is promised to the Messiah in Is. xlii. 2'.[62] This, he says, accounts for the *non sequitur* (or so it now appears) here, i.e. why Jesus' exorcisms should mean anything more than Pharisaic exorcisms. But if this is so, then the unwritten assumption is precisely what Cope claims the whole section is trying to prove, i.e. that the gift of the Spirit, promised to the Messiah in Is. xlii, has been given to Jesus. Cope's logical sequence would work if the only alternatives were the reaction of the crowd (Jesus is the Son of David) and that of the Pharisees (Jesus is in league with demonic powers). However, it is precisely verse 27 which opens up different possibilities, i.e. that exorcisms can be performed by Pharisees who are neither Messianic, nor in league with Beelzebub. Thus each account here is a collection of isolated sayings, and Mark is not easily derivable from the others.

Discussion is very fierce over the original form and the tradition-history of the blasphemy saying. Wellhausen proposed that an original logion spoke of sins being forgivable for the 'son of man' (meaning man in general); this was changed by Mark to 'sons of men' because of possible Christological objections, and was finally changed back by Q to blasphemy against the Son of Man (i.e. Jesus).[63] This has been criticised most recently by Tödt.[64] Wellhausen's general thesis of the dependence of Q on Mark is questionable in any case, and Tödt suggests that there is dependence the other way: the original form (i.e. the Q form) had 'speaking a word against the Son of Man' with a clear periodisation in mind, and Mark has tried rather unsuccessfully to alter this, making the saying more obscure in its context. However, the argument appealing to greater obscurity as a sign of a secondary text is dangerous here since there is a lack of close connection in all three gospels as they stand. Matthew's version, contrasting blasphemy against the Son of Man which is forgivable with blasphemy against the Holy Spirit which is not, stands somewhat incongruously after the claim that Jesus (who for Matthew at least is the Son of Man on earth) acts by the power of the Holy Spirit (xii. 28). In Luke the saying is in a totally different context, and is difficult after xii. 8f. which implies that whoever denies the Son of Man on earth and speaks against him will receive the same treatment at the final judgement. How this differs from the blasphemy against the Son of Man, which according to xii. 10 is forgivable, is not clear.[65] Mark's account is perhaps the least obscure: there is only the formal discrepancy between iii. 28 and 29 (all is forgivable – this is not forgivable) and the meaning is clearly 'all is forgivable except this one thing', the one thing being the denial of Jesus' power and authority here and now (with no added complication of a differentiation between a pre-Easter and a post-Easter situation).

Any Q form of the saying is difficult to recover; however, it is probable that its basic form is to be seen in Matt. xii. 32*ab*, with Matt. xii. 31 being parallel to Mark.[66] Luke's reference to 'blaspheming' against the Holy Spirit may be a secondary assimilation to the Markan form of the saying,[67] so that an original form of the saying behind Matt. xii. 32/Lk. xii. 10 may have run:

ὃς ἐὰν εἴπῃ λόγον εἰς τὸν υἱὸν τοῦ ἀνθρώπου, ἀφεθήσεται αὐτῷ
ὃς δ'ἂν εἴπῃ (λόγον) εἰς τὸ πνεῦμα τὸ ἅγιον, οὐκ ἀφεθήσεται αὐτῷ.[68]

It is now very difficult to see Mark as dependent on this saying. The verbal differences are enormous. Further, as Boring points out, the form of the two versions is different: the Q form is in antithetic parallelism of the form A B A′ B′, whereas Mark's version is a chiastic structure A B B′ A′.[69] Moreover, the content of the versions is quite different. There is nothing in Mark corresponding to the contrast between blasphemy against the Son of Man and blasphemy against the Holy Spirit, and the Q version is entirely built on this. Further, if Mark had objected to the ideas expressed in the Q version, he need only have changed τοῦ υἱοῦ τοῦ ἀνθρώπου to τῶν υἱῶν τῶν ἀνθρώπων and not changed the whole construction.[70] Thus there is no good reason to assume any direct literary relationship between the two versions. They differ widely in wording, form and content, and represent two quite independent versions.

In the rest of the pericope, as in the parable of the mustard seed, Mark and Luke have virtually no verbal agreements at all. Even Sanders, who is in general sceptical about the theory of overlapping sources, admits that 'the agreements between Mark and Luke are scant, and many of the agreements I have counted are not strong; that is, they are only single scattered words and the words are often in different grammatical forms'.[71] The cases of note are (1) the use of ἐπί in Mk. iii. 24f. (but Matthew's κατά as 'against' is Matthean[72] so that this is not very significant as an agreement between Mark and Luke); (2) the participle εἰσελθών in Mk. iii. 27 (ἐπελθών in Lk. xi. 22), but, as Hawkins says, 'this little grammatical resemblance can count for nothing in comparison with the mass of Marco–Matthaean identities which distinguish the records of this saying about "the strong man armed"';[73] (3) the ὅτι λέγετε clause in Mk. iii. 30/Lk. xi. 18.[74] At points where Mark and Luke can be different, they are different, and Streeter's later comment is justified: 'The verbal resemblances between the two accounts are no more than would be inevitable if they represent two quite independent traditions of the same original incident.'[75] Matthew, on the other hand, has agreements with both the other two. With Mark, he agrees in his version of the strong man saying and the first half of the blasphemy saying; with Luke, he agrees in the setting, the divided kingdom sayings, the saying about the Jewish exorcists, the saying about the presence of the Kingdom, and the second half of the blasphemy saying. Thus Matthew again occupies a 'medial' position. Although theoretically this could be explained by Matthew's being the source of both the others, this is very unlikely, for, as has been shown, one would have to give reasons why the second of the other two writers must have carefully avoided all the parts of Matthew which the first one had copied.[76] Thus the best solution is that Matthew is not a source of the other two accounts, but a later conflation of them.

There is thus good reason to believe that there are here, in Mark and Luke, two quite independent versions of the pericope, with Matthew as a later conflation of the two forms.

The accounts of the temptation story (Mk. i. 12f. and parallels) are perhaps easier to deal with in this context. There are here enormous difficulties for the GH, since Mark's account has virtually nothing in common with that of Matthew and Luke, and indeed presents major differences. Mark alone refers to the wild beasts, but he has nothing of the detailed account of the three-fold temptation which appears in almost identical wording in his alleged sources. He has the ministry of the angels, which appears in Matthew but not in Luke, but he implies that this ministry lasted throughout the forty day period, unlike Matthew. In Mark, the temptation itself takes place during the forty days, whereas in Matthew, the temptations only start after this period. Other attempts to derive Mark's version from the other two are unconvincing. Streeter argued that 'an original tradition is always detailed and picturesque'[77] (though, as Butler says, 'form critics would not agree'),[78] and that it 'would hardly record . . . a temptation to do nothing in particular'. However, the fact that there is very little verbal contact between the two accounts, and that Mark's account can be integrated into a coherent theological scheme,[79] suggests that Mark does not offer here simply an excerpt from Matthew, which requires Matthew's fuller account to make sense.[80] Schulz suggests that Mark abbreviated the Q account because he could not tolerate the implied polemic 'gegen die Wundermann-Christologie im Sinne des θεῖος ἀνήρ',[81] since the miracles are an integral part of his gospel. However, it is very doubtful whether Mark is really presenting a 'Wundermann-Christologie'. Recent studies on Mark have suggested precisely the opposite, i.e. that Mark was consciously trying to correct this sort of Christology.[82] Once again, the theory of an overlap of two independent sources seems to be the most satisfactory answer to the literary problems posed here.[83]

The final passage to be considered here is the collection of sayings in Mk. iv. 21–25 and parallels. The theory of a Mark–Q overlap is usually put forward here because there are doublets to each of the Markan sayings, rather than because of the existence of a parallel non-Markan account at this point. (Only Luke has parallels to the sayings in this context.) The place of these sayings in the middle of Mark's parable chapter presents problems of interpretation for Mark's theology; but for the limited purposes of deciding about the synoptic interrelationships, such questions are not directly relevant. What concerns us here is whether Mark derived this collection (of what were probably originally isolated sayings) from Matthew and/or Luke and/or Q. Arguments for literary priority on the basis of 'better context elsewhere' are dangerous.[84] Mark presumably had his own reasons for putting the sayings in this context, so that it is a moot point whether any other context is 'better'; also, if this sort of argument is used for the greater originality of Q rather than Matthew, one is faced with the uncertainty of not knowing what the original Q context was.

In the first two sayings, there is a Lukan parallel to Mark together with another Lukan version of each saying (in xi. 33; xii. 2); in both cases the second Lukan version is very close to Matthew's version (in Matt. v. 15; x. 26). The first Lukan version is fairly close to Mark, but with a few significant differences which, on the 2DH, can be easily explained as due to the influence of the non-Markan version. These are the phrases ἵνα οἱ εἰσπορευόμενοι βλέπωσιν τὸ φῶς in viii. 16 and ὃ οὐ μὴ γνωσθῇ in viii.17.[85]

However, it is just these small details which cause difficulty for the GH. According to Farmer's theory, Mark must have switched at this point to following Luke as his main source; but then, in the first two logia, he must have omitted very carefully all those small details which bring Luke's version closer to Matthew, i.e. just those details which were attributed on the 2DH to the influence from the non-Markan version: the aim of lighting the lamp in Lk. viii. 16, and the being 'known' in Lk. viii. 17. Far from reproducing the 'concurrent testimony' of his sources, Mark seems carefully to have avoided doing so at this point. Further, Mark must have made other small changes in Luke which make his version even more unlike Matthew's: the form of the introduction in Mk. iv. 21 (a rhetorical question instead of a statement with the 'lamp' as the subject of the clause, not the object), the οὐχ ἵνα construction instead of the use of ἀλλά in verse 21*b*, even though Mark uses ἀλλά in verse 22 (though this time not from Luke).

Some have sought to explain the Markan version of these sayings as derived from Q, the differences being due to MkR. (This would give only indirect help to the GH here, since the latter postulates dependence of Mark on Lk. viii. 16–18; these other theories make Mark dependent on Q as derived from the Lukan doublets to Lk. viii, the latter being in turn dependent on Mark.) Schneider has argued this for the case of Mk. iv. 21, and Lambrecht, following him closely, has tried to extend this to all of verses 21–25.[86] Thus for verse 21, Schneider claims that the double question may be an example of Markan duality, and the use of ἔρχεται and the article with λύχνος (which Jeremias takes as an Aramaism, and therefore a sign of a primitive tradition)[87] may be Christologically orientated.[88] This depends on whether the 'lamp' is meant to represent Jesus in Mark's interpretation. Almost all commentators are agreed that the reference in the middle of Mark's parable chapter must be to the preaching of the word, as described in the parable of the Sower. Schneider's interpretation then involves a very veiled identification of Jesus with the proclamation. Although it has been claimed that Jesus and the 'Gospel' are almost identified in Mk. i. 1, viii. 35, x. 29,[89] such an allusion here would be very much more veiled and obscure. One needs the identification of the 'lamp' with both Jesus and the proclamation simultaneously; and whilst the second is fairly clear from the context, the first would have to be derived independently, or from these small differences which involve very insignificant words (ὁ and ἔρχεται). The addition of 'under the bed' (which Jeremias also takes as secondary, though he does not think of dependence of Mark on any Q version)[90] is taken by Schneider as due to an effort to make the negative parts of the parable of the Sower correspond more closely with the negative parts here, as well as stressing the open nature of the proclamation.[91] However, parallels with the parable of the Sower are thin, apart from the three-fold failure of the seed, and the stress on openness is there already. The concluding phrase is said to be omitted because Mark already has a double final clause.[92] However, the double final clause itself is still unexplained: even with making the lamp the subject, Mark could have written καί with two finite verbs. Thus it is doubtful whether Schneider's attempt to deny the existence of two forms of the saying will succeed. Even if he is correct in all his assertions about Mark's theology in the details, there is still the methodological problem that the wording is so different in Mark that one cannot be certain that it is Q, and not some other tradition, which is Mark's source.

In Mk. iv. 22, it is again difficult to see all the differences between Mark and the other versions as due to MkR. Most assume that the Q version underlying Matthew and Luke has been preserved almost exactly in Matt. x. 26.[93] The change in construction to ἵνα clauses may well be Markan,[94] ἵνα being often used by Mark.[95] But why should he move κρυπτόν to the first half? Why change κεκαλυμμένον to ἐγένετο (ἀπόκρυφον occurs nowhere else in Mark, so that one cannot say that it is a Markan word)? Why change ἀποκαλύπτω to φανερόω (Mark never uses this verb elsewhere)? Moreover, the resultant version is a piece of near-perfect Semitic synonymous parallelism, which might suggest originality rather than a secondary version.[96] As far as the rest of the section is concerned, most would agree that the actual process of collecting these sayings is due to Mark, though it may be that verses 24f. formed a pre-Markan unit. Best argues for this on the grounds that verse 24 makes very little sense in context and is thus part of a tradition taken over by Mark.[97] If this is so, it certainly gives no support to the theory that Mark is dependent on Q, or on Matthew, or on Luke, where the sayings are separate. Thus, in this passage, the analysis above indicates that Mark probably has independent versions of the sayings, and one is indeed justified in talking of an overlap of sources.

In all the passages considered in this chapter, the synoptic interrelationships are very difficult to explain by the GH in the form advocated by Farmer. Mark's redactional motives cannot be what Farmer claims them to be. Either Mark followed a totally different plan of dealing with his sources in these passages from elsewhere in the tradition, or else the underlying theory of synoptic interrelationships is wrong. In all these passages there is evidence of the existence of two distinct versions, a Markan and a non-Markan, and these two are independent of each other. The best explanation of these passages remains the traditional solution of an overlap of Mark with an independent source lying behind Matthew and Luke. Since, therefore, the 2DH gives a more coherent, and self-consistent, picture of the overall redaction involved than does the GH, it must be preferred unless advocates of the GH can suggest a more convincing rationale behind Mark's alleged redactional procedure.

PART III   SOME PARTICULAR TEXTS

SECTION A   SELECTED MARKAN PASSAGES

INTRODUCTION

One of Farmer's fundamental criticisms of Streeter's treatment of the minor agreements is that Streeter divided the agreements into categories, and found a different explanation for each one. The danger of this method is that one might miss the possibility of a whole 'web' of agreements occurring in a single pericope.

So far I have discussed the evidence in a similar 'atomising' way. With the possible exception of the discussion of the Mark-Q overlaps, the phenomena have been considered within the context of similar examples within the gospel tradition. Farmer's criticisms of Streeter demand that one also look at the phenomena within the context of the pericopes in which they occur. Thus it is right that one should examine various individual pericopes within the gospels to see which hypothesis can best explain the texts.[1] Again, some sort of criterion of 'coherence' must be applied, for any hypothesis can give some explanation of the changes made. What is required is to see if one hypothesis gives a better, more consistent explanation of the redaction involved for the secondary writer(s). In the first section of this part of the study, various passages from Mark's gospel with their synoptic parallels will be examined in detail, with the opposing theories of Markan priority and the GH about the relative position of Mark in mind. In the second section, an attempt will be made to examine some of the 'double tradition' passages, bearing in mind the competing theories of the 'Q' hypothesis and the GH.

9 THE HEALING OF THE MAN WITH THE WITHERED HAND

(Matt. xii. 9-14/Mk. iii. 1-6/Lk. vi. 6-11)

This is one of the pericopes where Longstaff finds a pattern of 'alternating agreement'.[1] In the discussion of Longstaff's book, it was suggested that such a pattern is not only not surprising, but that it is the inevitable result of his method of analysing the texts. However, even Longstaff's detailed decisions are questionable. It was pointed out previously (and by Longstaff himself) that there are some disagreements between Mark and each of the other two gospels, and that even when Mark is (allegedly) closer to Matthew in verses 1-2, there are still twelve disagreements. Longstaff claims that these are far less significant than the disagreements between Mark and Luke, even if they are more in number (twelve as opposed to eight).[2] However, there is a very great difference between Matthew and Mark in these two verses in the way they end: Mark has Jesus' opponents silently watching, whereas Matthew has them explicitly asking Jesus if it is legal to heal on the Sabbath. The result is that the shapes of the two accounts are now widely different. In Mark, Jesus' call to the sick man is an act out of the blue, and the saying about doing good on the Sabbath (verse 4) is a polemical assertion. In Matthew, Jesus argues his case, and concludes with the saying about doing good, which answers the initial question about legality; with this firmly established, the healing now follows. Thus the difference between Matthew and Mark in the introduction is very far from being insignificant, and the question arises as to which is the more primitive tradition.

I start with the Matthean version. In form, Matthew's account is close to the structure of a *Streitgespräch*, with its question and counter-question.[3] The way that the pericope is constructed, starting with the question 'is it lawful?', followed by a reasoned argument and a conclusion 'therefore it is lawful', suggests that, in Matthew's view, Jesus' reply has given some legal justification for his action.[4] However, there are features here which make it very difficult to believe that this was the original form of the story.

First, the second half of verse 10 in Matthew is grammatically very

96

awkward. The final ἵνα clause must refer back to the verb ἐπηρώτησαν, but the words of the direct question intervene, and the result is that the ἵνα clause is left somewhat awkwardly appended at the end of the sentence. Apart from the grammar, the question about the legality of the proposed healing does not fit very well with the final reference to wanting to accuse Jesus, and indeed makes little sense according to Jewish presuppositions. For it was recognised, at least by the later Rabbis, that life could be saved on the Sabbath by doing work, but that in cases where life was not in danger, the Sabbath law could not be broken.[5] Thus, in the present situation, the Pharisees' question could have had only one answer: since the man had only a withered hand and hence was in no danger of his life, an act of healing would have been an illegitimate breach of the Sabbath law. Thus the Pharisees would accuse Jesus if he did heal the man, and they cannot have been genuinely asking if it was legal to do so. Rather, they must have been watching to see if he actually would heal the man. However, in Matthew's view, it does appear to be a real question, since the whole debate in verses 10–12 is structured to try to prove that it is legitimate to perform the cure. The question is taken seriously, and an attempt is made to answer it positively. Thus there is some discrepancy between the concrete details of the situation involved and Jesus' justification of his actions.

Further difficulties arise in verses 11f. First, in verse 12, there appear to be two quite separate conclusions. In verse 12*a*, the general rabbinic principle of קַל וְחוֹמֶר is applied to the illustration in verse 11. Since a man is of greater value than a sheep, whatever is allowed for a sheep is also allowed for a man. In terms of the actual example given, this implies that one can legitimately do work to rescue a man in dire circumstances on the Sabbath. However, this goes no further than the generally accepted view that life could be saved on the Sabbath. Certainly it does not lead to the completely general claim of verse 12*b* that it is legitimate to 'do good' on the Sabbath. This cannot be deduced from the argument in verses 11–12*a*. It can only be a polemical attack on the rules concerning Sabbath observance. Thus between verses 12*a* and 12*b* there appears to be a marked break, and the conclusion in verse 12*b* cannot belong to the same stratum of tradition as that which contains the deductive argument in verses 11–12*a*. This seam suggests a break in the sources used by Matthew, which is partly confirmed by the slightly unusual construction in verse 12*b* of ὥστε + indicative. Whilst by no means unknown in the New Testament, nor even in Matthew (cf. xix. 6; xxiii. 31),[6] it is a strange usage, and may confirm that Matthew is switching sources here.

If it is extremely difficult to derive the conclusion in verse 12*b* from the premiss in verse 11, it is equally difficult to see how the premiss itself can be used in a reasoned argument in the present context. The whole argument, given in the form 'granted A, does not B follow?', is useless if 'A' is not granted at all. In this case, it is certain that 'B' (the healing of a man not in imminent danger of his life) was not allowed by the Rabbis. If the premiss is not accepted either, the argument carries no conviction. Now Matthew's present version assumes that it is legitimate to draw out on the Sabbath a sheep that has fallen into a pit, but this seems to have been very far from being the case. At Qumran, it was expressly forbidden (cf. CD xi. 13f.); the later Rabbis were divided on the question: a stricter school allowed food to be provided for the animal, whilst a more lenient view allowed articles to be lowered into the pit, but only to enable the animal to escape of its own accord.[7] Thus there is no warrant for believing that the premiss in Matt. xii. 11 would have been accepted by anyone.[8]

A very similar saying occurs in Lk. xiv. 5 in the middle of another Sabbath-healing story, and hence this account must also be analysed. The story in Lk. xiv. 1-6 appears to be composite, in that it has two endings, one in verse 4 and another in verse 6. Daube isolates two forms of controversy stories in the gospels.[9] In one, a revolutionary action is followed by a protest and then by the silencing of the protest; in the other, the opponents question Jesus, Jesus replies to their criticisms and the action comes at the end. With this greater precision about the forms, it is clear that, as Daube says, 'Luke 14 seems to be a conflation of the two forms'.[10] The countering of the opponents is complete after verse 4*a*, and the story would end naturally after the healing itself in verse 4*b*. The saying in verse 5, and the second conclusion in verse 6, are therefore separable from the story of the healing.

Now it is very unlikely that the saying in verse 5 was a completely isolated saying. It demands some narrative framework to make sense, and indeed, it must have been part of a story which involved some breach of the Sabbath law. Its content implies that it answers a question of the form 'is it lawful to do X on the Sabbath?'. Exactly such a question occurs in verse 3, and thus it may be that verses 3 and 5 belong together in the same stratum of the tradition. Further consideration of verse 3 suggests that it too is part of an older tradition. The whole scene is sometimes held to be a Lukan creation, designed to act as a framework for the saying in verse 5, and based on the story in Mk. iii. 1-6.[11] However, verse 3 contains some un-Lukan features. The three verbs ἀποκριθείς . . . εἶπεν . . . λέγων overload the sentence,[12] and the use of ἀποκριθείς in a context where there is no real answer (because there is no explicit prior question) is un-Lukan.[13] There is too the use of νομικός. Luke generally uses γραμματεύς, and the use of νομικός therefore appears to be pre-Lukan.[14] Thus, although there are many Lukanisms here, so that Luke may have filled out many of the details, there are still traces of an earlier tradition in the question in verse 3, as well as in the answer in verse 5.

The main difficulty of verse 5 itself lies in the combination of υἱός and βοῦς. (The textual variants here are almost certainly attempts to alleviate the difficulty.) The conjunction of these two nouns is very odd. The OT texts which talk of helping an animal mention an ox and an ass (cf. Ex. xxiii. 4f.; Deut. xxii. 4). On this basis it might be assumed that the reference to the 'son' is secondary. The assonance in Aramaic between ברא (son), בעירא (ox), and בירא (pit), as well as בר חמרא (ass), suggests a Semitic original to the saying. Black's solution is that ברא has replaced בר חמרא, so that the original reference was to the biblical pair of 'ox and ass'.[15] Lohse believes that only בעירא was original, and the reference to the 'son' was a later expansion of the original pun in the course of the oral tradition.[16] The difficulty of both these theories is that it appears to have been accepted by all that one would not rescue an animal by actually pulling it out of a pit on the Sabbath. On the other hand, the suspension of the Sabbath rules to save a man in the same situation was generally accepted, probably even at Qumran (cf. CD xi. 16f.) where the Sabbath regulations were apparently interpreted even more strictly than elsewhere.[17] Thus, if the argument was to get off the ground at all, it must have referred to a human being falling into a pit so that 'son' is more likely to have been the original reference here. If this is so, then Strecker's suggestion, that ἤ βοῦς is an addition under the influence of Lk. xiii. 15, has much to recommend it,[18] especially if this was done at the Aramaic stage when the pun would have been more evident. (The reference to an animal fits very well in the illustration in Lk. xiii, since untying an animal and leading it to water was recognised as a legitimate breach of the Sabbath law.)[19]

Thus the original form of the saying concerned a man falling into a pit, and in the course of the tradition the figure of the animal was added. The textual tradition in Lk. xiv shows how incongruous later scribes found this, and it would be natural for the 'son' reference to be dropped altogether. It is precisely this that has happened in Matthew's version of the saying in Matt. xii. 11. Thus Matthew's version is the latest form,[20] where the original reference to a human being has been dropped completely. Further confirmation of this can be seen in the use of πρόβατον. Matthew is fond of the 'sheep' imagery, either to describe, or to compare, those who receive the divine mercy.[21] Thus the reference here is probably due to Matthew's own redactional work.

The conclusion of this is that the question 'is it lawful?', and the saying in reply, both stem from a tradition which is common to Matthew and Luke (though they differ in who puts the question: Matthew makes it a question by the opponents, Luke has it on the lips of Jesus).[22] It is highly unlikely that Matthew is Luke's source, since Matthew develops the tradition of the reply even further away from the original by using his favourite πρόβατον. Thus, behind Matthew and Luke lies a common source containing this material. If this is so, then this fragment gives part of an argument to show that Jesus' breach of the Sabbath law was, at the very least, reasonable. Although the argument would probably not have convinced a Qumran sectarian, nevertheless the attempt is made to provide some justification for Jesus' actions, and to show that Jesus did not arbitrarily break the Sabbath law. This will be seen to tie up very closely with some other passages in the 'double tradition', and thus may show that this part of the tradition had its own distinctive outlook, in this case over the question of the Law.[23]

It has been seen that Matthew's material does not fit the form of the logical argument into which it is being pressed. The question in verse 10*b* cannot, in the circumstances presented, be a genuine question, and the premiss assumed in verse 11 fits equally badly; finally the conclusion in verse 12*b* fails to follow logically. However, the above analysis of Lk. xiv eases some of these difficulties. The question in verse 10*b* and the argument in verses 11–12*a* are part of a separate tradition which Matthew shares with Luke, and the inappropriate premiss in verse 11 was seen to be due to MattR. When one now strips away all this from Matthew's account, one is left with a story which has Jesus' opponents standing ready to accuse Jesus if he actually healed the man, rather than asking his opinion on a question to which there could only be one answer. Jesus' 'justification' for his action is then a polemical assertion that it is lawful to 'do good' on the Sabbath. This is exactly the case in Mark, and hence Mark's account must be very similar to, if not identical with, one of Matthew's sources.

Mark's account is in fact clear and unconfused precisely where Matthew's account is not. In Mark, the Pharisees watch Jesus to see if he will heal on the Sabbath, thereby performing an illegal action, so that they can accuse him. This fits well with the circumstances of the story since there is now no question of a difference of opinion on what was really an undisputed question. Moreover, in Mark, the final ἵνα clause fits perfectly, both with regard to the grammatical structure of the sentence, and also with regard to its sense: the accusation will follow Jesus' action which is recognised by all as illegitimate, rather than following on anything that

Jesus says. There is now no reasoned argument, as in Matt. xii. 11f./Lk. xiv. 5, and Jesus' reply takes the form of a direct assertion.

The identification of Mark as one of Matthew's sources solves many of the difficulties of the Matthean version. Matthew alters Mark's παρετήρουν by substituting the direct question from his other tradition, thereby making for some of the historical difficulties noted above. The final ἵνα clause, which fits well in Mark, is taken over verbatim by Matthew, but his change of the previous clause disrupts the structure of the whole sentence, as well as making the two parts fit very badly with regard to their contents. The non-Markan tradition provides the saying in verses 11–12a which Matthew also redacts, and Matthew then switches back to Mark's account for his final conclusion in verse 12b. This is now, by the addition of ὥστε, cast in the form of a logical conclusion, with a statement at the end of what is, formally speaking, a structured argument. However, in context it can only be a polemical assertion, as in Mark.

Further differences between Matthew and Mark can also be explained quite satisfactorily if Matthew is redacting Mark. In verse 9 μεταβαίνω[24] and ἐκεῖθεν[25] are both Matthean, and the αὐτῶν qualifying συναγωγή is characteristic.[26] In verse 10 καὶ ἰδού is Matthean,[27] as is τότε in verse 13,[28] and συμβούλιον λαμβάνω in verse 14.[29] The omission of Mk. iii. 5 could be due to reverence for the person of Jesus and a wish to avoid any suggestion that Jesus was angry.[30] Thus it is relatively unproblematical to see Matthew's version as derived, in part at least, from Mark.

Similarly, a theory of Lukan dependence on Mark presents no particular problems. Luke re-writes the introduction,[31] adding the note that Jesus was teaching in the synagogue.[32] He mentions the opponents in the stylised grouping 'scribes and Pharisees', avoiding Mark's strange conjunction of Pharisees and Herodians. He adds the note that Jesus knew his opponents' thoughts in verse 8,[33] as well as the reference to the man's obeying Jesus' command to stand. This then necessitates the extra clause in verse 9a which is Lukan in language.[34] He omits Mk. iii. 5b as Matthew does (and the same reasons seem appropriate) and he re-writes the concluding verse in a typically Lukan way.[35] The accounts in Mark and Luke are in any case very close to each other, so that it is not easy to decide which way dependence lies, but certainly the theory of Markan priority presents no problems here.

On the other hand, a few small features suggest that any theory which makes Mark dependent on either of the others (as, for example, the GH does) has some awkward features to explain. If Mark is dependent on Matthew, he appears to have reached a form which is all but identical with one of Matthew's sources. Moreover, it is difficult to see why, if Mark knew Luke, he should have omitted Luke's διδάσκειν in Lk. vi. 6, when it is a frequent feature of the 'seam' passages in Mark to present Jesus as 'teaching'.[36] Why too should Mark have avoided using Luke's reference to Jesus knowing his opponents' thoughts when he himself mentions this in ii. 8? Why should he have avoided Luke's καὶ στῆθι and ἀναστὰς ἔστη when this would have been a neat example of a 'repetition of motif', which is often thought to characterise Mark's own style?[37] Why should Mark have avoided Luke's use of ἐπερωτάω in vi. 9, when the word is a Markan favourite (8 - 25 - 17 + 2)? The same consideration applies to the difference between Mark and Matthew in Matt. xii. 10, where Matthew also uses ἐπερωτάω (though here it is possible that Mark might be consciously changing Matthew's direct question for some reason). Finally, the use of περιβλεψάμενος in Mk. iii. 5/Lk. vi. 10 is an example of a part of Mark's characteristic vocabulary also appearing in Luke, thus showing dependence of Luke on Mark.[38]

The fact that περιβλεψάμενος is not characteristic of Luke also has implications for the question of the relationship between Matthew and Luke. The GH must presumably assert that Luke is dependent on Matthew here. Lk. vi. 10a must, on this theory, be a Lukan addition to Matthew (there being no Matthean parallel). However, the fact that περιβλέπομαι is not a Lukan word (this is its only occurrence in Luke-Acts) makes this very unlikely. Similarly, if Luke is redacting Matthew, it is hard to see why he has avoided Matthew's καὶ ἰδού in Matt. xii. 9 (16 times elsewhere in narrative in Luke, 8 times in Acts). Further, the use of the dative with εἶπεν in Lk. vi. 8, in what the GH must claim is a Lukan addition to Matthew, is also un-Lukan: Luke prefers πρός + accusative. Thus a theory that Luke is redacting Matthew has a number of awkward features to explain here.

This analysis shows that the evidence can be explained quite satisfactorily in terms of the 2DH, but not in terms of the GH. One of Matthew's sources as derived from an analysis of Matthew alone must have been very similar to Mark, and all the difficulties in Matthew's text can be explained if his source is Mark. In addition Matthew uses another tradition which he shares with Luke, but Luke's version is more primitive. On the other hand, the assumptions of the GH leave many unanswered questions. Matthew's difficult version remains unexplained; Luke's form of the saying in xiv. 5 is more original than Matthew's and hence is unlikely to be derived from Matthew; Mark's version looks too much like Matthew's source, and several omissions which Mark must have made from Luke are difficult to explain; finally, the one clear indication of priority (i.e. περιβλεψάμενος) implies Lukan dependence on Mark. Thus the 2DH provides a more adequate explanation of the texts than does the GH.

10 THE SYNOPTIC TRADITION ON UNCLEANNESS

(Matt. xv. 1–20/Mk. vii. 1–23)

The lack of any direct Lukan parallel to this pericope means that the discussion about the Synoptic Problem is confined to the question of the relationship between Matthew and Mark. In his discussion of this pericope, Farmer notes the gloss in Mk. vii. 3f., added to explain Jewish customs for Gentile readers, and he puts forward three considerations from which, he claims, 'it is clear that Mark's version of this tradition is secondary to that of Matthew'.[1] Two of these, as well as his note about Mk. vii. 3f., make implicit appeal to his criterion of 'Jewishness'. This has been considered earlier in general terms, and the result of that discussion was that no firm decisions could be made on the basis of one tradition being 'more Jewish' than a parallel one.[2] A 'Jewish' tradition need only imply that an author was part of, and writing for, a community well acquainted with Judaism. Thus when Farmer points to the two lists of vices at the end of the pericope and says that Matthew's is more Jewish and hence the more original, this is by no means a necessary conclusion.[3] It is equally possible that Matthew has altered Mark's list to conform to the commands of the Decalogue.[4] A simple comparison of the contents of the two lists cannot really determine anything about literary priority without further considerations.

It is essentially the same criterion which is being applied when Farmer says that Mark omitted the polemic against the Pharisees (Matt. xv. 12–14), since this meant little for the later Gentile church, whereas, in the early Palestinian church, such hostility would have been very real. However, anti-Jewish polemic of the same kind occurs in Pauline material written for non-Palestinian churches (cf. Ro. ii. 19; 1 Thess. ii. 16). Jewish-Christian conflict was not confined to the first few decades after the crucifixion, and hence not all texts reflecting anti-Jewish sentiments are necessarily early. The polemic in Matt. xv. 12–14 implies only that Matthew is a gospel written with Jews, in particular Pharisees, very much in mind. This is in itself not a very startling claim. Moreover, to suggest that Mark omitted these verses because such polemic meant little to the later Gentile church is in this case unconvincing. For the whole pericope is in effect a piece of anti-Jewish polemic, as it sets forward a view of cleanness in sharp contrast to the views of the scribes and Pharisees. Mark is no less polemical than Matthew (and indeed many would say that Mk. vii. 15 is considerably more so).

A study of Matthew alone in fact suggests that verses 12–14 are a redactional insertion into an existing source. In verse 15 Jesus is asked to interpret the 'parable', which, in Matthew's present form, most naturally refers to the saying in verse 14 about the blind leading the blind. One might, therefore, have expected an explanation to the effect that the 'blind' is meant metaphorically, and that 'leading' means teaching etc. Instead, Matthew's version continues by understanding Peter's request as referring to the saying in verse 11. Thus verses 12–14 interrupt the clear connection which exists between the parable in verse 11 and the request for its interpretation in verse 15.[5] The theory that verses 12–14 are a redactional insertion receives some support from considerations of vocabulary. Verse 12 is introduced by Matthew's favourite τότε, and the participle προσελθόντες is also a characteristic way of introducing new material.[6] The tradition history of verses 12–14 is probably more complicated. However, all that is being claimed here is that the connection between verses 11 and 15, and the redactional nature of the introduction in verse 12, both suggest that the sayings in verses 12–14 have been inserted by Matthew into a source where originally verse 15 followed immediately after verse 11. This is, of course, exactly the situation in Mark. Thus, in not containing verses 12–14, Mark's version is seen to be closer to Matthew's source, rather than secondary.

Farmer's last point, seeking to show that Mark is secondary to Matthew, brings in wider considerations of the unity of the whole pericope. He writes:

> In Matthew the point is that to eat with unwashed hands does not defile a man. The appropriate question is set forth in verse 2, and the answer fittingly comes at the end of the literary unit in verse 20. In Mark, however, the point is that Jesus declared all foods clean (19*b*), a point of special interest to Gentile churches.[7]

However, the interest of Mark's verse 19*b* for Gentile churches can hardly be taken as any indication that Mark is less Jewish than Matthew, and therefore secondary. Verse 19*b* could scarcely be said to be of little interest to a Jewish-Christian church. In fact, the whole debate, with its various themes of hand-washing, oral tradition, the Qorban practice, unclean foods etc., concerns customs and laws within Judaism, and the different issues must have been of concern to all Christians in contact with Judaism, and presumably to Jesus himself. The fact that the main point of Mark comes in verse 19*b*, whereas Matthew's version is centred on the theme of hand-washing, shows nothing about relative literary priority.

Farmer's other point, that Matthew's version has the appropriate question at the beginning and the answer coming fittingly at the end, goes rather further and brings in wider issues of the coherence and unity of each account. It is generally thought (at least by those who accept Markan priority) that Mark's version is composite. Whatever decision is made about further sub-divisions, there appears to be a definite break between verses 1-13 and verses 15-23. Verses 1-13 concern the validity of the oral tradition, and verses 15-23 deal with the written Law itself, especially the food laws. The two sections are connected by the link-word κοινός, and the seam between them is clearly visible at the literary level also in the characteristically Markan feature of Jesus' summoning a crowd in verse 14, together with the Markan vocabulary there (πάλιν, καὶ ἔλεγεν αὐτοῖς).[8] Although it is possible that verse 15 might be the original answer to the question in verse 5,[9] it is still the case that the terms of reference in verse 15 have been extended to cover a far wider scope than the more limited issue of the oral tradition in verse 5. Farmer apparently claims that this is not the case in Matthew, in that Matthew's version is said to be centred on the single theme of eating with unwashed hands. This therefore suggests that one should look at each account separately to see if one is more coherent than the other. I start with Mark's account.

In Mark, the disciples are questioned about their failure to wash before eating, which is said to contravene the 'tradition of the elders'. Mark adds a note in verses 3f., which not only explains the particular custom to Gentile readers (though with some notorious difficulties about historical accuracy), but also shows that the scope of the problem is wider than hand-washing.[10] Thus verses 3f. make it clear that, for Mark, it is primarily a question of the validity of the whole oral tradition, of which hand-washing simply happens to be a convenient example. With this assumption, the logic of the rest of the section down to verse 13 is reasonably clear. Jesus' reply in verses 6–8 is a straight polemical assertion, using the words of Is. xxix. 13 LXX: the oral tradition is of merely human origin, in contrast to the divine command. The climax is then the charge in verse 8 that Jesus' opponents are guilty of breaking God's law simply to keep their tradition. Verses 9–13 now give an example of this unsubstantiated claim: the Qorban practice leads to a breaking of the fifth commandment. Probably verses 6–8 and 9–13 are of separate origins: καλῶς is used literally in verse 6, ironically in verse 9; the tradition 'of men' becomes 'your' tradition;

verse 9 is a repetition of verse 8; further, the typically Markan phrase καὶ
ἔλεγεν αὐτοῖς indicates a seam in the tradition at this point.[11] The
relevance of the section on Qorban oaths is also uncertain, since the conflict between keeping oaths and honouring parents is not strictly one
between the oral tradition and the written Law: the command to keep
one's oaths is based firmly in the written Law itself (Nu. xxx. 2; Deut.
xxiii. 23).[12] Thus verses 9–13 probably originated in another part of the
tradition and were not initially integrated with this present context. However, the charge of verse 8 is generalised in verse 13*b* to cover all the oral
tradition (cf. the expansion in verse 4) so that the whole section now has
a reasonable unity and progression of thought.

Is Matthew's version any more coherent? Many have said that it is, and
that Matthew's version may be close to Mark's source (in which case
Matthew may be Mark's source).[13] Some also point to the way in which
Matthew's different arrangement brings the pericope closer to the form of
a *Streitgespräch* with the question followed by counter-question.[14] However, Matthew's overall presentation turns out to be far less coherent. It is
clear that, for Matthew, the central question is indeed the specific one of
hand-washing (cf. the *inclusio* between verses 2 and 20 which governs the
whole pericope). The initial charge against the disciples is even sharper
than in Mark: it is quite explicitly a case of their 'disobeying' the oral
tradition in question. (This in turn raises even more sharply the problem of
the historicity of this incident, since hand-washing does not appear to have
been a demand imposed on the laity prior to about 100 A.D.[15] Mark's
version – 'Why do they not walk according to the tradition of the elders?' –
is possibly susceptible to the interpretation that this tradition might not be
legally binding on the disciples,[16] and hence might be historically more
plausible.) However, Matthew's version does not, and logically cannot,
relate to this question. For the reply of Jesus, referring to the Qorban
practice, now has little relevance to the specific question of hand-washing.
The two oral traditions are quite different, and so, whilst verses 3–6 could
certainly show that the existing Qorban practice is invalid, the argument
cannot show that all oral tradition (and hence hand-washing) is also invalid.
All it can indicate is that the casuistry over the law of oaths needed
revision.[17] Thus verses 3–6 in Matthew cannot act as any proof for the
assertion in verses 7–9 that all oral tradition is of only human origin.
Verses 7–9 still function in the argument as a polemical assertion, and
verses 3–6 do not prove its validity. If however the logic is meant to go the
other way, i.e. if the quotation from Is. xxix is meant to give scriptural
backing to the claim of Jesus about Qorban oaths,[18] then (a) it is redundant, since the argument has already shown that, in this one case, the oral

tradition contradicts the will of God as expressed in the fifth commandment, and (b) it still does no more to relate the Qorban example any more
closely to the issue of hand-washing: it only reinforces the attack on
Qorban oaths. Thus, whilst it has sometimes been said that the Qorban
saying could be Jesus' reply to the Pharisees' question,[19] this can only be
the case if the issue is the validity of the whole oral tradition, as in Mark,
and not just the question of hand-washing, as in Matthew. It is more likely
that the Qorban saying was an isolated part of the tradition, which was
only introduced to this pericope when verses 3f. in Mark extended the
scope of the discussion to the whole oral tradition. If the issue is only that
of washing, the Qorban example is irrelevant. (The relevance is only slightly
greater when the issue is extended to cover all oral tradition, as seen above.)
Thus Matthew's logic is less tight than Mark's, and even in Matthew, it is
the quotation from Is. xxix which really speaks to the charge made against
the disciples. The Qorban example still only provides a supplementary
example of this general charge.

The centrality of the quotation from Is. xxix shows that Jesus' reply at
least has extended the scope of the discussion so that all oral tradition is
now being questioned. There is thus a discrepancy in Matthew between the
concentration on the hand-washing question and the form of Jesus' reply.
To assume that the latter is secondary would leave nothing as the original
reply to the question. It is more likely that the restriction of the issue to
washing is the secondary feature, and that originally the story was concerned with the wider question of the validity of the whole oral tradition.
The reply referring to Is. xxix is then the real answer to the question raised,
and the Qorban saying is only indirectly related. Mark's version is thus the
more coherent, since it initially extends the scope of the question to cover
all oral tradition, and it makes the immediate answer the quotation of Is.
xxix which is relevant to the problem. Mark's version therefore probably
represents the more primitive tradition, where the various elements are put
side by side, and where the seams between them are still clearly visible.
Matthew's account attempts to intermingle them in a way which gives a
good formal structure (the form of the *Streitgespräch*), but it is less
coherent, both as a result of the rearrangement and also because of the
attempt to limit the discussion to the issue of hand-washing.

In the second half of the pericope, it is even harder to see Matthew's
version as still dealing with the question of unwashed hands. Mark's
account has as its kernel the saying in verse 15, which many, even the most
sceptical, have regarded as one of the authentic sayings of Jesus.[20] However, it is quite likely that verses 17–19 and 20–23 are later interpretations
of the logion, the first rationalising Jesus' dogmatic pronouncement, the

second explaining what it is that 'comes out of a man' that defiles him.[21] Further, the device of the disciples asking Jesus to explain the meaning of a parabolic saying to them privately in a 'house' is typically Markan.[22] It is clear too, that, in Mark at least, the question of hand-washing and the oral tradition has been left far behind. Whether or not the original form of verse 15 included the phrase εἰσπορευόμενον εἰς αὐτόν,[23] the reference must now be to the prescriptions of the OT Law itself. With the phrase, the saying refers to foods, and thus to the food laws of Lev. xi. etc. Without the phrase, the reference is wider, but it must still include the food laws (as well as other laws on defilement).

In Matthew the situation is slightly different. Matt. xv. 11 explicitly speaks of things entering 'into the mouth', and thus the reference is clearly restricted to food alone. This in turn creates a difficulty in the request for an explanation in verse 15, for the 'parable' in verse 11 is now so clear that it hardly needs expounding.[24] One of the most recent attempts to show a logical cohesion in Matthew's account is that of Cope, who claims that in Matthew an explanation is still required, since what comes 'out of the mouth' needs clarification.[25] Yet Matthew still proceeds to give the (now unnecessary) explanation for the first half of the saying. Even the clarification in the second half leads Matthew into further trouble. It is unlikely (*contra* Cope) that breath and spittle need to be specifically excluded as defiling agents. (The context implies that it is one's own mouth that is being considered, and hence the possibility that another person's spittle could defile a man, which it could, does not arise.) However, what 'comes out of the mouth' has to be re-interpreted as 'out of the heart' so as to include more than just words, e.g. robbery and murder.[26] (Cope suggests that the stress is still on verbal sins in the list of vices of verses 19f., since these come first and last on the list;[27] but still the 'mouth' has to be modified, even by Matthew.) Both these difficulties stem from the reference to 'mouth' in verse 11 and thus imply that it is a secondary addition to the saying, and not, as Cope suggests, integral to the whole pericope picking up the בְּפִיו in the MT (but not the LXX) of Is. xxix. 13. Matthew's version of the saying therefore seems to be clarification of a version of the logion which had no such reference to the 'mouth', and hence, in this respect, appears to be secondary to that of Mark.

The question now arises of how far this is related to the issue of hand-washing. Matthew appears to keep this as the central issue by closing with verse 20*b*. It is possible that Matthew's different version in verse 11, limiting attention to food, is also due to his concentration on this issue.[28] Hübner claims that Matthew intends to restrict attention in verse 11 to food which has been touched by unwashed hands.[29] However, one would have then expected something to the effect that 'unwashed hands do not defile any food'. The eating would be irrelevant, since the point at issue would be whether the food itself had already been defiled. (Eating defiled food would make the eater unclean with the same degree of uncleanness as the food itself, cf. Toh. ii. 2). In verse 11, the contrast between what goes in and what comes out of a mouth is clearly not one between one food and another (food touched by unwashed hands which is pure, as opposed to other unclean food); rather it is between all food as a possible defiling agency and the true causes of defilement. The completely general reference to 'what goes into the mouth' means that the written Law itself comes into view. If hand-washing is still meant to be the main point at issue, then Matthew appears to have confused two quite separate matters: making food unclean by touching, and the Mosaic rules on the cleanness of food.[30] Once again, therefore, there is a tension between the limitation of the issue to hand-washing and the main part of the pericope. Since the wider perspective is essential to the rest of the unit (and removing it would involve removing almost all the material in it) it is easiest to assume that verse 20*b* is a secondary attempt to limit the scope of the discussion. Possibly Matthew's verse 11 represents a weakening of Mark's verse 15, but the principle still remains that the Mosaic food laws are implicitly questioned.[31]

It is thus very difficult to see Matthew's version as a coherent whole. In particular, the question and answer which surround the pericope and try to give unity to it do not succeed in this. Far from being the 'appropriate question' receiving its 'fitting answer' (to use Farmer's terminology), they seem to be part of a later attempt to limit the discussion to this one issue. The material itself makes it clear that questions of far wider scope are at issue here. Matthew's apparent coherence and unity are only superficial. In most of the points at issue, Matthew has been shown to be secondary, and Mark is closer to what must have been Matthew's source.

There are, moreover, a few linguistic features which suggest that Matthew is using Mark himself (and not just a source similar to Mark). In verse 1 Matthew speaks of the 'Pharisees and scribes', an ordering which is unique in Matthew. Elsewhere Matthew refers to the 'scribes and Pharisees' (in that order), and the phrase is one of Matthew's standard descriptions of Jesus' opponents (cf. Matt. v. 20; xii. 38; xxiii. 2, 13, 14, 15). Matthew's ordering here is easily explained if Mark is Matthew's source, since Mark does mention the groups separately and in this order ('Pharisees and scribes from Jerusalem'). The theme of 'scribes from Jerusalem' as constituting an important part of the opposition to Jesus may well be Markan.[32] Matthew characteristically joins both groups together to form a single deputation coming from Jerusalem, but the unusual ordering betrays the use of a source. Moreover, the fact that the Jerusalem origin of the opposition may be due to MkR suggests that it is Mark who is Matthew's source.[33]

In Mk. vii. 14/Matt. xv. 10 there is another characteristic of MkR which also appears in Matthew: for the new scene, Jesus summons a crowd to act as an audience for the new teaching to follow, and this is a characteristic Markan device.[34] But the same also occurs in Matthew, even though Matthew's verse 20*b* makes it clear that Matthew himself envisages the scene as a single unit. As Hübner says: 'An dieser Stelle belässt Matthäus also die markinische Zäsur.'[35] Finally, εἰσπορεύομαι is a favourite Markan word (8 times in Mark).[36] Matthew regularly uses εἰσέρχομαι and does so in verse 11; however, in verse 16 εἰσπορεύομαι appears for the only time in Matthew, and thus may show dependence on a source. Since Mk. vii. 18 also uses the word in the parallel verse, this is another case of a Markan characteristic appearing in Matthew, thus showing dependence of Matthew on Mark.

The result of this analysis is that Matthew is shown to be dependent on a source which is indistinguishable from Mark. The simplest solution is therefore to say that Matthew is dependent on Mark himself.

11 THE CLEANSING OF THE TEMPLE

(Matt. xxi. 12–13/Mk. xi. 15–19/Lk. xix. 45–8)

This pericope is analysed in some detail by Farmer, Longstaff and Orchard to see if the texts are susceptible to explanation along Griesbachian lines. There are some agreements between Matthew and Luke against Mark: both agree in omitting the whole of Mark's verse 16, and also the phrase 'for all the nations' at the end of the quotation of Is. lvi. 7; further, both agree that the incident took place on the same day as the entry into Jerusalem, unlike Mark who dates it a day later. The shorter texts of Matthew and Luke will be considered later. With regard to the different chronology, Farmer says that this indicates that 'Mark was not unwilling to exercise his freedom' in dealing with his sources.[1] However, this is very strange for an author trying to combine his two sources where they agree and to give their concurrent testimony.[2] An appeal to editorial freedom is scarcely sufficient to explain this anomaly for the GH. A satisfactory explanation must surely give a rather more substantial reason for this editorial change by Mark, if such it be. (Possible reasons why Matthew and Luke might have changed Mark will be considered later.)

Farmer starts by considering the 'sandwich' structure of Mk. xi. 12–20, in which the story of the cleansing interrupts the two halves of the story of the cursing of the fig-tree. On form-critical grounds, he says, Mark is shown to be secondary, since the original form of the story of the fig-tree must have been a unified whole.[3] This may be so, but it does not necessarily prove that it is Matthew who is Mark's source. Matthew's version could just as well represent a secondary 'improvement' of Mark. Mark's practice of 'sandwiching' is almost certainly characteristic of his own literary technique,[4] and this does probably represent the secondary interruption of an originally unified story. However, Matthew's differences from Mark here may well be redactional: for Matthew, the incident of the cursing of the fig-tree is a miracle pure and simple (cf. especially παραχρῆμα in xxi. 19, not in Mark, repeated in verse 20) which then acts as an illustration for the teaching on the power of prayer which follows.[5] Precisely in order to provide such an illustration, Matthew may well have altered

Mark's sandwich structure and re-united the two halves of the fig-tree story, thereby separating it from the incident of the cleansing of the temple.

Orchard introduces considerations of historicity. He claims that, although Matthew's is the more original form, the actual event must have included an interval between Jesus' curse and the physical withering of the tree. Hence Mark's version must be secondary, sorting out the historical problems created by Matthew's 'telescoping' of the incident.[6] This would mean that Mark's version is more accurate at the historical level, but, because of this, secondary at the literary level. However, if Mark's version is indeed more accurate historically then this should suggest the literary priority of Mark. In view of the fact that Matthew's different structure can be explained as due to MattR, there is no good reason, on form-critical grounds alone, to claim that the theory of Markan priority is unsatisfactory.

Farmer's analysis of the text of the pericope itself begins with a consideration of Lk. xix. 47f. This, he claims, is a Lukan creation based on Matt. xxvi. 55; it is designed to establish the historical basis for Jesus' condemnation of the manner of his arrest, since Matthew's version is defective as history 'in that the basis for Jesus' claim that he was daily in the temple teaching had not been previously established in Matthew's Gospel.' Luke then abstracted from Matt. xxi. 15 the opposition of the 'chief priests and scribes', and combined this with two items from Matt. xxvi. 47–55 (the 'chief priests and elders' sending the arrest party and Jesus' having been 'daily in the temple teaching') to produce Lk. xix. 47f.[7]

Now it may well be that Lk. xix. 47 is due in part to LkR, but if so the reasons cannot be exactly as Farmer claims. It is quite wrong to say that Matthew's history is defective, for Jesus does teach in the temple: in all the controversies which follow, the scene is the temple (cf. Matt. xxi. 23/ Mk. xi. 27 with no change of venue until after Matt. xxiii. 39/Mk. xii. 40).[8] Thus, although it may well be Luke's intention to stress Jesus' teaching in the temple on a regular basis, a desire to correct Matthew's 'defective' history cannot be Luke's reason.[9]

Matt. xxvi. 55 is almost identical with Mk. xiv. 49 (the only difference being that in Matthew Jesus says that he was 'sitting' in the temple). Hence dependence of Luke on Matthew here is indistinguishable from dependence on Mark.[10] Moreover, dependence on Mark is more plausible, since in Mark, the 'scribes' are included in the group who send the arrest party, whereas Matthew does not refer to the scribes here (Matt. xxvi. 47/ Mk. xiv. 43). Lk. xix. 47 speaks initially of the 'chief priests and scribes';

possibly this grouping is derived from Matt. xxi. 15, in which case
Matthew's version of who sent the arrest party in xxvi. 47 has only provided the reference to the 'elders' here. However, Matt. xxvi. 47 refers to
the πρεσβυτέροι, whereas Lk.xix. 47 refers to οἱ πρῶτοι. Luke appears to
have no objection to using the term πρεσβυτέροι to refer to the Jewish
leaders.[11] Now there is some evidence that οἱ πρῶτοι, referring to 'leaders',
is not uncharacteristic of Luke, and hence its presence here may be due to
LkR.[12] However, Lk. xix. 47 cannot be explained satisfactorily simply as
LkR based on Matt. xxi. 15 and xxvi. 47. The main problem lies in the
final phrase καὶ οἱ πρῶτοι τοῦ λαοῦ, which seems to be appended after the
sentence has really finished. Thus, whilst the statistics do give some support
for οἱ πρῶτοι τοῦ λαοῦ being a Lukan phrase, it appears to be an addition
to a whole sentence already existing in Luke's source. When this Lukan
phrase is peeled away, what is left is the clause 'the chief priests and
scribes sought to kill him', which is almost identical with Mk. xi. 18. If
Luke were freely redacting Matthew, one would have expected all three
nouns to come together, rather than the third being awkwardly appended
at the end of the clause. Thus Luke's text demands a source almost
identical with Mk. xi. 18. Lukan dependence on Mark is therefore much
easier to envisage than Luke's having produced the awkward syntax of
verse 47 by a free re-writing of Matt. xxi. 15, xxvi. 47-55. Further,
Matthew's own reference to the 'scribes' at xxi. 15 is slightly unexpected,
since compared with Mark, Matthew shows less antipathy to the scribes.[13]
The theory of Markan priority would explain both the Matthean and
Lukan texts very well, since Mk. xi. 18 refers to the scribes and would
therefore be the source for Matt. xxi. 15 and Lk. xix. 47. (However, on
the GH, Matthew's reference to the scribes could be accounted for by its
presence in Matthew's source, which remains unidentified.) Luke may have
added verse 47a on his own (possibly on the basis of Mk. xiv. 49/Matt.
xxvi. 55) and possibly rewritten verse 48;[14] but the analysis of verse 47b
has shown that Luke must have used a source for this half-verse which was
all but identical with Mark. It is easiest to assume that Luke is dependent
on Mark himself here.

Farmer makes little comment about Mk. xi. 15, though Longstaff sees
it as a typical case of the 'pattern of alternating agreement' which he finds
elsewhere. Mark's verse 15 was discussed earlier, and there it was seen that
the alternating 'agreement' is only one of degree, and also not very surprising.[15] The GH is by no means free from problems here either. Matthew's
alleged closeness to Mark in Mark's verse 15c involves the omission of τούς
with ἀγοράζοντας. This suggests that the buyers and sellers formed a single
group. Mark's account may show greater historical accuracy in distinguishing

two groups, traders and pilgrims, in which case Mark's version has greater claims to originality. Longstaff's 'alternating agreement' has to be explained on the GH as Mark's using Luke for verse 15*b* and Matthew for verse 15*c*. However, there is no substantial difference between Matthew and Luke here so it is not clear what might have led Mark to use Luke for verse 15*b*. Moreover, the Matthean parallel uses a paratactic construction which is one of Mark's favourites.[16] Thus the GH must envisage Mark's deliberately avoiding this here, when presented with the possibility of adopting this favourite construction from one of his sources. In fact, the one feature which might suggest which way dependence lies again implies dependence of Luke on Mark: the (probably) pleonastic ἤρξατο is retained in Lk. xix. 45, providing an example of a Markan characteristic reappearing in one of the parallels, thus showing the priority of Mark.[17] Moreover, since Matthew does not use the word at this point (the omission is easily explicable as MattR), the dependence of Luke must be on Mark, and not on Matthew.

Mk. xi. 16 is peculiar to Mark, and hence on the 2DH constitutes a minor agreement in omission. Reference is often made to possible analogies in Josephus (*Con. Ap.* 2.7) or the Mishnah (Ber. ix.5) for the same idea in Judaism, if not an exact parallel. Longstaff admits the validity of these parallels, with the possible inference that Mark here preserves early, authentic tradition. However, he claims that it is quite possible that Mark, although the latest gospel to be written, could still preserve earlier traditions; hence Mark could have added this verse to Matthew and Luke.[18]

Nevertheless, the difficulties for seeing verse 16 as a Markan addition are very great. The verse can hardly have been handed down as an isolated fragment of the tradition: it is too bald to make sense on its own and it demands a narrative setting. Further, it is difficult to imagine any other setting for the verse than the present one, and indeed it can be fitted in to make sense within this context. The historical difficulties associated with this story are notorious,[19] but the most convincing explanation of Jesus' motives in 'cleansing' the temple is that he was aiming to create the conditions of the new age as set out in Zech. xiv. 21: 'There shall be no longer any trader (כְּנַעֲנִי) in the house of the Lord'.[20] It is possible that verse 16 also reflects the same verse of Zechariah with its statement that all the vessels of Jerusalem shall be deemed to be holy and thus to be used for sacred purposes; hence they must not be taken out of the temple.[21] Alternatively, it may simply be parallel to the passage in Ber. ix.5, banning the use of the temple as a short-cut.[22] Whatever the precise background, Jesus appears here as defending the holiness of the temple, and insisting on its preservation for its proper use.[23]

This, however, is directly opposed to Mark's own interpretation of the story. For, by sandwiching it between the two halves of the story of the cursing of the fig-tree, Mark himself evidently intended that each story should illuminate the other. Hence the whole unit implies a rejection of the Jewish temple, and indeed of unfaithful Judaism.[24] There is thus a tension between verse 16 and Mark's total understanding of the scene, and so it is very unlikely that Mark himself would have added verse 16 alone to his sources (as the GH must say). Hence, verse 16 must have come to Mark in a source,[25] and, since the verse requires a narrative framework to make sense, the source must have already contained an account of the 'cleansing'. Mark is thus using a source for his story (i.e. not just for verse 16), and moreover, since verse 16 is not in either Matthew or Luke, that source cannot be either of those two gospels. It is therefore extremely hard to account for Mark's verse 16 on the GH, but relatively easy if Mark is prior and dependent on earlier, independent sources. Possibly the verse was not understood by Matthew and Luke and hence omitted as irrelevant.[26]

In verse 17 Farmer says that Mark adds the phrase πᾶσιν τοῖς ἔθνεσιν in the interests of the Gentile mission, but it is shown to be an addition by the fact that it 'is not necessary to the point being made in this context, where the contrast is between the right and wrong use of the temple'.[27] However, an alleged addition by Mark of the phrase can hardly be 'in the interests of the Gentile mission'. If this saying is meant to point to the later church's attitude to the Gentiles, then it fits very badly with later ideas: for this verse implies that the Gentiles are to be incorporated into the worshipping life of the Jewish temple. This was scarcely the dominant, and certainly not the Markan, view,[28] and hence it is very difficult to see this extra phrase as being due to MkR. The opposite change, whereby Matthew and Luke each omit the phrase from Mark, can be easily explained if both took the quotation of Is. lvi. 7 as a genuine prophecy which, after the destruction of the temple in 70 A.D., was manifestly incapable of fulfilment.[29]

The problem of what precisely is the contrast made in the two quotations of Is. lvi. 7 and Jer. vii. 11 is more difficult to decide. This raises the question of whether or not the quotations are integrally related to the story. It is unlikely that the point of the incident was to contrast prayer with the sacrificial cult. It was the synagogue, rather than the temple, which was the place of prayer; further, the allusion to Is. lvi. 7 is hardly appropriate for making such a point (the context is about Gentile sacrifices being acceptable), whereas there are a number of other prophetic texts which could have made the point much better (e.g. Is. i. 11; Jer. vii. 22; Hos. vi. 6; Am. v. 22; Ps. i. 9). The immediate problem concerns who is being addressed in Mark's verse 17 with ὑμεῖς. If it is directed to those whom Jesus has driven out of the temple, then it implies that those who sold and bought were scandalously abusing the place. But there is very little evidence for this. Possibly the incident here reflects a special situation,[30] but otherwise, the practice of exchanging money into the old Tyrian coinage, and selling the proper animals for sacrifice, was made necessary by the Law in order to enable pilgrims coming from afar to participate fully (and properly) in the cult. Futher, there is little evidence that those who acted as bankers and who sold the animals made any excessive gain from their activity: their profit margins were in fact strictly controlled by the Law.[31]

The most important difficulty in interpreting verse 17 in this way concerns the allusion to λῃσταί. In the context of Jer. vii. 11, the reference is to those who break the Law, and this cannot be the case with the merchants, who are doing their business precisely in order that the Law be kept. However, the word λῃστής does not mean 'thief', but a nationalist rebel, or guerrilla.[32] This meaning is well-established in Josephus and is also known to Mark (cf. xiv. 48; xv. 27), so one must assume, without any evidence to the contrary, that this is the meaning here too. It is now even more difficult to apply this only to the merchants in the temple, since, whatever they were, they can hardly have been the only group of guerrillas there. This meaning of λῃστής suggests that it is the watching by-standers still in the temple who are being addressed. If this is so, then the full quotation of Is. lvi. 7 can be fitted in with the Jer. vii quotation: Jesus is accusing those present of turning the temple into a nationalist stronghold when the true destiny of God's house should have been as a place of universal worship. Thus the contrast is not so much between right and wrong use of the temple as between right and wrong users, and the full form of Is. lvi. 7 is essential to the point being made.

This now makes it extremely difficult to see how the saying in verse 17 is directly related to the preceding story. The interpretation of Jesus' action as a purifying, or cleansing, does not really fit the facts: driving out the merchants would lead, not to a purified form of temple worship, but to a total suspension of the cult in the way previously prescribed. The most likely background is the saying in Zech. xiv. 21, which will account for the expulsion of the merchants, and possibly also for the ban on carrying vessels. But then verse 17, with its contrast of nationalism/universalism, must represent a different situation. The closest link between the saying and the action would be to see the latter as an implicit Messianic claim by Jesus, which nevertheless does not lead to the desired result (i.e. a new temple for universal worship), and so Jesus' rebuke in verse 17 follows. However, there is still a considerable gap (both logically and, implicitly, temporally) between the two.[33] There is thus some support, from considerations of content alone, for Bultmann's thesis that verses 15f. and 17 belong to different strata of the tradition.[34]

When one compares the parallel accounts in Matthew and Luke in the light of these considerations, it becomes apparent that Mark's version is more primitive. Matthew and Luke both omit 'all the nations' from Is. lvi. 7, so that the saying becomes an attack on the commercialisation of the temple. However, this does not fit well with the relatively innocent character of the proceedings. Moreover, the omission means that the allusion to Jeremiah loses all its force, since 'all the nations' is precisely the part of Is. lvi. 7 which contrasts with the reference to λῃσταί.[35]

Further, the seam, which from consideration of content is apparent between the action and the saying, is also visible at the literary level in Mark, but not in Matthew and Luke. The introduction of verse 17*a*, with the reference to a general teaching activity (ἐδίδασκεν) and the phrase καὶ ἔλεγεν αὐτοῖς, is Markan in both elements.[36] Farmer's suggestion that the reference to 'teaching' in Mark comes from Luke's ἦν διδάσκων in xix. 47[37] is rendered less likely by the fact that Mark must then have avoided using a periphrastic tense, which otherwise is a favourite construction of his.[38] In the second phrase, Mark's knowledge of Matthew is also rendered unlikely by the fact that Mark would then have avoided Matthew's use of the historic present λέγει, even though this also is generally favoured by Mark. However, both phrases in Mark are, in themselves, typical of his style, and are often used by him to introduce disparate elements in Jesus' teaching. This is not the case in Matthew and Luke, where the saying and the action are linked even more firmly.[39] Mark, therefore, appears to be combining two traditions (i.e. verses 15f. and 17), but these cannot be Matthew and Luke, since they have the two combined already. Thus the GH does not satisfactorily account for the pre-history of the Markan text. Moreover Mark's version is the more primitive, in that the seams between the different strata of the tradition are still clearly visible.

In verse 18, Farmer says that Mark conflates Luke's redactional summary in xix. 47f. with Matt. xxii. 33.[40] I have argued above that in fact Mark is probably prior to Luke, in view of Luke's awkward grammar here. Farmer's suggestion about the relationship between Mark and Matthew is not easy to accept. Matt. xxii. 33 comes after another whole chapter, and one would have to envisage Mark's looking ahead 66 verses to find this verse. The reverse change is more credible: Matthew may have taken slight exception to the fact that, in Mark, the positive reaction to Jesus' teaching occurs after only one verse of the content of that teaching has been given. Thus Matthew may have reserved this part of Mark's verse to use later in a context where Jesus had given an extended block of teaching. Farmer claims that this is a Matthean transitional statement, and refers to Matt. vii. 28f. However, this probably reflects the same process as Matt. xxii. 33: Mk. i. 22, in a context where no teaching has yet been specified, is transferred by Matthew to a more suitable position after some real instruction, i.e. the Sermon on the Mount. In fact Mk. xi. 18*b*/Matt. xxii. 33 is full of Markan, rather than Matthean, characteristics. διδαχη is probably Markan, as is ἐκπλήσσομαι, and explanatory γάρ clauses are also characteristic of Mark.[41] Thus it is far easier to see Matthew as dependent on Mark rather than vice versa: Matt. xxii. 33 preserves Markan characteristics, thus showing that it is the secondary text.[42]

The theory of Markan priority also gives a reasonably clear picture of Matthew's and Luke's redaction. Both have a more positive attitude to the temple. In Matthew, the story is the climax of Jesus' entry into the city as Messiah, and the cleansing itself is a Messianic act. This is brought out in xxi. 9 where the crowds acclaim Jesus as Son of David, and in xxi. 14-16 where Jesus performs miracles which are clearly meant to be Messianic (cf. xi. 2-6). Matthew avoids the possible implication that the temple is rejected by Jesus by changing Mark's perfect πεποιήκατε to a present ποιεῖτε: the temple is in the process of becoming (but has not yet become) a den of rebels.[43] In Luke, the incident is drastically shortened, the main point of the story being to show Jesus as taking possession of the temple. In line with this, Mark's perfect tense is also changed to avoid the implication of any permanent rejection of the temple at this stage, since, for Luke, the temple continues as the place of prayer for the early Christian church (Lk. xxiv. 53; Ac. iii. 1; xxii. 17). Thus the incident loses all significance as an eschatological act.[44] The fact that, for both evangelists, the incident acts as the climax of the entry scene may account for the agreement in placing the 'cleansing' on the same day as the entry.

All these theories depend partly on the theory of Markan priority, so that Mark supplies the yardstick by which to measure Matthew's and Luke's changes. Nevertheless, such redactional considerations are not wholly irrelevant to the question of the Synoptic Problem, since many of the features mentioned above (e.g. Matthew's and Luke's more positive attitude to the temple) could be deduced without Mark's account. Moreover, it is clear that Mark's interpretation of the story is different (especially in his negative attitude to the temple). Thus Matthew's and Luke's changes from Mark can be seen to be coherent and reasonably consistent. It is much harder to conceive of the reverse changes taking place, i.e. Mark, with his negative attitude, conflating Matthew and Luke, but introducing old motifs in verse 16 and the phrase 'all the nations' in verse 17. These considerations, together with the linguistic details noted above, combine to suggest that the theory of Markan priority gives a more plausible explanation of the texts than does the GH, and hence, by the criterion of coherence, is to be preferred.

12 TRIBUTE TO CAESAR

(Matt. xxii. 15–22/Mk. xii. 13–17/Lk. xx. 20–6)

Farmer claims that 'the question concerning tribute to Caesar affords a clear-cut test of the Marcan hypothesis as over against that of Griesbach'.[1] He starts by pointing out what must have happened if Mark was the common source. Mark's version of the statement leading up to the opponents' question to Jesus (Mk. xii. 14a) includes four phrases. Matthew must have transferred the final phrase to be the second of the four, and also slightly re-worded it. Luke, on the other hand, must have kept Mark's order, but omitted the second phrase entirely, re-worded the first and third, and copied faithfully only the final phrase. Farmer claims that 'there is no obvious explanation' for Matthew's behaviour. Moreover, Luke's changes in wording in contrast to his faithful preservation of Mark's order, as well as his total omission of one phrase, 'defy critical analysis'. Farmer also claims that the GH gives a much more adequate explanation: 'Luke freely reused the text of Matthew in this instance, as he characteristically did: omitting a phrase here, rearranging the order of a phrase there, and frequently rewording the whole in a rather free manner . . . The whole is freely recast in a typical Lucan fashion.' The transfer of the 'way of God' phrase to the end of the sentence is to stress this characteristically Lukan motif, and the omission of the 'care for no man' phrase is due to its redundancy in Matthew. 'The text of Luke, therefore, on the Griesbach hypothesis presents no special difficulty to the critic.' Mark, faced with both versions, chose Luke's order for the phrases, but decided to use Matthew's fuller wording, until the final phrase when he switched back to Luke. But this was 'quite understandable, since he took that phrase in the order presented by Luke and not that of Matthew'.

These arguments do not, however, show that the GH gives any better explanation than the theory of Markan priority. The fact is that Matthew and Mark are extremely close to each other in their forms of the question put to Jesus, and any explanation of how Luke might have derived his version from one of them as his source serves equally well to explain how he might have done so from the other. It is thus difficult to accept that

Luke's changes from Mark's text 'defy critical analysis', whereas Luke's use of Matthew 'presents no special difficulty to the critic'. If the claim that 'Luke freely reused the text of Matthew as he characteristically did' is considered a valid explanation for the differences between Luke and Matthew, and 'omitting a word here, re-arranging the order of a phrase there, and frequently rewording the whole in a rather free manner' is accepted, then such an explanation can be repeated exactly to show how the differences between Luke and Mark might have arisen on the Markan hypothesis. Further, the 'free re-casting' of Matthew 'in typical Lucan fashion' must have been even freer on the GH than the re-casting envisaged by the Markan hypothesis, since the GH must assume a transposition of the 'way of God' phrase as well as all the small changes in wording. Nor is Farmer's reason for this extra change entirely convincing. If Luke had wanted to emphasise this phrase, one might have expected him to put it first rather than last.

Farmer's explanation of Mark's alleged procedure solves very few problems and creates others. First, it is not at all clear why Mark should have taken the trouble to conflate his sources in this way. If, as Farmer suggests, Mark was trying to reconcile two competing congregations worried about the discrepancies between Matthew and Luke,[2] it is very hard to envisage partisan communities being concerned about such inconsequential details of what Jesus' opponents, rather than Jesus himself, said. Secondly, Mark's procedure as outlined by Farmer turns out to be inconsistent both with itself, and also with his alleged usual practice when conflating, viz. to adhere more closely to the wording of the source whose order he is following.[3] If the latter were the case, one would expect Mark, in using Luke's order of the phrases, to stay closer to Luke's wording. However, Farmer says that this is not so, in that Mark chose to use Matthew's wording for the first three phrases. But then comes an apparent *volte-face*, for Mark uses Luke's wording for the final phrase. Farmer says this is quite understandable, 'since he took that phrase in the order presented by Luke and not that of Matthew'. Thus Mark, on this theory, follows Luke's order and Matthew's wording for the first three phrases, and this is part of his conflationary process; but in the last phrase he uses Luke's wording precisely because he is using Luke's order. If the last reason is correct, Mark should have used Luke's wording throughout. The self-contradictory nature of Mark's redactional procedure according to the GH here must put into question the validity of the whole theory.

Farmer's claims about the redaction involved according to the Markan hypothesis are mostly negative statements. He says that 'there is no obvious explanation' for Matthew's version if it is derived from Mark. However, the two versions are almost identical and virtually no change has taken place. The difference in order can easily be explained on the theory of Markan priority as due to Matthew's wishing to bring together the two negative phrases and the two positive ones, thereby also bringing the two phrases about 'truth' together.[4] A reverse change (i.e. Mark altering Matthew) is equally possible: Mark's changes could be due to a desire to form a neat chiastic structure. However, the two versions are very close and it is not really possible to say that a change one way is inexplicable whilst a change the other way is not.

As far as Luke's version is concerned, nearly all the verbal differences must be explained by both the Griesbach and the Markan hypotheses: the former must explain them as changes from Matthew, the latter as changes from Mark. (However, the GH must also explain the change in the ordering of the phrases by Luke, which is not necessary for the theory of Markan priority.) These differences are in fact quite easy to explain as due to LkR. Luke's omission of the 'care for no man' phrase may be due to its redundancy in Mark/Matthew (as Farmer says). Alternatively, it may be due to reverence for the person of Jesus: the questioners' statements here are not challenged, so that it is assumed that Jesus does indeed 'care for no man'. But $\mu\acute{\epsilon}\lambda\epsilon\iota$ with personal objects is elsewhere used in a good sense, i.e. 'caring' is something that one ought to do.[5] Luke, therefore, may have wished to avoid any suggestion that Jesus was indifferent to other people. In either case, the somewhat clumsy repetition of $\delta\iota\delta\acute{\alpha}\sigma\kappa\epsilon\iota\varsigma$ in Luke counts against any theory that Luke is freely re-writing;[6] but since Matthew and Mark both have the extra phrase, this consideration cannot distinguish between Matthew and Mark as Luke's source here. The use of $\acute{o}\rho\theta\hat{\omega}\varsigma$ for $\dot{\alpha}\lambda\eta\theta\acute{\eta}\varsigma$ could be LkR.[7] The change from $\beta\lambda\acute{\epsilon}\pi\epsilon\iota\varsigma$ to $\lambda\alpha\mu\beta\acute{\alpha}\nu\epsilon\iota\varsigma$ would be in line with Luke's general tendency to write Septuagintal Greek.[8] $\beta\lambda\acute{\epsilon}\pi\omega$ $\epsilon\iota\varsigma$ $\pi\rho\acute{o}\sigma\omega\pi\sigma\nu$ does not appear to correspond to any Hebrew idiom. The phrase does not occur in the LXX, the closest parallel being 1 Kingd. xvi. 7 where the sense is different. (The meaning is looking at external things and not inner realities, rather than showing partiality.) $\lambda\alpha\mu\beta\acute{\alpha}\nu\omega$ $\epsilon\iota\varsigma$ $\pi\rho\acute{o}\sigma\omega\pi\sigma\nu$, on the other hand, is quite clearly a Hebraism, being a literal translation of נָשָׂא פָנִים , and used in this way in the LXX.[9] Although the significance of Luke's Semitisms is debated, especially with regard to their possible implications for sources behind Luke's gospel, nevertheless there does seem to be good reason for believing that many of the Semitisms (or Septuagintalisms) are redactional, and that they cannot all be indicative of sources.[10] All these changes could, of course, be used to explain Luke's use of Matthew. The GH would also have to explain the change in order of the phrases as well as the change from $\dot{\epsilon}\nu$ $\dot{\alpha}\lambda\eta\theta\epsilon\acute{\iota}\alpha$ to $\epsilon\pi$' $\dot{\alpha}\lambda\eta\theta\epsilon\acute{\iota}\alpha\varsigma$ (although neither of these is difficult to envisage). Thus, if Luke's use of Matthew presents no problems, as Farmer claims, then Luke's use of Mark as a source presents even fewer problems, since fewer changes are involved. The GH therefore fails to give any better explanation of the texts in this part of the pericope than the theory of Markan priority. Luke's changes can be satisfactorily explained on either hypothesis; Mark's procedure, on the other hand, appears to be inconsistent in his choice of wording, and hence this must count against the GH here.

Besides this one part-verse, there are other features in this pericope which are difficult to explain on the GH. If Mark is conflating Matthew and Luke, one must explain the use of ἀγρεύω in verse 13 and ἐκθαυμάζω in verse 17. Both are NT *hapaxes*. The former might be due to Mark's stylistic preference, the lack of similar contexts being why the word occurs nowhere else. However, the change which Mark must have made in verse 17 is more surprising, since both his alleged sources use θαυμάζω. Mark appears to have no objection to θαυμάζω (7 - 4 - 13 + 5), and of the four Markan uses, three would have to be judged as MkR by the GH.[11] If Mark wanted to use a word for astonishment, and disliked his sources' θαυμάζω, one would have expected the more characteristically Markan ἐκπλήσσομαι[12] or ἐκθαμβέομαι.[13] Thus the use of ἐκθαυμάζω may well indicate a pre-Markan source, but if so that source is neither Matthew nor Luke. According to the theory of Markan priority, on the other hand, the change by Matthew and Luke of the unusual Markan word to a more usual one would explain the differences well. Certainly too the Lukan version, using θαυμάζω with ἐπί and a dative impersonal object, is typically Lukan.[14] This would then be consistent with the theory of Markan priority (though also with the GH, since Luke could have changed Matthew in the same way).

Other differences are difficult for the GH. If Mark knew Matthew, why has he failed to take over from Matthew his favourite idiom of the historic present twice in Matt. xxii. 21/Mk. xii. 16f.? He must have just previously used Matthew, including Matthew's historic present καὶ λέγει αὐτοῖς in the preceding phrase, and so he must have had Matthew's version in view. Luke's account is not significantly different, so it is not at all clear why Mark should have avoided Matthew's λέγουσιν in favour of Luke's οἱ δὲ εἶπαν.[15] Another difference which is not easy to explain is Mark's failure to include Luke's ἐπηρώτησαν from Lk. xx. 21 if indeed he knew Luke. The word is a Markan favourite,[16] and Mark's parallel here καὶ ἐλθόντες is not apparently prompted by Matthew; thus it remains unexplained why Mark should not have used a favourite word of his when presented with the opportunity to do so by one of his sources. Finally, the parallels in the verb used by Jesus in the command to bring the money (Matt. ἐπιδείξατε, Mk. φέρετε, Lk. δείξατε) are not easy to explain on the GH. Luke has a general preference for compound verbs, so there is no good reason why he should have changed Matthew here to a simple verb, if he was in fact dependent on Matthew.[17] Further, there is no clear reason why Mark should have avoided the use of δείκνυμμι (or a compound) in both his sources, when he uses the verb twice elsewhere (i. 44; xiv. 13).

Other differences, not so far mentioned, are easily explicable assuming Markan priority. Matthew's introductory verse is full of Mattheanisms (the use of τότε, συμβούλιον λαμβάνω, ὅπως[18] as well as the concentration on the Pharisees as the chief opponents), so that a theory of Matthew's rewriting of Mark would explain this very well. The use of πονηρίαν in verse 18 in Matthew instead of Mark's ὑπόκρισιν is also explicable as due to MattR. The noun πονηρία itself is rare (1 - 1 - 1 + 1), but the adjective πονηρός is frequent in Matthew (24 - 2 - 12 + 8). Also, the use of ὑπόκρισις is rare (1 - 1 - 1 + 0), but the labelling of other people as ὑποκριτής is typically Matthean (10 - 1 - 3). Thus the addition of ὑποκριταί to Mark, and the replacement of Mark's ὑπόκρισιν with the πονηρ-root would be quite intelligible as MattR. Further, Matthew's use of the rhetorical question τί σοι δοκεῖ appears to be Matthean, ironically imitating Jesus' own manner of speaking.[19]

Some of the changes made by Luke have already been noted. In addition to these, ἐπιλαμβάνομαι in verses 20, 26 is a Lukan word (1 - 1 - 5 + 7),[20] so its use here by Luke is easily explicable; also the use of παρατηρέω (1 - 1 - 3 + 1) in verse 20 could be due to LkR. Indeed the whole of verse 20 links up with the charge laid before Pilate by the Jews in Lk. xxiii. 2 which is peculiar to Luke. Luke here seems to be consciously preparing for this, and showing in advance that the charge is false (cf. ἐσίγησαν in verse 26).[21] The use of κατανοήσας in verse 23 is also characteristic of Luke.[22] There is thus nothing difficult about explaining the Lukan redaction involved. (However, all the above considerations apply equally well as explanations of LkR of Matthew rather than of Mark.)

The result of this is that there is no good reason to doubt the theory of Markan priority here. The versions are very close, and in many cases the changes could have taken place either way. In particular, Matthew and Mark are so close that any theory about Luke's changes of Matthew is largely indistinguishable from a theory of Luke's changes of Mark. However, there are a few small details, noted above, which are difficult to explain if Luke is using Matthew, and rather more difficulties if Mark is using both the other accounts. Farmer's explanations of Mark's procedure in verse 14a are unsatisfactory, and other details are also difficult to explain on the GH. On the other hand, the relative consistency and coherence of the theory of Markan priority suggest that this is the more plausible hypothesis.

13 THE DOUBLE COMMANDMENT OF LOVE

(Matt. xxii. 34–40/Mk. xii. 28–34/Lk. x. 25–28; xx. 39f)

This pericope occurs in different contexts in the three gospels. Whilst the context in Matthew and Mark is the same, Luke has a story in his central section where the two-fold love command is given, and there is only a remnant of the pericope at the place equivalent to Matt. xxii. 34–40/ Mk. xii. 28–34. In discussions of the Synoptic Problem, attention has often been focused on the question of the relative priority of Matthew and Mark. However, it is also necessary to consider Luke's version, since this plays an important role in the GH which claims that Mark used Luke as one of his sources.[1]

When the accounts in Lk. x and Mark are compared, it is apparent that the verbal agreement between them is not extensive. Such agreement as exists is mostly confined to their OT quotations. Lk. x. 27 and Mk. xii. 30 both mention four faculties in their quotation of Deut. vi. 5, in contrast to three in the MT and LXX; moreover both agree in the naming of the four faculties concerned (although the order of the last two is different), and both differ from the LXX in having ἰσχύς rather than δύναμις to correspond to the Hebrew מְאֹד. However this is about as far as the agreement goes. Certainly if Lk. x is considered as parallel to Mark at all, agreement between Luke and Mk. xii. 30 is much closer than between Luke and Mk. xii. 32f.:[2] Luke agrees with the earlier Markan version in using ψυχή and not σύνεσις, in retaining the personal pronouns, and in following the LXX text exactly for the version of the command to love God (Mk. xii. 32 paraphrases). There is thus very little warrant for saying, as Orchard does, that Luke's text is closer to Mk. xii. 32f., and then claiming that Mark places side by side Matthew's account (where Jesus enunciates the love command) and Luke's (where the lawyer does).[3] The second half of the pericope in Mark has no parallel in either Matthew or Luke, and any verbal links which Lk. x may have with Mark must be with the earlier half of Mark's version of the pericope.

However, apart from the form of Deut. vi. 5 quoted here, the two accounts in Mk. xii and Lk. x appear to differ so widely in wording that it is difficult to envisage any close literary relationship between them. The main differences are that (a) the context is quite different, (b) the question put to Jesus is not the same, and (c) it is the lawyer in Luke, rather than Jesus himself as in Mark, who quotes the double commandment of love.[4] Thus, apart from the actual love command itself, without which both accounts would reduce to nothing, the two versions have virtually nothing in common. Whether they reflect two separate incidents in the life of Jesus,[5] or two independent lines of tradition[6] (possibly stemming from the same incident) is perhaps immaterial. What is important here is that Mark and Luke are largely independent of each other.

The only significant agreement between Mark and Luke thus lies in the form of the *Shema* quoted, but there are notorious problems associated with the forms of this quotation in the gospels. It is well known that none of the three gospels offers a text of Deut. vi. 5 which is attested elsewhere. The LXX manuscripts have probably suffered by assimilation to the gospel texts, and it is usually assumed that the original LXX wording was that of B: ἐξ . . . διανοίας . . . ψυχῆς . . . δυνάμεως.[7] The Lukan text itself is not certain. The usual printed text has one ἐκ and three ἐν's; further the last phrase ἐν ὅλῃ τῇ διανοίᾳ σου is omitted by D 1241 it Marc. If one accepts this Western 'non-interpolation' then one has a coherent text with three faculties mentioned which correspond in sense, if not in actual wording, to the texts of the MT and LXX of Deut. vi. 5, and it may well be that this is the original reading here.[8] The extra διάνοια phrase would then be an assimilation to the Markan (or conceivably to the Matthean) text in the early stages of the tradition history. (This could be an addition by a later scribe to an original three-fold text in Luke, or a Lukan addition to a pre-Lukan source.[9] In either case, the original version lying behind Luke would be three-fold, not four-fold.) The unusual four-fold form of Mark's version is therefore probably not part of the original in Luke, and if this disappears, then one of the most important agreements between Lk. x and Mark vanishes. Simpson claims that Luke's version shows knowledge of Matthew, by retaining Mark's four-fold form, but by placing διάνοια at the end, and by using ἐν with at least three nouns, as in Matthew.[10] However, this is not convincing. If Luke had been influenced by Matthew, one might have expected him to omit Mark's extra phrase; alternatively he could have followed Matthew's order (though this would have then produced Mark's version since Matthew and Mark are identical in the first three elements). The interchange of the last two phrases is only with difficulty derivable from Matthew, where the διάνοια phrase is indeed last from one point of view, but in third place from another. It seems preferable to see the original Lukan version as lacking the phrase and this being added later. If this is so,

then the only verbal point of contact between Luke and Mark is the use of
ἰσχύς instead of the LXX's δύναμις, and this might be due to independent
reminiscence by both writers of 2 Ki. xxiii. 25.[11] There is therefore very
little justification for any theory that Mark made use of Lk. x. 25–28 in
his composition of Mk. xii. The two accounts are quite different and use
independent traditions.

Many of the considerations above, which suggest that Lk. x and Mark
are independent, apply also to a comparison of Lk. x with Matthew. As
before, these differ in context, in the form of the question put to Jesus,
and in who enunciates the double love command. However, there are other
points at which Matthew and Luke agree. Both call the questioner a
νομικός; both say that he was 'testing' Jesus; both have him address Jesus
as 'Teacher'; both introduce Jesus' reply with the phrase ὁ δὲ ἔφη / εἶπεν
and both have the explicit reference to the Law (ἐν τῷ νόμῳ); finally both
use the preposition ἐν with at least some of the faculties mentioned in the
Shema. These small linguistic agreements suggest that there is some literary
relationship between Matthew and Luke, whether direct dependence of
one on the other, or dependence of both on a common source.[12]

A consideration of Luke's text alone suggests that Luke is indeed using
a source (whether it be Matthew or a common source). For Luke, the pericope serves as the introduction to the parable of the Good Samaritan, and
for this whole unit (i.e. the lawyer's question and the parable) it is clear
that what unites the material is the idea of 'doing' (verse 25 'What shall I
do?'; verse 28 'Do this'; verse 37 'Go and do likewise'). Thus the main concern of the unit is practical.[13] On the other hand, the debate in verses
25–28 concerns theoretical opinions on the Law. The juxtaposition of the
two is evident in verse 28: ὀρθῶς ἀπεκρίθης refers to the theoretical question, τοῦτο ποίει to the practical one.[14] This division within the material
is also shown by ἐκπειράζων in Luke; there is nothing in the practical
question that could be regarded as dangerous to Jesus so that this would
seem to belong to a different stratum of the tradition.[15] Again, there is a
slight discrepancy between the question and the answer: the lawyer asks
about how to obtain 'life', and the answer refers to two OT quotations
which say nothing about life explicitly. Am. v. 4 (which does have the
relevant word) might have been more appropriate.[16] There are thus at least
two strata visible here.

It is inherently more likely that a piece of theoretical argument with
Jewish opponents about the Law should be adapted to a piece of Christian
paraenesis rather than vice versa;[17] in any case, the practical interest
belongs to the stage of combining the pericope here with the parable
which follows,[18] and this must necessarily be later than the stage of the

composition of the units themselves. The form of the question may also
be redactional, assimilating it to the question of the rich young man in
xviii. 18.[19] The result of all this is that Luke is probably bringing out the
practical consequences of a pre-Lukan tradition, in which a hostile theoretical question was put to Jesus, and the double commandment emerged as
a reply. The existence of such a pre-Lukan tradition is also suggested by
the use here of νομικός (verse 25) and εἶπεν + dative (verse 28). Neither is
characteristic of Luke, and they probably reflect the use of a source.[20]
Thus there is evidence in Lk. x. 25–28 of a pre-Lukan tradition, taken over
and adapted by Luke to act as the introduction to the following parable,
with an overall paraenetic aim.

The facts that (a) Luke is dependent on a source, and that (b) some of
the features which appear to be pre-Lukan also belong to Matthew (e.g. the
'tempting') make it at least possible that it is Matthew who is Luke's
source. However, this will be seen to be unlikely when Matthew's version
is analysed in detail.

Whatever the relationship between Matthew and Luke, it is clear that
Matthew's version is very closely related to Mark's. The whole structure of
the pericope is identical at just the points where Luke is different: the
context is the same, the question put to Jesus is similar, the reply is given
by Jesus and not the questioner. Some literary relationship between the
two accounts is therefore demanded. Some have claimed that Matthew's
account is more original in a number of features. There is, first, the claim
that, in the question put to Jesus, Matthew's use of μεγάλη reflects a
Semitic use of a positive for a superlative.[21] However, Mark's πρώτη is
also a substitute for a superlative and hence is equally Semitic.[22] Some
have claimed that Matthew's version of Deut. vi. 5 is closer to the MT in
his use of ἐν, not ἐκ, (reflecting the Hebrew בְּ).[23] However it is very
unlikely that Matthew is more original than Mark. Matthew's triplet of
καρδία, ψυχή and διάνοια has nothing to correspond to the Hebrew מְאֹד
(= ἰσχυς in Mark and Luke, δύναμις in LXX). καρδία and διάνοια are
translation variants of לְבָב , and it appears that Matthew has failed to
notice this. Rather than implying any greater originality of Matthew, it
is more likely that Matthew is dependent on Mark. Possibly he has tried
to bring Mark into line with Deut. vi by reducing the number of faculties
from four to three, but he has not realised that he has duplicated 'heart'
and omitted 'strength' in the process.[24] Moreover, dependence on Mark
is much more likely than dependence on the Lukan version: a simple
omission of the last Markan phrase gives Matthew's text, whereas dependence on the present Lukan text would involve Matthew's choosing to

omit the third of the four, which is less easy to envisage. (Further, if Matthew knew only the original three-fold text which is probably the original behind the present Lukan version, Matthew's triplet becomes even more difficult to derive from this, since it would involve replacing ἰσχύς with διάνοια.) Thus the presence of the two synonyms here implies dependence on Mark.

The other main difference between Matthew and Mark, apart from the extra material in Mark's verses 32–34a, lies in Matthew's verse 40. In verse 40 Matthew has Jesus state that the whole Law and the prophets can be deduced from the one principle of the love-commands, κρέμαται reflecting the rabbinic term תָּלוּי .[25] Hultgren claims that there is a discrepancy between the question in verse 34 and the answer in verse 40. The question asks about one commandment in the Law that is 'greatest', a commandment which stands qualitatively above the rest; the answer speaks of one principle upon which not only the Law but also the prophets depend for their ultimate validity.[26] Hultgren's answer to this difficulty is to postulate two stages in the Matthean tradition: an earlier version giving only the double commandment and the conclusion in verse 40, and a later, somewhat unsuccessful, attempt to combine this with Mark's version which provides the introductory question. Hultgren says that the question to which verse 40 speaks

> is a question which was asked in the Matthean church, for it held that the casuistry of the Pharisees, as a means of interpretation, misses the true meaning of scripture . . . But if the Pharisees proceed wrongly, how can one proceed correctly? The double commandment of love is taken as a starting point – over against the Pharisees – from which exegesis can proceed.[27]

However, the correct deduction from this would appear to be the reverse of Hultgren's own reconstruction of the tradition-history of Matthew's version. If, as seems probable, verse 40 answers to a question of vital concern to Matthew and his church, then it is more likely that this verse is due to MattR, and is not part of a pre-Matthean source. That verse 40 is indeed Matthean is shown by the fact that Matthew appears to be fond of providing epigrammatic summaries of the Law (cf. Matt. vii. 12; ix. 13; xii. 7; xxiii. 23) as is the case here. Unlike Mark, there is no hint in verse 40 that the two love commands are qualitatively different from the rest of the Law,[28] and the use of 'the Law and the prophets' as a description of the sum of God's demand is Matthean, even if not original to him.[29] Undoubtedly verse 40 reflects a Semitic viewpoint, in that the OT law still retains its validity and is not completely abrogated. But this, as the discrepancy between this verse and the question shows, is a sign not of originality, but of the redactional work of the evangelist.[30]

The question of whether $\mu\epsilon\gamma\acute{\alpha}\lambda\eta$ or $\pi\rho\acute{\omega}\tau\eta$ is more original in the lawyer's question is not easy to answer. The idea of one commandment being qualitatively greater than any other one is foreign to rabbinic thought, if it implies that the others are unimportant or dispensable. In this sense $\pi\rho\acute{\omega}\tau\eta$ reflects presuppositions foreign to Judaism. Bornkamm has used this argument, as well as others, to show that the *Sitz im Leben* of the Markan account is not Palestinian Judaism, but the Hellenistic Judaism of the Diaspora.[31] He refers to the implied criticism of the cult, and to the stress on monotheism in Deut. vi. 4; he claims too that the interpretation of $\delta\iota\acute{\alpha}\nu\omicron\iota\alpha$ and $\psi\upsilon\chi\acute{\eta}$ by $\sigma\acute{\upsilon}\nu\epsilon\sigma\iota\varsigma$ points to the high value put on 'reason' in the Hellenistic environment, as does the use of the *hapax* $\nuo\upsilon\nu\epsilon\chi\tilde{\omega}\varsigma$; also, the good Greek phrase $\dot{\epsilon}\pi'$ $\dot{\alpha}\lambda\eta\theta\epsilon\acute{\iota}\alpha\varsigma$ indicates a non-Palestinian background. Matthew's version could be regarded as more Palestinian in some respects (in that most of the features noted by Bornkamm in connection with Mark's *Sitz im Leben* are peculiar to Mark) but still the whole basis of the discussion seems to be foreign to Judaism: for the fact that to love God is still called the 'first' (and great) commandment implies some sort of precedence of this over the others. If $\mu\epsilon\gamma\acute{\alpha}\lambda\eta$ is a Semitism with a superlative meaning, then Matthew's *Sitz im Leben* is just as un-Palestinian as Mark's. Even if $\mu\epsilon\gamma\acute{\alpha}\lambda\eta$ in verse 36 is not meant as a superlative, and Matthew's lawyer only asks what it is that makes a commandment great, Jesus still answers about a great 'and first' commandment. This implies that the whole dialogue is to do with the precedence of one commandment over others. This suggests that the references to 'great' may be secondary, and that 'first' stood in Matthew's source. If this was the case, Matthew may have taken exception to the idea of one commandment being qualitatively different from the others, thereby diminishing the importance of the others, and so changed $\pi\rho\acute{\omega}\tau\eta$ to $\mu\epsilon\gamma\acute{\alpha}\lambda\eta$. There are, moreover, no such difficulties in Mark: there Jesus is asked about the 'first' commandment, and answers in these terms. There are therefore reasonable grounds for assuming that Matthew's source was very similar to our Mark.[32]

It is also the case that Matthew and Luke have some verbal agreements, as seen above. Amongst these is the reference to the fact that the lawyer 'tests' Jesus. This was seen to fit rather uneasily in Luke, and is therefore probably part of Luke's source. It fits equally badly in Matthew, at least with those parts of Matthew's version which appear to be redactional. There is a discordant note between this and verse 40: if the question is about one commandment from which all the rest can be exegetically deduced, then there is nothing hostile about this. But if the question is about one commandment which is qualitatively different from the rest, with the implication that the others are unimportant, then this is a hostile question on Jewish presuppositions and the reference to 'testing' is appropriate. Thus the tension is due to verse 40, and since this is probably redactional, the reference to 'testing' must be prior to this, i.e. it is part of Matthew's source material. So too the use of νομικός here is unique in Matthew and certainly does not reflect normal Matthean usage. (Matthew always uses γραμματεύς elsewhere). If the word is not to be omitted as a scribal gloss from Luke,[33] it too must be part of Matthew's source material. There are also a number of unusual Semitisms in Matthew's account which also imply the use by Matthew of an earlier tradition.[34] Thus Matthew appears to have redacted both Mark and another source. Further, it is probably Matthew's source, rather than Matthew himself, which has been used by Luke. The use of νομικός and πειράζων are both source elements in Matthew; moreover, if it were Matthew, rather than Matthew's source, which Luke used, there is no explanation for Luke's failure to take over Matthew's ὁ δὲ ἔφη in verse 37. Luke uses ἔφη 7 times in the gospel and 11 times in Acts, so Luke clearly has nothing against the word. On the other hand, Matthew's 13 uses of the word suggest that its use here is due to MattR.[35] Luke thus shows links with Matthew's source, but not with Matthew himself even though one would expect him to do so (e.g. with ἔφη) had he known him. Both are therefore probably dependent on a common source, rather than one being dependent on the other. Matthew then conflates both his sources.

Bornkamm claims that Mark's version, with its Hellenistic orientation, can scarcely be Markan in construction, and that we have a pre-Markan unit, at least for the scribe's answer.[36] The fact that the positive attitude to the scribe reflected here is alien to Mark, who elsewhere is uniformly negative about the scribes,[37] must count heavily against the GH. For the latter must account for the extra expansion of the material in Mark's verses 32–34*a*, with its commendation of the scribe, as MkR. Burchard goes further and claims that the whole pericope has been constructed in a Hellenistic milieu, the idea of commandments ranked in order being in place there but foreign to a Palestinian setting.[38] However, it is precisely this 'foreignness' of the question which makes the hostility intelligible. Mark's account, where the hostility has vanished, may reflect an extra-Palestinian milieu, but this is no reason to deny the possibility of an earlier and/or different form of the tradition which could have its roots in a Palestinian setting. Bornkamm's view is that Matthew and Luke go back to an older form of Mark's text, lacking the apologetic aim. He claims that only in this way is it possible to explain the positive agreements between Matthew and Luke, and also the common omission of Deut. vi. 4.[39] However, the former are probably due to the parallel source, and the latter is due to the differing standpoints of the evangelists. For Mark, the interest is apologetic; for Matthew and Luke, it is the question of explicit commandments in the Law (of which the confessional statement in Deut. vi. 4 is not one) which predominates. Probably Matthew, at least, is writing for a church closely connected with Judaism, and the stress on monotheism can be assumed; the same may also be true for the source common to Matthew and Luke.

The case for some sort of Ur-Marcus is considerably weakened by the fact that Luke appears to know the presence of this pericope in its Matthean/Markan context, and in its present Markan (not Matthean) form. Although Luke omits the pericope here, he has two verses which speak of a favourable reaction by some of the scribes (γραμματεῖς, as in Mark, not νομικός as in Matthew) with the words καλῶς εἶπας (cf. Mk. xii. 32 καλῶς, no parallel in Matthew) prefaced by διδάσκαλε (as in Mk. xii. 32, no parallel in Matthew).[40] The final verse in Lk. xx. 40 is almost identical with Mk. xii. 34c, and the οὐκέτι makes no sense in Luke's present text, since it assumes that the scribes have already put at least one question, as in Mark.[41] Moreover the fact that it is the scribes who do not dare to put any more questions strongly suggests that it is Mark, rather than Matthew, who is Luke's source. (The parallel in Matthew comes after the following pericope in xxii. 46, and the subject of the verb is a general 'they' following a reference to the Pharisees, not the scribes, in verse 41.) The GH might explain Mark's version as an expansion of Matthew based on the ideas of these two verses in Luke; however, Luke's version itself would be unexplained and it is difficult to see MkR accounting for the necessary addition which is so un-Markan in both its ideas and its vocabulary.[42] Further, if Luke is dependent on Mark here, then his omission of the pericope in chapter xx is consistent with his usual method of dealing with doublets, as worked out by Schürmann.[43]

There are thus strong reasons for believing that there were two forms of this pericope in the tradition: a Markan one, and another known and used by Matthew and Luke. Luke used the second version in chapter x but rewrote it for his own ends; he therefore omitted the parallel version in Mark but xx. 39f. shows that he knew its presence here in its Markan, not Matthean, form. Matthew's version is best explained as a conflation of Mark and the other version, and the form of the *Shema* strongly suggests that Mark is one of Matthew's sources. The GH cannot easily explain the form of Lk. xx. 39f., nor the extended Markan version. (The difficulties of Matthew's version can be safely disregarded by the GH since the pre-Matthean tradition-history is irrelevant.) The texts thus need at least two basic sources to explain them. The 2DH can identify these sources as Mark and Q relatively easily, and thus this theory is preferable to one which involves Matthean priority.

14 THE WOES AGAINST THE SCRIBES AND PHARISEES

(Matt. xxiii. 5–7/Mk. xii. 38–40/Lk. xx. 45–7)

The long speech against the scribes and Pharisees in Matt. xxiii has a short parallel in Mk. xii. 38–40 and Luke xx. 45–7, as well as a longer parallel in Lk. xi. The material in Lk. xi is usually classified as 'Q' material (on the 2DH), but attention here will be concentrated on the shorter parallels in Mark and Lk. xx, with only passing reference to Lk. xi. According to the GH, Luke derived his version in xx. 46f. from Matt. xxiii. 5–7, and Mark then used Luke for his account. This is claimed by Farmer with additional reasons, and his detailed explanations deserve careful consideration.[1] Although use by Mark of Matthew is theoretically possible on the GH, this is rendered unlikely by the extremely close verbal agreement between Mark and Luke.

Farmer's first claim concerns Luke's choice of the material from Matt. xxiii. 'Having already utilized much of this material (or material parallel to it) back in 11: 39–52 of his Gospel, Luke here only took two verses from a section he had previously omitted, i.e. he took verses 6 and 7 from Matt. 23: 5–7.' However, this glosses over some of the problems of these texts, since Luke has not omitted this material, but has already used some of it in the earlier context: Lk. xi. 43 is closely parallel to Matt. xxiii. 6, and thus forms a doublet with Lk. xx. 46. On the 2DH, the presence of such a doublet can be easily explained as due to the presence of the saying in Luke's two sources, Mark and Q. Matt. xxiii. 6 is then a conflation of these two sources. (Cf. the reference to 'chief seats at feasts' which is in Mark, but not in Lk. xi; on the other hand, Matthew's order, with 'greetings' coming last, agrees with Lk. xi against Mark.)[2] However, the GH must explain why Luke chose to include a doublet of part of the material which he had already included,[3] and to ignore other material which he had not included in the earlier speech.

The following verse in Luke (verse 47) has no parallel in Matthew. Farmer says that Luke added further charges against the scribes here, and Luke's version is clearly secondary since (a) verse 47 reflects Luke's interest in widows, and (b) Matthew's version is more Jewish in provenance:

Matthew's reference to phylacteries and tassels fits well with Jewish laws and customs, whereas Luke's reference to 'long robes' is a secondary change intended to make Jesus' accusation more intelligible to Gentile readers. Thereafter, Mark copied Luke almost word for word.

Farmer's judgement, that the reference to long robes is simply a secondary re-writing of Matthew's 'phylacteries and tassels', is not at all certain, and in fact it is extremely questionable whether Matthew and Mark/Luke are related at all here. One of the main difficulties is to know what exactly is meant by Mark and Luke in the reference to στολαί.

The explanations usually given are that the στολή either refers to a special garment worn by the scribes,[4] or, more particularly, to a voluminous prayer-shawl (טַלִּית) which distinguished the scribes from others.[5] The suggestion has also been made that the criticism here concerns when the prayer-shawl was worn, i.e. not just at prayer, but ostentatiously at other times too.[6] Rengstorf has shown that independent evidence for a special scribal טַלִּית is virtually non-existent outside the New Testament itself, and he seeks to find an explanation by reference to the later practice of wearing special clothes on the Sabbath.[7] However, the evidence for such a practice is very late (mid-third century) and, as he himself says, the earlier texts speak rather of ensuring that one's everyday clothes are clean for the Sabbath.[8] Besides the fact that the evidence is so late, there is nothing in the text here to imply that Jesus' criticisms are explicitly directed against any form of Sabbath observance. Rengstorf deduces this from the references to synagogues and feasts, which, he says, were associated with the Sabbath. Nevertheless, all the evangelists were quite capable of understanding, and writing about, Jesus' polemical attitude to the Sabbath, and, in view of the absence of any hint in the gospels themselves that this was the point at issue, it seems unjustified to introduce this here. Perhaps the most unsatisfactory part of Rengstorf's article is the prior assumption, shared also by Farmer and others,[9] that both Matthew's verse 5 and Mark's στολαί refer to the same basic charge. Thus Rengstorf assumes that Matthew's verse 5 is shown by verse 4 to be directed against the scribes, and thus both Matthew's verse 5 and Mark's στολαί charge are about external dress which distinguished the scribes from the rest of the populace. Matthew's account can then be used to interpret Mark's version. He assumes that Matthew's verse 5 only makes sense if it is to do with a practice which was approved by the scribes' oral tradition interpreting the Mosaic Law, but which was not yet established as universal practice; the ostentatious nature of the scribes' behaviour was an attempt to have their practice universally adopted. This can then be used to interpret the Markan (or Lukan) text.[10]

This analysis, however, makes several assumptions, not the least of which is that Matthew's text is a unitary composition. It is universally recognised that Matthew's designation of the opponents as 'scribes and Pharisees' is a stereotyped formula, and it is clear that the opponents are not always the same in all parts of Matt. xxiii. Jeremias too recognises this, but his division seems too simple when he says that verses 1–22, 29–36 are directed against the scribes, and verses 23–28 against the Pharisees.[11] Haenchen has shown very clearly that there are different strata within the tradition in this chapter, and this is certainly the case in these few verses.[12] In verse 4 the charge is that the opponents tell others to do things but do not do them themselves. Verse 5 on the other hand assumes that they do perform the 'works', but for the wrong reasons. Verses 6f. are nothing to do with the performance or otherwise of works, but charge the listeners with vanity, ambition, and conceit. The different verses clearly embody different charges with quite different presuppositions about the opponents. Verse 4 is concerned with scribes, those who are in a position of authority to tell others what to do. Verses 6f. are probably directed against the same people: the charge concerns those who are vain and ambitious about their status in society, and chief seats etc. were the prerogative of the learned, i.e. the scribes.[13] However, verse 5 is quite different: it is about acts of excessive piety performed for the wrong reasons. The very close links with vi. 1–18, and with the overall charge of hypocrisy by which Matthew unites all the various charges in chapter xxiii, suggest that the insertion of this verse is due to MattR;[14] moreover, the stress on excess piety implies that this charge is directed against Pharisees rather than scribes.[15] Thus verse 5 is quite separate from verses 4 and 6f. Haenchen has pointed out the apparent irrelevance of the basic charge in verse 5a if it is to cover the charges in verses 6f., since no 'works of the Law' are referred to in the latter verses.[16] But they are referred to in verse 5b,[17] and so the two halves of verse 5 belong closely together. Moreover, after verse 7a there is a grammatical break, in that the construction changes abruptly from a direct accusative object to an infinitive ('love greetings' to 'love to be called').[18] This suggests the existence of another seam in Matthew's traditions. The result of this analysis is that verses 5, 6–7a, 7b come from different strata. Since verse 5 is probably redactional, verses 6–7a must be from one of Matthew's sources. It is also clear that the two charges, in verses 5 and 6–7a, are quite separate. It is therefore unjustified to interpret one with respect to the other.

Verses 38f. of Mark (or verse 46 of Luke) appear to be unitary in the sense that there is one single accusation of vanity and conceit. It is directed against those who have the high positions in society, the learned and the respected, i.e. the scribes. The clear implication of the Markan (and Lukan) text is that the scribes love to be recognised and honoured as such. This is certainly the case with the greetings and chief seats, and there is nothing to suggest that the reference to long robes is any different. Certainly Mark and Luke appear to have understood the wearing of the στολαί as nothing more than a piece of ostentatious vanity.[19] There is nothing in the gospel texts which implies that the ostentation was intended to encourage imitation. Rengstorf is right to oppose too easy a solution to the problem, and possibly one must admit to total ignorance about what practice is being described here, and what were the original motives. However, it is clear that what is being referred to is quite different from Matt. xxiii. 5. In Matthew, the practice is a specific requirement of the Law, being performed in an ostentatious way to earn praise, and thus the charge would appear to be anti-Pharisaic. In Mark and Luke, it is not a requirement of the Law, but a reference to the way clothes were worn, or to a particular article of clothing, which signified not excess zeal but the special status of the person wearing it.

The result of this is that there is virtually no justification for claiming that Mark's and Luke's charge about 'long robes' is derived from Matthew's about phylacteries and tassels. They are making different accusations against different people, and the only common feature is that both concern something that is worn. But the things worn, the people concerned, and the motives for wearing, all differ. Thus it is safest to assume that there is no literary relationship at all between Matt. xxiii. 5 and Mk. xii. 38*a*/Lk. xx. 46*a*.

It is also worth noting that the consideration of Matthew's text led to the conclusion that verses 6-7*a* were pre-Matthean. Since verses 6-7*a* are paralleled partly in Mark, partly in Lk. xi. 43, the 2DH would explain this very well. There is of course, nothing impossible for the GH since the pre-Matthean sources do not enter the discussion: Matthew is the first gospel to be written and the earlier developments are irrelevant to the later use of Matthew by Luke and then Mark. However, the analysis does suggest pre-Matthean sources here, and the 2DH can identify some of these sources, as well as accounting for the seam between verses 7*a* and 7*b* (since the parallels in Mark and 'Q' cease after verse 7*a*).

The problem associated with the charge about 'devouring widows' houses' (Mk. xii. 40/Lk. xx. 46) entails a discussion of the relationship between Mark and Luke. This charge has no direct verbal links with Matthew. It has been suggested that this is the same basic charge as Matthew's about broadening phylacteries, with translation variants of תְּפִילִין accounting for the different versions,[20] but this will not explain the differences between Greek texts in a direct literary relationship with each other. Certainly Luke's interest in widows would ensure that this appealed to Luke, but this does not necessarily imply that the introduction of the verse here is due to Luke, as Farmer suggests. It must first be noted that the charge is unrelated to the preceding verse. In Mk. xii. 38f./ Lk. xx. 46, it is the scribes who are addressed, but this is not the case here. Rather, the charge is against excess zeal in piety to be seen by others. This is very similar, therefore, in general terms, to Matt. xxiii. 5 (though quite different in detail), and thus fits the Pharisees better than the scribes. If so, the charge has a striking parallel in Josephus (*Ant.* 17.2.4) where there is a story of Pharisees tricking some gullible old women.[21] Alternatively the charge may be directed against those who exploited their position as legally appointed trustees looking after widows' estates, and who tried to convince others of their qualifications for this job by making an ostentatious show of piety.[22] In either case, the charge has nothing to do with the scribes as such. Thus between the two charges lies a seam in the tradition. The two accusations concern different people and have different presuppositions.[23]

This seam, recoverable by considering only the contents of the two charges, is also visible at the literary level in Mark, but not in Luke. Mark's account is grammatically very awkward, since the participle οἱ κατεσθίοντες in the nominative is in apposition to the genitive τῶν θελόντων.[24] This anacolouthon suggests that two independent sayings are juxtaposed here, and this supports the results obtained above from consideration of the content alone. But what is suggested by the contents, and is clearly visible at the literary level in Mark, is no longer visible in Luke's version. Luke has the grammatically impeccable relative pronoun with a finite verb, οἳ κατεσθίουσιν. A change by Luke of Mark's awkward sentence structure is easy to envisage.[25] The reverse change is much harder to imagine. If Mark realised that the two accusations were directed against different people, and he wanted to separate them, one would have expected him to do so by introducing a typically Markan phrase (e.g. καὶ ἔλεγεν αὐτοῖς), rather than by disrupting the grammar of the sentence in this way. Thus Mark's version appears to be the more primitive: the seams between the different units of the tradition are clearly visible at the level of both the contents and the grammatical structure. Luke improves the grammar, but confuses the two accusations by failing to distinguish between the two groups against whom the charges are directed.

Another small verbal difference suggests Markan priority. In verse 38 Mark has an awkward double construction with θελόντων: he follows this with an infinitive (περιπατεῖν) and then immediately with a direct accusative object (ἀσπασμούς). On the other hand, Luke's syntax is less abrupt since he has an extra verb φιλούντων, so that θελόντων now governs only the infinitive construction which follows. It is hard to envisage Mark's spoiling Luke's construction by omitting φιλούντων, whereas Luke's addition of the word is an intelligible improvement of Mark's Greek.[26] The 2DH would also explain the choice of vocabulary here in Luke very well, since φιλούντων may be a reminiscence of the Q version of the saying. The word is unusual in Luke (he uses it only once elsewhere, at xxii. 47, but there with the meaning 'kiss'), and its presence in Matt. xxiii. 6 indicates, on the 2DH, that this was the wording of Q.[27] The use of ἀγαπάω in Lk. xi. 43 could then be due to LkR, since this is a verb which Luke uses 9 times elsewhere.

The result of this comparison of Mark and Luke is that it is far more likely that Luke's is the secondary version. Farmer's statement, that 'there is no evidence in this instance that Mark did anything other than copy the text of Luke',[28] is thus highly questionable. The way that Luke improves Mark's grammar, and also mends the seams which are visible in Mark's version, suggests that it is Luke who is using Mark, and not vice versa. Moreover, Matthew's text cannot have been the source of the other two in the way Farmer suggests; what he describes as parallel texts turn out to be quite different, and indeed, independent examination of Matthew's text does give some justification for the view that Matthew is using Mark and another source known also to Luke. In short, the analysis above gives no support to the GH, Luke's choice of material from Matthew and Mark's disruption of Luke's grammar being especially difficult to explain. The 2DH encounters no such difficulties, and gives a more coherent account of the redactional activity involved.

15 THE WIDOW'S MITES

(Mk. xii. 41–4/Lk. xxi. 1–4)

This small pericope has no Matthean parallel, and thus the GH must claim that Luke first inserted the story into the Matthean structure and that Mark used Luke. Farmer argues that this indeed happened, and his case depends almost solely on form-critical evidence.[1] Farmer discusses the *'Chreia'* form as used by Greek rhetoricians, and claims that Luke's version is nearest to this pure form. Mark's version, on the other hand, clearly shows secondary features in the 'completely unnecessary' three-fold repetition of the term used for the 'temple treasury', the lack of conciseness in the introduction, the added detail that 'he called his disciples to him' which is 'but a literary effort at verisimilitude which adds nothing to the *Chreia*', and in the interpretative gloss explaining that two *lepta* in terms of Roman coinage amounted to a *quadrans*. 'On strictly form-critical grounds, Luke's form is clearly more original.'[2]

With regard to these form-critical considerations, it is very doubtful if they will bear the weight which Farmer puts on them. He claims that the unit is a *Chreia*, and quotes with approval the definition of Dibelius: 'It is a reproduction of a short pointed saying of general significance, originating in a definite person and arising out of a definite situation.'[3] Now it is not at all surprising that both the Christian evangelists and the Greek rhetoricians preserved memorable sayings of those whom they held in honour, with short introductions to make the sayings intelligible. However, Farmer seems to go further (and his argument demands this) in claiming that the *Chreia* had a definite form, which Luke follows more closely than Mark. This is by no means certain. Dibelius says: 'The typical short forms of the *Chreia* are those in which the saying is introduced either by a question, or by a personal remark, or by a very concise description of the circumstances in the genitive absolute.'[4] This fits very well with many of the secular examples given by Farmer, but it does not fit Luke's version. If Luke's account were to correspond strictly to the *Chreia* form, the introduction should be in the genitive absolute (which could have been done very easily). Moreover, Luke's version contains more than the very terse sentences which seem to characterise the Greek *Chreiai*. It is true that this is not essential: Dibelius says that 'the terse style of the *Chreia* tolerates many extensions without spoiling the form',[5] and Farmer too has to say that the final verse is an extension of the form, an *aitia*, explaining the saying itself.[6] However, this raises the question of what precisely it is which constitutes the form. If all that is being claimed is that pithy sayings were often handed on with a minimum of context, then this is surely indisputable; but if appeal is made to a definite 'form', which Luke is said to be significantly closer to, then one requires much more precision about the nature of this form.

Dibelius says that what distinguishes the *Chreia* is that 'the concentration upon the saying itself always remains recognizable: the striking phrase, full of spirit and wit, or full of pride or folly in a ridiculous degree, is preserved for special honour or as a characteristic mark of the speaker.'[7] This is, however, really moving away from the strict form of the anecdote in question and on to a consideration of the content. At this level too there is little to support the view that Luke gives a true *Chreia* (even without verse 4). As Dibelius says, most of the Greek *Chreiai* are of an entirely different nature from the gospel stories. Not only do the latter differ in giving rather more incidental information about the circumstances (e.g. here Luke's ἀναβλέψας), but also their content and the importance they attach to the saying vary greatly from the Greek examples. As Dibelius says,

> In the Greek texts there is a large number of examples of witty repartee without material content, such as appropriate answers, startling paradoxes, sayings with a double meaning... An essential side of Greek intellectual life comes forward here: the leaning to a clever play upon words, conceptions and thoughts... These pointed anecdotes are dominated by the εὐτραπελία, the dexterity in jocular speech.[8]

It is just this which is not found in the Christian tradition. There is no humorous play on words, no subtle verbal jousting, not even in this case a direct discomfiture of Jesus' opponents. There is, it is true, a certain paradox in what Jesus says about the widow ('she has put in more than the rest'), but precisely here the emphasis is completely different from that in the Greek texts. In the latter, the paradox (and indeed the whole incident) is meant to redound to the praise of the speaker, whereas here, attention is drawn not to Jesus as the great orator, but to the widow herself and her actions. It is considerations like these which led Dibelius to discount very heavily any similarity between the *Chreiai* and the pericopes of the gospel tradition.[9] He did admit the possibility that Luke may have altered some of the material to bring it closer to the *Chreia* form, but he does not mention this pericope. The only similarity between this pericope and the *Chreia* is that both contain short, striking sayings in a relatively short unit. But this of itself is unexceptional. In form, the *Chreia* turns out to be too imprecise to have value here (or, if a stricter definition is maintained, it does not correspond to Luke's account), and in content the *Chreiai* seem far removed from the gospel tradition.

In fact the differences between Mark and Luke here are very small. There is no extra information in Mark, and Mark's version is only longer because of its repetitious nature. Luke's version is certainly more concise, but a tendency of later writers to expand their sources, rather than to contract them, is not easily demonstrable.[10] Lukan dependence on Mark has only rarely been doubted in the past. One exception was Schmidt, who suggested that the pericope was a later insertion into Mark from Luke, and that this would then explain the absence of the pericope from Matthew.[11] However, this assumes Markan priority (and really seeks to explain Matthew's omission of the story on that assumption). Moreover, the omission by Matthew can be sufficiently accounted for by the fact that Matthew may have wished to draw attention to the connection between xxiii. 38f. and xxiv. 1ff.[12] Perhaps too Matthew's apparently negative attitude to women may be relevant.[13] Schmidt's theory is unnecessarily complicated and one does not need an Ur-Marcus to explain Matthew here.

The form-critical considerations, as I have suggested, are not decisive. In fact, it is extremely difficult to decide which way dependence lies; for where Mark and Luke differ, most of the changes could well be explained either as Mark's altering (mostly expanding) Luke in a typically Markan way, or as Luke's altering Mark in a typically Lukan way. Farmer cites as the clearest sign of the secondary character of Mark the 'interpretative gloss' of the *quadrans*. However, although this is almost certainly an addition to the original tradition, this probably says more about the differences between Mark and Luke and their audiences, than about their relative dates.[14] Mark's gloss implies that the *quadrans* was a coin in normal usage in the community for which he was writing. The style of the addition ($\ddot{o}$ $\dot{\epsilon}\sigma\tau\iota\nu$ . . .) is Markan,[15] but equally, Luke could be said to have a slight tendency to avoid foreign words.[16] It is thus quite possible that Luke omitted the reference to the *quadrans* here.

Mark's account contains considerable verbal redundancy, and this is generally recognised as a characteristic feature of Mark's style.[17] Mark may have expanded Luke's shorter version by adding typically Markan redundancies; but equally, Luke could have avoided Mark's repetitions.[18]

However, Mark's version is not only redundant: it is at times grammatically awkward. The opening phrase is more elegant in Luke. He has a single clause with a participial phrase as object, whereas Mark has a πῶς phrase, and then has to append an awkward extra phrase to mention the 'rich' explicitly. If Mark has expanded Luke, he has done more than simply add an extra, detachable phrase. The considerable re-writing necessary, and the awkward end-result, make this a rather implausible hypothesis. On the other hand, LkR of Mark would be easy to envisage.[19] Mark's final phrase is also awkward: ὅλον τὸν βίον αὐτῆς stands in apposition to πάντα ὅσα εἶχεν but is separated by the verb ἔβαλεν. Luke's version is much neater with the single phrase πάντα τὸν βίον ὃν εἶχεν.[20] That Luke has changed Mark seems much more likely than the other way round.

Farmer says that, in view of the concise nature of Luke's account, the burden of proof must rest with the critic who wants to maintain that Luke is secondary. 'He must show by appeal to the style and vocabulary of Luke that Luke's form of Mark 12: 41–44 is of Lucan construction. This would be difficult to do convincingly.'[21] However, this is not as difficult as Farmer suggests. In verse 42 of Mark (Luke's verse 2) the change from καί to δέ is in line with Lukan usage,[22] although the reverse change is equally possible. The change from θεωρέω to ἰδεῖν is also quite intelligible as LkR: the former is not very common (2 - 7 - 7 + 14), whilst the latter is extremely common (58 - 44 - 65 + 49). Thus, although Luke can (and does) use θεωρέω, a change to ἰδεῖν would be consistent with his apparent preference in choice of verbs of seeing.[23] Moreover, in this case, the reverse change would be very much harder to envisage. Mark uses ἰδεῖν 44 times, but θεωρέω only 7 times, so there is no apparent reason why Mark should prefer the latter when εἶδεν stood in his source. The use of τινα with χήραν represents a correction to more classical usage if Mark is Luke's source;[24] the reverse change is possible, since Mark often uses the numeral in this way, but the usage is a Semitism,[25] and hence may imply the existence of a more primitive tradition. The use of καὶ εἶπεν in verse 3 of Luke is unusual for Luke. He usually writes εἶπεν δέ[26] so that Luke's version here probably betrays the use of a source; it is significant that καὶ . . . εἶπεν occurs at precisely this point in Mark's parallel. The use of ἀληθῶς for ἀμήν would again be consistent with LkR, since Luke has not many 'amen' sayings (32 - 13 - 6). However, a reverse change is also possible. Luke misses out, or Mark adds, the reference to Jesus' summoning the disciples. The idea involved, and the vocabulary used, are certainly Markan,[27] but it is not at all clear that a simple addition by Mark to Luke's text would explain things very well. According to Luke xx. 45 Jesus is addressing the disciples. All that Mark would have needed to do if he wanted to make the disciples the recipients of the teaching would have been to copy Luke verbatim. Instead Mark has the woes against the scribes addressed to the general public (cf. the reference to the 'great crowd' in verse 37*b*), and in verse 41 there is a totally new beginning. Luke, on the other hand, links the two sections very closely (ἀναβλέψας implies that Jesus stays where he is and carries on teaching).[28] If Mark wanted to have Jesus' teaching as private instruction for the disciples alone, and if he was using Luke as his source, then this was already to hand for him. In fact, Mark's version appears to be the more primitive, since the two pericopes (verses 38-40, 41-44) are still clearly separate in the tradition, and Mark has to add verse 43*a* to include his characteristic idea of private instruction. In Luke, the two pericopes have been joined more closely together by identifying the audience and the occasion of both.

There is thus nothing difficult about explaining Luke's version as LkR of Mark. Further, although many of the changes could have taken place in reverse, the small details of the καὶ εἶπεν in Luke, the use of θεωρέω, and the problem of the disciples as the audience, all suggest that it is not Mark, but Luke who is secondary here. This, together with the negative results from the form-critical considerations, implies once again that the theory of Markan priority gives a better explanation of the texts than the GH.

INTRODUCTION

In much of the recent discussion about the revival of the GH, attention has been focussed on the relationship between Mark and the other two synoptic gospels. However, another important assertion of the GH is that Luke is directly dependent on Matthew. Now it would be quite possible to believe that Mark conflated Matthew and Luke without necessarily believing that Luke knew Matthew. Indeed precisely this position was adopted by de Wette and Bleek in the nineteenth century. Both believed that a direct literary relationship between Matthew and Luke was excluded by the fact that neither of these two gospels consistently gave the more original tradition.[1] Nevertheless, the two issues, i.e. the relationship between Matthew and Luke, and the relative position of Mark, are not completely separate. If there is a common source behind Matthew and Luke, there is the possibility of this source overlapping with Mark, and hence of accounting for some of the agreements between Matthew and Luke against Mark. On the other hand, if it could be shown that Luke knew and used Matthew in 'double tradition' passages, the same explanation might account for the agreements in passages where there is a Markan parallel as well.[2] The theory of Luke's dependence on Matthew also plays a vital hidden role within Farmer's total argument for the GH. The phenomenon of order, in particular the fact that Matthew and Luke do not agree against Mark in this respect, is regarded by Farmer as giving decisive support to the GH.[3] Yet, as seen above, this phenomenon is in itself quite consistent with a theory of independent use of Mark by Matthew and Luke. Thus before this phenomenon can support the GH, the possibility that Matthew and Luke are independent of each other must be excluded.[4] The theory of Lukan dependence on Matthew thus plays an important implicit role within the argument from order as given by Farmer to support the GH.

Griesbach himself never dealt with the problem of the relationship between Matthew and Luke in any detail. In the modern debate, the question was raised briefly in Farmer's book in 1964. He says that 'the most probable explanation for the extensive agreement between Matthew and Luke is that the author of one made use of the work of the other',[5] and that certain features suggest that it is Luke who is secondary. He appeals to their similarity in literary form, to the Lukan prologue with its explicit acknowledgement of a debt to sources, to the omission of some Jewish elements in Matthew, and to the external evidence. He does not consider in detail any passages of the double tradition. Similarly, in his recent article on the 'Q' material,[6] Farmer again only deals with the subject in broad outline and does not analyse any texts in detail. The same is true of the work of Orchard, who concentrates almost exclusively on the arrangement of whole pericopes within the gospel tradition. It is at this level, he believes, that the final redactor's hand is to be seen most clearly: 'The correct methodology is to begin with the comparison of the over-all plan and then to check with the individual units.'[7]

The analysis of the detailed wording of the texts in a discussion of the source question is felt by some advocates of the GH to be methodologically unsound, especially in the light of the insights gained from form-criticism. As seen above, the objections of de Wette and Bleek to a theory of direct dependence of Luke on Matthew were based on the fact that, as often as not, Luke's version appeared to be more primitive than Matthew's. Some have taken this as convincing proof of the independence of Matthew and Luke and their common dependence on a Q source.[8] However, Farmer and others believe that, in the light of form-criticism, this argument no longer has force. Each pericope has its own tradition-history, and it is quite possible for Luke, writing later than Matthew, to have had access to forms of the tradition earlier than Matthew's. Thus, Farmer says that the 'double tradition' includes what Luke took from Matthew '*plus* whatever Luke may have copied from other sources closely paralleling material copied from Matthew'.[9] Such sources may have contained the parables of the pounds, the great supper, and the lost sheep, as well as some parts of the apocalyptic discourse.[10] Thus the theory that Luke is dependent on Matthew does not preclude the possibility that, in some instances, Luke's version might be more primitive.

The theory of the possible existence of parallel traditions raises the problem of whether detailed analysis of the texts of the double tradition can have any value in a study of the GH. If the theory were that Luke had used Matthew as his only source, this would be very easy to test: if one could find a single case where Luke's version is more primitive (or at least independent), then this would disprove the theory. The possibility of parallel traditions destroys the force of this. Nevertheless, if the theory of Luke's use of Matthew is to have any significance, then it must hold true at some point. For if at every point in the double tradition Luke used independent earlier traditions, then one is left with a very strange form of dependence of Luke on Matthew: Luke will have used Matthew's structure but preferred an independent form of the wording every time. Such a theory would in any case be virtually indistinguishable from the Q hypothesis. Parallel traditions may be required by the GH to explain the widely different wording in the two versions of the parables of the talents/pounds and the great supper. However, this explanation becomes less plausible when the Matthean and Lukan wordings are very close. It is in these cases that direct dependence of Luke on Matthew must presumably hold true if it exists anywhere. Thus attention will initially be focussed on those parts of the double tradition where there is extensive verbal agreement between Matthew and Luke.

If Luke is dependent on Matthew, all the differences between the two accounts must be due to LkR. Thus at all the points where Luke differs from Matthew, Luke's version should be characteristically Lukan. Instances where this is not the case suggest that the initial source theory is wrong. Further, in cases where the agreement is extremely close, instances where Luke's version cannot be explained as LkR will be even more significant. A decision by Luke to use an independent parallel tradition would be plausible if this were widely different from the version in Matthew. However, if the two differ in small insignificant ways, such a decision by Luke would be less easy to understand. If, on the other hand, the different Matthean version can be accounted for as MattR of the version in Luke, then this will suggest that both have used a common source, rather than that Luke is dependent on Matthew. If, in addition, one can discover various strands of the double tradition which are shown to be part of source material common to Matthew and Luke, and if these have common thematic links which are distinctive in themselves, then this is an indication that behind the double tradition lies not an amorphous mass of unrelated source material, but rather a more unified tradition with its own characteristic ideas.

16 WISDOM MOTIFS IN THE DOUBLE TRADITION

The parable of the playing children (Matt. xi. 16–19/Lk. vii. 31–35) is part of one of the passages listed by Farmer as exhibiting 'the kind of verbal similarity . . . which suggests the possibility of direct copying',[1] and it affords a useful starting point for the present discussion. Certainly the verbal agreement here is very close, but the two accounts are by no means identical. However, if Luke is dependent on Matthew alone for his version, then all the differences between the two must be due to LkR. These must therefore be examined in detail.

Although the parable itself forms the end of a much longer section of double tradition material dealing with the Baptist's question to Jesus, attention here will be focussed on the parable and its immediate introduction in each gospel (Matt. xi. 12–19/Lk. vii. 29–35). In what immediately precedes the parable, Matthew and Luke differ widely. If Luke is dependent on Matthew, then the following are the most important changes which Luke must have made: (1) the omission of Matt. xi. 12–15 here, and the transposition of verses 12f. in a significantly different version to Lk. xvi. 16; (2) the insertion of Lk. vii. 29f. presenting a different version of Matt. xxi. 32; (3) the change of 'works' to 'children' in Lk. vii. 35. It is clear that, in the present Lukan version, verse 35 refers to the saying in verses 29f.,[2] identifying 'Wisdom's children' with 'all the people and the tax-collectors'. This is primarily shown by the parallel uses of the verb δικαιόω in both verses. Is this link then Lukan or pre-Lukan? The GH must assume that 'children' in verse 35, and also the insertion of verses 29f., are both due to LkR, so that the link must, on this hypothesis, be due to Luke himself. Consideration of this demands an excursion into the problem of the relationship between verses 29f. and Matt. xxi. 32.

Clearly Lk. vii. 29f. and Matt. xxi. 32 are closely related,[3] but it is doubtful if Luke's version can be seen as simply LkR of Matthew. There are certainly some traces of LkR: 'all the people' is a Lukan phrase,[4] and βουλή is also Lukan.[5] However, there are also signs of a pre-Lukan layer in these verses, viz. (a) the use made of δικαιόω, (b) the reference to νομικοί, and possibly (c) the clear (Semitic?) parallelism here. The first two are sometimes regarded as characteristic of LkR[6] but this ignores a careful study of the occurrence of these words. The sense of δικαιόω here is unparalleled elsewhere in Luke-Acts. Unlike the other usages of the verb, the sense in Lk. vii. 29, 35, with a divine person as object (God/Wisdom) is one of 'acknowledging to be in the right', a nuance which will fit none of the other occurrences in Luke-Acts (Lk. x. 29; xvi. 15; xviii. 14; Ac. xiii. 39), but which is very similar to a usage prominent in the Psalms of Solomon.[7] Thus the usage here is not characteristic of Luke himself and is therefore probably due to a source. So too the use of νομικός is not characteristic of Luke, but it is used frequently in double tradition passages in Luke.[8] The parallel structure of Luke's version is not a strong point, but Semitic parallelism may be significant for determining primitive traditions.[9]

Now none of these features appears in Matt. xxi. 32, so that Luke's source, visible at these points, cannot be Matthew. The only slight link is the use of δικαιοσύνη in Matthew, but this is used in a way that is thoroughly characteristic of Matthew himself, referring to the right behaviour demanded by God.[10] It is easy to see a use of δικαιόω in Matthew's source leading to Matthew's use of δικαιοσύνη here; it is very difficult to see the process reversed, with δικαιοσύνη in Matthew being changed by Luke to δικαιόω with a meaning not attested elsewhere in Luke. Other features of Matthew's version are also probably redactional and show how the saying has been adapted to fit the present Matthean context: μεταμελοῦμαι is used by Matthew only of the Synoptics (3 times), and here it echoes Matt. xxi. 29; ὕστερον (7 - 0 - 1) is Matthean as is the use of τοῦ + infinitive in a final or consecutive clause;[11] πιστεύω here may pick up the reference in Matt. xxi. 25.

Internal considerations suggest that the verse is not in its original position in Matthew, since it fits rather poorly with the preceding parable. The story itself in Matt. xxi. 28-31 is perfectly coherent. with its central theme of the importance of putting words into practice, and with its climax in verse 31. Verse 32 then adds another conclusion, which on form critical grounds alone appears to be secondary. The content of verse 32 also fits uneasily with the parable: it introduces the person of John, and yet nothing is known of any change of mind concerning John on the part of the Jewish leaders. This verse is probably, therefore, an isolated logion, only loosely linked with its context here.[12] Matthew appears to have adapted the wording to the context and thus the saying exhibits several secondary features. The only phrase which is not Matthean is οἱ τελῶναι καὶ αἱ πόρναι. Tax-collectors are never mentioned with approval elsewhere in Matthew (cf. Matt. v. 46, 47; xviii. 17) and πόρνη is a Matthean *hapax*.

One can now bring these results back to Lk. vii. 29f. The link between verses 29f. and verse 35 is primarily via the similar usages of δικαιόω. Since this usage in verses 29f. was seen to be pre-Lukan, and cannot easily be explained as LkR of Matt. xxi. 32, the link between verses 29f. and 35 must also be pre-Lukan. This shows that Luke's source already contained verses 29f. in some form at this point.[13] Further, some of Luke's redaction can easily be removed. The phrase 'all the people having heard' with the following καί is very clumsy grammatically,[14] and, in view of the Lukan nature of the vocabulary, is probably an addition by Luke to his source. The presence of 'harlots' in Matt. xxi. 32 suggests that originally the source may have read simply αἱ πόρναι καὶ οἱ τελῶναι. In view of the Matthean nature of the rest of Matthew's version, it is probable that Luke preserves the remainder of his source unaltered. (Luke's reference to God's 'will' may be secondary, but since Matthew's parallel 'not believing him' is probably redactional, the source's precise wording may not be recoverable). Hence the source may have run:

> αἱ πόρναι καὶ οἱ τελῶναι ἐδικαίωσαν τὸν θεόν,
> βαπτισθέντες τὸ βάπτισμα Ἰωάννου:
> οἱ δὲ Φαρισαῖοι καὶ οἱ νομικοὶ (τὴν βουλὴν τοῦ θεοῦ ἠθέτησαν
> εἰς ἑαυτούς), μὴ βαπτισθέντες ὑπ' αὐτοῦ.

The link between verses 29f. and 35 in Luke implies that Luke's 'children' in verse 35 is more original. The parallel with verses 29f. demands a personal subject for the 'justifying', and only 'children', not 'works', will satisfy this. The secondary nature of Matthew's version here is supported by other considerations. It is clear that, for Matthew at least, the 'works of Wisdom' are the 'works of Christ', verse 19 echoing verse 2, and the two verses forming an *inclusio* around the whole section.[15] Thus ἔργων in verse 19 brings Jesus and Wisdom into a very close relationship, to the point of identification.[16] Thus, in Matthew the sense is clear: given the close association of Jesus and Wisdom, the works of Jesus justify his claims. But this is a powerful theme in Luke's own writings: the idea that the miracles are important for providing the basis for faith is a recurring theme.[17] If, therefore, Matthew's 'works' was in Luke's source (i.e. if Luke read Matthew) it is hard to see why Luke should have wanted to change it. It is much more probable that Luke did not know Matthew, that the link between verses 29f. and 35 is in Luke's source, and that it is Matthew who has altered τέκνων to ἔργων.[18]

In the common source which appears to lie behind Matthew and Luke, Wisdom's children are identified as the tax-collectors (? and harlots) who listen and respond to John. Even though the πάντων in verse 35 may well be a Lukan addition,[19] so that Luke clearly excludes the possibility of Wisdom's children being John and Jesus,[20] this possibility is equally unlikely for the source.[21] In the Wisdom literature, Wisdom's 'sons' are always those who listen and respond to her call, rather than those who actually proclaim it.[22] Nevertheless John and Jesus still have a special role in relation to Wisdom: the response to them is the same as the response to Wisdom herself, so that they are representatives of Wisdom and proclaim her message.[23] This theme of Jesus as one of Wisdom's representatives will have important consequences later.

The result of the analysis so far is that Luke's version in verses 29f. and 35 reflects a pre-Lukan source, which manifestly cannot be Matthew. Moreover, Matthew has parallels to both these verses, and the differences between Matthew and the pre-Lukan source can easily be explained as due to MattR. Thus the probability is that Matthew knows Luke's source also and changes it characteristically. However, Matthew must also have removed verses 29f. from their original context here and instead he has the collection of sayings in Matt. xi. 12-15 as the immediate introduction to the parable in verses 16-19. Luke has no parallel to these verses here, but he does have a parallel to verses 12f. in Lk. xvi. 16. The question arises, therefore, of whether the change in contexts, as well as the change in wording involved, can be adequately explained as due to LkR. Some of the small verbal differences may well be Lukan changes: in Lk. xvi. 16*b* εὐαγγελίζεται and πᾶς are Lukan words, and the use of βιάζεται in the middle-active sense is probably a secondary attempt to modify Matthew's more difficult version.[24] However, the problem of Matt. xi. 13/Lk. xvi. 16*a* is more complex and demands a consideration of the wider context in Lk. xvi.

The problem of the sequence of thought in Lk. xvi is notoriously complex. Verses 16-18 are clearly related to each other (in that they concern the Law) but fitting them into the wider context is more difficult. However, even verses 16-18 do not constitute a homogeneous unit. For verse 17 appears to be an attempt to correct possible antinomianist interpretations of verse 16*a*; in turn verse 18 looks like an attempt to correct any rigidly legalistic interpretation of verse 17.[25] Could all this be due to LkR, as the GH must assume? Matthew has parallels to these sayings elsewhere, so the different context here must be due to LkR, on this hypothesis. In particular, the concern to correct any dangers of antinomianism in verse 16*a* must be due to Luke. But, according to the GH, verse 16*a* receives such a possible interpretation only as a result of LkR: Matt. xi. 13 has no suggestion that the Law has now lost its validity. Hence, on this hypothesis, Luke must have adapted verse 16*a*, but then felt obliged to correct it

immediately. This seems somewhat implausible. The fact that verse 16*a* is
felt to need some sort of 'explanation' suggests that it was already formu-
lated in this way (i.e. open to possible interpretations about the Law's
validity) prior to verses 16 and 17 being combined.[26] Thus verse 16*a* must
be pre-Lukan in wording and so Luke's source cannot be Matthew.

If verse 16*a* is indeed the wording of a pre-Lukan source, then there is
no difficulty in seeing Matt. xi. 13 as the end-result of MattR of the same
source. The characteristically Matthean stress on the prophetic nature of
the OT (cf. the formula quotations) leads to the 'prophets' being mentioned before the 'Law', and in the same way πάντες and ἐπροφήτευσαν
are added. The wish to avoid any idea that the Law is no longer valid
would be good reason for removing the saying from its context in a series
of logia concerning the validity of the Law to one about John. Further,
the stress on John leads naturally to Matthew's explaining precisely how
John fulfils scripture: he is Elijah (verse 14, cf. xvii. 13, if Markan priority
is assumed, this latter verse is a Matthean addition and hence redactional;
if not, it still remains true that the explicit equation of John with Elijah is
peculiar to Matthew.)[27] Thus, at all the points where Matthew's version
diverges from Luke's, the differences can be accounted for by MattR.[28]
This strongly suggests that Luke preserves the more original wording of his
source in verse 16*a*, and that this source was also used by Matthew.

Lk. xvi. 17, which seeks to correct verse 16, has a parallel in Matt. v. 18.
Analysis of the latter suggests that this verse has undergone some redaction
by Matthew. Ἀμὴν γὰρ λέγω ὑμῖν is Matthean (30 - 12 - 6).[29] The final
ἕως ἂν πάντα γένηται phrase in verse 18*d* fits badly after the other
temporal ἕως phrase in verse 18*b*; this, together with the fact that there is
a close parallel to the phrase in Matt. xxiv. 34 (diff. Mk. xiii. 36) suggests
that 18*d* is also a redactional addition.[30] The precise meaning of the
addition is very difficult to determine. Matthew may have believed that
Jesus' teaching went beyond the old written Law, but not in a destructive
way, i.e. he came not to destroy but to 'fulfil' the Law. The whole of verse
17 has clearly undergone some redaction: for the construction μὴ νομίσητε
ὅτι ἦλθον . . . οὐκ ἦλθον . . . ἀλλά cf. x. 34, (diff. Lk. xii. 51); for 'law and
prophets' cf. vii. 12; xxii. 40 (but see later); for πληρῶσαι cf. the formula
quotations.[31] The meaning of πληρῶσαι is much debated, but the linguistic
evidence would seem to exclude a simple meaning of to confirm the validity
of the Law. Possibly verse 18*d* should be taken in conjunction with verse
17: Matthew did think that 'all things' had come with Jesus, and so Jesus'
teaching now 'fulfils' the old law which, in its immutable character, has
now by implication had its day.[32] This therefore suggests that 18*d* is a
redactional attempt to counter the ideas in the rest of verse 18. If this is

so, then Lk. xvi. 17 preserves basically the same logion, but without Matthew's additions. Thus Luke is closer to Matthew's source, in which the eternal validity of the Law is very forcibly stressed.[33] This change is unlikely to be due to Luke himself, who, though he may have a deep concern for the ethical values within the OT Law, does not stress the eternal validity of the Jewish Law elsewhere.[34] The same reasoning suggests that the position of Lk. xvi. 17, acting as a corrective to verse 16, is also due to Luke's source, rather than to Luke himself. It is probable that verse 18 in turn corrects verse 17. Unless one is going to have a very large number of stages in the pre-Lukan tradition between Jesus and the final redactor, it seems most plausible to attribute verse 16*a* to Jesus himself, with the implied radical stance against the Law; this was then toned down by an early conservative group stressing the abiding validity of the Law. The same concern can be seen in other 'double tradition' passages. In Matt. xxiii. 23*d*/Lk. xi. 42*d*, there appears to be a similar attempt to modify Jesus' radicalism by claiming that the demands of the Law are not abrogated,[35] as is also the case in the 'double tradition' fragment visible in Matt. xii. 10–12/Lk. xiv. 3, 5.[36] There is thus a stratum of the tradition visible, which appears in 'double tradition' passages, but which is pre-Matthean and pre-Lukan, and has its own distinctive ideas about the validity of the Law. Luke and Matthew have both preserved it, yet in contexts which modify its conservatism considerably.

The total extent of the pre-Lukan source here is uncertain. Verses 16 and 17 were joined already in the pre-Lukan source, and Schürmann has sought to show that the source (which he believes to be Q) extended to cover all of verses 14–18 with Matt. v. 19 included after Lk. xvi. 17.[37] He believes that there are a number of reminiscences of this Q passage in Matt. v. 17–20, but not all his arguments are convincing. Lk. xvi. 14 is probably redactional.[38] It is difficult, too, to fit Matt. v. 19 into this complex. It is considerably less conservative than Matt. v. 18/Lk. xvi. 17: those who disregard a commandment are down-graded but still in the Kingdom. Schürmann says that the stricter verse 18 does not exclude the laxer verse 19, but nevertheless the presuppositions are different.[39] Further, the τούτων only links with μία κεραία with difficulty;[40] also, if Matt. v. 19 were part of Luke's source it is hard to see why Luke should have omitted it.[41] Thus Schürmann's thesis is difficult to sustain for verse 14 of Luke and verse 19 of Matthew.

Nevertheless, the possibility remains that verses 15–18 form a pre-Lukan unit, also known to Matthew. The reminiscence of 'the Law and the prophets' in Matt. v. 17 from Lk. xvi. 16[42] is more significant than the others adduced by Schürmann, since (a) the context in Matt. v is concerned mostly with the legal prescriptions of the Law, rather than the prophets, and (b) the phrase is not very common in Matthew. The close proximity of the divorce saying in both Matthew and Luke is also very striking. Thus there is a common collocation of motifs which seems too significant to be coincidental: the era of the Law is in some sense past (Matt. v. 17/Lk. xvi. 16) but the Law itself is still valid (Matt. v. 18/Lk. xvi. 17); yet Jesus' teaching shows the true will of God which at times contradicts the letter of the Law e.g. on divorce (Matt. v. 21ff./Lk. xvi. 18), for what really matters is not outward observance of the letter but inner obedience from the heart (Matt. vi. 1; v. 20/Lk. xvi. 15). Perhaps the last is the weakest link, but verse 15 in Luke does not fit well into its present Lukan context. Most assume that verses 14–18 prepare for the following parable: verses 14f. for the first part (verses 19–26) and verses 16–18 for the second part (verses 27–31).[43] Clearly verse 14 fits well with the parable, both being concerned with the question of wealth; further verses 16f. are related to verses 29–31, both concerning the sufficiency of the Law. However, verse 15 does not fit well here: there is a transition between verses 14 and 15 from the sin of loving money to the question of inner/outer obedience.[44] Moreover, verse 15 does not correspond with anything in the parable (it is not suggested that the rich man was guilty of self-justification). Similarly, if verses 16f. are to lead up to verses 29–31, verse 18 does not fit here either. If verses 29–31 are about the sufficiency of the Law, verse 18 is implicitly a radical attack on the Law. Conversely, the detailed concern of verse 18, i.e. the question of divorce, is totally unrelated to the parable. Thus, in view of the parallels in Matthew, and the fact (noted by Schürmann) that the central concern of these verses is different from the wider context in Luke,[45] it seems most plausible to regard these verses in Lk. xvi. 15–18 as a pre-Lukan unit which was also known to Matthew.

Schürmann is thus probably right to isolate these verses as part of a common source of Matthew and Luke, but wrong to regard them as homogeneous. He claims that the whole passage is a piece of unified teaching on the need for even greater efforts to obey the Law in the new age.[46] (This depends on the originality of Lk. xvi. 16b; if, as argued above, Matthew's version is more original here, this argument loses force.)[47] Probably there are different layers here, with Lk. xvi. 16a being a saying from the historical Jesus, with a very reactionary reply in verse 17, this in turn being corrected by verses 18 and possibly 15.[48] Thus the original source may have run

ὁ νόμος καὶ οἱ προφῆται μέχρι Ἰωάννου· ἀπὸ δὲ τῶν ἡμερῶν
Ἰωάννου ἕως ἄρτι ἡ βασιλεία τοῦ θεοῦ βιάζεται, καὶ βιασταὶ ἁρπάζουσιν

αὐτήν. ἕως ἂν παρέλθῃ ὁ οὐρανὸς καὶ ἡ γῆ, ἰῶτα ἕν ἢ μία κεραία οὐ μὴ παρέλθῃ ἀπὸ τοῦ νόμου.

(A decision about the different wordings in Matt. v. 18/Lk. xvi. 17 is difficult. The awkward nature of Matthew's double ἕως phrases, however, suggests that Matthew is more original). Luke preserves the unit almost unchanged, except for altering the wording of verse 16*b*. Matthew separates the sayings into widely different contexts, and hence the fact that the first saying in Matt. xi. 12f. occurs alone means that this is no longer in its original context within this unit. (Matt. v. 17 may represent a Matthean re-writing of the first saying, to introduce Matthew's edited form of the second saying in verse 18.) Thus the fact that Matthew splits this unit up, whereas it is retained as a whole in Luke, indicates that Matthew is secondary.

The further question of what was the original context of the whole unit is more difficult. It is possible that it did originate in Matt. xi/Lk. vii, and has been transferred *en bloc* by Luke to chapter xvi, and split up by Matthew between chapters v and xi. However, this raises the problem of why Luke should have omitted the unit here and placed it in what appears to be a less appropriate context. Certainly a change by Matthew, to bring verses 12f. from elsewhere into this section about John, would be perfectly intelligible, whereas the reverse change is hard to visualise.[49] However, Lk. vii. 29f. has been seen to be original here; Matthew's omission may have been due to his having no interest in the source's equation of Wisdom's children with the tax-collectors. For him the association of Jesus with Wisdom is more important, and what justifies Jesus/Wisdom are the works of Jesus themselves, not the independent acknowledgement of a third party. Thus it is easiest to assume that Matt. xi. 12f. has replaced Lk. vii. 29f. as the immediate introduction to the parable of the playing children.

The result of the analysis so far is that, in many respects, Luke's version is more original, and the evidence can only be explained if Matthew and Luke are dependent on a common source which Matthew has often changed. What then of the wording of the parable itself? It is quite likely that ὁ βαπτιστής, ἄρτον, οἶνον are secondary additions by Luke.[50] So too Luke's ἐκλαύσατε is probably secondary to Matthew's ἐκόψασθε.[51] But what of the difference between ἑτέροις (Matt) and ἀλλήλοις (Lk)? Matthew's version implies that there is one group of children who both pipe and wail and who complain to other children outside their group; Luke implies that the piping, wailing and complaining all take place within one group. The question of which is more original is also connected with the question of whether the interpretation in terms of Jesus and John is original to the parable or not. It is often said that the allegorisation in terms of Jesus and John betrays a later stage, as does the ἦλθον clause which looks back on Jesus' ministry as a completed whole. Further, the interpretation is said not to fit well: Jesus and John come in the wrong order (John coming first corresponds to the wailers who come second); also, the 'children' are compared to 'this generation' in the introduction, but to John and Jesus in the interpretation.[52] Thus Luke's version, with its two groups of children, is often said to be part of the later allegorising process.

However, this is not all valid as a criticism of Luke's version. Most would agree that the parable refers to the refusal of the Jewish leaders to respond to Jesus and John.[53] Now in Matthew's version, there are certainly difficulties. The Jews are compared to the children who pipe and wail, but the group who do not respond are other children (different in Matthew).[54] However, in Luke's version, there is an undifferentiated group of children, all of whom refuse invitations to play with each other. The children cannot correspond to Jesus and John, but they can correspond to the Jews as a whole who reject John's and Jesus' call. There is no need to see any allegorisation originally: the parable tells of children who refuse to respond to invitations to play, and their general refusal corresponds to that of the Jews in the face of Jesus and John despite their very different appeals.[55] This also fits well with the wider context of verses 29f. and 35, for the parable portrays the attitude of those who refuse to be 'Wisdom's children'. As a single group, in their refusal to play when called, the Jewish leaders contrast with the others (tax-collectors etc.) who respond positively. There is thus no need to separate verses 31f. and 33f. in Luke from each other. Matthew's ἑτέροις may then be the start of a process of allegorisation, attempting to make the correspondence between the two activities (piping and wailing) and the two preachers closer. Thus the original form of the parable may have run as follows:

Matthew		Luke
	τίνι οὖν ὁμοιώσω τὴν γενεὰν ταύτην;	
	ὁμοία ἐστὶν παιδίοις καθημένοις ἐν ταῖς	
ἑτέροις	ἀγοραῖς καὶ προσφωνοῦσιν ἀλλήλοις λέγοντες	
	ηὐλήσαμεν ὑμῖν καὶ οὐκ ὠρχήσασθε	
	ἐθρηνήσαμεν καὶ οὐκ ἐκόψασθε.	
	ἦλθεν γὰρ Ἰωάννης	+ ὁ βαπτιστής
	μήτε ἐσθίων μήτε πίνων	+ ἄρτον, οἶνον
	καὶ λέγετε δαιμόνιον ἔχει.	

Matthew Luke

ἦλθεν ὁ υἱὸς τοῦ ἀνθρώπου ἐσθίων καὶ πίνων
καὶ λέγετε ἰδοὺ ἄνθρωπος φάγος καὶ οἰνοπότης,
φίλος τελωνῶν καὶ ἁμαρτωλῶν.
καὶ ἐδικαιώθη ἡ σοφία
ἔργων   ἀπὸ τῶν τέκνων αὐτῆς.   + πάντων

(Not all the minute disagreements are noted, but different decisions about some of them would not affect the basic argument here, which is that Matthew shows at least two important secondary features.)

The conclusion of this survey is that, at some points, Luke's version in vii. 29–35 is more original than Matthew's parallel account. Matthew, therefore, cannot be Luke's source, and the pre-Lukan source is still visible in (a) the introduction in vii. 29f., (b) the wording of verse 35, (c) parts of the wording of the parable itself. The presence of Matt. xi. 12f. represents a secondary disruption of an original unit which is still visible in Lk. xvi. 15–18, and Matt. v makes it probable that Matthew knows these verses in the form of this unit rather than separately. Here too Luke's version is more original at some points. This by no means precludes the possibility that Luke's version is secondary at other points, as it does indeed appear to be. Hence Luke himself cannot be Matthew's source. The fact that, at those points where Luke seems to be more original, Matthew's version appears to be redactional suggests that both evangelists are using a common source. Thus the Q hypothesis explains these texts satisfactorily. The GH, which must claim that all the differences are due to LkR, does not. (The extremely close verbal agreement between Matthew and Luke, especially in the parable itself, really excludes the possibility of the existence of independent parallel traditions.) It remains to be seen if similar themes to those discovered here can be discerned elsewhere in the double tradition. In particular, attention will be concentrated on the idea of Jesus as the representative of Wisdom being rejected by men.

II

I turn now to two other passages in which many scholars have found traces of a 'Wisdom myth'. Sayings which may have been originally ascribed to personified Wisdom are found in Matt. xxiii. 34–36/Lk. xi. 49–51, and Matt. xxiii. 37–39/Lk. xiii. 34–35, and here again one must ask whether all the differences between the two versions can be explained as due to LkR.

In the doom oracle, Matt. xxiii. 34–36/Lk. xi. 49–51, there are a great number of differences which are very difficult to explain in this way. In fact, at almost every point, Matthew's version appears to be secondary. The smaller, less substantial changes will be considered first. In verse 49 Luke has simply 'kill and persecute', whereas Matthew has in addition references to 'crucifying, flogging in your synagogues', and persecuting 'from city to city'. The reference to crucifying is clearly difficult,[56] but the rest seem to be redactional additions by Matthew which now correspond more closely to the predictions of persecution for the Christian church as recorded in Matt. x. Moreover, the extra features here correspond with the parts of Matt. x which are peculiar to Matthew. For 'floggings', there is a parallel in x. 17. Matthew, unlike Mark, uses the technical Jewish term $\mu\alpha\sigma\tau\iota\gamma\acute{o}\omega$, and only he of the Synoptists refers to the disciples, as well as Jesus, being flogged. Thus the reference here is probably due to MattR. 'Your' synagogues is also Matthean,[57] and 'from city to city' recalls x. 23 (peculiar to Matthew). Thus Matthew's extra phrases are probably all Matthean additions, and Luke's shorter version is more original. In Luke's verse 50 $\dot{\epsilon}\kappa\zeta\eta\tau\epsilon\hat{\iota}\sigma\theta\alpha\iota$ with $\tau\dot{o}$ $\alpha\hat{\iota}\mu\alpha$ is unique in the NT, but corresponds with the Hebrew idiom דָּרַשׁ הַדָּם .[58] Matthew's $\ddot{\epsilon}\lambda\theta\eta$ corresponds with a similar phrase (though not precisely this verb) in Matt. xxvii. 25 (peculiar to Matthew) and hence is probably redactional; further, Luke's use of the similar phrase $\dot{\epsilon}\pi\alpha\gamma\alpha\gamma\epsilon\hat{\iota}\nu$ $\tau\dot{o}$ $\alpha\hat{\iota}\mu\alpha$ in Ac. v. 28 makes it unlikely that he would have changed Matthew's phrase had he known it. Thus Luke's Semitic idiom is probably original. Again in verse 50 of Luke, the phrase 'the blood of all the prophets' fits awkwardly with the reference in verse 51 to Abel and Zachariah, since Abel is never said to be a prophet in any known Jewish tradition. (The question of whether Zachariah was a prophet depends on the identity of the person concerned; on this, see later.) Moreover, if Luke's is the original version, Matthew's account can easily be seen as an attempt to avoid this difficulty by referring to 'righteous blood' and 'Abel the righteous'. $\delta\acute{\iota}\kappa\alpha\iota\sigma$ is a favourite Matthean word (10 - 1 - 4), so a theory that Matthew is secondarily altering Luke's version is perfectly plausible. The reverse change is much harder to envisage: besides the creation of the difficulty mentioned above, there is no good reason why Luke should have wanted to change Matthew's $\delta\acute{\iota}\kappa\alpha\iota\sigma$ since he uses the word redactionally in the same sense in Lk. xxiii. 47. (This is a change of Matthew on the GH, of Mark on the 2DH.)

The three $\dot{\alpha}\pi\acute{o}$ phrases of verses 50f. in Luke are very awkward grammatically, and it is hard to envisage so skilful a writer as Luke creating such difficulties himself. These, too, probably reflect Luke's source rather than LkR. The lack of article with $\alpha\ddot{\iota}\mu\alpha\tau\sigma$ in verse 51 reflects a Semitic construct-state construction, and Matthew's extra article seems to be secondary. The absolute use of $\sigma\ddot{\iota}\kappa\sigma$ for Matthew's $\nu\alpha\acute{o}\sigma$ is hard to explain as LkR of Matthew: this usage of οἶκος is unique in the NT, and there is no apparent reason why Luke should have wanted to alter ναός in this way. (He uses ναός 4 times, which is admittedly not very often, but ἱερόν (9 - 8 - 14 + 24) would have been a more characteristically Lukan word to use.) In verse 51*b* ναὶ λέγω ὑμῖν is not Lukan (3 times in Luke, perhaps significantly always in double tradition passages, cf. Lk. vii. 26; xii. 5) whereas Matthew's phrase ἀμὴν λέγω ὑμῖν is used by Luke 5 times, so there is no good reason why Luke should have wanted to change Matthew here. On the other hand, a change by Matthew would be consistent with Matthew's preference elsewhere. Finally, there is the repeated use of ἐκζητεῖσθαι in verse 51 of Luke, for which Matthew has ἥξει. Again, as in verse 50, this is un-Lukan and hence a change by Luke is hard to imagine. Matthew's parallel may be due to a reminiscence of Lk. xiii. 35 (which I shall try to show later is original), and this might strengthen the case for a connection between the two logia in the pre-Matthean tradition. (ἥκω (4 - 1 - 5) is not particularly characteristic of Matthew). In all these insignificant details, Luke's version cannot be easily explained as LkR of Matthew. In places where they differ, Luke is un-Lukan, whereas Matthew's version can be explained as due to MattR. Rather than Luke using Matthew as a source, it appears that both are using a common source, with Luke preserving the source's wording more faithfully.[59]

Besides these relatively trivial differences, there are others, which significantly affect the interpretation of the saying. The main difference concerns the identity of the speaker. In Matthew, the saying is a word of Jesus in the present directly addressed to the listeners. In Luke, the saying is on the lips of Wisdom in the past, with the verb in the future and the recipients of the prophets' mission in the third person. Further, the people sent with the prophets are 'wise men and scribes' in Matthew, 'apostles' in Luke. Could all these changes be due to LkR, as the GH must presumably claim? In Matthew, it is clear that (a) Jesus is speaking of a commissioning of his own in the present, and (b) the violence predicted for the messengers refers to the violence experienced in the later Christian church. Why should Luke have changed Matthew? It is possible that 'apostles' is due to LkR, if one restricts attention to statistical data alone. (The word occurs 6 times in Luke, 30 times in Acts.) However, if it is redactional, then one must interpret the word in the sense which it always has elsewhere in Luke, i.e. referring to Christian figures and almost always to the Twelve. If it refers to pre-Christian figures here, then this is a meaning unique in Luke, and hence is unlikely to be redactional. (At the very least, one cannot appeal to the other 35 Lukan uses of the word to prove that it is so.) But if the reference to 'apostles' is Lukan, this raises the question of why Luke has changed the speaker from Jesus to Wisdom. In fact this makes it very unlikely that 'apostle' here means what it does elsewhere in Luke, since Luke almost defines an apostle as one who was with Jesus and was sent out by him (cf. Ac. i. 8 etc.). Thus it is very difficult to see both these changes as LkR.

It is in fact agreed by most scholars that Luke's version, in making Wisdom the speaker, is more original.[60] One exception is Kümmel, who says that Matthew's version is so striking that it cannot but be original;[61] but this does not explain how Luke's version, which is just as striking and distinctive, has arisen. Others have said that Luke, interpreting the 'prophets' as OT figures, could not thereby retain Jesus as the subject, and so, wanting God as the originator of the prophets' mission, chose 'Wisdom' as a periphrasis.[62] Now it is probable that in Luke's present version, the prophets are OT figures, but there is no reason why Luke should have read Matthew in this way. He clearly knows that there are Christian prophets (cf. Ac. xi. 27; xiii. 1; xv. 32; xxi. 10), while the persecution of the Christian church by the Jews is a recurrent theme in Acts. There is thus no reason why Matthew's version, referring to the suffering of prophets and others in the period following Jesus, should have caused Luke any difficulty or forced him to re-interpret the saying in terms of the pre-Christian era. Further, the motif of Wisdom as a personal subject has no parallel elsewhere in Luke: sometimes it is God (with no periphrasis felt to be necessary) who sends the prophets, or who speaks through them,[63] sometimes prophets are filled with the Holy Spirit.[64] A reference here to God, or the Holy Spirit, sending the prophets would have been typically Lukan. The unusual reference to 'Wisdom' thus suggests that this is not LkR of Matthew, but shows Luke's source. Matthew's change would then be consistent with his practice, noted already, of associating Jesus and Wisdom very closely, almost to the point of identification.[65]

An examination of Luke's version in its present context makes it clear that, not only is Wisdom speaking in the past, but also the recipients of the messengers include the present generation's predecessors. This is implied by the third person αὐτούς in verse 49, and also by the connection with the preceding woe in verse 47f. There it is said that the present generation show that they share in their forefathers' guilt by building the tombs, but the two groups are clearly distinguished.[66] Hence in the present Lukan context (whether this is Lukan or pre-Lukan does not matter) the present generation are not the recipients of Wisdom's messengers referred to in verse 49. Thus the messengers, and the violence done to them, belong to the pre-Christian era. This now leads to certain conclusions about the interpretation of Luke's version. First, 'Zachariah' must be a pre-Christian figure, and thus cannot be the man whose murder by the Zealots in A.D. 68 is recorded by Josephus (*B.J.* 4.5.4). The most likely candidate is the priest, son of Jehoiada, whose murder is recorded in 2 Chr. xxiv.[67] Secondly, the 'apostles' must also be pre-Christian figures, and hence cannot be apostles in the normal Lukan sense of the word.[68] The usage is thus non-Lukan and so pre-Lukan. Luke therefore preserves the wording of his source faithfully, and clearly that source cannot be Matthew.

Matthew's different version is now explicable if he too is using the same source as Luke. The difference in speakers, noted already, entails the change of 'them' to 'you' as well as the alteration of the tense of the verb. The reference to 'wise men' and 'scribes' may reflect positions of importance within Matthew's own church.[69] The addition of 'son of Barachiah' to 'Zachariah' may be a natural slip: his source spoke of prophets and so Matthew supplies the name of the father of Zachariah the prophet (cf. Zech. i. 1 LXX). Alternatively, and perhaps more plausibly, it may be a reference to the man murdered by the Zealots in A.D. 68, Matthew thus extending the period for which the Jews are guilty right up to what is for him the final judgement on them, viz. the events of A.D. 70 (cf. xxii. 7).[70] The second alternative is possibly more convincing since it is clear that the time span included in verse 35 must include the Christian era as well.

Luke's version does not appear to be original, in the sense of being free from any adaptation in the pre-Lukan tradition. For example, on the Q hypothesis, Steck believes that verse 51 is an addition by Q, and that the reference to 'this generation' in verse 50*b* is an early, pre-Lukan gloss to an original Jewish saying.[71] Hoffmann rightly criticises the excision of verse 50*b*, since the saying must include some reference to who is being held responsible for the blood of the prophets, and verse 50*b* supplies this. However, he agrees that verse 51 may be a subsequent addition by Q to the original saying.[72] This would then explain some of the clumsiness of the three $\dot{\alpha}\pi\dot{o}$ phrases; also verse 51 adds nothing to verse 50, except to stress the responsibility of 'this generation', a theme which is prominent in other double tradition passages.[73] Nevertheless, for the limited purposes here, it is sufficient to note that, at almost every point, Luke's version is more original than Matthew's.[74] In view of the un-Lukan nature of Luke's version in the points where Matthew and Luke differ, and in view of the ease with which Matthew's version can be explained as redactional, the theory of a Q source used by both gospels seems better than any hypothesis which makes Luke dependent on Matthew. The Q version used by Matthew and Luke may have been as follows:

διὰ τοῦτο ἡ σοφία τοῦ θεοῦ εἶπεν, Ἀποστελῶ εἰς αὐτοὺς προφήτας καὶ
ἀποστόλους, καὶ ἐξ αὐτῶν ἀποκτενοῦσιν (? καὶ σταυρώσουσιν?) καὶ
διώξουσιν, ἵνα ἐκζητηθῇ τὸ αἷμα πάντων τῶν προφητῶν τὸ ἐκκεχυμένον
ἀπὸ καταβολῆς κόσμου ἀπὸ τῆς γενεᾶς ταύτης, ἀπὸ αἵματος Ἀβελ ἕως
αἵματος Ζαχαρίου τοῦ ἀπολομένου μεταξὺ τοῦ θυσιαστηρίου καὶ τοῦ
οἴκου· ναὶ λέγω ὑμῖν, ἐκζητηθήσεται ἀπὸ τῆς γενεᾶς ταύτης.

III

The final text to be discussed in this chapter is the lament over Jerusalem
in Matt. xxiii. 37–39/Lk. xiii. 34f. The level of verbal agreement between
the two versions is very high, and it is thus difficult to deny Lukan dependence on Matthew at this point if such dependence exists anywhere.[75]
However, once again detailed consideration suggests that Luke's version is
more original. In particular, the introduction to the final saying in Luke
ἕως ἥξει ὅτε[76] (ἀπ' ἄρτι ἕως ἄν in Matthew) is difficult to explain as due
to LkR. Elsewhere Luke usually uses ἕως with οὐ.[77] Thus Luke is probably
preserving the wording of his source, which therefore cannot be Matthew.
The use of ἥξει in Matt. xxiii. 36 may also be a reminiscence of ἥξει in
Lk. xiii. 33 if the word were in Matthew's source, and this gives additional
support to the theory of the existence of a common source here. This also
implies, and is suggested by many independently of this theory, that the
doom oracle and the lament belong together originally in the pre-Matthean
tradition. This would mean that the lament was also originally a saying of
Wisdom.[78] Many others believe that this is so, even though the link with
the doom oracle may be due to Matthew.[79] The speaker appears to be a
supra-historical figure referring to attempts over the whole history of
Israel to 'gather her children' together.[80] That God is the subject seems to
be excluded by the divine passive ἀφίεται in the third person, in contrast
to the first person of the speaker.[81] A theory of Wisdom as the speaker
would, however, fit very well: the image of Wisdom making her nest is
paralleled in Sir. i.15, and the motif of Wisdom being no longer seen, as
part of the punishment for rejecting her, appears in Prov. i. 28; Sir. xv. 7;
li. 19. So too the idea of Wisdom sending prophets and messengers is
clearly part of the same tradition as Lk. xi. 49. The main argument against
an original connection between the sayings is the different point in time
assumed by the speakers: in Lk. xi. Wisdom looks forward from before the
start of history, in Lk. xiii the speaker looks back over Israel's history in
the past.[82] However, as Suggs points out, the nature of the form really
determines the tenses: a doom oracle requires a future tense, as does a
lament a past tense.[83] Thus there is no insurmountable problem in

accepting both logia as Wisdom sayings, already joined together in the pre-Matthean tradition.

If the theory that the ἥξει phrase is Lukan presents difficulties from a linguistic point of view, the same is also true when the ideas implied here are considered. The phrase implies that the 'coming one' is a different person from the speaker.[84] However, this can scarcely be due to LkR. Luke makes Jesus the speaker here, and elsewhere clearly identifies Jesus as the 'coming one' (cf. Lk. vii. 20; xix. 38). It may be that Luke understood the subject of ἥξει to be 'the time',[85] but everything is much clearer with the Wisdom background in mind. For if it is Wisdom speaking, then the 'coming one' is a final eschatological figure different from Wisdom herself (possibly the Son of Man) who will be the final judge. If this is so, then Luke has preserved the saying uncritically and put it on the lips of Jesus. What is important for him is the opening 'Jerusalem'.[86] Steck points out that, within the deuteronomistic scheme of the violent fate of all the prophets which this saying clearly presupposes, it is always all Israel which is the object of the prophets' address, never Jerusalem. The introduction of Jerusalem here is only explicable by the link with the Wisdom tradition, whereby the speaker is Wisdom who makes her home in Zion (cf. Sir. xxiv. 10).[87] Thus for the source, Jerusalem represents all Israel, whereas for Luke, she is one city in Israel distinct from the others (a prophet must die there and not in another Israelite city). Luke's main stress is thus quite different from that of the source.

If Luke's version is indeed original at these points, then Matthew's version is easily explicable as due to MattR. In Matthew there is nothing to suggest that the coming one is different from the speaker (hence it is hard to see why Luke should have changed things if he knew Matthew). Instead, Jesus is clearly the speaker, and the departure of Jesus from the temple is closely related to the departure of the speaker mentioned in the oracle. Matthew's ἀπ' ἄρτι points to the time of the absence of Jesus between his death and the Parousia, and the phrase is used in a similar way in Matt. xxvi. 29, 64 (both unique to Matthew). This is therefore easy to envisage as MattR. Further, by having γάρ in verse 39 instead of δέ, as in Luke, the final saying is now made the basis for the claim in verse 38: the desertion of the house is explained in verse 39 as being the departure of Jesus, and this then occurs in xxiv. 1.[88] This tight nexus of ideas fits well with Matthew's tendency to associate Jesus and Wisdom very closely. The link between Wisdom and the Shekinah is also traditional (cf. Sir. xxiv. 8) so that Jesus' presence is on a par with that of the Shekinah.[89] In Luke, on the other hand, the two sayings are really separate.

The result of this analysis is that Luke's version is un-Lukan at the points where Matthew and Luke differ, whereas Matthew is Matthean there. The Q hypothesis, with Luke preserving Q and Matthew redacting the same source, fits these facts well. The GH, which must assume that Luke is redacting Matthew, does not. The common source may therefore have run as follows:

Ἰερουσαλήμ, Ἰερουσαλήμ, ἡ ἀποκτείνουσα τοὺς προφήτας καὶ λιθοβολοῦσα τοὺς ἀπεσταλμένους πρὸς αὐτήν, ποσάκις ἠθέλησα ἐπισυνάξαι τὰ τέκνα σου ὃν τρόπον ὄρνις τὴν ἑαυτῆς νοσσιὰν ὑπὸ τὰς πτέρυγας, καὶ οὐκ ἠθελήσατε. ἰδοὺ ἀφίεται ὑμῖν ὁ οἶκος. λέγω δὲ ὑμῖν, οὐ μὴ ἴδητέ με ἕως ἥξει ὅτε εἴπητε, Εὐλογημένος ὁ ἐρχόμενος ἐν ὀνόματι κυρίου.

IV

The analysis of these texts has shown that Luke's version has a number of features which are more primitive than Matthew's version, and which are also uncharacteristic of Luke. If, therefore, the possibility of Matthean dependence on Luke is excluded (and in any case it is unlikely since Luke does not always offer the more original version), it is most probable that Luke is using source material which is also common to Matthew. Further, in all the passages considered so far, there is a distinctive theme running through all of them. In this, Wisdom appears as a personified being who sends messengers: the prophets and others in the past, and John and Jesus in the present. Linked with this is the theme of the violent fate suffered by all the prophets as a result of their call to repentance, set within a deuteronomistic view of history. Steck has shown how this theme of the prophets' fate was an on-going, living tradition, re-appearing in writing at many points of Jewish history. So too the idea of personified Wisdom, making her appeal to men, and either being totally rejected (1 En. xlii), or else making her home in Israel (Bar. iii–iv, Sir. xxiv), is well attested outside the NT. What is distinctive about these sayings here is the combination of these two streams of tradition, so that Wisdom herself becomes the agent in sending out the prophets who suffer violence at the hands of Israel.[90] It is clear that the seeds of such a combination were to hand: in the Wisdom tradition, Wisdom herself can call directly to men (Prov. i. 22ff.; viii. 32ff.; Sir. xxiv. 19ff.) and is also identified as the Torah (Sir. xxiv. 23; Bar. iv. 1), so that there is a possible link with the prophets' call to obey the Law. Yet such a link, in particular the idea that Wisdom sends out messengers to represent her, is not attested prior to these sayings.

Bultmann's claim, that the idea of Wisdom's sending envoys was a well-established motif in Jewish tradition,[91] has been effectively criticised by

Johnson.[92] Johnson points out that in nearly all the tradition, it is Wisdom herself who speaks directly, and there is no idea of any other envoys in mind. Even the much-quoted verse in Wisd. vii. 27 may not be totally relevant. The context concerns the status of those seeking Wisdom, not their revelatory function: the link between 'friend of God' and 'prophet' suggests mystical union with God (cf. Philo, *De Vit. Mos.* 1.152), and the man so described is one who lives with Wisdom (vii. 28), loves her (viii. 2) and finds rest with her (viii. 16).[93] The idea of an oracle-giving prophet, who is the representative of Wisdom and who hands on her message, is thus hard to establish in Judaism.

This criticism of Bultmann's thesis about the Jewish background is justified. However, it is then all the more striking when the idea of Wisdom's sending envoys does appear, as it clearly does in Lk. xi. 49–51, and by implication in Lk. vii. 31–35, and xiii. 34f.[94] Certainly this idea is not particularly congenial to Luke. Nowhere else does he use the theme of personified Wisdom. In Lk. ii. 40, 52, the boy Jesus is said to be 'full of wisdom' but there is no need to read any Wisdom myth into this: being full of wisdom is equivalent to being wise and accepting wise instruction (cf. Prov. iii. 4). Nor is there any need to read a Wisdom myth into Lk. xxi. 15 (diff. Mk. xiii. 11) or Ac. vi. 3, 10, where being full of wisdom leads to 'theologically informed and irresistible utterance'.[95] Ac. vii. 10 falls into the same category, and Ac. vii. 22 refers to secular wisdom. (There are no other uses of the noun in Luke–Acts). Thus the idea of personified Wisdom is not characteristic of Luke.

Now it was seen earlier that the fact that Luke's version is more primitive is not of itself fatal to the GH, since the possibility remains in theory that Luke and Matthew used independent, parallel traditions. Although this seems rather unlikely in the cases of Lk. vii. 31–35 and xiii. 34f. in view of the very close verbal agreement with Matthew, it is theoretically possible in Lk. xi. 49–51, where the versions are not so similar. However, the considerations above about the un-Lukan nature of the ideas involved make even this option highly improbable. It is very hard to envisage Luke's choosing an independent version of the logion which does not fit his overall ideas, if in fact he knew Matthew as well. It is much more likely that he did not know Matthew, and preserved his source more faithfully than Matthew did.

The sayings examined in this chapter thus form a set with a unifying thread through them. They presuppose a tradition which sees Wisdom as the agent in sending the prophets who all suffer, and which sees John and Jesus as part of the same line of suffering messengers. This is pre-Matthean and pre-Lukan, and often it is Luke who has preserved the more original tradition. The hypothesis of a single source Q, used by both Matthew and Luke, and with its own distinctive ideas, seems to be demanded by the evidence. Several small linguistic features also support this hypothesis, since there are some words and phrases which appear to be peculiar to the double tradition passages.[96] The GH, which postulates direct use of Matthew by Luke, or else the choice by Luke of an independent parallel tradition, gives no satisfactory explanation of the texts.

17 THE APOCALYPTIC DISCOURSES

The material contained in the apocalyptic discourse in Mk. xiii presents many difficulties in a study of the Synoptic Problem. Not only are there parallels to Mk. xiii in the similar contexts of Matt. xxiv and Lk. xxi, but there is also a considerable body of related material elsewhere, e.g. in Lk. xii and xvii. Farmer devotes more space to this speech than to any other pericope in seeking to explain the changes in the texts on the GH.[1] Before dealing with Mark's version, he considers the Lukan parallel in the light of Matthew's gospel, and claims that Lk. xxi can be easily explained as LkR of Matt. xxiv. Thus, Luke followed Matthew closely up to Matt. xxiv. 8. Then, noticing the doublet in Matt. xxiv. 13 with Matt. x. 22, he turned back to use the material in Matt. x. 17–22 instead of using Matt. xxiv. 9–14, possibly because he preferred Christians being 'hated by all' (Matt. x. 22) to being 'hated by all the Gentiles' (Matt. xxiv. 9). Other smaller changes are then easily intelligible. In Lk. xxi. 14f., 22, Luke paraphrases Matthew, since he has already used the Matthean material in xii. 11f. and xvii. 31 respectively, and he wishes to avoid creating doublets. Similarly he omits Matt. xxiv. 23–28 because he has already drawn on this material in chapter xvii. Finally, the changes in Lk. xxi. 20–24 are due to Luke's writing after the events of A.D. 70.[2]

Those who assume Markan priority have to explain Luke's version in chapter xxi in relation to Mk. xiii. Some of these explanations can serve just as well if one is seeking to account for Luke's differences from Matthew, since Matthew and Mark are very close here. Hence, many of Farmer's explanations of Luke's procedure have the implicit agreement of many other scholars. For example, the differences in Lk. xxi. 20–24 can be (and are) explained as due to Luke's writing after the fall of Jerusalem, and this accounts for the differences between Luke and Mark just as well as those between Luke and Matthew.

However, this is not the case in the whole pericope. On the 2DH, Luke's source for xxi. 12–19 is Mk. xiii. 9–13 with no change of context involved. On the GH, Luke's source is Matt. x. 17–22, which involves Luke's turning back fourteen chapters in Matthew. Farmer's explanation of why Luke might have done this is scarcely convincing. That Luke should have looked ahead five verses, and then have been influenced by the doublet to switch back to the earlier context for the five verses prior to the doublet verse, is very strange. Further, if Luke preferred 'hated by all' to 'hated by all the Gentiles', he could have simply omitted τῶν ἐθνῶν from Matt. xxiv. 9 without making this elaborate change.

On the theory of Markan priority, Matt. x. 17–25 is usually explained as Matthew's anticipating material from Mk. xiii, taking the persecutions (which Matthew's church is presumably facing) out of the apocalyptic context, and thereby ensuring that they need no longer be a sign of the imminent end. Matt. x. 17 does seem to start a new section in Matthew, and the link with verses 1–16 is not strong. The situation presupposed here changes suddenly from a mission, where the disciples play a very active role, to one of persecution, where they can only be passive. The nature of the discourse also changes from direct instructions (with imperatives) to predictions (with indicatives). Although there is some link between the two sections in that both involve acts of witness by the disciples, there appears to be a seam in the tradition here, indicating that Matthew has changed sources at this point. On the 2DH, these sources are readily identifiable: Matthew has switched from conflating the mission charges of Mark and Q to using Mk. xiii. A change of sources can, of course, be accommodated within the GH, but these sources cannot be identified. However, given the fact that (a) Luke's alleged procedure in switching back from Matt. xxiv to Matt. x is not satisfactorily explained, and (b) Matthew's reverse changes are intelligible, the 2DH gives a better explanation of the relationship between Matt. x, xxiv and the other two gospels.

Farmer's other claim, that Luke paraphrases or omits material in Matt. xxiv which he has used elsewhere, is also the explanation of others who assume Markan priority.[3] In itself, this is quite plausible. However, what is left unexplained is the literary relationship involved in the earlier Lukan contexts where Luke has used material either directly from, or parallel to, Matt. xxiv. Thus, given the present forms of Lk. xii. 11f. and xvii. 22f., Farmer's explanations are plausible. The question arises, therefore, of whether this earlier material can be adequately explained on the GH.

I

I start with a consideration of Lk. xvii. 22–37. This section of Luke is of special interest in any study of the 'double tradition' on the GH, since it is one of the places where it is conceded by many advocates of that hypothesis that Luke's version is more original than Matthew's.[4] This is also one of the passages used by McKnight to show that Luke is more original than Matthew, and hence not dependent on him.[5] Buchanan too admits that 'it seems reasonable to suggest that Matthew and Luke are not directly related here but have instead used a common source'.[6] As has been seen, such phenomena can be accommodated within the Griesbach hypothesis, using the insights of form-criticism. Indeed, writing in general terms, Farmer says that 'it would be quite possible to extend considerably the list of such passages in Luke and Matthew which call for a common source or sources, and one would still not be required to hypothecate anything like the "Q" that has traditionally and conventionally been required by the two-document theory'.[7] Farmer himself apparently thinks that only verses 26–30 in Lk. xvii. 22–37 are to be explained in this way, and that Luke drew on Matt. xxiv for verses 21–24, 37.[8] However, in the light of his more general remarks, he would presumably see no anomaly for the GH if more of Lk. xvii could be shown to be more original than its Matthean parallel. Nevertheless, this will be seen to have important implications when Matt. xxiv and Mk. xiii are considered.

In considering Lk. xvii. 22–37, I take as a starting point verses 26–30. The Matthean form is probably secondary in referring to the παρουσία. (The word appears only in Matthew, and 4 times in this chapter.)[9] Further, it is probable that the saying about Lot was also in Luke's source. Lührmann shows how the two stories of the flood and the destruction of Sodom were frequently coupled in the Wisdom literature as examples of divine judgement.[10] In view of this, there is no good reason for not ascribing both examples (of Noah and Lot) to the original source.[11] The double comparison forms a couplet in parallelism, which may also be a sign of greater originality.[12] The repetition of the phrase 'so will be the parousia of the Son of Man' in Matthew's version (verses 37, 39) may be a further indication that Luke's double comparison is more original and part of the source known to Matthew as well.[13] Some have claimed that Luke's version is secondary in referring to the 'days' (plural) of the Son of Man in verse 26.[14] This, it is said, creates a discrepancy with the rest of the pericope which speaks of the 'day' of the Son of Man, clearly referring to the Parousia, whereas 'days' in verse 26 must refer to the time before the Parousia. However, the apparent tension causes no difficulty in interpreting the saying, and the discrepancy is purely formal. In fact, the comparison with the 'days of Noah' demands, strictly, a plural expression. Certainty is not possible, but there is no compelling reason for thinking that Luke has altered his source in any substantial way.

The meaning of the verses is clear. The coming of the Son of Man will be a sudden, unexpected event. Many people will be pursuing their ordinary daily activities, and will be caught unawares by the sudden disaster, which, if they are not prepared for it, will mean total destruction for them. Moreover, 'since none of the activities mentioned in verses 27, 28 are bad in themselves the critique must be fastening on the absorption in everyday affairs and lack of eschatological awareness'.[15] Thus the saying functions in part as a warning against complacency in the face of the eschatological crisis which might break in at any moment. Further, the comparison with the destruction wrought by the flood, and by the fire and brimstone, implies that the Son of Man's coming will be judgemental. Just as the majority of men perished in the catastrophes in the past, so the coming of the Son of Man will be equally catastrophic for those who are not ready. It remains to be seen how far this idea of the day of the Son of Man as sudden and judgemental links up with the other verses in the context.

I consider first Lk. xvii. 23f./Matt. xxiv. 26–28 and the comparison with lightning. Two interpretations of the metaphor have been suggested: it could imply that the Son of Man's coming will be either (a) temporally sudden, or (b) universally visible.[16] Now it is fairly clear that the second interpretation fits Matthew's version better: the fact that the lightning is said to go 'from East to West' suggests that spatial, rather than temporal, ideas are predominant. Moreover, the warnings are more specific in Matthew, with explicitly geographical details ('in the desert/in the inner chamber'). Clearly, in Matthew, what is being corrected is any wrong idea of *where* the Son of Man will arrive: it is no good looking for him in the desert or in an inner room, since, when he arrives, he will be universally visible. It is sometimes said that Matthew's version is more original because it is 'more concrete',[17] but greater 'concreteness' is not necessarily a sign of greater originality.[18] In fact, it is just these concrete details which make for difficulties here.

In Matthew, the saying is placed in the middle of the apocalyptic discourse, immediately after the prediction of false Messiahs and before the description of the Parousia itself. However, verses 26–29 also refer to the Parousia (using the imagery of lightning rather than clouds), but this now comes too early, prior to verse 29.[19] Further, verses 26–28 do not follow on very easily from what precedes in verses 23–25. There, the appearance of false Messiahs is predicted, and their falseness appears to lie simply in the fact that they are not Jesus,[20] even though they may do all the things expected of the Messiah (hence the possibility of leading people astray). However, in verses 26–28 the point is that they will appear in the wrong way, and one will therefore be able to test their claims by the way in which they appear. Thus, in verses 23–25, it is a question of the wrong people appearing in the right way, whereas in verses 26–28 it is a question of people appearing in the wrong way. The presuppositions are quite different for the two warnings. Verses 26-28 therefore do not fit very well in their present Matthean context.

Further there is some internal incoherence within these verses. The 'concrete details' of verse 26 refer to specifically Messianic expectations, i.e. that the Messiah would appear in the desert or in secret.[21] This does not cohere very easily with verse 27 which refers to the Parousia of the Son of Man, not of the Messiah. (There is no evidence that the Son of Man was expected in the desert, or in a hidden way.) Thus Vielhauer's objections to the authenticity of this saying, viz. that it presupposes the post-Easter identification of Jesus with the figures of both the Messiah and the Son of Man,[22] have relevance to Matthew's version. But it is only in Matthew that the warning cries concern specifically Messianic claims, and these considerations do not affect Luke's account. Thus, in Matthew, verses 26-28 fit well with neither verses 23-25, nor with verses 29ff. Moreover, the Messianic references in verse 26 do not fit with the Son of Man saying in verse 27. The easiest solution to the problems found here is to say that verses 26-28 are a secondary insertion into Matt. xxiv, and that the Messianic details have been superimposed on verse 26 to try to link these verses more closely with the warnings of false Messiahs in verses 23-25. The 'concrete details', of the desert and the inner room, are probably secondary additions by Matthew, and Luke's shorter version may therefore be original.

This solution to the literary problems would also account for some of the smaller verbal differences between Matthew and Luke. Luke's μηδὲ διώξητε is parallel to Matthew's μὴ πιστεύσητε. Matthew's change from Luke's version would be explicable as an assimilation to the very similar saying in verse 23, whereas Luke's use of διώκω is very unusual, so that LkR is not easy to envisage. Further, the secondary nature of Matthew's verse 28 may be indicated by the use of φαίνω and ἀπό . . . ἕως, both of which could be due to MattR.[23] Thus, the explicitly spatial ideas here, i.e. the geographical details of verse 26 and the 'East to West' phrase in verse 27, are all probably redactional in Matthew, and the use of the lightning metaphor to imply universal visibility may therefore be partly Matthean.

Luke's version has not escaped redactional activity either. In Luke, what is compared with the lightning flash is not the coming of the Son of Man, or his day (Matthew's 'Parousia' is again almost certainly secondary), but the Son of Man himself. Similarly, in the Transfiguration story, Luke says that Jesus' clothing was ἐξαστράπτων (ix. 29. This is an addition to Mark on the 2DH, or to Matthew on the GH. Either way, it is LkR.)

Grundmann comments: 'Für Lukas ist die göttliche Welt lichthafte Wirklichkeit, und ihr Aufleuchten im irdischen Bereich geschieht blitzhaft'.[24] Luke's interest, therefore, seems here to be primarily Christological and his source may have simply said 'so will be the day of the Son of Man'.

Thus, the original source compares the day of the Son of Man with a lightning flash. Moreover, Lk. xvii. 23, which tells Christians to ignore any warning cries, need only imply that there will be no time for such advance notice when the event happens: there will not even be a moment to say 'Look here!' since the day will come with the speed and suddenness of a lightning flash. Thus the original use of the lightning metaphor may have been temporal rather than spatial.[25] Each evangelist appears to have altered it independently: Luke by interpreting it Christologically, so that Jesus himself appears to radiate lightning, Matthew by linking it with other Messianic expectations, so that the universal visibility is stressed. The original source may therefore have simply warned that the day of the Son of Man could come at any time with no advance notice, and that when it does come, it will be with the speed of lightning.

This now links up extremely closely with Luke's verses 26-30. If in verses 23f., the Parousia is said to come suddenly, then verses 26-30 draw out some of the consequences of this in view of the judgemental nature of the event. Schürmann sees a seam between these two, in that verses 23f. describe the event itself, whereas verses 26-30 interpret it as judgement: 'eine Diskrepanz . . . die eine sekundäre Anfügung erkennen lässt'.[26] Thus he sees here (as elsewhere in the Son of Man sayings in Q) two layers, with the Son of Man saying belonging to the earlier stratum of the tradition. But driving such a wedge between verses 23f. and 26-30 is unnecessary. Verses 23f. do not describe the nature of the Parousia for its own sake: there is an implied warning even here, and verses 26-30 only draw the consequences more clearly. However, an idea of universal visibility in the lightning metaphor would not fit so well here. If this were the point of verses 23f., then these verses would be directed against people who are eschatologically aware, but who are looking for the wrong thing, whereas verses 26-30 are a warning to those who are totally unaware of the eschatological possibilities. If, however, verses 23f. are concerned with suddenness, then the two sayings cohere extremely closely, both sayings acting as warnings for what might happen at any moment. This connection of thought must be that of the pre-Lukan, and pre-Matthean, source, since Matthew and Luke both alter the perspective as has been seen. Moreover, both verses 23f. and 26-30 are couched in the same formal structure.[27] Even though it would probably be wrong to build too much on the pure form, the rarity of such a form does at least suggest that the two sayings belong together in a single source. Thus the common theme and common form imply that the source which Luke used in verses 26–30 must have included verses 23f. as well. Matthew's secondary elements also show that Luke's source cannot have been Matthew.

One can now consider verses 22 and 25. Verse 22*a* is almost certainly redactional, εἶπεν δέ and εἶπεν + πρός + accusative both being characteristic Lukanisms.[28] The problem of the origin of the rest of the verse depends on its interpretation, in particular the meaning of 'one of the days' of the Son of Man. The context implies that the reference must be to the future. There is no sign of a change between verses 22 and 23, from looking back (to Jesus' earthly life) to looking forward (to the Parousia); rather, both appear to be looking in the same direction. Hence the interpretation which sees verse 22 as saying that the disciples will look back with longing to Jesus' earthly days is excluded.[29] Zmijewski tries to correlate verses 22 and 26, and interprets verse 22 as referring to the time before the Parousia, but with the stress on 'seeing': one will have to believe in, without actually seeing, the exalted status of the Son of Man.[30] But in that case, one would not expect 'one of the days of the Son of Man' to be the direct object of the verb 'to see'; rather, one would expect that it is the Son of Man himself whom the disciples will long to see. Thus the only remaining possibility is that the reference is to the Parousia itself. The odd plural may, however, be explicable as LkR, i.e. as part of Luke's tendency to divide events into a sequence of successive parts.[31] Further, the final phrase, 'you will not see', has the effect of predicting a delay of the Parousia events. This may be not so much an apology, as an attempt to curb any over-enthusiastic anticipation of the Parousia.[32] Nevertheless, while this fits in well with Luke's overall perspective, it does not fit in so well with verses 23f., 26–30. For these verses are directed to those who are content to carry on as normal and who are unaware of the imminence of the crisis. These verses therefore aim to arouse some eschatological enthusiasm, whereas verse 22 tries to dampen this down. Thus verse 22 is mostly a Lukan addition to the source, modifying its ideas considerably, and in a way which is typically Lukan.[33]

Verse 25 is also probably due to LkR. In the use of πρῶτον (8 out of the 10 usages in Luke are in 'L' material) and δεῖ,[34] Luke's hand can be seen. The idea of suffering as the necessary prelude to glory is Lukan (cf. Lk. ix. 31; xxiv. 26, 46; Ac. iii. 18; xvii. 3; xxvi. 23), whereas the suffering motif is really alien in the context. The verse is thus best explained as a Lukan addition to his source. The Christological stress corresponds with Luke's redaction of the lightning saying, and the verse fits well with Luke's *heilsgeschichtlich* perspective, presenting the saving facts as part of a continuous time-line.[35]

In the rest of the section, verses 31–33 have more in common with Luke's redactional verses than with the source.[36] These verses suggest that there will still be time for people to forfeit their status even after the Son of Man has come, in this case by clinging on to worldly possessions. This does not cohere well with the theme of the day of the Son of Man being a single, sudden event, coming with the speed of lightning and bringing in the final judgement itself; however, it does fit with the idea that the coming of the Son of Man will be a temporally extended affair, as the redactional verse 22 implies. Further, verse 32, in the second person plural, fits uneasily grammatically with verses 31 and 33, both of which are in the third person.[37] This suggests that verse 32 has a different origin from that of verses 31, 33. On the 2DH, verse 32 is LkR, verse 31 is from Mk. xiii, and verse 33 is a Q doublet of the saying in Mk. viii. 35. Nevertheless, even without assuming Markan priority, it is clear that these verses are an intrusion into the source used by Luke in verses 23f. and 26–30. The thematic affinity with Luke's redactional verse implies that their position here is due to Luke's own work, even if their ultimate origin remains undetermined.

With verse 34 the theme of sudden judgement re-appears, suggesting the use of the source once more. There is some evidence that Luke again gives the more original version. Luke's ταύτῃ τῇ νυκτί does not correspond with Luke's normal usage: one would expect an ἐν, and ἐκείνῃ rather than ταύτῃ.[38] Zmijewski denies this, referring to xii. 20 for a parallel phrase, and Ac. xii. 6 for a similar lack of ἐν. He thinks that Luke's reference to 'night' is redactional, and related to the use of the lightning metaphor and the parallel in the Transfiguration story, which, in Luke, may be a night scene.[39] However, Lk. xii. 20 and Ac. xii. 6 only show that Luke can use this phrase, but it still remains uncharacteristic and one would expect him to write differently if he were redacting a source. Moreover, the link with the lightning saying is somewhat remote: one would expect a reference to the 'night' in verse 23 itself, rather than ten verses later, if this was Luke's intention. If Luke's version is pre-Lukan, Matthew's is thoroughly Matthean in its use of τότε. Thus a change by Matthew is easy to envisage, whereas the reverse change is much harder to conceive, given the un-Lukan nature of Luke's version. If Luke's 'night' is original, this implies that the 'two on one bed' is also original in verse 34, since only they of the examples given are engaged in a specifically night-time activity. Matthew's different example of men working in a field could then be due to an allusion to the imagery of Matt. xxiv. 18.[40] With verse 37, the precise interpretation of the saying is again uncertain. Luke's introductory question may well be redactional,[41] but it is at least possible that the vultures' coming represents again a sudden event (cf. Job ix. 26; Hab. i. 8),[42] so that the saying links up with the other verses in Luke's source.

The result of this analysis of Lk. xvii. 22-37 is that Luke is probably dependent on a single source for verses 23f., 26-30, 34f., 37*b*,[43] and that Luke himself has made various additions to this. Moreover, there is a difference in outlook between Luke and his source. For Luke, the End is a protracted affair, with the possibility of a delay in its initial arrival; for the source, on the other hand, the 'day of the Son of Man' is a single, sudden, judgemental act, and the source tries to arouse its listeners to readiness since the End may arrive at any moment.[44] Thus eschatological enthusiasm has to be damped down by Luke, whereas for the source it is sadly lacking. The distinctive outlook, visible in these source verses,[45] suggests very strongly that Luke is here dependent on a single source, rather than on a set of unconnected logia.

When one now compares the parallel version in Matt. xxiv, it becomes apparent that Matthew has parallels to Lk. xvii here in just those verses which the analysis of Luke alone suggested had come from Luke's source. Moreover, these same verses are separable from their Matthean contexts, and this implies that they come to Matthew in a source different from the rest of Matt. xxiv. This has already been seen in the case of Matthew's verses 26-28. The other parallel comes in verses 37-41, and here too a seam between the traditions in Matthew is evident, for the whole discourse changes its nature abruptly after verse 36.[46] Up to verse 36, the point has been that the Parousia (A) cannot come until various disasters and troubles (B) have occurred. Nobody knows the date of A, but the presence of B is not to cause anxiety since B is the necessary prelude to A, and A will put right the ills of the present.[47] In verses 37ff., the theme changes to a warning that A can come at any moment, and that it may be disastrous if men are unprepared, and hence one must watch.[48] Thus in verses 1-36 the expectation of the Parousia inspires confidence and hope, whereas in verses 37ff., it functions as a warning. The two ideas are separable and suggest that between verses 36 and 37 there is a change of source. Thus, these verses which are common to Matt. xxiv and Lk. xvii are separable from both their contexts. Further, in many cases, Luke's wording has been seen to be more original than Matthew's. All this implies that Matthew and Luke are both dependent on a single common source for these verses, with Luke often preserving the wording of the source more faithfully than Matthew. Thus the concession of advocates of the GH, that Lk. xvii. 26-30 may be dependent on a tradition parallel to Matthew, rather than on

Matthew himself, must be extended to cover all the material common to Matt. xxiv and Lk. xvii. The theory of a single source, common to Matthew and Luke, is, of course, essentially the Q hypothesis. (For a suggested reconstruction of this common source, see the appendix at the end of this chapter.)

All this now has important implications in a consideration of the relationship between Matt. xxiv and Mk. xiii. Farmer's theory is that Luke, in chapter xxi, omitted or paraphrased anything he had already used which was either borrowed from, or parallel to, Matt. xxiv. However, in the case of the 'omissions', these have been seen to be the same verses as those which he had used in chapter xvii, but which he had derived from Matthew's source rather than from Matthew. This theory is not impossible, since Luke may have recognised Matthew's use of their common source and so omitted the relevant part. However, it is perhaps easier to see these verses simply as additions by Matthew from one of his sources to other pre-Matthean tradition, without also having to postulate subsequent omission of these verses by Luke. Certainly if Luke is using Matthew, he has managed to get back to the shape of the discourse in one of Matthew's sources. Nevertheless, things become much more problematical for the GH when the Matthew–Mark relationship is considered.

Farmer suggests that Mark's procedure, assuming the use of Matthew and Luke as his sources, is easily intelligible. Basically he followed Matthew's wording, but was strongly influenced by Lk. xxi for his choice of what to include: 'The general shape of Luke's version of the discourse was preserved, but ... the text was revised to bring it into accord with the text of Matthew.'[49] The fact that the verses which Mark omits from Matt. xxiv are also omitted by Luke indicates 'that Mark was not only following the text of Matthew as closely as a copyist might, but that he was also shaping his version ... in the light of the parallel version in Lk. 21: 5–33'.[50] It is this choice of the material which, in Farmer's view, weighs so heavily in favour of the GH. The Augustinian hypothesis, he claims, can give no reason for Mark's omissions from Matthew.[51] The 2DH is equally unsatisfactory:

Since there are minor but significant agreements between Matthew and Luke against Mark in Matthew 24: 1–7 and 24: 30–35 which ... require these verses, as well as 24: 26–28; 24: 37–41; and 24: 43–51, to be attributed to 'Q', it is difficult to know why Mark would have omitted from 'Q' exactly those literary units which Luke does not have in common with Matthew 24, in Luke 21, but does include elsewhere.[52]

All this is, however, open to serious objections. Mark's alleged procedure, in following Matthew's wording but Luke's choice and ordering of material, is not only slightly inconsistent with the facts (e.g. Mk. xiii. 21-23 is included though not in Luke), it is also somewhat at variance with Farmer's claim, made elsewhere in his book, that there is a general correlation of agreement in wording and agreement in order in Mark's use of Matthew and Luke: where Mark follows the order of one source he is closer to the wording of that source.[53] Although such a claim is difficult to establish, Farmer appears to be saying that precisely the opposite happens here. Further, Farmer claims that Mark followed Matthew's wording 'as closely as a copyist might', and that 'wherever the text of Luke followed that of Matthew, Mark copied the common text so closely that the agreements between Matthew and Luke against Mark were reduced to insignificance'.[54] But this is now very difficult to correlate with the alleged number of 'minor but significant agreements between Matthew and Luke against Mark' in Matt. xxiv. 1-7, 30-35 which necessitate ascribing these verses to Q on the 2DH. These agreements are never specified in detail. Hardly any reconstruction of Q has ever included these verses; nor do these verses provide any examples of what various scholars have regarded as the most significant minor agreements.[55] In fact, such agreements are hard to find. Neirynck lists some, but they are hardly impressive, and most concern agreements in omission without any positive agreements between themselves.[56] (E.g. 'one of the disciples' in Mark's verse 2, and the inner group of four in verse 3, both disappear in Matthew and Luke, but Matthew has οἱ μαθηταί, whereas Luke has τινες. This is really a case of all three being different, not of any minor agreement against Mark.) The positive agreements are very trivial:οὐ καταλυθήσεται for οὐ μὴ καταλυθῇ in verse 2 of Mark, δέ for καί in verse 3; εἶπεν for λέγει in verse 5; γάρ in verses 6 and 7; πολλῆς qualifying 'glory', not 'power' in verse 28; ἕως for μέχρις in verse 30 and an extra μή in verse 31. These can scarcely be described as 'significant' agreements, and the disagreements far outweigh the agreements. There is little justification for postulating a Q version in these verses. A Mark-Q overlap is only really a justifiable theory when there are a number of agreements in important words between Matthew and Luke against Mark, but this in turn makes it extremely difficult to establish any literary contact between Mark and Q.[57] Here there is a great deal of verbal agreement between Mark and the other two gospels, and very little significant disagreement, and this makes the hypothesis of a Q version very unlikely.

Mark is also shorter than Matthew elsewhere in this discourse, and there are some verses in Matt. xxiv peculiar to Matthew. On the 2DH, these are simply Matthean additions. Farmer says:

> It is incumbent upon those who think that Matthew so proceeded (i.e in the way demanded by the 2DH) to consider the possibility that instead of being added by the Evangelist to what he found in Mark and 'Q', the following verses were an organic part of the material available to him when he composed his Gospel[58]

and he quotes Matt. xxiv. 10–12, 30*a*. However, verses 10–12*a* exhibit a number of features characteristic of Matthew: τότε is a Matthean favourite; the idea of 'stumbling' is frequent in Matthew (σκανδαλίζω: 14 - 8 - 2 + 0, σκάνδαλον: 5 - 0 - 1 + 0); ψευδοπροφήτης occurs more frequently in Matthew than in the other synoptists (3 - 1 - 1 + 1); παραδίδωμι is not uncharacteristic of Matthew (31 - 20 - 17 + 14); πλάναω is Matthean (8 - 4 - 1 + 0) as is ἀνομία (4 - 0 - 0). Moreover, these verses very largely repeat the warnings of Matt. vii. 15–23, where there is a similar prediction of 'false prophets' who are rejected because of their 'lawlessness'. This looks like a link between these two sections being consciously created by Matthew. Thus verses 10–12 appear to be Matthew's own creation, bringing out what is a matter of concern to him, but in no way an 'organic part' of his source material here. Again in verse 30*a*, the same result emerges. The phrase is too short to make certainty possible, but φαίνω is Matthean (13 - 1 - 2) and σημεῖον is used frequently by Matthew (13 - 5 - 9). The link with verse 3 may be redactional, but in any case the idea of a warning 'sign' is not integral to the context: the climax is the coming of the Son of Man himself (unless the 'sign' here is the Son of Man himself, the genitive being epexegetic), so that, again, this is not an 'organic part' of the discourse. The reference to Zechariah could well be redactional, Matthew being fond of alluding to the OT, and the introductory καὶ τότε is Matthean. The public nature of the Son of Man's coming (visible to 'all the tribes of the earth') may also be redactional.[59] Thus, verses 10–12 and 30*a*, far from being integral to their context, are probably MattR.

When one now compares Mark's version with Matthew, including the material in Matt. x. 17–22, the result is that Mark xiii is identical in extent with Matthew's account when the latter has been pruned of redactional additions, and of the verses taken from the source used also by Luke in chapter xvii. Moreover, the relationship of Matt. x. 17–22 to Mark and Luke has been shown to be more easily explained if it is Matthew who has secondarily changed the contexts. In the rest of Matt. xxiv, what Mark has 'omitted' comprises Matthew's own additions and the material which belongs to Matthew's other source. Thus, on the GH, Mark has succeeded in a piece of source-critical surgery of Matthew worthy of any Jeremias 1900 years before his time, in that he has carefully pruned Matthew down to one of the latter's sources. The same could be said of Luke in chapter xxi, since he could be consciously doing this, knowing the extent of Matthew's other source from chapter xvii, and then Mark could have followed him. However, the presence of Mk. xiii. 21-23 (which does not appear in the source common to Matthew and Lk. xvii) means that Mark has done his job even better than Luke. Mark's inclusion of these verses, as well as his adherence to Matthew's wording, not only means that he has 'not slavishly' followed Farmer's rule: he has also done perfectly what Luke did only imperfectly in restoring one of Matthew's sources. It is very much easier to see dependence as running the other way round: it is Mark who is Matthew's source and Matthew adds to this the material which he shares with Lk. xvii as well as making some redactional additions. The GH must postulate this happening to a source very similar to Mark, and Mark subsequently subtracting Matthew's additions. This is unnecessarily complicated and the theory of Markan priority gives a much simpler solution.

That the dependence is this way is suggested also by a few linguistic details. It is easier to explain Matthew's omission of the awkward τοιαύτη from Mk. xiii. 19, than Mark's addition of this to Matthew; the lack of the typically Markan εὐθέως[60] in Mk. xiii. 24 counts heavily against any theory of Markan dependence on Matthew in view of the fact that Matt. xxiv. 29 uses the word here; Mark's ἔσονται πίπτοντες in xiii. 25 is paralleled by Matthew's πεσοῦνται, and again, Matthew's account seems to be a secondary improvement (Is. xxxiv. 4 LXX has the simple verb); in Mk. xiii. 22 Mark's change of Matthew's πλανῆσαι to ἀποπλανᾶν is hard to visualise: Mark uses the former 4 times, but this is the only occurrence in Mark of the latter; on the other hand, Matthew never uses ἀποπλανᾶν but he uses πλανῆσαι 8 times, so a Matthean change is easy to envisage. All these considerations suggest, therefore, that Matthew is secondary to Mark, and that Mark cannot be secondary to Matthew.

The net result of this analysis is that Matthew, in reproducing the material in x. 17-22 and chapter xxiv, is dependent on Mk. xiii and on a source which he shares with Lk. xvii. This gives at least some justification for the phrase two-'document' hypothesis. The problem of how far this second source extended can be investigated further by an analysis of the later parts of Matt. xxiv and their relationship to the end of the apocalyptic discourse in Mk. xiii. 33-37, and the parallels in Lk. xii. It is to these that I now turn.

II

The small unit in Mk. xiii. 33–37, with which Mark closes his apocalyptic discourse, is a very appropriate section with which to test the GH. In these few verses Mark appears to be mixing elements from various parables (the returning master, the burglar, the servants entrusted with authority, and the talents), and the secondary nature of Mark's account seems clear. (Secondary to what is another matter.) In its present form, Mark appears to be confusing at least two quite different stories: the 'giving authority to the servants' and the 'going away' of the master presuppose a long absence (of the order of days or weeks); the command to the doorkeeper to watch, and the reference to the different watches of the night, presuppose a night out by the master (with an absence lasting a few hours). Clearly then Mark's account is secondary, and this is frequently noted in the commentaries and elsewhere.[61] Moreover, what are apparently the same parables, which appear in Mark truncated and conflated, all appear in Matthew and/or Luke. Three of them come in Lk. xii. 35–46, and in two of them (the burglar and the servants entrusted with authority, Matt. xxiv. 43–51/Lk. xii. 39–46), the agreement in wording between Matthew and Luke is extremely close. This section therefore affords a good example for testing the contention of the GH that Luke is dependent on Matthew. (An appeal to the possible use by Matthew and Luke of independent parallel accounts is very unlikely in view of the high level of verbal agreement: if dependence of Luke on Matthew occurs anywhere, it must occur here.) Thus these texts provide a good place to test the GH in both its main assertions: for it ought to be able to explain these facts – a very close literary relationship between Matthew and Luke, and a manifestly secondary account in Mark – very well.

I consider first the relationship between Matthew and Luke in the material in Lk. xii. On this, Farmer simply says that Luke 'took the material in Matthew 24: 43–51 and joined it with a parable from his special source material'.[62] However, the Matthean and Lukan versions are not identical. Now if Luke is here dependent on Matthew, then all the minute differences in wording etc. must be due to LkR, and it only needs one such change to be inexplicable in this way for the theory to run into difficulties. It is certainly the case that nearly all the differences can be accounted for if Luke is secondary,[63] but one of these causes problems, viz. ἀπίστων in Lk. xii. 46 parallel to ὑποκριτῶν in Matt. xxiv. 51. ὑποκριτής is a favourite word of Matthew's (13 - 1 - 3), whereas ἄπιστος is not characteristic of Luke (1 - 1 - 2 + 1). (The other occurrence in Luke is ix. 41 which is derived from Mk. ix. 19 on the 2DH, or from Matt. xvii. 17

on the GH. Either way it comes to Luke from his tradition. Ac. xxvi. 8 uses the word in a different sense of 'incredible'). Thus a change by Luke is extremely difficult to envisage since (a) Luke's word here is not Lukan, and (b) Luke was not apparently averse to using Matthew's ὑποκριτής (cf. Lk. vi. 42; xii. 56; xiii. 15). On the other hand, if Luke's wording is original here, a redactional change by Matthew presents no problems, since Matthew's wording is typically Matthean.[64] The very triviality and the isolated nature of this difference make it all the more significant in considering the GH. Presumably, that hypothesis would have to say that Luke has known and used an independent form of the tradition at this point. However, it is hard to see why Matthew's use of 'hypocrite' should have made him use this independent tradition rather than Matthew himself, if indeed he knew Matthew. It is much easier to assume that Luke did not know Matthew, and that both have used a common source. Each evangelist has introduced changes into the source, and in this case Matthew has preserved the source's wording more faithfully than Luke. However, Matthew's 'hypocrite' shows that Matthew has made at least one change, and the un-Lukan nature of Luke's parallel excludes the possibility that Luke is dependent on Matthew himself.

This now leads on to a consideration of the parable of the waiting servants in Lk. xii. 35–38. It is almost certain that verse 37*b* is a later addition to the parable: it disrupts the sense of reality in the story, and the master of the house clearly becomes the Lord of the church in the role of a servant (cf. Lk. xxii. 27; Jo. xiii. 4ff.)[65] The language is very close to that of Lk. xvii. 8 (cf. περιζωσάμενος διακόνει μοι) and ἀνα/κατα - κλίνω is Lukan (1 - 1 - 7). Thus verse 37*b* is probably a Lukan allegorising feature.[66] So too verse 35 is probably (but not certainly) Lukan. The vocabulary is not un-Lukan,[67] but the rarity of the words used makes the use of statistics uncertain. However, the introductory καὶ ὑμεῖς ὅμοιοι in verse 36 suggests that verse 35 is not an integral part of the parable which follows. Thus verses 35 and 37*b* are probably additions by Luke to his source. Clearly their aim is to relate the parable to the situation of the disciples. (Whether the disciples in turn correspond to the whole church, or only to later church leaders, need not be decided here.) This now explains the unusual feature in the parable of the many servants, when there is need for only one person to wait up and unlock the door. Luke's evident interest in relating the parable to the situation of the disciples, and presumably to the later church, provides the motive for extending the number of servants in the story from one to several (though this may also have occurred in the pre-Lukan tradition). Thus, an original parable, about a master giving instructions to a servant to watch up for him, has been expanded to refer to several servants in the course of the tradition. This will become important when Mark's version is considered.

It is probable that the source which provided Luke with the parable also contained the following parables of the burglar and the servants entrusted with authority. For, first, Matthew appears to give evidence that the parable of the waiting servants was also known to him: two features in Matt. xxiv. 43, ἐγρηγόρησεν and φυλακῇ (diff. Luke) may be reminiscences of Lk. xii. 37 and 38 respectively.[68] Certainly the reference to 'watching' in the parable of the burglar is somewhat out of place: if one knew when the thief was coming, one would not bother to watch for all the time prior to his coming.[69] Further, φυλακή implies that the thief comes in the night, whereas the point of the parable is that the time is completely unknown, hence day or night. Both these features are thus secondary elements in Matthew, and hence instances where Luke is more original. (This again presents difficulties for the GH, since the high measure of verbal agreement excludes the possibility of independent parallel traditions.) Thus Matthew and Luke are probably dependent on a common source for both the parables of the burglar and the servants entrusted with authority, and, in view of the reminiscences in Matthew, the same is probably true of the parable of the waiting servants.

But secondly, it is also apparent that all three parables are closely related thematically, both to each other and to similar material in the double tradition. All imply that the Parousia will be a sudden unexpected event with no prior warning.[70] This is very closely related to the material common to Lk. xvii and Matt. xxiv, which the earlier analysis indicated as also stemming from a single source. There, as here, the theme is of the sudden coming of the Son of Man without prior warning. So too the prediction of the Parousia functions not so much as a promise of vindication to the persecuted, but rather as a threat to the present audience of the dire consequences which will ensue if they are caught unawares: hence the unusual comparison of the Son of Man with a thief, the references to the punishment dealt out to the wicked servant, and to the destruction wrought by the flood in Noah's time and the fire and brimstone in Lot's. This motif also links very closely with yet another 'double tradition' passage, viz. the woes against the Galilean cities in Lk. x. 13-15/Matt. xi. 21-23. (Further, the close verbal similarity renders any theory of independent parallel traditions unlikely, and yet Luke's version is un-Lukan in his use of ἐν τῇ κρίσει whereas Matthew's ἐν ἡμέρα κρίσεως is Matthean.[71] Thus, once again, literary dependence of Luke on Matthew is rendered unlikely in a 'double tradition' passage where there is a high level of verbal agreement.) Nowhere in this material is there an idea that the

Parousia will be particularly joyful, in contrast to Mk. xiii, Matt. xxiv. 4-36, and the redactional addition in Lk. xii. 37*b*. Nowhere in these parables, as in the apocalypse of Lk. xvii, is there any detailed description of the events leading up to, or accompanying, the Parousia. All that is said is that it will come with terrifying suddenness. This is all explicable on the 2DH: all these passages stem from Q, and the common themes are due to the distinctive ideas of that source. The linguistic considerations have shown that Luke cannot be dependent on Matthew, and yet the high measure of verbal agreement excludes the possibility of independent parallel traditions. Hence the GH fails to give a satisfactory explanation of these texts. The evidence demands a hypothesis of a common source, used by both Matthew and Luke, i.e. a 'Q' hypothesis, and the common thematic links between different parts of the double tradition material suggest that 'Q' was a single source, rather than a cipher for a body of amorphous, unrelated material. (For a suggested reconstruction of this source, see the appendix at the end of this chapter.) With all these results in mind, one can now turn to Mk. xiii. 33-37.

On any source hypothesis, verse 33 in Mark is largely a redactional addition.[72] Βλέπετε is frequently used by Mark in this discourse (e.g. verses 5, 9, 23); ὁ καιρός is unlikely to be original and seems to be a technical term for the eschaton: it is related to Mk. i. 15 which is probably a Markan redactional summary; the link with verse 32 is weak since verse 33 largely repeats verse 32; γάρ explanatory clauses are typical of Mark; only ἀγρυπνεῖτε here may be traditional, as Mark seems to prefer γρηγορέω (3 times here, and 3 times in the Gethsemane scene; the relationship between these is very difficult to determine). ἀγρυπνέω occurs only here and at Lk. xxi. 36 in the synoptics; Luke's version will be considered later. Hence it is probable that verse 33 is MkR.

In verse 34*a*, the reference to the servants all being given authority could, on the GH, be seen partly as Mark's using Matthew's introduction to the parable of the talents in Matt. xxv. 14f. The language is very similar, and the reference to 'giving authority' (as opposed to Matthew's 'handing over possessions') may be redactional (cf. Mk. vi. 7).[73] However this cannot explain Mark's version completely. The adjective ἀπόδημος is a NT *hapax* and does not appear in the LXX, although the verb (used here by Matthew) does appear elsewhere in the gospels (3 - 1 - 2); there is no obvious reason why Mark should have changed Matthew's ἀποδημῶν. Further, ἔργον is not a particularly Markan word (6 - 2 - 2, and elsewhere in Mark, at xiv. 6, the meaning is different), so that again it is not clear why Mark should have changed Matthew here.[74] Thus Mark's verse 34*a* cannot be seen simply as MkR of Matthew. In any case such a theory hardly explains why Mark should include only the start, but no more, of Matthew's parable.

With verse 34*b*, Mark is now closer to Lk. xii. 35–38, with the explicit command to 'watch'. However, once again it is difficult to see this as due to MkR of Luke. For Mark has the figure of the single door-keeper, and is thus closer to what was almost certainly the original form of the parable, the many servants being due to secondary adaptation.[75] Thus Mark gives an earlier form than Luke and, far from being dependent on Luke, must be dependent on a source lying somewhere in the pre-history of Luke's version. The wide difference in wording (apart from the use of γρηγορέω) excludes a direct literary relationship between Mark and Luke, and the use of ἐντέλλομαι by Mark again suggests Mark's use of a source (the word is not Markan: 5 - 2 - 3). Since the word does not occur in Matthew or Luke in this context, that source cannot be either of those two gospels.

Verse 35*a* could, theoretically, be due to Mark's dependence on Matt. xxiv. 32, although if so, he has partly adapted Matthew's version to fit the story: 'which day' has become a simple 'when', and 'your Lord' is 'the master of the house'. However, this makes for some confusion in Mark, as it is not clear how far the details of the parable are being interpreted and how far they are still part of the story. 'The lord of the house' still seems to be part of the story, but the second person plural address suggests that the parable is starting to be applied to those listening. It is perhaps easier to see dependence the other way round, with Matthew tidying up Mark and clearing up any possible ambiguity. The process of interpreting the parable, started in Mark, is finished in Matthew, and Matthew keeps only the interpretation, so that it is quite clear that 'your Lord' is Jesus, returning as Son of Man on his 'day'. In verse 35*b* the four-fold division of the night could be a Markan adaptation of Luke's three-fold division in Lk. xii. 38, and the fact that Mark reflects a Roman, rather than a Jewish, milieu is often noted. However, in view of the absence of any other verbal parallels between Mk. xiii and Lk. xii it is precarious to argue that Mark's version here is due to Mark's adapting Luke, rather than some other source.

Verse 36 could, on the GH, be seen as dependent on Lk. xxi. 34–36 in some way, but only the words 'sudden' (and even here not quite identical: ἐξαίφνης in Mark, αἰφνίδιος in Luke) and 'watch' (ἀγρυπνέω in Lk. xxi. 36 and in Mk. xiii. 34 if not verse 36) are close enough to suggest literary dependence. However, the differences far outweigh the similarities. It is possible that Mark's version is redactional, partly assimilating this to the Gethsemane scene. Nevertheless, in terms of the limited question of the relationship between Mark and Luke, it is easier to see Lk. xxi. 34–36 as an expansion of Mark. Προσέχετε ἑαυτοῖς is Lukan (cf. Lk. xii. 1; xvii. 3; Ac. v. 35; xx. 28) as is ἐφίστημι, and there is a large number of Pauline words in this passage, which may at the very least suggest a use of standard Hellenistic Christian paraenesis.[76] The whole passage can plausibly be seen as a Lukan construct, built out of the material in Mark.[77] If Mark were dependent on Luke, one would have to imagine Mark's carefully excising all those features which imply a Lukan origin of these verses, and also abbreviating Luke almost to vanishing point. Thus although verse 36 may be partly due to MkR, this need not imply redaction of Luke, and it is more plausible to see Luke as dependent on, and expanding, Mark. Finally, Mark's verse 37 must, on virtually any source hypothesis, be MkR,[78] but this does not assist in any way in deciding between the merits of the GH and the theory of Markan priority.

The result of this analysis gives no support to the GH. The relationship between Mark and Lk. xii is too remote, and the verbal contacts too slight, to suggest any direct literary dependence, and, in fact, Mark has an earlier form of the parable. Thus there are two independent forms of the parable of the doorkeeper. Moreover, the analysis of Lk. xii showed that Luke is here using a pre-Lukan source which also included material used by Matthew too. The fact that Mark has not used Matthew either means that there are two traditions visible here: one used by Mark, the other used by Matthew and Luke. This is effectively the 'two-document hypothesis', and the result of the investigation of the material in Lk. xii and xvii suggests that the non-Markan source, common to Matthew and Luke, is a single source with its own distinctive ideas. One is therefore driven to some sort of Q hypothesis.

CONCLUSION

In the study of the Synoptic Problem, no conclusions can have complete certainty, and any solution is theoretically possible. One can never prove with mathematical rigour that one solution is right, or that another is wrong. Nevertheless, various phenomena considered in this discussion have suggested that the GH is considerably less viable as a solution to the Synoptic Problem than the 2DH. Farmer's work on the history of the study of the Synoptic Problem has been seen to be unsatisfactory at a number of points: any extra-scientific factors allegedly at work in the minds of source critics in the past are very difficult to substantiate; moreover, Farmer's work ignores the very real criticisms which led to the rejection of the GH. Many of those criticisms are still applicable to the contemporary revival of the GH by Farmer and others.

When some of the general phenomena were considered in detail, no evidence was found to support the GH. Moreover, in some cases the evidence was found to tell strongly against the GH and in favour of the 2DH (e.g. in the use of the historic present, in some of the minor agreements, and in the discussion of the 'overlap' passages). The inconsistent redactional procedure (especially by Mark) which the GH has to envisage must be more adequately explained if the contemporary revival of the GH is to be taken seriously.

In the detailed examination of the wording of individual pericopae, the results frequently suggested some form of 2DH. Matthew and Luke appear to have had access to common source material, and independent use of a common source, rather than direct dependence of Luke on Matthew, was seen to be a necessary hypothesis. Further, several passages of such common source material were seen to exhibit a number of distinctive, characteristic features, at the level of the vocabulary used and the ideas expressed. On the 2DH this can be easily explained as common dependence on source material 'Q', and the distinctive features suggest that at least some parts of Q probably stem from a unified source. The theory of a direct literary relationship between Matthew and Luke was seen to play a very important role within the argument from order used to support the GH, and hence the theory of the independence of Matthew and Luke has implications for the GH's theories about the relative position of Mark. If Matthew and Luke are independent, then the argument from order (as propounded by Farmer) is logically inconclusive, and it gives no support for the theory that Mark was the last, rather than the first, gospel to be written. Further, the detailed studies of the wording of various Markan passages showed that the evidence was most easily explained if Mark was prior rather than secondary.

In all this, it is a matter of weighing probabilities. The GH can give an explanation of the texts at one level, but it fails to account for the reasons why the changes allegedly made by the later writers (i.e. Luke and Mark) were made in the way in which the hypothesis must assume. Insofar as the 2DH can often apparently give a more coherent and consistent set of explanations of why the later changes were made (i.e. by Matthew and Luke on the 2DH), that hypothesis is to be preferred. In many cases, good reasons could be seen why Matthew and Luke might have changed Mark in triple tradition passages; further, the study of the 'overlap' passages and the double tradition material suggested that the source also used by Matthew and Luke was to a certain extent a unified source. This then gives some justification for talking of a two-'document' hypothesis: even if 'Q' was not a document written on a single scroll, it does seem to make sense to talk about it as a unity with its own characteristic features.

If the GH is to continue to be a serious rival to the 2DH as a viable solution to the Synoptic Problem, then its adherents must give a more detailed explanation for Luke's and Mark's behaviour. Clearly Luke and Mark could have done what the hypothesis claims: what is still lacking is a detailed explanation of why they might have done this. Until this is shown convincingly, there seems little reason for reviving the hypothesis. The conclusion of this study, therefore, is that there seems to be no good reason for abandoning the traditional 2DH, i.e. the theory of independent use by Matthew and Luke of Mark and Q; in addition, perhaps more attention should be given to the distinctive features of Q than has traditionally been the case in past study of the gospels.

APPENDIX

A suggested reconstruction of the common source used by Matthew and Luke in Matt. xxiv. 43–51/Lk. xii. 35–46

Matthew		Luke
omits	καὶ ὑμεῖς ὅμοιοι ἀνθρώποις προσδεχομένοις τὸν κύριον ἑαυτῶν, πότε ἀναλύσῃ ἐκ τῶν γάμων, ἵνα ἐλθόντος καὶ κρούσαντος εὐθέως ἀνοίξωσιν αὐτῷ. μακάριοι οἱ δοῦλοι ἐκεῖνοι, οὓς ἐλθὼν ὁ κύριος εὑρήσει γρηγοροῦντας. ἀμὴν λέγω ὑμῖν ὅτι ?Uncertain. κἂν ἐν τῇ δευτέρᾳ κἂν ἐν τῇ τρίτῃ φυλακῇ ἔλθῃ καὶ εὕρῃ οὕτως, μακάριοί εἰσιν ἐκεῖνοι.	Luke changes v. 37b
φυλακῇ + ἐγρηγόρησεν	τοῦτο δὲ γινώσκετε, ὅτι εἰ ᾔδει ὁ οἰκοδεσπότης ποίᾳ ὥρᾳ ὁ κλέπτης ἔρχεται, οὐκ ἂν ἀφῆκεν διορυχθῆναι τὸν οἶκον αὐτοῦ. καὶ ὑμεῖς γίνεσθε ἕτοιμοι, ὅτι ᾗ ὥρᾳ οὐ δοκεῖτε ὁ υἱὸς τοῦ ἀνθρώπου ἔρχεται.	? + v. 41.
	τίς ἄρα ἐστὶν ὁ πιστὸς δοῦλος καὶ φρόνιμος, ὃν κατέστησεν ὁ κύριος ἐπὶ τῆς οἰκετείας αὐτοῦ τοῦ δοῦναι αὐτοῖς τὴν τροφὴν ἐν καιρῷ. μακάριος ὁ δοῦλος ἐκεῖνος ὃν ἐλθὼν ὁ κύριος αὐτοῦ εὑρήσει οὕτως ποιοῦντα. ἀμὴν λέγω ὑμῖν ὅτι ἐπὶ πᾶσιν τοῖς ὑπάρχουσιν αὐτοῦ καταστήσει αὐτόν. ἐὰν δὲ εἴπῃ ὁ (κακὸς?) δοῦλος ἐκεῖνος ἐν τῇ καρδίᾳ αὐτοῦ· χρονίζει μου ὁ κύριος, καὶ ἄρξηται τύπτειν τοὺς συνδούλους αὐτοῦ, ἐσθίῃ δὲ καὶ πίνῃ μετὰ τῶν μεθυόντων, ἥξει ὁ κύριος τοῦ δούλου ἐκείνου ἐν ἡμέρᾳ ᾗ οὐ προσδοκᾷ καὶ ἐν ὥρᾳ ᾗ οὐ γινώσκει, καὶ διχοτομήσει αὐτόν, καὶ τὸ μέρος	οἰκονόμος σιτομέτριον ἀληθῶς ? + ἔρχεσθαι
ὑποκριτῶν	αὐτοῦ μετὰ τῶν ἀπίστων θήσει.	

A suggested reconstruction of the source used by Matthew and Luke in Matt. xxiv. 26–28, 37–41/Lk. xvii. 22–37

Matthew		Luke
	ἐλεύσονται ἡμέραι	+ v. 22
ἐρήμῳ/ταμιείοις	καὶ ἐροῦσιν ὑμῖν· ἰδοὺ ἐκεῖ, ἰδοὺ ὧδε· μὴ ἀπέλθητε μηδὲ διώξητε. ὥσπερ γὰρ ἡ ἀστραπὴ	
ἀνατολῶν/δυσμῶν παρουσία	ἀστράπτουσα ἐκ τῆς ὑπὸ τὸν οὐρανὸν εἰς τὴν ὑπ᾽ οὐρανὸν λάμπει, οὕτως ἔσται ἡ ἡμέρα τοῦ υἱοῦ τοῦ ἀνθρώπου.	ὁ υἱὸς τοῦ ἀνιθρώπου ἐν τῇ ἡμέρᾳ αὐτοῦ. + v. 25

188

Matthew

Luke

παρουσία

ὥσπερ αἱ ἡμέραι τοῦ Νῶε, οὕτως ἔσται καὶ ἐν
ταῖς ἡμέραις τοῦ υἱοῦ τοῦ ἀνθρώπου. ἤσθιον,
ἔπινον, ἐγάμουν, ἐγαμίζοντο, ἄχρι ἧς ἡμέρας

καθὼς ἐγένετο

οὐκ ἔγνωσαν

εἰσῆλθεν Νῶε εἰς τὴν κιβωτόν, καὶ ἦλθεν ὁ
κατακλυσμὸς καὶ ἀπώλεσεν πάντας.

Omits

ὁμοίως ὥσπερ αἱ ἡμέραι Λώτ· ἤσθιον, ἔπινον,
ἠγόραζον, ἐπώλουν, ἐφύτευον, ᾠκοδόμουν· ᾗ δὲ
ἡμέρᾳ ἐξῆλθεν Λώτ ἀπὸ Σοδόμων ἔβρεξεν πῦρ
καὶ θεῖον ἀπ' οὐρανοῦ καὶ ἀπώλεσεν πάντας.

καθὼς ἐγένετο

παρουσία

κατὰ τὰ αὐτὰ ἔσται ᾗ ἡμέρᾳ ὁ υἱὸς τοῦ
ἀνθρώπου ἀποκαλύπτεται.

v. 40

ταυτῇ τῇ νυκτὶ ἔσονται δύο ἐπὶ κλίνης μιᾶς,
ὁ εἷς παραλημφθήσεται, καὶ ὁ ἕτερος ἀφεθήσεται.
ἔσονται δύο ἀλήθουσαι ἐπὶ τὸ αὐτό, ἡ μία
παραλημφθήσεται, καὶ ἡ ἑτέρα ἀφεθήσεται.

+ v. 37a

ὅπου ἐὰν ᾖ τὸ πτῶμα, ἐκεῖ συναχθήσονται
οἱ ἀετοί.

σῶμα

(Some of the smaller differences are difficult to judge.
However, they do not affect the argument.)

NOTES

Part 1. Some Aspects of the History of the Study of the Synoptic Problem

1 Henry Owen, *Observations on the Four Gospels* (London, 1764).
2 The theory was proposed briefly in J. J. Griesbach, *De Resurrectione* of 1783, where the author considered only the resurrection narratives; it was worked out more fully in his *Commentatio* of 1789. This is included in J. P. Gabler (ed.), *J. J. Griesbachii Opuscula Academica*, vol. II (Jena, 1825). ET by B. Orchard in B. Orchard and T. R. W. Longstaff (eds.), *J. J. Griesbach: Synoptic and Text-Critical Studies 1776–1976* (Cambridge, 1978), pp. 103–35.
3 Cf. W. R. Farmer, *The Synoptic Problem* (2nd ed., Dillsboro, N. C., 1976), p. 201. All references are to the second edition of this work unless otherwise stated.
4 See Stoldt, *Geschichte und Kritik der Markushypothese*.
5 Sieffert, *Ueber den Ursprung des ersten kanonischen Evangeliums*.
6 Farmer, *Synoptic Problem*, pp. 18f.
7 *Synoptic Problem*, p. 58. See also his claim: 'The fate of various hypotheses concerning the gospels was intimately bound up with the fate of the theological schools and ecclesiastical parties which found one or other of these hypotheses useful.' ('Skeleton', p. 30). Cf. too 'Criterion', p. 393. Stoldt's thesis is that the rejection of the GH was part of the violent reaction against the work of D. F. Strauss alone. (See his *Markushypothese*, esp. pp. 206–14.)
8 *Synoptic Problem*, p. 22.
9 'Skeleton', p. 41; see too the similar claims made in *Synoptic Problem*, p. 37; 'Criterion', pp. 393f.
10 *Synoptic Problem*, pp. 178f.; 'Criterion', pp. 393f.; 'Response', p. 429.
11 His section on 'The Fate of the Griesbach Hypothesis' (*Synoptic Problem*, pp. 67–85) deals only with the later discussion in England by Woods, Abbott and Stanton.
12 *Synoptic Problem*, p. 201.
13 I have dealt with this aspect of the subject more fully in my article 'The Griesbach Hypothesis in the 19th Century'. What follows is a very brief summary of the argument in that article.
14 Cf. Strauss, *Life of Jesus*; Schwegler, *Das nachapostolische Zeitalter*; Baur, *Kritische Untersuchungen*.
15 See especially his article 'Neue Untersuchung über das Markus-Evangelium'.
16 Ritschl, 'Ueber den gegenwärtigen Stand'.

17 Köstlin, *Der Ursprung und die Komposition der synoptischen Evangelien.*
18 Volkmar, *Die Religion Jesu.* Cf. Fuller's comment: 'Not only Hilgenfeld and Ritschl, but also Volkmar and Köstlin gave up the Griesbach-Saunier position. With Schwegler's abandonment of theology after 1846, that left Baur to all intents and purposes alone.' ('Baur versus Hilgenfeld', p. 369).
19 See Storr, *Ueber den Zweck der evangelischen Geschichte.*
20 Lachmann, 'De ordine narrationum' (ET in Palmer, 'Lachmann's Argument').
21 Wilke, *Der Urevangelist*; Weisse, *Die evangelische Geschichte.*
22 See his earlier article of 1826, 'Ueber die Parabel von den Arbeitern im Weinberge'. Strauss' *Leben Jesu* first appeared in 1835.
23 *Urevangelist*, p. 684.
24 Weisse, *Evangelische Geschichte*, pp. 64-6, 69.
25 *Ibid.*, pp. 4 and 10. Cf. Reicke, 'Griesbach's Answer', *Griesbach Studies*, p. 66.
26 Holtzmann, *Die synoptischen Evangelien*, pp. 366-373.
27 Weiss, 'Entstehungsgeschichte', pp. 63-8, 665-72.
28 Weiss, 'Entstehungsgeschichte', pp. 680-9 for the first, 689-92 for the second. See the similar division in his *Introduction*, II, pp. 242-4, 245f. See too the clear distinction recognised by Holtzmann, *Die synoptischen Evangelien*, p. 113.
29 See Wilke, *Urevangelist*, p. 446; Holtzmann, *Die synoptischen Evangelien*, p. 114.
30 See his *Commentatio*, pp. 370-7. (ET in *Griesbach Studies*, pp. 108-10, and especially the notes on pp. 209-12.) Very often Griesbach claimed that Mark wished to avoid long teaching discourses.
31 Weiss, 'Entstehungsgeschichte', pp. 680f. For example, if Mark wished to avoid Matthew's Sermon on the Mount, why did he switch from Matthew to Luke after Matt. iv. 22, rather than after Matt. iv. 24 which is the point at which the Sermon begins?
32 See *Synoptic Problem*, chs. 3 and 4; also Farmer's own summary in 'Criterion', pp. 387f.
33 The argument is now usually known as the 'Lachmann Fallacy'. The name appears to derive from the chapter in Butler's book, *Originality*, pp. 62-71, where the fallacious nature of the argument was pointed out.
34 For a fuller treatment of this, see my article, 'The Argument from Order and the Synoptic Problem'.
35 The difference between the two arguments is well brought out by Palmer, 'Lachmann's Argument', p. 377; also Wenham, 'The Synoptic Problem Revisited', p. 8. Lachmann's form of argument was that used by Holtzmann, *Einleitung*, p. 347; Wrede, *Messianic Secret*, p. 149 (referring to Holtzmann); Sanday, 'Gospels', p. 1224a; Woods, 'Origin and Mutual Relation', pp. 68-79. (Woods' essay in fact presents both arguments from order: see pp. 61-6 for what is essentially an appeal to the fact that Matthew and Luke do not agree against Mark in order. However, the rest of his essay should not be ignored.)
36 Farmer has evidently confused these two arguments when he says that Wrede's and Woods' arguments from order are invalid when Mark is identified with the *Grundschrift* (see 'Criterion', p. 388, and *Synoptic*

Problem, p. 65 respectively). In his later article, 'Modern Developments',
pp. 293f., Farmer recognises the distinction between the two arguments.
However, he does not say that this has important consequences for his
presentation of the history of the study of the Synoptic Problem.

37 Butler, *Originality*, p. 66; Styler, 'The Priority of Mark', p. 225; Neirynck,
'Argument from Order', p. 796.

38 Woods, 'Origin and Mutual Relation', pp. 66f.; Abbott, *Common Tradition*,
p. vii, referring to his earlier article, 'Gospels', p. 791.

39 See *Commentatio*, p. 397. (ET in *Griesbach Studies*, p. 120).

40 Cf. Nineham's comment: 'It is one thing to show that Marcan priority has
not been proved, quite another to show that it is not a fact.' (See his
review of Farmer's *Synoptic Problem*, in *J.T.S.* 28 (1977), 548.)

Part II. General Phenomena

1 Criteria

1 See Perrin, *Rediscovering*, pp. 37–49; Carlston, 'Positive Criterion';
McArthur, 'Basic Issues' and 'Burden of Proof'; Walker, 'Quest'; Hooker,
'Christology and Methodology'; McEleney, 'Authenticating Criteria', as
well as many others.

2 Farmer, *Synoptic Problem*, pp. 227–9; also Burton, *Principles*, p. 6 (198).

3 Fuller, 'After Ten Years', p. 68; see too the longer form of this essay, 'Die
neuere Diskussion', p. 148.

4 *Synoptic Problem*, p. 228. Cf. Sanders, *Tendencies*.

5 Cf. *Synoptic Problem*, p. 243.

6 Cf. Hengel, *Judaism and Hellenism*, passim.

7 Cf. Catchpole, 'Divorce Material', pp. 98f.

8 See Walker, 'Quest', p. 43; McEleney, 'Authenticating Criteria', pp. 439f.

9 See Zeller, 'Vergleichende Uebersicht', pp. 527–35, where he gave long lists
of words said to be characteristic of Matthew/Luke and also appearing in
Mark. However, his list is less impressive in detail: often words were
included simply because they appeared more often in Matthew/Luke than
in Mark, but without necessarily being characteristic. See my article, 'The
Griesbach Hypothesis in the 19th century', p. 57.

10 See his 'Ueber den gegenwärtigen Stand', p. 515. Ritschl appealed not to
redactional elements, but to 'Elemente, welche der einen Gesammt-
anschauung dienen'. However, the criterion is essentially the same.

11 Fuller, 'Baur versus Hilgenfeld', pp. 369f.

12 See Hooker, 'Christology and Methodology', p. 482; McEleney, 'Authenticating Criteria', p. 441.

13 See Cadbury, *Style*, p. 73: 'The starting point for any study of Luke's
method of using sources is a comparison of Luke and Mark.'

14 Farmer himself believes that many of the studies of redaction criticism on
Luke are still valid. Referring to Cadbury's work together with
Conzelmann's work on Luke's theology, he writes that their findings are

'not dependent on the two-document hypothesis (although both
Cadbury and Conzelmann have assumed it), but rather upon the
hypothesis that Luke used and modified texts that are found in Mark
and Q. But since substantially the same texts are found in Matthew, it is
possible to reach fundamentally the same results on any hypothesis

which recognizes that Luke may have used Matthew.' ('Criterion', p. 392; see too 'Notes', p. 301, with regard to Cadbury's work again.)

Nevertheless, this must be tested in each case: Luke's changes from Mark can only be viewed as changes from Matthew where Matthew and Mark agree.

15 Hawkins' lists of characteristic words and phrases in his *Horae Synopticae*, based primarily on total numbers of occurrences, are thus very valuable in this context.

16 See especially Carlston, 'Positive Criterion'.

17 Walker, 'Quest', p. 50.

18 H. E. W. Turner, *Historicity*, p. 68.

19 Cf. the similar remarks made by Fee, 'Modern Text Criticism', *Griesbach Studies*, p. 168:

> The real question is not whether it (the GH) can be falsified, any more than whether the two-source theory can (if indeed either could be; then of course we must look elsewhere). The real question is, which theory best explains the phenomena ... Although all things are theoretically possible, not all possible things are equally probable.

20 See Wilke, *Urevangelist*, p. 443; Lachmann, 'De ordine narrationum', p. 372; Weiss, 'Entstehungsgeschichte', pp. 680f.

21 Woods, 'Origin and Mutual Relation', pp. 66f.; Streeter, *Four Gospels*, pp. 157f. Such a form of argumentation is, of course, at best inconclusive: the fact that no reasons can be discerned by a modern critic does not prove that such reasons did not exist.

22 Stoldt, *Markushypothese*, pp. 129f., referring to Holtzmann, *Einleitung*, p. 347.

23 *Markushypothese*, pp. 185f., and see the whole section, pp. 184–201. Cf. too Farmer's similar criticisms of the circularity in the arguments of Schmid and others, which claim that Matthew and Luke have 'improved' Mark. ('Response', pp. 427f.).

24 *Markushypothese*, p. 201.

25 This is not necessarily so, since some features in one gospel may be identifiable as redactional independently of theories about the Synoptic Problem. For example, one can probably say that, on the basis of the total number of usages, τότε (90 − 6 − 15 + 22) is a favourite Matthean word, and ἀνήρ (8 − 4 − 27 + 100) is a favourite Lukan word, on almost any source hypothesis.

26 When redactional elements can be identified independently of one's solution to the Synoptic Problem (cf. preceding note), these can be used as a control on the otherwise circular argument.

27 *Synoptic Problem*, p. 200.

28 In *Matthew, Luke & Mark*, pp. 39–68.

29 *Evidence of Conflation*, *passim*.

30 'Marcion, Tatian, Mark', *passim*.

2 Mark's Duplicate Expressions

1 See Weiss, 'Entstehungsgeschichte', pp. 646–51; Holtzmann, *Synoptischen Evangelien*, pp. 280–4; Taylor, *Mark*, pp. 50–2; Neirynck, *Duality*, *passim*

2 Bleek, *Introduction*, p. 261.

3 De Wette, *Lehrbuch*, pp. 148f. He listed Mk. i. 11, 32, 42, 44; ii. 11, 13f., 19, 21f., 23f.; iii. 2; iv. 15, 21; v. 22f., 25–8; vi. 7, 14f., 36; viii. 27, 30, 33, 37f.; ix. 5f., 18, 22, 42; x. 29–31, 33f., 46; xi. 1–3, 15; xii. 1, 8, 11, 14, 26; xiii. 3f.; xiv. 1f., 12–16, 70.

4 Schwarz, *Neue Untersuchungen*, p. 293.

5 Bleek, *Introduction*, p. 262.

6 Wilke, *Urevangelist*, p. 446. Holtzmann, *Synoptischen Evangelien*, p. 114.

7 Wilke, *Urevangelist*, p. 446; Weiss, 'Entstehungsgeschichte', pp. 683f.; Streeter, *Four Gospels*, pp. 163f.

8 *Synoptic Problem*, p. 82; cf. Stanton, *The Gospels as Historical Documents* Part II, pp. 35f.

9 *Synoptic Problem*, p. 76; cf. Abbott, 'Gospels', p. 791.

10 *Synoptic Problem*, pp. 99f.

11 *Synoptic Problem*, p. 155.

12 *Matthew, Luke & Mark*, p. 14.

13 Dungan, 'Mark – The Abridgement', pp. 66f.

14 *Horae Synopticae*, pp. 139–42.

15 Sanders, *Tendencies*, p. 271.

16 *Horae Synopticae*, p. 139.

17 Cf. Allen, *Matthew*, pp. xxiv–xxvi; Cadbury, *Style*, pp. 83–90; Schmid, *Matthäus und Lukas*, pp. 64–9.

18 *Duality, passim.*

19 *Duality*, pp. 75–89.

20 *Duality*, pp. 112–31.

21 *Duality*, pp. 89–112. This classification into groups is Neirynck's own: see pp. 33–6.

22 *Duality*, pp. 94–106.

23 *Duality*, p. 35 n. 84.

24 Mk. i. 32, 42; ii. 18; iv. 21; v. 2f., 12, 14–16, 30; vi. 14–16; viii. 27; x. 46; xi. 1, 2; xiv. 27, 30; xv. 26, 42.

25 Mk. ii. 20; iv. 9, 30, 39; v. 14; vi. 11, 36; xiv. 1, 12, 47, 49.

26 Mk. i. 17; ii. 1; iii. 22, 28, 29; iv. 1, 19, 31 bis; v. 23, 39f.; vi. 3, 4, 6, 21, 45, 49f., 51; vii. 15, 18, 24, 41; viii. 4, 9–13, 17; ix. 2, 28; x. 6, 16, 38f.; xi. 11f., 13, 14; xiii. 3, 15, 19, 20, 21, 24, 34; xiv. 6, 18, 45, 54; xv. 16, 32.

27 Mk. i. 5, 39; iii. 33; iv. 5 bis, 40; v. 1, 13, 38; vi. 11, 32; x. 42; xi. 11; xii. 14; xiii. 28, 29; xiv. 25.

28 Mk. i. 21, 28, 31, 38, 45; ii. 4 bis; iii. 8; iv. 35; v. 11, 15, 19 bis, 33, 34, 38, 39, 42; vi. 30; ix. 38; x. 30; xii. 42, 44; xiv. 15; xv. 21.

29 Mk. i. 2f., 12; ii. 3, 25; iii. 13–16, 14–16, 16f., 21f., 26; iv. 7, 8 bis; 11, 15, 16, 39; vi. 35; x. 22, 24, 27, 30, 49, 52; xi. 15, 17, 27, 28, xii. 2, 14, 23; xiii. 33; xiv. 16, 35, 43, 61, 68; xv. 24, 44; xvi. 2.

30 Mk. i. 3; iv. 12; x. 47f.; xi. 1; xii. 16; xiii. 2.

31 Mk. iv. 17; vi. 1f., 45f.; x. 1, 8; xi. 24; xiii. 11; xiv. 3, 9, 22, 31, 33, 66, 71.

32 Mk. v. 15.

33 Mk. i. 45; ii. 4; iii. 5, 9, 31, 34; iv. 2, 38; v. 3f., 5 bis; vi. 25, 31, 51, 52. vii. 3, 3f., 17, 26, 33; ix. 12f., 26, 27, 33, 35, 48; xi. 4; xii. 23, 45; xiii. 1, 37; xiv. 52, 56f.; xv. 7, 19, 44; xvi. 8.

34 Cf. the criticisms of Wilke and Holtzmann noted above on p. 17.

35 *Synoptic Problem*, p. 82.

3 The Historic Present
  1 Cf. *Synoptic Problem*, pp. 122f. (Mark's use of ὅταν + indicative, and interrogative ὅτι), p. 130 (his use of κεντυρίων, κράββατος, θυγάτριον.)
  2 As Farmer himself says, *Synoptic Problem*, p. 122; but he still says that these affinities are 'interesting' (pp. 122 and 130) and hence, presumably, significant. What was said in ch. 1 about Semitisms applies equally well to Latinisms.
  3 Paul's letter to Rome shows the existence of an established church there.
  4 *Synoptic Problem*, p. 124.
  5 See *Synoptic Problem*, pp. 135f.
  6 *Synoptic Problem*, p. 136.
  7 *Ibid.*
  8 See *Horae Synopticae*, p. 213.
  9 Matt. ii. 13, 19; iii. 15; iv. 5, 6, 8 (two cases), 10, 11; viii. 7, 20, 32; ix. 28 (two cases), 37; xiii. 51; xiv. 31; xv. 12; xvii. 20, 25; xviii. 22; xix. 10; xxi. 16, 31 (two cases); xxvi. 52; xxviii. 10.
 10 Matt. viii. 4; ix. 6, 9, 14; xii. 13; xiv. 17; xv. 1; xvii. 1 (two cases); xxii. 16, 20; xxvi. 31, 36 (two cases), 38, 40 (three cases), 45 (two cases); xxvii. 38.
 11 Cf. *Synoptic Problem*, ch. VII. Matt. iii. 13; viii. 26; xix. 18, 20; xx. 33; xxi. 41, 42; xxii. 21 (two cases), 42, 43.
 12 Matt. xiv. 8; xv. 33, 34; xvi. 15; xxvi. 35; xxvii. 13, 22.
 13 Matt. iii. 1; iv. 19; xix. 7, 8; xx. 21, 22, 23; xxi. 13, 19; xxvi. 64, 71; xxvii. 22. In the majority of these there is no Lukan parallel. In xxi. 13; xxvi. 71; xxvii. 22, it is just possible that Mark could be following Luke instead of Matthew. But if he has used Luke here, then he has still avoided Matthew's very closely related version with its use of the historic present.
 14 Mk. i. 21, 30, 37, 38; ii. 4; iii. 3, 13 (two cases), 19, 20, 32; iv. 13, 36; v. 9, 15, 19, 23, 35, 36, 40, 41; vi. 1, 30, 31, 38 (two cases); vii. 32, 34; viii. 19, 20, 22 (three cases); ix. 35; x. 11, 24, 46, 49; xi. 4, 15, 27; xiv. 13, 51; xvi. 4.
 15 Mk. ii. 3, 5, 8, 15, 17, 25; iii. 4, 33, 34; iv. 1, 37, 38; v. 15, 39; vi. 45, 48; vii. 18, 28; viii. 1, 12, 17, 29, 33; ix. 5, 19; x. 1, 23, 27, 35, 42; xi. 1 (two cases), 22, 27, 33 (two cases); xii. 18; xiv. 13, 30, 45, 61, 66; xv. 2, 17, 20, 21, 24; xvi. 2, 6.
 16 Mk. i. 44; ii. 10, 14, 18; iii. 5; vi. 37; vii. 1; ix. 2 (two cases); xii. 13, 36; xiv. 27, 32 (two cases), 34, 37 (three cases), 41 (two cases); xv. 27. (These are, of course, the same texts as in n. 10 above).
 17 Mk. i. 40, 41; ii. 18; iv. 38; v. 7, 22, 38 (two cases), 40; vi. 1, 7, 50; vii. 5, 32; viii. 6; xi. 2, 21, 27; xii. 14; xiv. 12, 33, 63, 67; xv. 24.
 18 Mk. i. 12; iii. 31; iv. 35; x. 1; xi. 7 (two cases); xiii. 1; xiv. 7, 43, 53; xv. 16, 17, 22.

4 The Order and Choice of the Material
  1 See p. 6 above.
  2 See p. 13 above.
  3 See Butler, *Originality*, pp. 62–71.
  4 'Modern Developments', p. 280.
  5 'Modern Developments', p. 293.
  6 'Modern Developments', p. 294.

7   See *Synoptic Problem*, p. 209.
8   'Modern Developments', p. 293.
9   *Ibid.*
10 *Synoptic Problem*, p. 213. Cf. too Dungan, 'Mark – the Abridgement', p. 63.
11 Neirynck, 'Argument from Order', p. 792.
12 *Statistische Synopse*, p. 283. This depends, in part, on how one judges the relation of Lk. iv. 16–30; v. 1–11; vii. 36–50; x. 25–8 in relation to Mark, i.e. whether these are rearrangements of Mark, or independent versions.
13 *Origin*, pp. 10f. In view of this quotation, it is wrong of Dungan to cite Jameson in support of his theory that the phenomenon of alternating support for Mark's order is too much of a coincidence to be true, cf. 'Mark – The Abridgement', pp. 62f. See too J. A. T. Robinson, 'Wicked Husbandmen', pp. 458f.: 'A conspiracy theory is out of place.'
14 'Criterion', p. 389.
15 Cf. Fitzmyer's similar objections, 'Priority of Mark', p. 161.
16 *Synoptic Problem*, p. 236.
17 *Synoptic Problem*, p. 239.
18 'Modern Developments', pp. 284f. Already partly in *Synoptic Problem*, p. 236, but not given so much prominence there. The argument is not new: cf. Schwarz, *Neue Untersuchungen*, p. 275.
19 'Modern Developments', p. 285.
20 Cf. Schweizer, 'Theologische Leistung', pp. 340f.; Best, *The Temptation and the Passion in Mark*, p. 71. Farmer, 'Modern Developments', p. 285, says that 'this does not preclude an interest in Mark in Jesus as "Teacher"', but that 'Mark's "Teacher", like Aesclepius, does not deliver long discourses, rather he heals the sick'. But this still does not explain the editorial references to Jesus' specifically 'teaching' in Mk. i. 21, 22; ii. 13; iv. 1f.; vi. 6; viii. 31; ix. 31; x. 1; xi. 17; xii. 35.
21 'Modern Developments', p. 286.
22 *Synoptic Problem*, p. 81, cf. also p. 176.
23 'Criterion', p. 389.
24 Cf. Farmer, 'Fresh Approach', p. 41.
25 Cf. Kümmel, *Introduction*, pp. 59f.
26 Kümmel, *Introduction*, p. 60.
27 'Modern Developments', p. 283.
28 Cf. his article, 'J. A. T. Robinson and the Synoptic Problem', p. 351.
29 *Matthew, Luke & Mark*, p. 39.
30 *Ibid.*, p. 40.
31 *Ibid.*, pp. 48, 52, 66.
32 *Ibid.*, p. 48.
33 *Ibid.*, p. 66.
34 *Ibid.*, p. 66.
35 *Ibid.*, p. 45.
36 *Ibid.*, p. 49; cf. too pp. 43 and 66.
37 *Ibid.*, pp. 43, 48f., 66.
38 *Ibid.*, p. 58.
39 Cf. Held, 'Miracles', p. 256. Busse, *Wunder*, pp. 112f., points out that Jesus' power in his word (cf. 'hear' in v. 15), as well as his dependence on

God in prayer (v. 16), are also important for Luke.

40 Orchard, *Matthew, Luke & Mark*, p. 51, cf. also p. 59.
41 *Ibid.*, p. 50.
42 *Ibid.*
43 *Ibid.*, pp. 58f.
44 *Ibid.*, p. 51.
45 *Ibid.*, p. 60.
46 *Ibid.*, p. 52.
47 *Ibid.*
48 *Ibid.*, p. 61.
49 Taylor, 'The Order of Q', and 'The Original Order of Q', *passim*.
50 Orchard, *Matthew, Luke & Mark*, p. 61.
51 *Ibid.*, p. 62. Orchard gives Lk. xii. 49–50; xiv. 25–33 wrongly for the parallels.
52 *Ibid.*, p. 63.
53 *Ibid.*, p. 53. Schürmann's solution to the problem of the Lukan doublets is that Luke avoids them if the second half of the doublet is in his Markan source, i.e. Luke appears to be less familiar with his Markan source than with his other source. See Schürmann, 'Dubletten' and 'Dublettenvermeidungen'. However, such a distinction is not possible for the GH, since the Markan material is not necessarily part of a separate source for Luke.

5 Conflated Texts

1 *Evidence of Conflation*.
2 Abbott, 'Gospels', p. 791; Beare, *J.B.L.* 84 (1965), 296.
3 Longstaff, *Evidence of Conflation*, pp. 106–13.
4 *Ibid.*, p. 201.
5 Farmer, 'Modern Developments', p. 281.
6 Longstaff, *Evidence of Conflation*, p. 107.
7 *Ibid.*, pp. 107f.; cf. too the remarks quoted there of Sanders, *Tendencies*, p. 264.
8 *Evidence of Conflation*, p. 108.
9 *Ibid.*, p. 109.
10 *Ibid.*, pp. 106f.
11 *Ibid.*, pp. 19–22; cf. Kraeling, *Greek Fragment*.
12 *Evidence of Conflation*, p. 17; cf. Metzger, 'Tatian's Diatessaron', pp. 264f.
13 J. H. Hill, *Earliest Life of Christ*.
14 See Higgins, 'Arabic Version'.
15 Longstaff, *Evidence of Conflation*, p. 28.
16 *Ibid.*, pp. 28 and 109.
17 *Ibid.*, pp. 51, 55; 51f., 57. (The double page references are to Longstaff's commentary and to the place where he prints the texts synoptically.)
18 *Ibid.*, pp. 50 and 54f.
19 *Ibid.*, pp. 53, 54, 56, 57, 67, 68 (John); pp. 69f. (*Passio*).
20 *Ibid.*, pp. 68f. (John). Benedict's use of the *Passio* is more sporadic.
21 *Ibid.*, p. 58.
22 *Ibid.*, pp. 85 and 93.
23 For *Passio*, see *ibid.*, pp. 86, 94; 86, 95; for Benedict pp. 87, 95 etc.

24 Stenton, 'Roger of Howden and Benedict'.
25 See Gransden, *Historical Writing*, pp. 222-30; also Stubbs, *Benedict*, p. liv.
26 Longstaff, *Evidence of Conflation*, p. 105.
27 *Ibid.*, pp. 85f., 94.
28 Thus Roger clearly did not see the two accounts as the same. Cf. p. 44 above and n. 18.
29 Cf. Stubbs, *Benedict*, p. 9. See p. xxvi for the relationship between the MSS.
30 Longstaff, *Evidence of Conflation*, pp. 88 and 99.
31 *Ibid.*, pp. 87 and 96.
32 *Ibid.*, pp. 89 and 99.
33 *Ibid.*, pp. 91 and 103.
34 See the similar criticisms of Longstaff made by Throckmorton, 'Mark and Roger of Hovedon', in reply to Longstaff's earlier article, 'Minor Agreements'. Longstaff has now replied to this criticism (in 'Mark and Roger of Hovedon: A Response') by appealing once again to Roger's very varied method of conflation, and by referring to the examples given in his book over and above those given in his previous article. Nevertheless, all these examples have been examined above, and if the argument given here is valid, they do not justify the claim that Roger wove together sources in any intricate way.
35 Longstaff, *Evidence of Conflation*, p. 111.
36 *Ibid.*, pp. 64 and 67.
37 A third could be added on p. 96: at the note of Thomas edifying all with his conversation, rather than a careful comparison of sources (cf. p. 45, and n. 31, above), this is probably just a straight switch between sources, but it does occur at a point of verbal agreement between the two sources.
38 *Evidence of Conflation*, pp. 86 and 95.
39 *Ibid.*, pp. 90 and 101.
40 *Ibid.*, p. 112.
41 As Longstaff does in dealing with Mk. i. 32-4, *ibid.*, p. 152.
42 *Ibid.*, pp. 112f.
43 *Ibid.*, p. 39.
44 *Ibid.*, p. 138; cf. similar remarks on pp. 167, 178, 188, 200f.
45 Cf. p. 28 above.
46 Longstaff, *Evidence of Conflation*, pp. 200f.
47 *Ibid.*, p. 157.
48 *Ibid.*, pp. 155f.
49 *Ibid.*, pp. 154f.
50 See the detailed discussion of this pericope, pp. 96ff.
51 Longstaff, *Evidence of Conflation*, p. 157.
52 *Ibid.*, p. 181.

6 Patristic Evidence

1 See the criticisms on this point in the reviews of Farmer's *The Synoptic Problem* by Beare, *J.B.L.* 84 (1965), 297; F. C. Grant, *Interpretation* 19 (1965), 354; Snape, *Modern Churchman* 9 (1966), 189; Mitton, *E.T.* 77 (1965), 3; Nineham, *J.T.S.* 28 (1977), 549; also Fitzmyer, 'Priority of Mark', p. 135.

2 See his articles 'Mark – The Abridgement' and 'Marcion, Tatian, Mark'.
3 Farmer, 'Modern Developments', pp. 281f.
4 'Modern Developments', p. 288.
5 See 'Marcion, Tatian, Mark', pp. 184ff.
6 *Ibid.*, p. 192. Cf. Irenaeus, *A.H.* I.10.2; Tertullian, *De Praescr.* 32.
7 'Marcion, Tatian, Mark', p. 199.
8 R. M. Grant, *Earliest Lives,*, p. 12.
9 Cf. Kelly, *Early Christian Doctrines*, pp. 35–41.
10 'Marcion, Tatian, Mark', p. 200; 'Abridgement', p. 95.
11 *A.H.* III.11.7. However, the historicity of this is uncertain: von Campenhausen, *Formation*, p. 197 n. 250, calls it 'highly improbable'.
12 'Modern Developments', p. 290.
13 *Ibid.*
14 Eusebius, *E.H.* III.39.
15 Irenaeus, *A.H.* III.11.11.
16 In Eusebius, *E.H.* VI.14. For further examples of problems raised by the differences between John and the synoptics in the second century, see Merkel, *Widersprüche*, pp. 34ff.
17 One exception might be Clement's statement that the gospels with genealogies were written first (in Eusebius, *E.H.* VI.14): it is possible that this claim is an attempt to justify the reliability of Matthew and Luke in the face of criticisms about their conflicting genealogies (cf. Farmer, *Synoptic Problem*, p. 226). However, it is not clear how a claim that both gospels were written first would resolve the problem of their mutual differences. There is certainly evidence that the different genealogies caused problems for later Christians (e.g. Origen: see Merkel, *Widersprüche*, pp. 110f.), as well as providing the focus of attack for anti-Christian writers (e.g. Julius Africanus: see Merkel, *Widersprüche*, pp. 125ff.). However, all these examples date from a time much later than the date of composition of Mark postulated by the GH.
18 'Marcion, Tatian, Mark', p. 202.
19 'Modern Developments', p. 291.
20 Fuller, 'Neuere Diskussion', p. 145.
21 See *Synoptic Problem*, pp. 224f.
22 Irenaeus, *A.H.* III.1.1; Origen, *Comm. in Mt.* I.1; Eusebius, *E.H.* III.24; Jerome, *Prol. Quatt. Ev.*
23 *Synoptic Problem*, p. 226.
24 See *A.H.* III.9.1-11, 6; III.11.7 respectively.
25 *A.H.* III.1.1. For this as intended to be a chronological order, see von Campenhausen, *Formation*, p. 195.
26 *Adv. Marc.* IV.2.1–5; IV.5.3 respectively.
27 'Marcion, Tatian, Mark', p. 201.
28 *Synoptic Problem*, p. 225.
29 *A.H.* III.1.1. Cf. von Campenhausen, *Formation*, pp. 188f.
30 Von Campenhausen, *Formation*, pp. 254ff.
31 See Ac. xx. 35; Did. i. 2–ii. 3; viii. 2; ix. 5; 1 Clem. xiii. 2; xlvi. 8; 2 Clem. iv. 2, 5; v. 2–4; vi. 1; viii. 5; ix. 11; xii. 2; Barn. iv. 14; Ign. Eph. xiv. 2; Pol. ii. 2; Pol. Phil. ii. 3; vii. 2.
32 Cf. Massaux, *Influence de saint Matthieu*, pp. 647ff.
33 Note, however, the recent suggestion of Kennedy about Clement's precise

meaning here: 'The passage could also be understood as a tradition that the two gospels with genealogies . . . and also Mark . . . were *progegraphthai*, "written before". Before what? The Greek particle *de* in 6.14.6 can perfectly well associate Mark with the other two gospels rather than with John, which is specifically said to be the last in order; thus we have a contrast of the Synoptics with John.' (See his essay 'Classical and Christian Source Criticism', p. 150.)

34 See von Campenhausen, *Formation*, p. 244. A much later date has been proposed recently by Sundberg, 'Canon Muratori', mainly on the grounds that the attitude of the Canon to Hermas, Wisdom and Revelation has close parallels in the attitudes of Eastern church fathers in the fourth century to these documents. However, this is not altogether convincing. Alleged doubts about the status of Revelation may refer only to the Apocalypse of Peter. Further, von Campenhausen's points still stand, viz. that the relatively small number of Catholic epistles recognised by the Canon fits an earlier date better, as does the fact that the heresies mentioned are from the second century.

35 Cf. *E.H.* II.15; VI.14.

36 Cf. n. 22 above.

37 Eusebius, *E.H.* II.16; Jerome, *De Vir. Illus.* 8; *Ap. Const.* VII.46; Epiphanius, *Haer.* LI.6.

38 Cf. *E.H.* VI.14.

39 'Skeleton', p. 28.

7 The Minor Agreements

1 Sanders, 'Overlaps', p. 453.

2 *Four Gospels*, pp. 295–331.

3 Burton, *Principles*, p. 9 (201). However, it should be noted that for Burton 'conceivably' was meant ironically and he never included this possibility in his discussion. Farmer evidently takes the word literally.

4 See *Synoptic Problem*, pp. 78f., 83, 217.

5 Even if the 'concurrent testimony' is interpreted even more strictly to allow only material which is in the same order in both gospels, there are still unexplained omissions by Mark. See p. 30 above.

6 Farmer, *Synoptic Problem*, p. 217.

7 Cf. Holtzmann, *Einleitung*, p. 339; Morgenthaler, *Statistische Synopse*, pp. 301–3; Farrer, 'On Dispensing with Q'.

8 See Sanday, *Oxford Studies*, p. 21.

9 *Synoptic Problem*, p. 95.

10 *Ibid.*, pp. 139f.

11 *Ibid.*, pp. 136f. Farmer incorrectly attributes Sanday's theory to Abbott as well. Abbott believed that Matthew and Luke might have used a modified text of Mark; but he never claimed that this text was the work of a single editor. Rather, Mark's gospel might have gone through a number of stages of 'improvement': see his *Corrections*, p. 55. The theory of a single mind was peculiar to Sanday. See Neirynck, *Minor Agreements*, p. 18.

12 Sanday, *Oxford Studies*, pp. 21f.

13 Cf. Taylor, *Mark*, pp. 46–9.

14 See p. 24 above.

15 This is the argument of Goulder, 'Putting Q to the Test'.
16 *Synoptic Problem*, p. 137.
17 See Neirynck, 'Les accords mineurs', pp. 224ff.
18 Taylor, *Mark*, p. 48; Pryke, *Redactional Style*, pp. 79ff.
19 The anomaly is also noted by Thomas, 'Investigation', p. 105. See also Neirynck, *Minor Agreements*, p. 203.
20 N. Turner, 'Minor Verbal Agreements', p. 226.
21 So Schmid, *Matthäus und Lukas*, p. 104.
22 *Four Gospels*, pp. 298f.
23 Cf. Fitzmyer, 'Agein and Pherein', p. 156. Fitzmyer also points out the difficulty of seeing ἄγω as an older usage, with φέρω as a later development. Cf. Farmer's discussion, *Synoptic Problem*, pp. 128–30. Further, some of Farmer's (and Streeter's) statistics are corrected by Fitzmyer.
24 Cf. Taylor, *Mark*, p. 428. Farmer, *Synoptic Problem*, p. 161, says: 'the fact that the list does not conform to any particular Old Testament list of prohibitions, being rather the result of both selection and compilation, somewhat weakens the plausibility of this suggestion.' However, both Matthew and Luke do not have the one item on Mark's list which is not a command from the Decalogue. Farmer's comment is thus difficult to understand.
25 So Taylor, *Mark*, p. 468; Lohmeyer, *Markus*, p. 240; Grundmann, *Markus*, p. 235; Haenchen, *Weg*, p. 393.
26 For the details of this, see the discussion of the pericope of the cleansing of the temple in Part III, esp. p. 115.
27 See pp. 114f. below.
28 Taken as part of the original text of Mk. i. 1 by Lohmeyer, *Markus*, p. 9; Taylor, *Mark*; p. 152. Grundmann, *Markus*, p. 26, apparently takes it as not original, but recognises the importance of the title for Mark.
29 Farmer, *Synoptic Problem*, p. 120; cf. also pp. 110 and 143. Streeter, *Four Gospels*, p. 296.
30 Streeter, *Four Gospels*, pp. 180 and 295f.
31 *Ibid.*, pp. 169ff.
32 See the similar criticisms of Vaganay's use of the minor agreements in omission (in *Le Problème Synoptique*) by Levie,'L'Évangile araméen', 820–33. Levie shows how the omissions cause no decrease in the amount of information given.
33 Farmer, *Synoptic Problem*, p. 106.
34 *Ibid.*, p. 119.
35 *Ibid.*
36 Farrer, 'On Dispensing with Q', p. 62.
37 See Morgenthaler, *Statistische Synopse*, p. 303; Schramm, *Markus-Stoff*, pp. 72–7.
38 Cf. Hawkins, *Horae Synopticae*, p. 208; Streeter, *Four Gospels*, pp. 305f.
39 *Synoptic Problem*, pp. 105f.
40 Thomas, 'Investigation', pp. 105–7.
41 Cf. too Fitzmyer, 'Priority of Mark', pp. 145f.
42 See *Synoptic Problem*, pp. 131–9.
43 Morgenthaler, *Statistische Synopse*, p. 303, thinks that this is one of the passages where Luke used Matthew; Schramm, *Markus-Stoff*, pp. 99–103,

thinks that Luke and Matthew had access to a parallel source.
44 So Schmid, *Matthäus und Lukas*, p. 78; cf. also Neirynck as in n. 17 above.
45 *Synoptic Problem*, p. 134.
46 *Ibid.*, p. 228. Cf. Sanders, *Tendencies*.
47 See p. 24 above.
48 Streeter, *Four Gospels*, pp. 299f.
49 Cf. Neirynck, *Duality*, pp. 97–101.
50 For this distinction, see Neirynck, 'Les accords mineurs', p. 215; also McCloughlin, 'Les accords mineurs', p. 19.
51 For the historic present, see chapter 3 above; for the Mark–Q overlaps, see chapter 8 below; for the use of ἄγω see n. 23 above; for Mk. ii. 1–12, see above.
52 Streeter, *Four Gospels*, pp. 309f.
53 Farmer, *Synoptic Problem*, pp. 144f.
54 Cf. Taylor, *Mark*, p. 187.
55 Cf. Schmid, *Matthäus und Lukas*, pp. 88f.
56 Beare, *J.B.L.* 84 (1965), 296.
57 *Synoptic Problem*, p. 147.
58 *Four Gospels*, pp. 325–8. Streeter is following Stanton, *The Gospels as Historical Documents* Vol. 2, p. 149; C. H. Turner, *Study of the New Testament*, p. 47. He is followed by Schmid, *Matthäus und Lukas*, p. 159, and McCloughlin, 'Les accords mineurs', pp. 31–5.
59 *Synoptic Problem*, pp. 148–50.
60 Gundry, 'I Q Isaiah a 50, 6', p. 564.
61 Lohmeyer, *Markus*, p. 330; Grundmann, *Markus*, p. 303; Haenchen, *Weg*, p. 515; Schweizer, *Mark*, p. 327.
62 Cf. Suhl, *Funktion*, pp. 58f.
63 ῥάπισμα in NT only in Mk. xiv. 65; Jo. xviii. 22; xix. 3; in LXX only in Is. 1. 6. ῥαπίζω occurs only three times in the LXX; in the NT only in Matt. v. 39; xxvi. 67. ἐμπτύω in the NT only in references to Jesus' passion (Matt. xxvi. 67; xxvii. 30; Mk. x. 34; xiv. 65; xv. 19; Lk. xviii. 32); in the LXX it occurs in Nu. xii. 14; Deut. xxv. 9. ἐμπτύσμα only in Is. 1. 6.
64 See Streeter, *Four Gospels*, p. 326; Gundry, 'I Q Isaiah a 50, 6', p. 564. The shorter reading is accepted by Taylor, *Mark*, pp. 570f.; Schneider, *Verleugnung*, p. 39; Catchpole, *Trial*, p. 175.
65 Grundmann, *Lukas*, p. 418; Schneider, *Verleugnung*, p. 41; Catchpole, *Trial*, pp. 174ff.
66 Catchpole, *Trial*, pp. 180f.; cf. Lampe, 'Holy Spirit', pp. 177–80.
67 Streeter, *Four Gospels*, p. 327; Taylor, *Mark*, p. 571; Catchpole, *Trial*, p. 175. However, Goulder, 'Putting Q to the Test', p. 228, says that this meaning is 'unexampled in the NT'.
68 See Juel, *Messiah and Temple*, pp. 71f.
69 See Catchpole, *Trial*, p. 183. Juel, *Messiah and Temple*, p. 70, casts some doubt on the parallel, pointing to the fact that bar Kochba was asked to judge by smell. However, the basis of the test is Is. xi. 3, and it could be that this was put into practice in slightly different ways on different occasions. The smelling is not specifically part of the test, but only one way of putting the conditions specified into practice. Juel still recognises that there is 'a clear difference between the scene in Mark and the scene in Luke'.

70 Catchpole, *Trial*, p. 183; for the redactional nature of v. 65 see Schneider, *Verleugnung*, pp. 103f.

71 See *Synoptic Problem*, pp. 149f.

72 Indeed Jameson, *Origin*, p. 129, argued that Matthew's version is so incoherent that it cannot be secondary. Goulder's attempt to see Matthew as making Mark clearer here by adding the question also seems to founder because of the incoherence brought about by the simultaneous omission of the blindfold ('Putting Q to the Test', p. 227).

73 Arguments about Lukan independence from Mark also, in this case, show independence from Matthew, since Matthew too has the allusions to Is. 1. Cf. n. 63 above.

74 Farmer, *Synoptic Problem*, p. 150.

75 Schneider, *Verleugnung*, pp. 55 and 102f., postulates the existence of a common tradition. This, however, is not necessary, and the existence of a tradition which contains so little seems unlikely.

8 The Mark–Q Overlaps

1 *Four Gospels*, pp. 305f.

2 Devisch, 'Marc et le document Q', p. 60.

3 It was advocated by Wellhausen, *Einleitung*, pp. 64–79. He assumed that some direct relationship must be involved, and argued that, since Q is more 'developed' and 'Christianized', Q must be the later work. However, this theory is hardly convincing: it excludes *a priori* the possibility of independence, and also makes no allowance for Matthean or Lukan redaction. See the criticism by Harnack, *Sprüche*, pp. 136–57.

4 Honey, 'Did Mark use Q?'; Brown, 'Mark as Witness'.

5 Sanday, *Oxford Studies*, p. xvi; Streeter, 'St. Mark's Knowledge and Use of Q'; Burney, *Poetry*, p. 8; Dibelius, *Tradition*, pp. 259–65; Schulz, *Q*, pp. 182 and 254.

6 Burkitt, *Gospel History*, pp. 147–66; Streeter, *Four Gospels*, pp. 186–91; Throckmorton, 'Did Mark know Q?'; Grundmann, *Markus*, p. 9; Kümmel, *Introduction*, p. 70; Devisch, 'Marc et le document Q', p. 91.

7 Farmer, *Synoptic Problem*, pp. 221–3; also 'Fresh Approach', pp. 46f.; see too Orchard, *Matthew, Luke & Mark*, pp. 39–68, and the discussion in chapter 4 above.

8 Devisch, 'Marc et le document Q', pp. 65f.

9 See Devisch, 'Le document Q, source de Matthieu', p. 73.

10 Streeter, *Four Gospels*, p. 291.

11 Dungan, 'Mark – The Abridgement', p. 73. Cf. too Farmer, *Synoptic Problem*, p. 142.

12 Farmer, *Synoptic Problem*, pp. 248 and 272; also 'Fresh Approach', pp. 46f.

13 Cf. Jeremias, *Eucharistic Words*, p. 186.

14 Farmer, *Synoptic Problem*, p. 142.

15 *Four Gospels*, p. 306.

16 Cf. Wilson, 'Farrer and Streeter on the Minor Agreements'.

17 Sanders, 'Overlaps', p. 455.

18 *Ibid.*, p. 457 n. 6.

19 *Synoptic Problem*, p. 248.

20 Cf. Lohmeyer, *Markus*, p. 88.

21 Cf. Neirynck, *Duality*, p. 56.

22 Cf. *Synoptic Problem*, pp. 78f., 83, 217, 264.

23 Swete, *Mark*, p. 86; Lohmeyer, *Markus*, p. 88.

24 Matthew's construction is less abrupt because of the fact that the clause starts a new sentence.

25 In fact the use of ἀναβαίνει here is unusual: see Taylor, *Mark*, p. 270; Crossan, 'Seed Parables', p. 257, takes it as an indication of a pre-Markan source; Lambrecht, 'Mark IV', p. 300, takes it as redactional, as at iv. 8, where he claims that it is a case of (redactional) duality.

26 Cf. Jeremias, *Parables*, p. 31.

27 Sanders, 'Overlaps', p. 458. Note too that his method must count ὁ κλάδος as a triple agreement, even though it occurs in a different context within the Markan account compared with the other two.

28 Hawkins, 'Three Limitations', *Oxford Studies*, p. 51; Bartsch, 'Zitierung', claims that this is a conscious allusion in Mark, but this probably reads too much into the Markan text; Schramm, *Markus-Stoff*, p. 50, thinks that the two forms of the double question are independent.

29 Sanders, 'Overlaps', p. 460; Hawkins, 'Three Limitations', p. 53.

30 'St. Mark's Knowledge and use of Q', p. 173.

31 *Four Gospels*, p. 190. That the two parables were already linked in the pre-Markan tradition may be shown by the introductory καὶ ἔλεγεν, which seems to be non-Markan, as opposed to the more characteristically Markan phrase καὶ ἔλεγεν αὐτοῖς (cf. Jeremias, *Parables*, p. 14). The non-Markan nature of the phrase also renders unlikely any theory that Mark is freely re-writing his sources with rather more freedom than usual.

32 Lambrecht, 'Mark IV', pp. 293–6.

33 The argument becomes circular when later (p. 296) Lambrecht suggests that βάλῃ in verse 26 is an adaptation to the Q wording of the parable of the mustard seed (cf. Lk. xiii. 18).

34 Lohmeyer, *Markus*, p. 88; followed by Grundmann, *Markus*, p. 100.

35 'The Synoptic Problem Revisited', pp. 20–2 and 31–5.

36 Crossan, 'Seed Parables', p. 256. The size references are taken as later additions to the original story by Taylor, *Mark*, p. 270 and Schweizer, *Mark*, p. 104, among others.

37 Cf. McArthur, 'Mustard Seed', p. 199. Wenham tries to weaken the link between Matthew and Mark. He says that Matthew and Mark have nothing in common beyond the size references: Matthew 'is supposed to have conflated Mark and Q, but he appears to have preferred Q almost every time' ('The Synoptic Problem Revisited', p. 31). Besides ignoring the similarities noted above, this leads him into some ambiguity, since the differences between Matthew and Mark are said to be so great as to preclude dependence of Matthew on Mark, yet the similarities are apparently large enough to suggest dependence of Mark on Matthew.

38 Hawkins, 'Three Limitations', pp. 50f.

39 Jeremias, *Parables*, p. 102. See Matt. xiii. 24, 31, 33, 44, 45, 47; xx. 1; xxii. 2; xxv. 1.

40 In Acts the only occurrences are xiv. 11; xvii. 29, both strict comparisons of like with like.

41 Cf. Schürmann, 'Sprachliche Reminiszenzen', p. 206; see too Schmid, *Matthäus und Lukas*, p. 301; Schulz, *Q*, p. 299.

42 It is too a natural change: 'throwing' seed is unusual, so that a change by Luke would be unexpected.
43 Kil. iii. 2; Tos. Kil. ii. 8.
44 Cf. Jeremias, *Parables*, p. 27.
45 Suhl, *Funktion*, pp. 154f.; McArthur, 'Mustard Seed', p. 204; Crossan, 'Seed Parables', pp. 254ff.
46 Cf. Funk, 'Looking-Glass Tree', *passim*. The extraordinary aspects of the imagery are recognised by Jeremias, *Parables*, p. 149; and Schweizer, *Matthew*, pp. 306f.
47 For Luke's 'garden' as original, see Schürmann, 'Sprachliche Reminis-zenzen', p. 206; Schulz, *Q*, p. 299.
48 So most scholars: see Taylor, *Mark*, p. 269; Grundmann, *Markus*, pp. 99f.; Schweizer, *Mark*, p. 103; Schramm, *Markus-Stoff*, pp. 31 and 76; Haenchen, *Weg*, p. 171.
49 Sanders, 'Overlaps', p. 457.
50 See the discussion of the 'Lachmann fallacy' on pp. 6f. and 26f. above.
51 Farmer, *Synoptic Problem*, p. 224, regards Semitic parallelism as a good criterion for distinguishing primary traditions from secondary ones. However, the Gospel of Thomas and other apocryphal sayings of Jesus show that this criterion can only be used very circumspectly. Cf. Wilson's comment: 'Parallelism is a feature of Semitic usage, and is characteristic of many of the sayings of Jesus, but the mere occurrence of a parallelism is no criterion of authenticity. It may be due to mere delight in word-play on the part of a later redactor.' (Wilson, *Thomas*, p. 143).
52 Boring, 'Unforgivable Sin', pp. 261–5, gives a similar critique of the GH.
53 'Mark and the Relatives of Jesus', pp. 82–98.
54 *Ibid.*, pp. 87f. (the omission of the exorcism), p. 89 (the wording of the scribes' accusation) etc.
55 'The Relatives of Jesus in Mark'.
56 Crossan, 'Relatives', p. 87, thinks that Mark added verse 21, and adapted the charge made by the family to correspond formally with verse 22 (ἔλεγον ὅτι in both); but then in verse 22 he claims that the extra charge of madness, as well as demonic collusion, is an adaptation to verse 21 (p. 89). However, this makes both the accusations that Jesus is mad assimilations to each other. It is simpler to assume that only one at most of them is MkR and, in view of Mark's known proclivity for forming 'sandwiches', it is easiest to assume that verse 21 is MkR.
57 Crossan, 'Relatives', p. 86.
58 See Barrett, *Holy Spirit*, pp. 60ff.
59 Streeter, 'St. Mark's Knowledge and Use of Q', p. 171; Butler, *Originality*, p. 11.
60 Cope, *Matthew*, pp. 36–9.
61 *Ibid.*, pp. 39f.
62 *Ibid.*, p. 38.
63 *Einleitung*, pp. 66f.
64 *Son of Man*, pp. 118–20 and 312–18.
65 Cf. Wrege, *Bergpredigt*, p. 156.
66 See Holst, 'Reexamining Mk 3: 28f. and Its Parallels'.
67 Cf. Tödt, *Son of Man*, pp. 315f.

68 See Boring, 'Unforgivable Sin', p. 267; Holst, 'Reexamining Mk. 3', p. 124, also points out that Luke's πᾶς construction is probably redactional. Matthew's κατά is probably Matthean, cf. Hawkins, *Oxford Studies*, p. 40; Schulz, *Q*, p. 246. Although, as Boring says, the difference is negligible ('Unforgivable Sin', p. 266), it does give an instance where Luke's version is more original, and hence is not dependent on Matthew.

69 'Unforgivable Sin', pp. 267–70.

70 Cf. Colpe, 'Lästerung', p. 66.

71 'Overlaps', p. 460. He thinks that this is one of the passages where a theory of overlapping sources is justified.

72 See n. 68 above.

73 *Oxford Studies*, p. 45.

74 All these are taken by Schramm, *Markus-Stoff*, p. 46, as signs of Markan reminiscences in Q material. However, except for possibly (iii), the similarities seem too insignificant to infer this.

75 *Four Gospels*, p. 189.

76 This is worked out in detail above if Mark is third. Exactly the same result emerges if Luke is placed third: Luke must have abstracted from Matthew just those parts which are not in Mark. See Downing, 'Rehabilitation of Q', pp. 170–6.

77 'St. Mark's Knowledge and Use of Q', p. 168.

78 *Originality*, p. 112.

79 Cf. J. M. Robinson, *Problem of History*; Best, *The Temptation and the Passion*.

80 Cf. Butler, *Originality*, p. 113.

81 *Q*, p. 182.

82 See Keck, 'Mark 3: 7–12'; Weeden, 'Heresy'; Achtemeier, 'Isolation of Pre-Markan Miracle Catenae' and 'Origin and Function of Pre-Marcan Miracle Catenae'.

83 Sanders, 'Overlaps', p. 459 also agrees.

84 Cf. Butler, *Originality*, pp. 8f.

85 Schürmann, *Lukas*, pp. 467f.; Schramm, *Markus-Stoff*, pp. 24–6; Schulz, *Q*, p. 474.

86 Schneider, 'Bildwort'; Lambrecht, 'Mark IV', pp. 285–90.

87 Jeremias, 'Lampe', p. 237.

88 'Bildwort', pp. 188 and 197f.

89 Cf. Marxsen, *Mark*, p. 128.

90 'Lampe', p. 237.

91 'Bildwort', p. 199.

92 *Ibid.*, p. 194.

93 See Schulz, *Q*, p. 461.

94 So Lambrecht, 'Mark IV', p. 289; cf. Neirynck, *Duality*, p. 82.

95 Hawkins, *Horae Synopticae*, p. 14.

96 Burney, *Poetry*, p. 15; but see n. 51 above.

97 'Mark's Preservation of the Tradition', pp. 31f. If this is so, then the phrase καὶ ἔλεγεν αὐτοῖς would be Mark's own (cf. n. 31 above) introduction to the unit he has taken over from his tradition.

Part III. Some Particular Texts

Section A Selected Marcan Passages

Introduction

1 Farmer has recently stated that this approach is not particularly helpful. He says that such an analysis of the detailed wording in each pericope could never be completed since it would require too much time and effort; also there is no scholarly consensus that such an analysis could ever solve the Synoptic Problem. Rather, other considerations (e.g. the argument from order, external evidence, redactional factors) must be considered. (See his 'A Response to Roland Frye', in Walker (ed.), *Relationships*, p. 310.) However, these reasons seem to be scarcely sufficient for denying the value of such analysis. Clearly other arguments must be allowed their proper place. Nevertheless, if a source hypothesis is to be accepted as a viable solution to the Synoptic Problem, then it must be capable of explaining the detailed wording of the gospel texts of each pericope, as well as explaining other phenomena such as order. A hypothesis which fails to account for the detailed wording within each pericope can hardly be said to be satisfactory.

9 The Healing of the Man with the Withered Hand

1 See Longstaff, *Evidence of Conflation*, pp. 153ff., and the discussion of Longstaff's book above, esp. pp. 49f.

2 *Ibid.*, pp. 154f.

3 Grundmann, *Matthäus*, p. 322; Roloff, *Kerygma*, p. 63; Hübner, *Gesetz*, p. 130; Banks, *Jesus and the Law*, p. 126.

4 Cf. Barth, 'Law', p. 79; Hummel, *Auseinandersetzung*, p. 45, thinks that the Sabbath law still retains its validity here: 'kontrovers ist nur ihre Auslegung and konkrete Anwendung.' Cf. too Davies, *Setting*, p. 104: the argument in Matt. xii. 11 is 'designed to place beyond any doubt that Jesus was within the Law'.

5 See Lohse, art. σάββατον, *T.D.N.T.* VII, p. 14. Cf. Shab. xviii. 3; Yom. viii. 6; DeutR 10, and other texts cited in *S.-B.* I, pp. 622–9.

6 Matthew uses the more usual infinitive construction 12 times.

7 See the discussion in b. Shab. 128b; cf. Banks, *Jesus and the Law*, p. 126.

8 This is noted by Strecker, *Weg*, p. 19, who concludes that Matthew was a Gentile Christian unacquainted with Judaism. Hübner, *Gesetz*, p. 140, however, warns against reading later rulings back into the time of Jesus. Lohse, 'Jesu Worte über den Sabbat', p. 88, claims that the saying reflects a laxer Galilean viewpoint, but this is undocumented. Banks, *Jesus and the Law*, pp. 126f., and Roloff, *Kerygma*, pp. 78f., assume that Matthew is not arguing but is still being just as polemical as Mark; but then the illustration of the sheep has no relevance at all. It is assumed here that the sheep would be rescued, and that this implies (ὥστε) a legal justification for Jesus' actions.

9 *Rabbinic Judaism*, pp. 170–5.

10 *Ibid.*, p. 172.

11 It is taken as a *Gemeindebildung* based on Mk. iii to form a framework for v. 5 by Bultmann, *History*, p. 12; Lohse, 'Jesu Worte', p. 81; Roloff,

Kerygma, p. 66. That the whole pericope is of Lukan origin is claimed by Busse, *Wunder*, pp. 304ff.

12 Luke does use λέγω twice in this way in the same sentence in xii.16; xx. 2, but there is no parallel to his having three verbs, as here.

13 Cf. Cadbury, *Style*, pp. 170f.

14 See Kilpatrick, 'Scribes'. Cf. also Rehkopf, *Sonderquelle*, p. 95, who claims that νομικός is characteristic of proto-Luke. In his critique of Rehkopf, Schürmann, 'Protolukanische Spracheigentümlichkeiten?', p. 276, claims that it is characteristic of Q. This assumes that Lk. xiv. 1–6 is a Q passage, which Schürmann here asserts on the basis of the parallel in Matt. xii. 11f. (*ibid.*, p. 270). This, however, would be a circular argument here, and it may be that not all the pericope is known to Matthew. Nevertheless, both Rehkopf and Schürmann implicitly agree that νομικός is an un-Lukan word, and hence pre-Lukan.

15 Black, *Aramaic Approach*, pp. 168f.

16 Lohse, 'Jesu Worte', p. 87.

17 Hübner, *Gesetz*, p. 141. There is, however, some doubt about the precise interpretation of the text in CD xi. 16f., which at first sight appears to forbid the pulling out of a man. The text is emended in the translations of Ginzberg, Vermes and Gaster, so that this breach of the Sabbath law is explicitly sanctioned. Schiffman accepts the present text, but suggests that the point of the regulation is only to forbid the use of the various articles of equipment mentioned, rather than to question the basic principle of allowing work to be done in order to save life on the Sabbath. (*The Halakah at Qumran*, pp. 126f.)

18 *Weg*, p. 19.

19 See Hengel, art. φάτνη *T.D.N.T.* IX, p. 53.

20 Cf. too Roloff, *Kerygma*, p. 79; Busse, *Wunder*, pp. 308ff.; *contra* Lohse, 'Jesu Worte', p. 87.

21 11 – 2 – 2 + 1. See Hawkins, *Horae Synopticae*, p. 7.

22 Cf. Schürmann, as in n. 14 above.

23 See p. 153 below, on Matt. v. 18/Lk. xvi. 17.

24 6 – 0 – 1. Hawkins, *Horae Synopticae*, p. 6.

25 12 – 5 – 3 + 4.

26 Kilpatrick, *Origins*, pp. 110f. Cf. Matt. iv. 23; ix. 35; x. 17; xiii. 54; xxiii. 34.

27 Cf. Neirynck, 'Les accords mineurs', pp. 224ff.

28 90 – 6 – 15 + 21; Hawkins, *Horae Synopticae*, p. 8.

29 Only in Matthew; Hawkins, *Horae Synopticae*, p. 33.

30 So Taylor, *Mark*, p. 223.

31 Cf. the typically Lukan ἐγένετο construction.

32 Cf. Lk. iv. 15, 31; xiii. 10, 22; xix. 47; xx. 1; xxi. 37; xxiii. 5.

33 διαλογισμός is Lukan: cf. Hawkins, *Horae Synopticae*, p. 17.

34 For εἶπεν + πρός, cf. Hawkins, *Horae Synopticae*, pp. 45f.; Cadbury, *Style*, p. 203.

35 Schramm, *Markus-Stoff*, p. 112, points to πλήθειν (2 – 0 – 13 + 9), πρός with a verb of speaking, and the use of the optative.

36 Schweizer, 'Theologische Leistung', pp. 340f.; Best, *The Temptation and the Passion*, p. 71.

37 Neirynck, *Duality*, pp. 97–101.
38 Cf. Hawkins, *Horae Synopticae*, p. 13, for this as Markan; further, this is the only occurrence of the verb in Luke–Acts. See Farmer, *Synoptic Problem*, p. 228, for the criterion. The difficulty for the GH is noted by Longstaff, *Evidence of Conflation*, p. 167.

10 The Synoptic Tradition on Uncleanness

1 See *Synoptic Problem*, p. 243. All references here unless otherwise stated.
2 See pp. 10f. above.
3 Note too Paschen, *Rein und Unrein*, pp. 187–94, who says that Mark's list is not based on similar Hellenistic lists, but on Prov. vi. 16–19, and hence has its basis in the early Palestinian church.
4 So Grundmann, *Matthäus*, p. 374; Carlston, 'Things that Defile', p. 90.
5 McNeile, *Matthew*, p. 227; Schweizer, *Matthew*, p. 326.
6 Held, 'Miracles', p. 227; Schweizer, *Matthew*, p. 326.
7 *Synoptic Problem*, p. 243.
8 See the analyses of Bultmann, *History*, p. 17; Kümmel, 'Traditionsgedanke', p. 122; also 'Reinheit', p. 37; Taylor, *Mark*, p. 343; Carlston, 'Things that Defile', p. 91; Merkel, 'Markus 7, 15', p. 341; Paschen, *Rein und Unrein*, pp. 156–60; Dupont, *Béatitudes* III, p. 578; Hübner, *Gesetz*, pp. 164f.
9 So Banks, *Jesus and the Law*, p. 140; also Lambrecht, 'Jesus and the Law', p. 56, who does, however, recognize that the scope has been broadened. Berger, *Gesetzesauslegung*, pp. 463f., claims that v. 15 is the answer to v. 5, and that the discrepancy is due to the fact that v. 5 has been secondarily created to fit the answer in v. 15. However, one would then expect a better correspondence between question and answer.
10 Suhl, *Funktion*, p. 80; Berger, *Gesetzesauslegung*, p. 464; Banks, *Jesus and the Law*, p. 132.
11 See Bultmann, *History*, p. 17; Taylor, *Mark*, p. 339; Carlston, 'Things that Defile', p. 91; Banks, *Jesus and the Law*, p. 135.
12 Cf. Kümmel, 'Traditionsgedanke', pp. 123f. This is denied by Berger, *Gesetzesauslegung*, p. 493; Banks, *Jesus and the Law*, p. 136; Lambrecht, 'Jesus and the Law', pp. 54f., who all say that, at least for Mark, the point at issue was the contrast between written Law and oral tradition. This may be so, but it does not solve the historical difficulties.
13 Berger, *Gesetzesauslegung*, p. 498: 'Der jetzige Mt-Text kommt also dem ursprünglichen Mk-Text wieder näher', referring to the lack of Mark's vv. 3f. in Matthew.
14 Cf. McNeile, *Matthew*, p. 222; Barth, 'Law', p. 87: 'Matthew has immensely tightened up the section'; Cope, *Matthew*, p. 61: the whole section shows a 'demonstrable, logical cohesion'.
15 See Büchler, 'Purification'; Montefiore, *Synoptic Gospels* Vol. 1, pp. 133–44. However, common practice may have preceded the formal codification of the rule, cf. Banks, *Jesus and the Law*, p. 133.
16 For Matthew's version as stronger, see McNeile, *Matthew*, p. 222; Lohmeyer, *Matthäus*, pp. 244f.
17 As indeed the Jews were quite prepared to do, not only with the oral tradition, but also with the written Law: cf. 1 Macc. ii, where the Sabbath law is set aside in special circumstances. See Kümmel, 'Traditionsgedanke', p. 116.

18 So Lohmeyer, *Matthäus*, p. 246; Hübner, *Gesetz*, p. 176; Cope, *Matthew*, p. 56.

19 Kümmel, 'Traditionsgedanke', pp. 122f.; Hübner, *Gesetz*, p. 145. Cope, *Matthew*, p. 60, appeals to Kümmel for support for the view that Matthew's version is a coherent whole. But this answer only makes sense in Mark's version.

20 Cf. Bultmann, *History*, p. 147; Käsemann, *Essays*, p. 101; Perrin, *Rediscovering*, pp. 149f. For a discussion of the possible interpretations, see Merkel, 'Markus 7, 15', pp. 341–50.

21 Bultmann, *History*, p. 17; Carlston, 'Things that Defile', p. 91; Berger, *Gesetzesauslegung*, p. 464; Hübner, *Gesetz*, p. 168.

22 See Kuhn, *Ältere Sammlungen*, pp. 113f.

23 It is regarded as a Markan addition by Taylor, *Mark*, p. 343; Merkel, 'Markus, 7, 15', p. 354.

24 McNeile, *Matthew*, p. 226; Haenchen, *Weg*, p. 269.

25 *Matthew*, p. 58.

26 Cf. Haenchen, *Weg*, p. 269.

27 Also Berger, *Gesetzesauslegung*, p. 503.

28 So Banks, *Jesus and the Law*, p. 139; Dupont, *Béatitudes* III, p. 583.

29 *Gesetz*, p. 180.

30 Cf. Neusner, *Purity*, p. 62: Matthew is 'linking – and mixing up – two quite separate matters in his concluding summary'.

31 Cf. Schweizer, *Matthew*, p. 326: Matthew 'could not have written v. 11 if the community had not considered the OT dietary laws to be binding.' Cf. too Banks, *Jesus and the Law*, p. 139, who says that Matthew is just as comprehensive as Mark.

32 Crossan, 'Mark and the Relatives of Jesus', pp. 88f.; Lambrecht, 'Jesus and the Law', p. 44.

33 Cf. McNeile, *Matthew*, p. 221.

34 Cf. n. 8 above.

35 *Gesetz*, p. 177.

36 Cf. n. 23 above; also Hawkins, *Horae Synopticae*, p. 12. Kümmel, 'Reinheit', pp. 137f., denies that this is Markan, since its use here is 'übertragen' and not 'wörtlich'. However, it is difficult to see such a distinction here. In Baur's *Lexicon*, a metaphorical use is listed for Mk. iv. 29, but not here.

11 The Cleansing of the Temple

1 *Synoptic Problem*, p. 258.

2 Cf. *ibid.*, pp. 78f., 83, 217.

3 *Ibid.*, p. 259.

4 Kuhn, *Ältere Sammlungen*, pp. 200f.; Kümmel, *Introduction*, p. 86; Schweizer, *Mark*, p. 230.

5 Cf. Grundmann, *Matthäus*, p. 452; Held, 'Miracle Stories', p. 289; Catchpole, 'Answer of Jesus', p. 225.

6 *Matthew, Luke & Mark*, pp. 97f.

7 *Synoptic Problem*, p. 260.

8 In the first edition of his book, Farmer included the sentence: 'Matthew only represented Jesus healing in the temple, and that but on one occasion

(Mt. 21: 14–17).' This is rightly omitted in the second edition, but Farmer still leaves the sentence saying that Jesus's teaching daily in the temple had not been established by Matthew.

9 Neirynck, 'Urmarcus redivivus', p. 110, shows how Mk. xiv. 49 can easily be seen as a redactional summary of the events in chs. xi–xii. He is opposing the theories of Boismard that Mark is dependent on Luke here, but his remarks apply equally well to Matthew's account: Matt. xxvi. 55 acts as a perfectly reasonable summary of the earlier events, and there is no 'defective history'.

10 Farmer says that 'it would be very difficult indeed to explain the redactional history of Luke 19: 47–48 on the Marcan hypothesis because of its verbal agreements with Matthew 26: 55' (*Synoptic Problem*, p. 262), but this ignores the agreement between Matt. xxvi. 55 and Mk. xiv. 49.

11 5 times in Luke, 8 times in Acts.

12 The usage is confined to Luke of the synoptists: cf. Lk. xix. 47; Ac. xiii. 50; xxv. 2; xxviii. 17.

13 Hummel, *Auseinandersetzung*, pp. 17f.; Goulder, *Midrash*, pp. 13ff., 413; Bornkamm, art. πρέσβυς, *T.D.N.T.* VI, p. 659 n. 46.

14 Creed, *Luke*, p. 243; Schramm, *Markus-Stoff*, p. 149, points to the Lukanisms τὸ καθ' ἡμέραν, εὑρίσκω, τὸ τί ποιήσωσιν, λαός, ἅπας.

15 See p. 50 above, and the whole discussion in that chapter.

16 Taylor, *Mark*, pp. 48f.; 'Parataxis . . . is one of the most noticeable characteristics of Mark's style.'

17 For this as Markan, see Taylor, *Mark*, p. 48; Pryke, *Redactional Style*, pp. 79ff. For the criterion, see Farmer, *Synoptic Problem*, p. 228. Hunkin, 'Pleonastic ἄρχομαι', p. 392, lists this as only a 'doubtful' case of an auxiliary use; however, Doudna, *Greek*, p. 52, says that it is definitely quasi-auxiliary. There is a parallel in Mk. xii. 1/Lk. xx. 9.

18 Longstaff, *Evidence of Conflation*, p. 182. Farmer's suggestion, that this verse reflects scandalous abuse of pagan temples known to Mark's readers (*Synoptic Problem*, p. 261), is quite undocumented. It is hard to see how Jesus' words about the Jewish temple could be taken as having any relevance for pagan temples.

19 See Lohmeyer, *Markus*, p. 237; Haenchen, *Weg*, pp. 382–9.

20 See Roth, 'Cleansing of the Temple', p. 175; Jeremias, *Theology*, p. 145; Roloff, *Kerygma*, p. 96; Schweizer, *Mark*, p. 231.

21 Cf. Roth, 'Cleansing of the Temple', pp. 177f.

22 Cf. Abrahams, *Studies*, p. 84; Grundmann, *Markus*, p. 231. Barrett, 'House of Prayer', pp. 14f., mentions other possibilities.

23 Cf. Taylor, *Mark*, p. 463; Schweizer, *Mark*, p. 233; Haenchen, 'Johanneische Probleme', p. 39.

24 Schweizer, *Mark*, p. 230; Catchpole, *Trial*, p. 130; Roloff, *Kerygma*, pp. 99f.; Trocmé, 'L'Expulsion', p. 4; Barrett, 'House of Prayer', p. 14.

25 Cf. Best, 'Mark's Preservation of the Tradition', p. 26.

26 Haenchen, 'Johanneische Probleme', p. 41.

27 *Synoptic Problem*, pp. 261f. Longstaff, *Evidence of Conflation*, pp. 183f., regards it as very appropriate in its context, and therefore it is quite possible to see it as an addition by Mark. However, the same observations about this sort of argument apply as in the case of Orchard, noted above.

28 The idea of the eschatological journey of the Gentiles to Jerusalem may have been part of Jesus' view (cf. Jeremias, *Promise*), but it is not Mark's. Rather, Mark has 'historicized' the Gentile mission (cf. Wilson, *Gentiles*, pp. 30f.) by breaking the connection between the mission and the End. Cf. Mk. xiii. 10.

29 So most commentators, e.g. for Matthew, Strecker, *Weg*, p. 22; for Luke, Wilson, *Gentiles*, p. 50; for both, Haenchen, 'Johanneische Probleme', p. 41; Barrett, 'House of Prayer', p. 12. Trocmé, 'L'Expulsion', p. 12, thinks that the phrase is omitted because it is so un-Christian in its view of the Gentiles.

30 So Eppstein, 'Historicity'.

31 Abrahams, *Studies*, pp. 82–9; Barrett, 'House of Prayer', p. 16.

32 Cf. Buchanan, 'Brigands'.

33 Cf. Barrett, 'House of Prayer', pp. 18f.

34 Bultmann, *History*, p. 36; also Roloff, *Kerygma*, p. 91. Barrett, 'House of Prayer', p. 19, says: 'We can only say with confidence that the incident and the pronouncement both have deep, though divergent, roots in the tradition.'

35 Barrett, 'House of Prayer', p. 18.

36 Bultmann, *History*, p. 36. For 'teaching', see Schweizer, 'Theologische Leistung', pp. 340f.; for καὶ ἔλεγεν αὐτοῖς see Jeremias, *Parables*, p. 14, and Kuhn, *Ältere Sammlungen*, pp. 130f.; for the use of διδάσκω + λέγω, see Kuhn, *Ältere Sammlungen*, p. 138.

37 *Synoptic Problem*, p. 261; cf. too Longstaff, *Evidence of Conflation*, pp. 184f.

38 Taylor, *Mark*, p. 45; Pryke, *Redactional Style*, 103–6.

39 Cf. Roloff, *Kerygma*, p. 91.

40 *Synoptic Problem*, p. 262.

41 See Pryke, *Redactional Style*, pp. 44, 126f., 145; Lambrecht, *Markus-Apokalypse*, p. 33; Kuhn, *Ältere Sammlungen*, p. 137.

42 Cf. Farmer, *Synoptic Problem*, p. 228, for the criterion.

43 Cf. Trilling, 'Einzug'; Trocmé, 'L'Expulsion', p. 7; Catchpole, 'Answer of Jesus', p. 225; Roloff, *Kerygma*, p. 101.

44 Conzelmann, *Theology*, pp. 76f.; Grundmann, *Lukas*, pp. 369f.; Trocmé, 'L'Expulsion', p. 5; Catchpole, *Trial*, pp. 130f.

12 Tribute to Caesar

1 See *Synoptic Problem*, p. 262. All references to Farmer's views are to pp. 262–4, unless otherwise stated.

2 *Ibid.*, pp. 280–3.

3 Cf. *ibid.*, pp. 217–19.

4 Cf. McNeile, *Matthew*, p. 318; also Grundmann, *Matthäus*, p. 472, for the first.

5 Cf. Mk. iv. 38; Lk. x. 40; Jo. x. 13; xii. 6; 1 Co. ix. 9; 1 Pe. v. 7; 1 Macc. xiv. 42f.; Wis. xii. 13.

6 Cf. Schramm, *Markus-Stoff*, pp. 168f.

7 ὀρθῶς meaning 'correctly' is used 3 times in the NT, all in Luke (vii. 43; x. 28; xx. 21). It is used once elsewhere, in Mk. vii. 35, with the meaning 'distinctly, clearly'.

8 Cf. Sparks, 'Semitisms', p. 134.
9 Lev. xix. 15; Ps. lxxxii. 2; Mal. ii. 9; Sir. iv. 22; xxxv. 13; 1 Esd. iv. 35.
10 See Neirynck, 'La matière marcienne', pp. 179–93, who points out that many of the Semitisms occur in introductory verses, where other considerations often suggest that Lukan redaction has occurred.
11 See p. 66 above.
12 Cf. Kuhn, *Ältere Sammlungen*, p. 172. According to Pryke, *Redactional Style*, p. 136, all five occurrences of the word in Mark are in redactional verses.
13 Cf. Hawkins, *Horae Synopticae*, p. 12.
14 *Ibid.*, p. 33.
15 For the general inconsistency of Mark's use of the historic present on the GH, see pp. 24f. above.
16 Cf. Hawkins, *Horae Synopticae*, p. 14.
17 See Schmid, *Matthäus und Lukas*, p. 142. For Luke's preference for compound verbs, see Cadbury, *Style*, pp. 166f.
18 See Hawkins, *Horae Synopticae*, pp. 8, 33, 6 respectively.
19 Schmid, *Matthäus und Lukas*, pp. 141f.
20 Hawkins, *Horae Synopticae*, p. 18.
21 Conzelmann, *Theology*, p. 85.
22 Hawkins, *Horae Synopticae*, p. 19.

13 The Double Commandment of Love

1 Stated explicitly for this pericope by Farmer, *Synoptic Problem*, p. 252.
2 *Contra* Orchard, *Matthew, Luke & Mark*, p. 109; Burchard, 'Das doppelte Liebesgebot', pp. 48f.; Fuller, 'Doppelgebot', p. 319.
3 Orchard, *Matthew, Luke & Mark*, p. 109. The only similarity between Mk. xii. 32f. and Lk. x. 27 is in the identity of the speaker.
4 Cf. Hawkins, 'Three Limitations', *Oxford Studies*, p. 42; Hultgren, 'Double Commandment of Love', p. 373.
5 Manson, *Sayings*, p. 259; Jeremias, *Parables*, p. 202.
6 Bultmann, *History*, p. 23; Strecker, *Weg*, pp. 135f.; Haenchen, *Weg*, pp. 412f.; Schramm, *Markus-Stoff*, pp. 47f.; Burchard, 'Das doppelte Liebesgebot', p. 42.
7 See S. E. Johnson, 'Biblical Quotations', p. 147.
8 *Ibid.* Johnson also points out that there is some Western support for reading ἐν in the first phrase. This would then also eliminate the confusion in the prepositions. Cf. too Grundmann, *Lukas*, pp. 221f.
9 For the latter possibility, see Jeremias, 'Muttersprache', p. 272. Berger, *Gesetzesauslegung*, p. 182, suggests a conscious assimilation of Mark by Luke to 2 Ki. xxiii. 25. However, if this was Luke's aim, one might have expected him to omit the διάνοια phrase altogether.
10 Simpson, 'Major Agreements', p. 280.
11 So Hawkins, *Oxford Studies*, p. 43.
12 Dependence on Q is assumed by Strecker, *Weg*, pp. 26, 135f.; Taylor, *Mark*, p. 484; Haenchen, *Weg*, pp. 412f.; Grundmann, *Matthäus*, p. 476. Schramm, *Markus-Stoff*, p. 47, thinks there is a non-Markan tradition.
13 Burchard, 'Das doppelte Liebesgebot', p. 49; Schramm, *Markus-Stoff*, p. 48.

14 Linnemann, *Parables*, p. 142, though she thinks that Luke is dependent on Mark.
15 *Ibid.*, p. 142.
16 Cf. Burchard, 'Das doppelte Liebesgebot', p. 48.
17 *Ibid.*, p. 49.
18 That these were not integrally linked from the start is shown by the well-known change in the reference to 'neighbour', from one to whom love is shown, to one by whom love is shown. See Crossan, 'Parable and Example', p. 288.
19 Cf. Banks, *Jesus and the Law*, p. 166.
20 See pp. 98f. above for the non-Lukan nature of νομικός. For εἶπεν + dative as un-Lukan, see Rehkopf, *Sonderquelle*, p. 93. If Luke were redacting freely, one would have expected εἶπεν πρὸς αὐτόν.
21 Butler, *Originality*, p. 137; Black, *Aramaic Approach*, p. 117.
22 Black, *Aramaic Approach*, p. 117.
23 Butler, *Originality*, p. 137; cf. Jeremias, 'Muttersprache', p. 272; Goulder, *Midrash*, p. 125.
24 Stendahl, *School*, p. 75; Strecker, *Weg*, p. 26; Simpson, 'Major Agreements', 280; Berger, *Gesetzesauslegung*, p. 181.
25 See *S.-B.* I, pp. 907f.; Hummel, *Auseinandersetzung*, p. 52; Burchard, 'Das doppelte Liebesgebot', p. 60. It is presumably on this basis that Butler, *Originality*, p. 137, says that 'v. 40 is plainly Semitic and original'. Some have rejected this interpretation of v. 40 on the grounds that, if exegetical deduction is the point at issue, then there is no element of testing in the question, and this does not fit the stress on μεγάλη. (Cf. Barth, 'Law', p. 77; Banks, *Jesus and the Law*, p. 169.) However, the first objection assumes that the 'testing' reference comes from the same stratum of tradition as v. 40, and the second is simply Hultgren's observation (see above) that the question and answer do not fit very well together. This need only show that Matthew's version is not unitary.
26 Hultgren, 'Double Commandment of Love', p. 377.
27 *Ibid.*, p. 377.
28 Cf. Schulz, 'Markus und das alte Testament', p. 193: 'Dieser Reduktion auf das monotheistische Bekenntnis und die Gottes- und Nächstenliebe sind alle übrigen Gebote des Alten Testaments entweder unterzuordnen bzw. zu annulieren.'
29 Hummel, *Auseinandersetzung*, p. 51; Fuller, 'Doppelgebot', p. 322.
30 Similar attempts to alleviate Jesus' radicalism with respect to the Law can be seen in Matt. xii. 5–7, 11f.; xix. 1ff. Cf. also the opposition to any wholly negative views on the Law as reflected in Matt. v. 17; xxiii. 23.
31 Bornkamm, 'Das Doppelgebot der Liebe'.
32 Fuller, 'Doppelgebot', p. 321, takes μεγάλη as a Semitism and as part of Matthew's non-Markan source, but this seems unnecessary.
33 So Hawkins, *Oxford Studies*, p. 44; Streeter, *Four Gospels*, p. 320, but the textual evidence (1 118 209 e syr[sin] arm Or) is weak.
34 Fuller, 'Doppelgebot', p. 321, points to εἶς ἐκ = מִן אַחַד, the inversion of the subject and verb in v. 35, and the lack of verb in v. 36.
35 See Fuller, 'Doppelgebot', p. 321.
36 'Das Doppelgebot der Liebe', p. 92.

37 Cf. Trocmé, *Formation*, pp. 94ff.
38 'Das doppelte Liebesgebot', pp. 51–5.
39 'Das Doppelgebot der Liebe', pp. 92f.; followed by Barth, 'Law', p. 76; Lührmann, *Redaktion*, p. 32.
40 See Suhl, *Funktion*, p. 89; Grundmann, *Markus*, p. 250; Burchard, 'Das doppelte Liebesgebot', p. 42.
41 Cadbury, *Style*, p. 102.
42 Cf. Bornkamm, 'Das Doppelgebot der Liebe', p. 92. In fact Farmer himself asserts that Mark is using Lk. x rather than Lk. xx (*Synoptic Problem*, p. 252).
43 See especially 'Dublettenvermeidungen', p. 84. According to Schürmann, Luke generally avoids doublets when he comes across a doublet in his Markan source to material which he has already included from his non-Markan source(s).

14 The Woes against the Scribes and Pharisees

1 See *Synoptic Problem*, pp. 265f. All references here unless otherwise stated.
2 Cf. Manson, *Sayings*, p. 99, who includes this in his section on Q; also Schürmann, 'Dubletten', p. 341; Schulz, *Q*, p. 104. Schramm, *Markus-Stoff*, p. 29, thinks that there is a variant tradition, if not Q.
3 Orchard, *Matthew, Luke & Mark*, p. 137, says that a desire to avoid doublets is one of the reasons for explaining Luke's omissions from Matthew.
4 So Jeremias, *Jerusalem*, p. 244; Wilckens, art. στολή *T.D.N.T.* VII, pp. 690f.; Grundmann, *Markus*, p. 256 (partly).
5 Daube, *Rabbinic Judaism*, p. 125; Manson, *Sayings*, p. 231; Grundmann, *Markus*, p. 256 (partly).
6 Manson, *Sayings*, p. 231.
7 Rengstorf, 'Die ΣΤΟΛΑΙ der Schriftgelehrten'.
8 *Ibid.*, pp. 398f.; cf. Haenchen, *Weg*, p. 420.
9 Cf. also McNeile, *Matthew*, p. 331; Manson, *Sayings*, p. 230.
10 'Die ΣΤΟΛΑΙ der Schriftgelehrten', pp. 386f.
11 *Jerusalem*, p. 254; repeated in his *Theology*, pp. 144f., though he adds v. 15 to the second group.
12 See 'Matthäus 23', pp. 41f.; also *Weg*, pp. 419–21.
13 Jeremias, *Jerusalem*, p. 244.
14 Haenchen, 'Matthäus 23', pp. 41f.; for hypocrisy as the main charge in this chapter, *ibid.*, p. 58.
15 See Jeremias, *Theology*, p. 146 for ch. vi, though not for xxiii. 5.
16 Haenchen, *Weg*, p. 419.
17 For phylacteries, see Ex. xiii. 16; Deut. vi. 8; xi. 18. For tassels, see Nu. xv. 38; Deut. xxii. 12.
18 Haenchen, *Weg*, p. 421.
19 *Ibid.*, p. 420.
20 Cf. Manson, *Sayings*, p. 230. תפילין could = 'phylacteries' or 'prayers'.
21 Cf. too Ass. Mos. vii. 3ff., though there is uncertainty about who is addressed here.
22 Cf. Derrett, 'Eating up the Houses of Widows'.

23 Lohmeyer, *Markus*, p. 263; Taylor, *Mark*, p. 495.
24 Lohmeyer, *Markus*, p. 263; also Schweizer, *Mark*, p. 255.
25 Cf. Hawkins, *Horae Synopticae*, p. 136; Cadbury, *Style*, p. 148; Taylor, *Mark*, p. 495.
26 Cf. Lohmeyer, *Markus*, p. 264; Taylor, *Mark*, p. 494.
27 Cf. Haenchen, *Weg*, p. 421; Schulz, *Q*, p. 104, is undecided.
28 *Synoptic Problem*, p. 266.

15 The Widows' Mites

1 *Synoptic Problem*, pp. 267–70.
2 *Ibid.*, p. 269.
3 *Ibid.*, pp. 266f., quoting Dibelius, *Tradition*, p. 152.
4 *Tradition*, p. 153. Dibelius cites Diogenes Laertius' *Lives of Eminent Philosophers* II, 8, 69; V, 1, 19; VI, 2, 59, and he refers to similar examples in Lucian's *Life of Demonax* 12–62, and Xenophon's *Memorabilia* III, 13.
5 *Tradition*, p. 155.
6 *Synoptic Problem*, p. 268.
7 *Tradition*, p. 156.
8 *Ibid.*, p. 157.
9 *Ibid.*, p. 161.
10 Farmer's whole argument here is very close to simply appealing to greater 'specificity' as a sign of a secondary tradition; however, this was the criterion which he withdrew in the second edition of his book, *Synoptic Problem*, p. 228.
11 Schmidt, *Rahmen*, p. 277.
12 Cf. McNeile, *Matthew*, p. 342; Schweizer, *Matthew*, p. 448; Lambrecht, 'Parousia Discourse', p. 317.
13 West, 'Primitive Version', pp. 80–2. Also Matthew may have a more positive attitude to wealth (*ibid.*, pp. 86f., though West does not refer to this passage explicitly).
14 See pp. 10f. above.
15 Hawkins, Horae˙ Synopticae, p. 34.
16 Cadbury, *Style*, pp. 154–6. Cadbury's results all assume Markan priority. Farmer himself makes a blanket assumption that all Cadbury's work is still valid if one assumes only that all three gospels are mutually dependent, and that Luke is not first. (See 'Notes', 301). Nevertheless, this must be tested in each case: Luke's changes from Mark can only be viewed as changes from Matthew when Matthew and Mark agree. However, in this case, Cadbury's lists include many examples where Luke appears to feel obliged to 'apologize' for using foreign words or names, all of which come from Luke's special source material, so that they may indeed indicate a Lukan *Tendenz*.
17 Neirynck, *Duality, passim*; cf. the examples listed from this passage: βάλλω (pp. 80, 118), χήρα (p. 82), synonymous expressions in v. 44 (p. 105).
18 Cf. Cadbury, *Style*, pp. 84 (γαζοφυλάκιον), 85 (χήρα πτωχή).
19 Taylor, *Mark*, p. 497: 'In Luke's more elegant version the roughness of Mark's narrative disappears.'
20 Cadbury, *Style*, p. 151, speaks of a 'better and more compact sentence' in Luke.

21 *Synoptic Problem*, p. 270.
22 Cadbury, *Style*, p. 142.
23 *Ibid.*, pp. 176f.
24 *Ibid.*, p. 193.
25 Taylor, *Mark*, p. 60. Cf. Mk. v. 22; x. 17; xii. 42; xiv. 47, 66.
26 Cadbury, *Style*, p. 169; Hawkins, *Horae Synopticae*, p. 39.
27 Mk. iii. 13, 23; vi. 7; x. 42; xii. 43. See Taylor, *Mark*, p. 229; Kuhn, *Ältere Sammlungen*, p. 159 (though he takes this as the one pre-Markan use of προσκαλέομαι).
28 Cf. Grundmann, *Lukas*, p. 377.

Section B. The Double Tradition

Introduction

1 See de Wette, *Lehrbuch*, pp. 150ff.; Bleek, *Introduction*, pp. 279f.
2 See Farmer, *Synoptic Problem*, pp. 20, 40; also Dungan, 'Mark – The Abridgement', p. 75.
3 See 'Modern Developments', pp. 280, 293.
4 See p. 28 above.
5 *Synoptic Problem*, p. 220. See the argument in 'Steps X–XIII', on pp. 220–5.
6 'Fresh Approach'.
7 *Matthew, Luke & Mark*, p. 34. For a discussion of Orchard's work, see Part II, chapter 4 above.
8 E.g. Streeter, *Four Gospels*, p. 183; Kümmel, *Introduction*, p. 64.
9 'Fresh Approach', p. 41; see also Orchard, *Matthew, Luke & Mark*, p. 20.
10 'Fresh Approach', pp. 41, 47; also *Synoptic Problem*, pp. 248, 272.

16 Wisdom Motifs in the Double Tradition

1 See *Synoptic Problem*, pp. 203, 207. He refers to the whole section Matt. xi. 2-19/Lk. vii. 18-35.
2 See Creed, *Luke*, p. 108; Schürmann, *Lukas*, p. 420; Suggs, *Wisdom*, p. 35; Christ, *Jesus Sophia*, p. 35.
3 A common source is accepted by Grundmann, *Matthäus*, p. 457; Strecker, *Weg*, p. 153; Wink, *John the Baptist*, p. 18; Hummel, *Auseinandersetzung*, pp. 23f.; Lührmann, *Redaktion*, p. 28. All these assume that it is a Q saying. This is denied by Manson, *Sayings*, p. 70; Hoffmann, *Studien*, pp. 194f.
4 10 times in Luke, 6 in Acts; cf. Hawkins, *Horae Synopticae*, p. 45; Conzelmann, *Theology*, p. 164. Schürmann, *Lukas*, p. 423; Hoffmann, *Studien*, pp. 194f.
5 0 - 0 - 2 + 8. Schürmann, *Lukas*, p. 422; Christ, *Jesus Sophia*, p. 78; Hoffmann, *Studien*, pp. 194f.
6 Cf. Hoffmann, *Studien*, p. 194; Goulder, *Midrash*, p. 358.
7 Cf. Schrenk, art. δικαιόω, *T.D.N.T.* II, p. 214; Manson, *Sayings*, p. 70. See Ps. Sol. ii. 16; iii. 3, 5; iv. 9; viii. 7, 27. Rehkopf, *Sonderquelle*, p. 93, says that it is proto-Lukan. Schürmann, 'Protolukanische Spracheigentümlichkeiten', p. 275, says that it is characteristic of Q, and also not unusual enough to justify Rehkopf's claims, since the word occurs frequently elsewhere, including Acts; but this latter point ignores the

special nuance of the word here. Also, even if it is characteristic of only Q, it appears to be pre-Lukan, and hence not redactional.

8 See pp. 131, 100 above for Lk. x. 25 and Lk. xiv. 3 being 'double tradition' passages. The other occurrences are Lk. xi. 45, 46, 52 in a context which is clearly part of the double tradition.

9 Cf. Farmer, *Synoptic Problem*, p. 224; but see p. 86 and n. 51 above.

10 See Schrenk, art. δικαιόω, *T.D.N.T.* II, pp. 198f.; Barth, 'Law', pp. 138f.; Strecker, *Weg*, pp. 149ff.

11 See Strecker, *Weg*, p. 153; Goulder, *Midrash*, p. 414; Merkel, 'Ungleichen Söhnen', p. 256. Goulder and Merkel believe that the whole parable is a Matthean construct.

12 See Grundmann, *Matthäus*, p. 457; Schweizer, *Matthew*, p. 410; Jeremias, *Parables*, pp. 80f. Jeremias thinks that v. 32 is a secondary addition, but believes that it must be pre-Matthean, since Matthew's reason for putting the parable here is the link with the preceding pericope via the theme of John. Against this, the link could easily be that both this and the following parable are vineyard parables, and this would account for the positioning here. See Hummel, *Auseinandersetzung*, p. 23; Schürmann, *Lukas*, p. 422.

13 Catchpole, 'On Doing Violence', p. 56, also points to possible reminiscences of the Matt. xi/Lk. vii context in Matt. xxi. 32. (For 'John came', cf. Lk. vii. 33; for 'way', cf. Lk. vii. 27). This adds further support for the theory that the Lukan context for the saying in Matt. xxi. 32/Lk. vii. 29f. is more original.

14 Strecker, *Weg*, p. 153.

15 So Lührmann, *Redaktion*, pp. 29f.; Schürmann, *Lukas*, p. 428; Christ, *Jesus Sophia*, p. 76; Suggs, *Wisdom*, p. 37; Schweizer, *Matthew*, p. 265; Goulder, *Midrash*, p. 358.

16 For the theory that this is an identification, see Christ, *Jesus Sophia*, p. 76; Suggs, *Wisdom*, pp. 56f. Strecker, *Weg*, p. 102, says that the claim of Jesus is that of Wisdom.

17 See Conzelmann, *Theology*, pp. 191–3; Achtemeier, 'Lukan Miracles'.

18 So most scholars: see Schmid, *Matthäus und Lukas*, p. 286; Strecker, *Weg*, p. 102; Lührmann, *Redaktion*, pp. 29f.; Schürmann, *Lukas*, p. 428; Hoffmann, *Studien*, p. 198.

19 Hoffmann, *Studien*, p. 197; Schulz, *Q*, p. 380.

20 Catchpole, 'Tradition History', p. 169.

21 *Contra* Bultmann, 'Hintergrund', p. 15; Suggs, *Wisdom*, p. 55.

22 Prov. viii. 32; Sir. iv. 11; xv. 11. See Wilckens, *Weisheit*, p. 198; Lührmann, *Redaktion*, pp. 29f.; Catchpole, 'Tradition History', p. 170.

23 Wilckens, *Weisheit*, p. 198; Hoffmann, *Studien*, p. 229; Schulz, *Q*, p. 386.

24 See Schmid, *Matthäus und Lukas*, p. 285; Schrenk, art. βιάζομαι, *T.D.N.T.* I, pp. 609–13; Barth, 'Law', p. 63; Strecker, *Weg*, pp. 167f.; Hoffmann, *Studien*, p. 51; Schulz, *Q*, p. 262; Kümmel, 'Lukas 16, 16', pp. 95f.

25 Dupont, *Béatitudes* III, pp. 166f. For v. 18 as very radical in relation to the Law, see Catchpole, 'Divorce Material', p. 112.

26 Cf. Hübner, *Gesetz*, pp. 20f.

27 See Trilling, 'Täufertradition', p. 279, followed by Barth, 'Law', p. 63; Strecker, *Weg*, p. 167; Schulz, *Q*, p. 261; Kümmel, 'Lukas 16, 16', p. 97; Hübner, *Gesetz*, p. 28.

28 Lührmann, *Redaktion*, pp. 27f., claims that the explicit Matthean interpretation only comes in v. 14, but this ignores the MattR in v. 12. Cf. Catchpole, 'Tradition History', p. 179, and 'On Doing Violence', pp. 52f. A similar criticism applies to Hoffmann, who argues that Matthew is more original here, and that it is Luke who alters the saying to fit his theme of *Heilsgeschichte (Studien*, pp. 51-60). He claims that a change by Luke is easily explicable since, for Luke, the era of fulfilment begins with Jesus, not with John. This relies very heavily on the theories of Conzelmann about Luke's view of John, and these are not at all certain. A detailed consideration of the material in Luke about John, including the birth stories, would suggest that John belongs within the era of fulfilment. See Wink, *John the Baptist*, pp. 51-7; Kümmel, 'Lukas 16, 16', pp. 98-102. For further criticisms of Hoffmann, see Catchpole, 'On Doing Violence', pp. 52f.

29 See Trilling, *Israel*, p. 169, who offers arguments against Jeremias' view that this is characteristic of Jesus himself, cf. Jeremias, 'Kennzeichen', pp. 89-93. See too Banks, *Jesus and the Law*, p. 213; Meier, *Law*, p. 58.

30 So Barth, 'Law', p. 66; Strecker, *Weg*, p. 143; Trilling, *Israel*, p. 168; Dupont, *Béatitudes* I, pp. 134-6; Wrege, *Bergpredigt*, p. 38; Banks, *Jesus and the Law*, p. 215; Meier, *Law*, p. 58.

31 This casts some doubt on the theory of Bultmann, *History*, p. 138, that vv. 17 and 18f. are from the same stratum of the tradition. See Barth, 'Law', p. 67; Strecker, *Weg*, pp. 143ff.

32 So Schweizer, 'Matth. 5, 17-20'; for the link of 17 with 18*d*, see too Barth, 'Law', p. 70; Wrege, *Bergpredigt*, p. 38; Trilling, *Israel*, p. 170.

33 For this as the meaning of the original logion, see Kümmel, 'Traditionsgedanke', pp. 127f.; Barth, 'Law', p. 65; Trilling, *Israel*, p. 168; Banks, *Jesus and the Law*, pp. 214f. Hübner, *Gesetz*, p. 21, sees here two independent versions, since Luke's is not couched in temporal terms; however, this probably drives too deep a wedge between the two versions: both assert the abiding validity of the Law. Meier, *Law*, p. 59, sees Luke's version as due to LkR, implying that the Law will change, though only with great eschatological travail. However, the lack of temporal reference here seems to make this difficult. Meier points to Lk. xvi. 18 as inconsistent with the view that the Law is immutable, but this need only imply that vv. 17 and 18 come from different strata in the tradition. Meier's interpretation would perhaps fit Matthew's version better than Luke.

34 *Contra* Jervell, 'Law'. Luke records two extra Sabbath healing stories, the story of Cornelius, and he presents Paul's circumcision of Timothy as simply a conciliatory act to placate the Jews.

35 Cf. Hoffmann, *Studien*, p. 170, and his review of Schulz' book in *B.Z.* 19 (1975), p. 114.

36 See pp. 98-100 above.

37 Schürmann, 'Mt 5, 19', *passim*.

38 Luke likes φιλ-compounds; ὑπάρχω is Lukan (3 - 0 - 15 + 25); ἐκμυκτηρίζω occurs only here and at Lk. xxiii. 35 in the NT; Luke is also prone to making such transitional sentences. See Dupont, *Béatitudes* III, pp. 62f; Kümmel, 'Lukas 16, 16', p. 91.

39 Schürmann, 'Mt 5, 19', p. 242; cf. Strecker, *Weg*, p. 145; Hübner, *Gesetz*,

p. 23. Dupont, *Béatitudes* I, p. 138, also points out the change in vocabulary (λύω for καταλύω, ἐντολαί for νόμος) which suggests a seam between v. 19 and what precedes.

40 Trilling, *Israel*, pp. 182f.; Hummel, *Auseinandersetzung*, p. 67; Wrege, *Bergpredigt*, p. 41; Dupont, *Béatitudes* I, p. 138.

41 Schürmann, 'Mt 5, 19', pp. 248f., says that Luke retained v. 17 to act as an introduction to v. 18 which he wanted to retain, but that Matt. v. 19 was too nomistic for him. However, Matt. v. 19 is less nomistic than Lk. xvi. 17: see Hübner, *Gesetz*, pp. 24f.; Meier, *Law*, p. 103.

42 Schürmann, 'Mt 5, 19', p. 244.

43 Dupont, *Béatitudes* III, p. 164 n. 1, and other authors cited there.

44 *Ibid.*, p. 165.

45 Schürmann, 'Mt 5, 19', p. 247: '... das eigentliche Interesse des Luk deutlich die in 16, 1–13 (14). 16–31 erkennbare Armutsfrage ist, keineswegs aber die Gesetzesfrage.'

46 *Ibid.*, p. 247.

47 Hoffmann, *Studien*, p. 54.

48 This implies at least a two-stage development in the 'Q' material, as Schulz does. However, Schulz does not think that the Q community, even in its later stage, relinquished its firm adherence to the Law; in fact, he attributes the divorce saying to the first stage of the Q redaction (*Q*, pp. 166ff.) as well as the previous saying. See Hübner, *Gesetz*, p. 31, for a similar reconstruction of the development of the tradition here.

49 Cf. Schmid, *Matthäus und Lukas*, p. 284; Trilling, 'Täufertradition', pp. 275f.

50 Schürmann, *Lukas*, p. 426; Hoffman, *Studien*, p. 197; Schulz, *Q*, pp. 379f.

51 Jeremias, *Parables*, p. 27; Schürmann, *Lukas*, p. 424; Hoffmann, *Studien*, p. 197; Schulz, *Q*, p. 379.

52 Cf. Bultmann, *History*, p. 172; Lührmann, *Redaktion*, p. 29; Schulz, *Q*, pp. 380f.

53 Cf. Dodd, *Parables*, p. 25; Jeremias, *Parables*, p. 162.

54 Linton, 'Children's Game', suggests that the Jews correspond to the first group, and that the piping and wailing correspond to their complaints against Jesus and John. But there is nothing in the parable to suggest that the piping and wailing are in themselves bad: the fault seems to lie in the lack of response by the other group(s).

55 Cf. Hoffmann, *Studien*, p. 226, but he still separates parable and interpretation. This seems unnecessary for the Lukan version: there is a good correspondence between the children in the story and the Jews who reject Jesus and John.

56 The best solution seems to be that of Hare, *Jewish Persecutions*, p. 91: the reference may have been in Q when the saying was still attributed to Wisdom, and hence looked forward to the fate of Jesus.

57 Cf. Kilpatrick, *Origins*, p. 110; Strecker, *Weg*, p. 30; Hummel, *Auseinandersetzung*, p. 29.

58 Cf. Chapman, 'Zacharias', p. 408.

59 For all these small details, see Steck, *Geschick der Propheten*, pp. 31f.; Schulz, *Q*, pp. 337f.

60 Cf. Bultmann, *History*, p. 114; Schmid, *Matthäus und Lukas*, p. 331;

Haenchen, 'Matthäus 23', p. 53; Wilckens, art. σοφία, *T.D.N.T.* VII, p. 515; Strecker, *Weg*, p. 30; Steck, *Geschick der Propheten*, p. 29; Lührmann, *Redaktion*, p. 46; Suggs, *Wisdom*, p. 14; Hoffmann, *Studien*, p. 164; Schulz, *Q*, p. 336.

61 Kümmel, *Promise*, p. 80.
62 Goulder, *Midrash*, p. 428.
63 Cf. Lk. i. 70; Ac. ii. 17; iii. 18, 21, 22; vii. 37, 48f., xiii. 20.
64 Lk. i. 15-17; i. 67; Ac. ii. 18; xix. 6; xxvii. 25.
65 Cf. Suggs, *Wisdom*, passim.
66 Cf. the contrast αὐτοὶ μέν ... ὑμεῖς δέ in v. 48.
67 Cf. Chapman, 'Zacharias', pp. 407f.; Steck, *Geschick der Propheten*, pp. 33-40; Grundmann, *Lukas*, pp. 249f.; Hoffmann, *Studien*, p. 165; Schulz, *Q*, p. 344.
68 Steck, *Geschick der Propheten*, p. 29, also points out that the lack of article here is un-Lukan.
69 For 'scribes', cf. Matt. xiii. 52: see Hummel, *Auseinandersetzung*, p. 27; Strecker, *Weg*, pp. 29-31. 'Wise men' are harder to parallel. For Matthew as secondary here, see Steck, *Geschick der Propheten*, pp. 29f. Christ, *Jesus Sophia*, p. 122; Schulz, *Q*, pp. 336f.
70 So Steck, *Geschick der Propheten*, pp. 39f. Steck also answers objections about the slight discrepancies involved in this identification.
71 *Ibid.*, p. 32.
72 *Studien*, pp. 166-8; cf. too Lührmann, *Redaktion*, p. 47.
73 Cf. Lührmann, *Redaktion*, pp. 24-48.
74 Schulz, *Q*, p. 339, refers to the Lukan text 'der ... ohne redaktionelle Überarbeitungen die Q-Tradition repräsentiert'.
75 This is also one of the passages listed by Farmer, *Synoptic Problem*, p. 207, as exhibiting a degree of verbal similarity which suggests direct copying.
76 See Lindars, *Apologetic*, p. 172; Suggs, *Wisdom*, p. 70, for this as the true reading.
77 Lk. xii. 50; xiii. 8, 21; xv. 8; xxii. 16, 18; xxiv. 49; Ac. xxi. 26; xxiii. 12, 14, 21; xxv. 21. See Steck, *Geschick der Propheten*, p. 50; Schulz, *Q*, p. 346. The future is also unique in Luke.
78 Cf. Bultmann, *History*, pp. 114f.; Grundmann, *Lukas*, p. 287; Wilckens, *Weisheit*, pp. 163f.
79 Cf. Haenchen, 'Matthäus 23', p. 57; Steck, *Geschick der Propheten*, pp. 230ff.; Schulz, *Q*, p. 347.
80 Bultmann, *History*, p. 114.
81 Steck, *Geschick der Propheten*, p. 230; Christ, *Jesus Sophia*, p. 138.
82 Haenchen, 'Matthäus 23', p. 56; Steck, *Geschick der Propheten*, p. 47; Schulz, *Q*, p. 347.
83 Suggs, *Wisdom*, p. 65.
84 Lindars, *Apologetic*, p. 173; Suggs, *Wisdom*, p. 70.
85 So Grundmann, *Lukas*, p. 290.
86 It is this which provides the link with the previous saying, cf. Conzelmann, *Theology*, p. 133; Lührmann, *Redaktion*, p. 45; Schulz, *Q*, p. 347.
87 *Geschick der Propheten*, pp. 227, 232.
88 Haenchen, 'Matthäus 23', pp. 55f.; Strecker, *Weg*, p. 113; Steck, *Geschick der Propheten*, p. 293. For Matthew's γάρ as redactional, see Schmid,

Matthäus und Lukas, p. 334; Strecker, *Weg*, p. 114; Steck, *Geschick der Propheten*, p. 50; Schulz, *Q*, p. 346.

89 Cf. Strecker, *Weg*, p. 113. Cf. Matt. i. 23; xviii. 19f.; xxviii. 20.
90 Steck, *Geschick der Propheten*, pp. 107, 224f.; Schulz, *Q*, p. 340.
91 See 'Hintergrund', pp. 15–18; followed by Wilckens, art. σοφία *T.D.N.T.* VII, p. 516; Suggs, *Wisdom, passim*; Schulz, *Q*, pp. 340, 386.
92 M. D. Johnson, 'Wisdom Approach'.
93 *Ibid.*, pp. 45–53.
94 Johnson plays down the importance of the idea, even in the New Testament.
95 Wilckens, art. σοφία, *T.D.N.T.* VII, p. 514.
96 See, for example, the discussion above on νομικός, ναὶ λέγω ὑμῖν, δικαιόω.

17 The Apocalyptic Discourses

1 *Synoptic Problem*, pp. 271–8.
2 *Ibid.*, pp. 271–3.
3 Cf. Klostermann, *Lukas*, p. 197; Schürmann, 'Dublettenvermeidungen', 84. For Lk. xxi. 14f. as LkR, using many of the ideas featured later in Acts, see Fuchs, *Sprachliche Untersuchungen*, pp. 171–91; also Zmijewski, *Eschatologiereden*, pp. 169–72. There is thus no need to postulate the existence of a proto-Luke source here as is done by Taylor, *Behind the Third Gospel*, pp. 101ff.; Gaston, 'Luk. 21'; cf. too Schramm, *Markus-Stoff*, pp. 175–8.
4 Cf. Farmer, *Synoptic Problem*, p. 272, with regard to Lk. xvii. 26–30.
5 Talbert and McKnight, 'Can the Griesbach Hypothesis be falsified?', pp. 364–7.
6 Buchanan, 'Has the Griesbach hypothesis been falsified?', p. 572. However, he seems to think that the GH is safeguarded by the fact that Matthew's use of Luke has not been proved: 'McKnight has succeeded in showing that Luke has preserved the tradition in its earlier form, but that is not enough to prove that Matthew used Luke as his source for this pericope.' (p. 571). However, this is beside the point: the thrust of McKnight's observation was that Matthew was dependent on Luke's source, not necessarily on Luke. If Matthew's immediate source is Luke's source, then this is effectively the Q hypothesis, and it presents an anomaly for the GH which asserts that Luke knew, and used, Matthew. The reference to the possibility that Matthew used Luke is quite irrelevant.
7 'Fresh Approach', p. 48. Quite what is meant by the 'traditional and conventional' Q hypothesis is not clear. Many have claimed that there are different strata within the Q material: cf. Bussmann, *Synoptische Studien* II, pp. 110–56; Barrett, 'Q: A Re-examination'; Schulz, *Q*, esp. pp. 47–53.
8 *Synoptic Problem*, p. 273.
9 So Schmid, *Matthäus und Lukas*, p. 336; Vielhauer, 'Gottesreich', p. 74; Lührmann, *Redaktion*, p. 73; Schulz, *Q*, p. 279.
10 Lührmann, *Redaktion*, pp. 75–83.
11 Cf. Catchpole, 'Son of Man's Search for Faith', p. 84. Lührmann himself takes the Lot saying as a secondary addition, added in the pre-Lukan source. This, however, seems unnecessarily complicated. The Lot saying is also

taken as secondary by Bultmann, *History*, p. 117; Tödt, *Son of Man*, p. 49; Vielhauer, 'Gottesreich', p. 74; Zmijewski, *Eschatologiereden*, p. 454. It is taken as part of Q by Schnackenburg, 'Lk 17, 20–37', p. 223; Schürmann, 'Menschensohntitel', p. 139.

12 Farmer, *Synoptic Problem*, p. 272; Talbert and McKnight, 'Can the Griesbach Hypothesis be falsified?', pp. 364f. Schnackenburg, 'Lk 17, 20–37', p. 223, points out that double comparisons occur elsewhere, though it is not clear whether he thinks they are characteristic of Q or of Jesus. Catchpole, 'Son of Man's Search for Faith', p. 84, says that they are characteristic of Q and he gives a number of examples; but Lk. x. 10f.; xiv. 28–32; xv. 4–9 are not all obviously in Q.

13 Schürmann, 'Menschensohntitel', p. 139; Catchpole, 'Son of Man's Search for Faith', p. 84.

14 Colpe, art. ὁ υἱὸς τοῦ ἀνθρώπου, *T.D.N.T.* VIII, p. 434; Tödt, *Son of Man*, p. 51; Schulz, *Q*, p. 279; Zmijewski, *Eschatologiereden*, p. 449; Schürmann, 'Menschensohntitel', p. 139; Schneider, 'Menschensohn', p. 276. It is taken as traditional by Lührmann, *Redaktion*, p. 73; Schnackenburg, 'Lk 17, 20–37', p. 223.

15 Catchpole, 'Son of Man's Search for Faith', p. 85; cf. also Manson, *Sayings*, pp. 143f.; Tödt, *Son of Man*, pp. 50f.; Schulz, *Q*, pp. 284f.

16 For (a) Bultmann, *History*, p. 122; Grässer, *Parusieverzögerung*, p. 170; Conzelmann, *Theology*, p. 124; Jeremias, *Theology*, p. 272. For (b): *S.-B.* I, p. 954; Foerster, art. ἀστραπή, *T.D.N.T.* I, p. 505; Colpe, *art. cit.*, p. 433; Tödt, *Son of Man*, p. 49.

17 So Tödt.

18 Greater detail was taken as a sign of a secondary, not original, tradition by Farmer, *Synoptic Problem*, p. 228, in his first edition. He withdrew this in his second edition in the light of the work of Sanders, concluding that greater detail implies nothing about the relative ages of the texts.

19 Klostermann, *Matthäus*, p. 194; Schmid, *Matthäus und Lukas*, p. 335.

20 Cf. Lambrecht, 'Parousia Discourse', p. 323: the point is 'the identification of the true Christ'.

21 For the first, see Jeremias, art. Μωυσῆς, *T.D.N.T.* IV, p. 862; for the second, see *S.-B.* I, p. 955; Justin, *Dialogue with Trypho*, 8.

22 'Gottesreich', p. 75.

23 φαίνω: 13 – 1 – 2; ἀπό . . . ἕως: 8 – 2 – 2.

24 Grundmann, *Lukas*, p. 192; see too Schürmann, *Lukas*, p. 556; Zmijewski, *Eschatologiereden*, pp. 405, 413.

25 Both interpretations have parallels: for universal visibility, see Bar. liii; for speed and suddenness, see Ps. xviii. 14; cxlvi. 6; Nah. ii. 4.

26 'Menschensohntitel', pp. 139f.

27 Cf. Edwards, 'Eschatological Correlative', pp. 11f.

28 See Hawkins, *Horae Synopticae*, pp. 39, 45f.; Cadbury, *Style*, pp. 169, 203; Zmijewski, *Eschatologiereden*, p. 398; Schulz, *Q*, p. 278.

29 Hence *contra* Conzelmann, *Theology*, p. 105, n. 3; Grundmann, *Lukas*, p. 343; Colpe, *art. cit.*, p. 458.

30 *Eschatologiereden*, pp. 399–403.

31 Schnackenburg, 'Lk 17, 20–37', p. 227; followed by Schneider, 'Menschensohn', pp. 274f.; Catchpole, 'Son of Man's Search for Faith', p. 83; cf. too

Schulz, *Q*, p. 278.

32 Cf. Wilson, *Gentiles*, pp. 83f.; Catchpole, 'Son of Man's Search for Faith', p. 83.

33 So Schnackenburg, 'Lk 17, 20–37', pp. 220f., who thinks however that the phrase "the days are coming" may be from Q. (It is a standard introduction to prophetic oracles.) Cf. also Catchpole, 'Son of Man's Search for Faith', p. 83. The verse is regarded as LkR by Bultmann, *History*, p. 130; Vielhauer, 'Gottesreich', pp. 61f.; Schulz, *Q*, p. 278; Schürmann, 'Menschensohntitel', p. 139; Schneider, 'Menschensohn', p. 274.

34 Cf. Grundmann, art. δεῖ, *T.D.N.T.* II, pp. 22f.

35 The verse is taken as Lukan by Bultmann, *History*, p. 122; Grundmann, *Lukas*, p. 342; Lührmann, *Redaktion*, p. 72; Tödt, *Son of Man*, p. 48; Zmijewski, *Eschatologiereden*, p. 419; Schnackenburg, 'Lk 17, 20–37', p. 222; Schneider, 'Menschensohn', pp. 275f.; Catchpole, 'Son of Man's Search for Faith', p. 84. It is taken as an old logion by Kümmel, *Promise*, p. 71, and by Schramm, *Markus-Stoff*, pp. 131f., on account of the lack of reference to the resurrection. But the same occurs in Lk. ix. 44, which must be LkR of Mark or Matthew (depending on which is prior).

36 See Zmijewski, *Eschatologiereden*, p. 465: 'Mit den vv. 31–33 unterbricht Lukas deutlich den ursprünglichen Textzusammenhang.' Cf. too Bultmann, *History*, p. 117; Manson, *Sayings*, p. 144. Lührmann, *Redaktion*, p. 74.

37 Zmijewski, *Eschatologiereden*, pp. 465f.

38 See Strobel, 'In dieser Nacht', p. 21.

39 *Eschatologiereden*, pp. 499f.

40 Schmid, *Matthäus und Lukas*, pp. 338f.; Schulz, *Q*, p. 280.

41 Bultmann, *History*, p. 336; Lührmann, *Redaktion*, p. 72; Zmijewski, *Eschatologiereden*, pp. 506f.; Schulz, *Q*, pp. 280f.; Schnackenburg, 'Lk 17, 20–37', pp. 225f.

42 Cf. Manson, *Sayings*, p. 147.

43 Similarly, Lührmann, Schnackenburg, Schulz and Zmijewski.

44 Similar summaries in Schnackenburg, 'Lk 17, 20–37', p. 229; Zmijewski, *Eschatologiereden*, p. 524.

45 Manson, *Teaching*, p. 261, and Schulz, *Q*, p. 286, both point to the complete lack of any detailed descriptions of the End events, in contrast to Mk. xiii and other Jewish apocalypses.

46 Cf. Lambrecht, 'Parousia Discourse', p. 311: 'Where Matthew leaves his "Markus-Vorlage" a new part begins.' Such a judgement is usually made assuming Markan priority. However, the seam was noticed already in 1826 by Wilke, 'Ueber die Parabel', pp. 76f., long before Markan priority was assumed.

47 Lambrecht, 'Parousia Discourse', p. 311: this part 'exhorts the disciples to faith and perseverance'.

48 *Ibid.*, p. 326: this part is 'a descriptive announcement of the unexpected coming that will hit the unprepared catastrophically'.

49 *Synoptic Problem*, p. 278.

50 *Ibid.*, p. 277. Nevertheless, Mark does not follow this rule exactly, since he adds Mk. xiii. 21–3/Matt. xxiv. 23–5. Farmer says that this shows that Mark was 'not slavish' in his adherence to this rule (p. 273).

51 *Ibid.*, p. 273.

52 *Ibid.*, pp. 273f.
53 *Ibid.*, pp. 218f.
54 *Ibid.*, p. 277.
55 Cf. McLoughlin, 'Les accords mineurs', who collects all those agreements which various scholars have considered the most difficult to explain on the theory of Markan priority. None of them appears in these verses.
56 Neirynck, *Minor Agreements.*
57 Hence references to Mark's omissions from Q, which imply that Mark knew Q, are problematical.
58 *Synoptic Problem*, p. 274.
59 Cf. pp. 169ff. above on Matt. xxiv. 26–8, and Matthew's redaction of the tradition to stress universal visibility. See also Matt. xvi. 27 (diff. Mark).
60 Cf. Hawkins, *Horae Synopticae*, p. 12.
61 Cf. Bultmann, *History*, p. 119; Taylor, *Mark*, p. 524; Jeremias, *Parables*, p. 54; Schweizer, *Mark*, pp. 279f.; Haenchen, *Weg*, p. 453; Grässer, *Parusieverzögerung*, pp. 86f.; Schulz, *Q*, p. 288; Dupont, 'Parable du maître', pp. 95f.; Lambrecht, *Markus-Apokalypse*, pp. 249ff.; Pesch, *Naherwartungen*, pp. 197–9; Weiser, *Knechtsgleichnisse*, pp. 131ff.
62 *Synoptic Problem*, p. 273.
63 See Schmid, *Matthäus und Lukas*, p. 340; Schulz, *Q*, pp. 268, 271f.
64 For Luke as original, see Schmid, *Matthäus und Lukas*, p. 341; Jeremias, *Parables*, p. 57; Weiser, *Knechtsgleichnisse*, pp. 201f.; Schulz, *Q*, p. 272. For 'hypocrite' as Matthean, see Haenchen, 'Matthäus 23', p. 58; Strecker, *Weg*, pp. 139f. Betz, 'Dichotomized Servant', p. 45, claims that 'hypocrite' is more original, the strange punishment of διχοτομεῖν referring to being 'cut off' from one's appointed lot, as in 1 QS ii. 16f. However, although the Qumran parallel may well illuminate the use of διχοτομέω, there is no mention of 'hypocrites' explicitly in the 1 QS text. (Cf. Weiser, *Knechtsgleichnisse*, p. 202). The fate of the man expelled from the covenant is to be with 'those who are cursed for ever', and this certainly does not demand an original ὑποκριτής rather than ἄπιστος.
65 Cf. Jeremias, *Parables*, pp. 53f.; Grässer, *Parusieverzögerung*, p. 89; Dupont, 'Parable du maître', p. 104; Weiser, *Knechtsgleichnisse*, pp. 169–71; Schneider, *Parusiegleichnisse*, pp. 34f.
66 Cf. Weiser, *Knechtsgleichnisse*, pp. 170f.; Schneider, *Parusiegleichnisse*, p. 35.
67 See Weiser, *Knechtsgleichnisse*, pp. 161–4; Schneider, *Parusiegleichnisse*, pp. 32f.
68 Schürmann, 'Sprachliche Reminiszenzen', p. 208; followed by Weiser, *Knechtsgleichnisse*, p. 168; Schneider, *Parusiegleichnisse*, p. 32. ἐγρηγόρησαν could be derived from Mk. xiii. 33–7 on the 2DH, but φυλακῇ cannot be from that source.
69 Alternatively this may be due to assimilation by Matthew to v. 42 (so Schulz, *Q*, p. 268). However, this still means that Matthew is secondary, and this again is difficult for the GH.
70 Thus Hoffmann, *Studien*, pp. 43–50, is more convincing in his claim that these parables are determined more by an imminenet expectation of the End, rather than by an experience of delay, contra Grässer, Schulz, Schneider and others.

71 For Matthew as secondary here, see Schmid, *Matthäus und Lukas*, p. 267; Lührmann, *Redaktion*, p. 62; Schulz, *Q*, p. 361. The Lukan phrase occurs only here, and in another 'double tradition' passage, Lk. xi. 31f. On the Q hypothesis, this is therefore a characteristic of Q.

72 Bultmann, *History*, p. 130; Grässer, *Parusieverzögerung*, p. 85; Pesch, *Naherwartungen*, p. 195; Weiser, *Knechtsgleichnisse*, pp. 131f.

73 Pesch, *Naherwartungen*, p. 198; Weiser, *Knechtsgleichnisse*, p. 137.

74 These examples are taken from Weiser, *Knechtsgleichnisse*, p. 138, who seeks to show that Mark's version is dependent on a pre-Markan tradition. His other examples, δοῦλος and ἕκαστος, could be explained by the GH as due to dependence on Matthew, but this will not work for the examples given above.

75 So Jeremias, *Parables*, p. 54; Grässer, *Parusieverzögerung*, pp. 86f.; Dupont, 'Parable du maître', pp. 106f.; Weiser, *Knechtsgleichnisse*, p. 172; Schneider, *Parusiegleichnisse*, p. 31; Crossan, 'Servant Parables', p. 21.

76 Cf. Bultmann, *History*, p. 119.

77 See Dupont, 'Parable du maître', pp. 93f.; Zmijewski, *Eschatologiereden*, pp. 291–4; Schneider, 'Menschensohn', p. 269.

78 Bultmann, *History*, p. 130; Lambrecht, *Markus-Apokalypse*, p. 248; Weiser, *Knechtsgleichnisse*, p. 144.

ABBREVIATIONS

A.T.R.	*Anglican Theological Review*
B.J.R.L.	*Bulletin of the John Rylands Library*
B.R.	*Biblical Research*
B.Z.	*Biblische Zeitschrift*
C.B.Q.	*Catholic Biblical Quarterly*
E.H.R.	*English Historical Review*
E.T.	*Expository Times*
Ev.Th.	*Evangelische Theologie*
E.T.L.	*Ephemerides Theologicae Lovanienses*
H.T.R.	*Harvard Theological Review*
H.U.C.A.	*Hebrew Union College Annual*
I.E.J.	*Israel Exploration Journal*
J.B.L.	*Journal of Biblical Literature*
J.E.T.S.	*Journal of the Evangelical Theological Society*
J.S.N.T.	*Journal for the Study of the New Testament*
J.T.S.	*Journal of Theological Studies*
J.T.S.A.	*Journal of Theology for Southern Africa*
N.R.T.	*Nouvelle Revue Théologique*
N.T.	*Novum Testamentum*
N.T.S.	*New Testament Studies*
Rev.Q.	*Revue de Qumran*
S.-B.	H. L. Strack and P. Billerbeck, *Kommentar zum Neuen Testament aus Talmud und Midrasch* (Munich, 1922–8)
St.Ev.	*Studia Evangelica*
T.D.N.T.	*Theological Dictionary of the New Testament*
T.J.	*Theologische Jahrbücher*
T.L.Z.	*Theologische Literaturzeitung*
Th.St.u.Kr.	*Theologische Studien und Kritiken*
T.U.	Texte und Untersuchungen
T.Z.	*Theologische Zeitschrift*

Z.K.T.	*Zeitschrift für katholische Theologie*
Z.N.W.	*Zeitschrift für die neutestamentliche Wissenschaft*
Z.R.G.G.	*Zeitschrift für Religion und Geistesgeschichte*
Z.Th.K.	*Zeitschrift für Theologie und Kirche*

BIBLIOGRAPHY

Abbott, E. A., art. 'Gospels', *Encyclopaedia Britannica* (9th ed., Edinburgh, 1879), vol. 10, pp. 789–843.
The Corrections of Mark adopted by Matthew and Luke (London, 1901).
Abbott, E. A., and Rushbrooke, W. G., *The Common Tradition of the Synoptic Gospels* (London, 1884).
Abrahams, I., *Studies in Pharisaism and the Gospels* (First Series. London, 1917).
Achtemeier, P. J., 'Toward the Isolation of Pre-Markan Miracle Catenae', *J.B.L.* 89 (1970), 265–91.
'The Origin and Function of the Pre-Marcan Miracle Catenae', *J.B.L.* 91 (1972), 198–221.
'The Lucan Perspective on the Miracles of Jesus: A Preliminary Sketch', *J.B.L.* 94 (1975), 547–62.
Allen, W. C., *A Critical and Exegetical Commentary on the Gospel according to St. Matthew* (Edinburgh, 1907).
Banks, R., *Jesus and the Law in the Synoptic Tradition* (Cambridge, 1975).
Barrett, C. K., *The Holy Spirit and the Gospel Tradition* (London, 1947).
'The House of Prayer and the Den of Thieves', in E. E. Ellis and E. Grässer (eds.), *Jesus und Paulus*, Festschrift for W. G. Kümmel (Göttingen, 1975), pp. 13–20.
'Q: A Re-examination', *E.T.* 54 (1943), 320–3.
Barth, G., 'Matthew's Understanding of the Law', in G. Bornkamm, G. Barth and H. J. Held, *Tradition and Interpretation in Matthew* (ET, London, 1963), pp. 58–164.
Bartsch, H.-W., 'Eine bisher übersehene Zitierung der LXX in Mark 4, 30', *T.Z.* 15 (1959), 126–8.
Baur, F. C., *Kritische Untersuchungen über die kanonischen Evangelien, ihr Verhältnis zu einander, ihren Charakter und Ursprung* (Tübingen, 1847).
Beare, F. W., Review of Farmer, *The Synoptic Problem*, in *J.B.L.* 84 (1965), 295–7.
Berger, K., *Die Gesetzesauslegung Jesu* (Neukirchen-Vluyn, 1972).
Best, E., 'Mark's Preservation of the Tradition', in M. Sabbe (ed.), *L'Évangile selon Marc. Tradition et Rédaction* (Louvain, 1974), pp. 21–34.
The Temptation and the Passion: The Markan Soteriology (Cambridge, 1965).

Betz, O., 'The Dichotomized Servant and the End of Judas Iscariot', *Rev.Q.* 5 (1964), 43–58.

Black, M., *An Aramaic Approach to the Gospels and Acts* (3rd ed., Oxford, 1967).

Bleek, F. J., *An Introduction to the New Testament* (ET, Edinburgh, 1869).

Boring, M. E., 'The Unforgivable Sin Logion Mk III 28–29/Matt XII 31–32/ Lk XII 10. Formal Analysis and History of the Tradition', *N.T.* 18 (1976), 258–79.

Bornkamm, G., 'Das Doppelgebot der Liebe', in W. Eltester (ed.), *Neutestamentliche Studien für Rudolf Bultmann* (Berlin, 1954), pp. 85–93.

Brown, J. P., 'An Early Revision of the Gospel of Mark', *J.B.L.* 78 (1959), 215–27.

'Mark as Witness to an Edited Form of Q', *J.B.L.* 80 (1961), 29–44.

Buchanan, G. W., 'Has the Griesbach hypothesis been falsified?', *J.B.L.* 93 (1974), 550–72.

'Mark 11. 15–19. Brigands in the Temple', *H.U.C.A.* 30 (1959), 169–77.

Büchler, A., 'The Law of Purification in Mark vii. 1–23', *E.T.* 21 (1909), 34–40.

Bultmann, R., 'Der religionsgeschichtliche Hintergrund des Prologs zum Johannes-Evangelium', in H. Schmidt (ed.), ΕΥΧΑΡΙΣΤΗΡΙΟΝ, Festschrift for H. Gunkel (Göttingen, 1923), pp. 3–26.

The History of the Synoptic Tradition (ET, Oxford, 1968).

Burchard, C., 'Das doppelte Liebesgebot in der frühen christlichen Überlieferung', in E. Lohse (ed.), *Der Ruf Jesu und die Antwort der Gemeinde*, Festschrift for J. Jeremias (Göttingen, 1970), pp. 39–62.

Burney, C. F., *The Poetry of Our Lord. An Examination of the Formal Elements of Hebrew Poetry in the Discourses of Jesus Christ* (Oxford, 1925).

Burton, E. deW., *Some Principles of Literary Criticism and their Application to the Synoptic Problem* (The Decennial Publications of the University of Chicago. 1st Series. vol. V, Chicago, 1904).

Busse, U., *Die Wunder des Propheten Jesus. Die Rezeption, Komposition und Interpretation der Wundertradition im Evangelium des Lukas* (Stuttgart, 1977).

Bussmann, W., *Synoptische Studien. II. Zur Redequelle* (Halle, 1929).

Butler, B. C., *The Originality of St. Matthew* (Cambridge, 1951).

Cadbury, H. J., *The Style and Literary Method of Luke* (Cambridge, Mass., 1920).

Campenhausen, H. von, *The Formation of the Christian Bible* (ET, London, 1972).

Carlston, C. E., 'A *Positive* Criterion of Authenticity?', *B.R.* 7 (1962), 33–44.

'The Things that Defile (Mark vii. 14) and the Law in Matthew and Mark', *N.T.S.* 15 (1968), 75–95.

Catchpole, D. R., 'The Answer of Jesus to Caiaphas (Matt. xxvi. 64)', *N.T.S.* 17 (1971), 213–26.

'On Doing Violence to the Kingdom', *J.T.S.A.* 25 (1978), 50–61.

'The Son of Man's Search for Faith (Luke xviii. 8b)', *N.T.* 19 (1977), 81–104.

'The Synoptic Divorce Material as a Traditio-Historical Problem', *B.J.R.L.* 57 (1974), 92–127.

'Tradition History', in I. H. Marshall (ed.), *New Testament Interpretation* (Exeter, 1977), pp. 165–80.

The Trial of Jesus (Leiden, 1971).

Chapman, J., 'Zacharias, Slain between the Temple and the Altar', *J.T.S.* 13 (1912), 398–410.

Christ, F., *Jesus Sophia. Die Sophia-Christologie bei den Synoptikern* (Zürich, 1970).

Colpe, C., 'Der Spruch von der Lästerung des Geistes', in E. Lohse (ed.), *Der Ruf Jesu und die Antwort der Gemeinde*, Festschrift for J. Jeremias (Göttingen, 1970), pp. 63–79.

'ὁ υἱὸς τοῦ ἀνθρώπου', *T.D.N.T.* VIII, 400–77.

Conzelmann, H., *The Theology of St. Luke* (ET, London, 1960).

Cope, O. L., 'The Death of John the Baptist in the Gospel of Matthew; or, the Case of the Confusing Conjunction', *C.B.Q.* 38 (1976), 515–19.

Matthew: A Scribe Trained for the Kingdom of Heaven (Washington, 1976).

Creed, J. M., *The Gospel according to St. Luke* (London, 1930).

Crossan, J. D., 'Mark and the Relatives of Jesus', *N.T.* 15 (1973), 81–113.

'Parable and Example in the Teaching of Jesus', *N.T.S.* 18 (1972), 285–307.

'The Seed Parables of Jesus', *J.B.L.* 92 (1973), 244–66.

'The Servant Parables of Jesus', *Semeia* I (1974), 17–62.

Daube, D., *The New Testament and Rabbinic Judaism* (London, 1956).

Davies, W. D., *The Setting of the Sermon on the Mount* (Cambridge, 1963).

Derrett, J. D. M., '"Eating up the Houses of Widows": Jesus' Comment on Lawyers?', *N.T.* 14 (1972), 1–9.

Devisch, M., 'Le document Q, source de Matthieu. Problématique actuelle', in M. Didier (ed.), *L'Évangile selon Matthieu. Rédaction et Théologie* (Gembloux, 1972), pp. 71–97.

'Le relation entre l'évangile de Marc et le document Q', in M. Sabbe (ed.), *L'Évangile selon Marc. Tradition et Rédaction* (Louvain, 1974), pp. 59–91.

Dibelius, M., *From Tradition to Gospel* (ET, London, 1934).

Dodd, C. H., *The Parables of the Kingdom* (London, 1961).

Doudna, J. C., *The Greek of the Gospel of Mark* (Philadelphia, 1961).

Downing, F. G., 'Towards the Rehabilitation of Q', *N.T.S.* 11 (1965), 169–81.

Dungan, D. L., 'Mark – The Abridgement of Matthew and Luke', *Jesus and Man's Hope*, vol. 1 (Pittsburgh, 1970), pp. 51–97.

'Reactionary Trends in the Gospel Producing Activity of the Early Church: Marcion, Tatian, Mark', in M. Sabbe (ed.), *L'Évangile selon Marc. Tradition et Rédaction* (Louvain, 1974), pp. 179–202.

The Sayings of Jesus in the Churches of Paul (Oxford, 1971).

Dupont, J., *Les Béatitudes* (3 vols., Paris, 1969–73).
'La parabole du maître qui rentre dans la nuit (Mc. 13, 34–6)', in A. Descamps (ed.), *Mélanges Bibliques*, Festschrift for B. Rigaux. (Gembloux, 1970), pp. 89–116.
Edwards, R. A., 'The Eschatological Correlative as a *Gattung* in the New Testament', *Z.N.W.* 60 (1969), 9–20.
Eppstein, V., 'The Historicity of the Gospel Account of the Cleansing of the Temple', *Z.N.W.* 55 (1964), 42–58.
Farmer, W. R., 'Basic Affirmation with some Demurrals: A Response to Roland Mushat Frye', in W. O. Walker (ed.), *The Relationships among the Gospels* (San Antonio, 1978), pp. 303–22.
'A Fresh Approach to Q', in J. Neusner (ed.), *Christianity, Judaism and Other Greco-Roman Cults. Studies for Morton Smith at Sixty. Part One, New Testament* (Leiden, 1975), pp. 39–50.
'Kritik der Markushypothese', *T.Z.* 34 (1978), 172–4.
'The Lachmann Fallacy', *N.T.S.* 14 (1968), 441–3.
'Modern Developments of Griesbach's Hypothesis', *N.T.S.* 23 (1977), 275–95.
'Notes on a Literary and Form-Critical Analysis of Some of the Synoptic Material Peculiar to Luke', *N.T.S.* 8 (1962), 301–16.
'The Present State of the Synoptic Problem', *Perkins Journal* 32 (1978), 1–7.
'A Response to Robert Morgenthaler's *Statistische Synopse*', *Biblica* 54 (1973), 417–33.
'A "Skeleton in the Closet" of Gospel Research', *B.R.* 6 (1961), 18–42.
The Synoptic Problem (London–New York, 1964. 2nd ed., Dillsboro, N.C., 1976).
'The Two Document Hypothesis as a Methodological Criterion in Synoptic Research', *A.T.R.* 48 (1966), 380–96.
Farrer, A. M., 'On Dispensing with Q', in D. E. Nineham (ed.), *Studies in the Gospels. Essays in Memory of R. H. Lightfoot* (Oxford, 1955), pp. 55–88.
Fee, G. D., 'Modern Text Criticism and the Synoptic Problem', in B. Orchard and T. R. W. Longstaff (eds.), *J. J. Griesbach: Synoptic and Text-Critical Studies 1776–1976* (Cambridge, 1978), pp. 154–69.
Fitzmyer, J. A., 'The Priority of Mark and the "Q" Source in Luke', *Jesus and Man's Hope*, vol. 1 (Pittsburgh, 1970), pp. 131–70.
'The Use of *Agein* and *Pherein* in the Synoptic Gospels', in E. H. Barth and R. E. Cocroft (eds.), *Festschrift to Honour F. Wilbur Gingrich* (Leiden, 1972), pp. 147–60.
Foerster, W., 'ἀστραπή', *T.D.N.T.* I, 505.
Fuchs, A., *Sprachliche Untersuchungen zu Matthäus und Lukas* (Rome, 1971).
'After Ten Years: The Synoptic Problem', *Perkins Journal* 27 (1975), 63–74.
Fuller, R. H., 'Baur versus Hilgenfeld: A Forgotten Chapter in the Debate on the Synoptic Problem', *N.T.S.* 24 (1978), 355–70.
'Die neuere Diskussion über das synoptische Problem', *T.Z.* 34 (1978), 129–48.
'Das Doppelgebot der Liebe. Ein Testfall für die Echtheitskriterien der

Worte Jesu', in G. Strecker (ed.), *Jesus Christus in Historie und Theologie*, Festschrift for H. Conzelmann (Tübingen, 1975), pp. 317-29.

Funk, R. W., 'The Looking-Glass Tree is for the Birds. Ezekiel 17: 22-24; Mark 4: 30-32', *Interpretation* 27 (1973), 3-9.

Gaston, L., 'Sondergut und Markusstoff in Luk 21', *T.Z.* 16 (1960), 161-72.

Goulder, M. D., *Midrash and Lection in Matthew* (London, 1974).

'On Putting Q to the Test', *N.T.S.* 24 (1978), 218-34.

Gransden, A., *Historical Writing in England c. 550-c. 1307* (London, 1974).

Grant, F. C., Review of Farmer, *The Synoptic Problem*, in *Interpretation* 19 (1965), 352-4.

Grant, R. M., *The Earliest Lives of Jesus* (London, 1961).

Grässer, E., *Das Problem der Parusieverzögerung in den synoptischen Evangelien und in der Apostelgeschichte* (Berlin, 1960).

Griesbach, J. J., 'Commentatio qua Marci Evangelium totum e Matthaei et Lucae commentariis decerptum esse monstratur', in J. P. Gabler (ed.), *J. J. Griesbachii Opuscula Academica*, vol. II (Jena, 1825), pp. 358-425. ET by Orchard, *Griesbach Studies*, pp. 103-35.

'Inquisitio in fontes, unde evangelistae suas de resurrectione domini narrationes hauserint', in J. P. Gabler (ed.), *J. J. Griesbachii Opuscula Academica*, vol. II (Jena, 1825), pp. 241-56.

Grundmann, W., 'δεῖ', *T.D.N.T.* II, pp. 21-5.

Das Evangelium nach Matthäus (Berlin, 1968).

Das Evangelium nach Markus (Berlin, 1973).

Das Evangelium nach Lukas (Berlin, 1974).

Gundry, R. H., '1 Q Isaiah a 50, 6 and Mark 14, 65', *Rev.Q.* 2 (1960), 559-67.

Haenchen, E., 'Johanneische Probleme', *Z.Th.K.* 56 (1959), 19-54.

'Matthäus 23', *Z.Th.K.* 48 (1951), 38-63.

Der Weg Jesu (Berlin, 1968).

Hare, D. R. A., *The Theme of Jewish Persecution of Christians in the Gospel according to St. Matthew* (Cambridge, 1967).

Harnack, A. von, *Sprüche und Reden Jesu* (Leipzig, 1907).

Hawkins, J. C., *Horae Synopticae* (2nd ed., Oxford, 1909).

'Three Limitations to St. Luke's Use of St. Mark's Gospel', in W. Sanday (ed.), *Oxford Studies in the Synoptic Problem* (Oxford, 1911), pp. 29-94.

Held, H. J., 'Matthew as Interpreter of the Miracle Stories', in G. Bornkamm, G. Barth and H. J. Held, *Tradition and Interpretation in Matthew* (ET, London, 1963), pp. 165-299.

Hengel, M., *Judaism and Hellenism* (ET, London, 1974).

'φάτνη', *T.D.N.T.* IX, 49-55.

Higgins, A. J. B., 'The Arabic Version of Tatian's Diatessaron', *J.T.S.* 45 (1944), 187-99.

Hilgenfeld, A., 'Neue Untersuchung über das Markus-Evangelium, mit Rücksicht auf Dr. Baur's Darstellung', *T.J.* 11 (1852), 102-32 and 259-93.

Hill, J. H., *The Earliest Life of Christ Ever Compiled from the Four Gospels, Being the Diatessaron of Tatian* (London, 1894).

Hoffmann, P., Review of Schulz, *Q – Die Spruchquelle der Evangelisten* in *B.Z.* 19 (1975), 104–15.

Studien zur Theologie der Logienquelle (Münster, 1971).

Holst, R., 'Reexamining Mk 3: 28f. and Its Parallels', *Z.N.W.* 63 (1972), 122–4.

Holtzmann, H. J., *Lehrbuch der historisch-kritischen Einleitung in das Neue Testament* (Freiburg, 1885).

Die synoptischen Evangelien. Ihr Ursprung und geschichtlicher Charakter (Leipzig, 1863).

Honey, T. E. F., 'Did Mark use Q?', *J.B.L.* 62 (1943), 319–31.

Hooker, M. D., 'Christology and Methodology', *N.T.S.* 17 (1971), 480–7.

Hübner, H., *Das Gesetz in der synoptischen Tradition* (Witten, 1973).

Hultgren, A. J., 'The Double Commandment of Love in Mt 22: 34–40. Its Sources and Composition', *C.B.Q.* 36 (1974), 373–8.

Hummel, R., *Die Auseinandersetzung zwischen Kirche und Judentum im Matthäusevangelium* (München, 1963).

Hunkin, J. W., '"Pleonastic" ἄρχομαι in the New Testament', *J.T.S.* 25 (1924), 390–402.

Jameson, H. G., *The Origin of the Synoptic Gospels* (Oxford, 1922).

Jeremias, J., *The Eucharistic Words of Jesus* (ET, London, 1966).

Jerusalem in the Time of Jesus (ET, London, 1969).

Jesus' Promise to the Nations (ET, London, 1958).

'Kennzeichen der ipsissima vox Jesu', in J. Schmid and A. Vögtle (eds.), *Synoptische Studien*, Festschrift for A. Wikenhauser (München, 1953), pp. 86–93.

'Die Lampe unter dem Scheffel', *Z.N.W.* 39 (1940), 237–40.

'Die Muttersprache des Evangelisten Matthäus', *Z.N.W.* 50 (1959), 270–4.

New Testament Theology. Part One. The Proclamation of Jesus (ET, London, 1971).

The Parables of Jesus (ET, London, 1963).

Jervell, J., 'The Law in Luke–Acts', *H.T.R.* 64 (1971), 21–36.

Johnson, M. D., 'Reflections on a Wisdom Approach to Matthew's Christology', *C.B.Q.* 36 (1974), 44–64.

Johnson, S. E., 'The Biblical Quotations in Matthew', *H.T.R.* 36 (1943), 133–53.

Juel, D., *Messiah and Temple. The Trial of Jesus in the Gospel of Mark* (Missoula, 1977).

Käsemann, E., *Essays on New Testament Themes* (ET, London, 1964).

Keck, L. E., 'Mark 3: 7–12 and Mark's Christology', *J.B.L.* 84 (1965), 341–58.

Kelly, J. N. D., *Early Christian Doctrines* (London, 1958).

Kennedy, G., 'Classical and Christian Source Criticism', in W. O. Walker (ed.), *The Relationships among the Gospels* (San Antonio, 1978), pp. 125–55.

Kilpatrick, G. D., *The Origins of the Gospel according to St. Matthew* (Oxford, 1946).

'Scribes, Lawyers, and Lucan Origins', *J.T.S.* 1 (1950), 56–60.
Klostermann, E., *Das Matthäusevangelium* (Tübingen, 1927).
Das Lukasevangelium (Tübingen, 1929).
Köstlin, K. R., *Der Ursprung und die Komposition der synoptischen Evangelien* (Stuttgart, 1853).
Kraeling, C. H., *A Greek Fragment of Tatian's Diatessaron from Dura* (London, 1935).
Kuhn, H.-W., *Ältere Sammlungen im Markusevangelium* (Göttingen, 1971).
Kümmel, W. G., 'Äussere und innere Reinheit des Menschen bei Jesus', in H. Balz and S. Schulz (eds.), *Das Wort und die Wörter*, Festschrift for G. Friedrich (Stuttgart, 1973), pp. 35–46.
'"Das Gesetz und die Propheten gehen bis Johannes" – Lukas 16, 16 im Zusammenhang der heilsgeschichtlichen Theologie der Lukasschriften', in O. Böcher and K. Haaker (eds.), *Verborum Veritas*, Festschrift for G. Stählin (Wuppertal, 1970), pp. 89–102.
Introduction to the New Testament (ET, Rev. ed., London, 1975).
'Jesus und der jüdische Traditionsgedanke', *Z.N.W.* 33 (1934), 105–30.
Promise and Fulfilment (ET, London, 1957).
Lachmann, K., 'De ordine narrationum in evangeliis synopticis', *Th.St.u.Kr.* 8 (1835), 570–90. ET in Palmer, 'Lachmann's Argument'. All page references to this.
Lambrecht, J., 'Jesus and the Law. An Investigation of Mk 7, 1–23', *E.T.L.* 53 (1977), 24–82.
'The Parousia Discourse. Composition and Content in Mt., XXIV–XXV', in M. Didier (ed.), *L'Évangile selon Matthieu. Rédaction et Théologie* (Gembloux, 1972), pp. 309–42.
'Redaction and Theology in Mark IV', in M. Sabbe (ed.), *L'Évangile selon Marc. Tradition et Rédaction* (Louvain, 1974), pp. 269–307.
Die Redaktion der Markus-Apokalypse (Rome, 1967).
'The Relatives of Jesus in Mark', *N.T.* 16 (1974), 241–58.
Levie, J., 'L'évangile araméen de S. Matthieu est-il la source de l'évangile de S. Marc?', *N.R.T.* 76 (1954), 689–715, 812–43.
Lindars, Barnabas., *New Testament Apologetic* (London, 1961).
Linnemann, E., *Parables of Jesus. Introduction and Exposition* (ET, London, 1971).
Linton, O., 'The Parable of the Children's Game', *N.T.S.* 22 (1976), 159–79.
Lohmeyer, E., *Das Evangelium des Matthäus* (Göttingen, 1956).
Das Evangelium des Markus (Göttingen, 1957).
Lohse, E., 'Jesu Worte über den Sabbat', in W. Eltester (ed.), *Judentum Urchristentum Kirche*, Festschrift for J. Jeremias (Berlin, 1960), pp. 79–89.
'σάββατον', *T.D.N.T.* VII, 1–35.
Longstaff, T. R. W., 'A Critical Note in Response to J. C. O'Neill', *N.T.S.* 23 (1976), 116–7.
Evidence of Conflation in Mark? A Study in the Synoptic Problem (Missoula, 1977).
'Mark and Roger of Hovedon: A Response', *C.B.Q.* 41 (1979), 118–20.
'The Minor Agreements: An Examination of the Basic Argument',

C.B.Q. 37 (1975), 184–92.

Lührmann, D., *Die Redaktion der Logienquelle* (Neukirchen-Vluyn, 1969).

McArthur, H. K., 'Basic Issues. A Survey of Recent Gospel Research', *Interpretation* 18 (1964), 39–55.

'The Burden of Proof in Historical Jesus Research', *E.T.* 82 (1971), 116–19.

'The Parable of the Mustard Seed', *C.B.Q.* 33 (1971), 198–210.

McCloughlin, S., 'Les accords mineurs Mt-Lc contre Mc et le problème synoptique', in I. de la Potterie (ed.), *De Jésus aux Évangiles. Tradition et Rédaction dans les Évangiles synoptiques* (Gembloux, 1967), pp. 17–40.

McEleney, N. J., 'Authenticating Criteria and Mark 7: 1–23', *C.B.Q.* 34 (1972), 431–60.

McNeile, A. H., *The Gospel according to St. Matthew* (London, 1915).

Manson, T. W., *The Sayings of Jesus* (London, 1949).

The Teaching of Jesus (Cambridge, 1935).

Marxsen, W., *Mark the Evangelist* (ET, New York, 1970).

Massaux, E., *Influence de l'Évangile de saint Matthieu sur la littérature chrétienne avant saint Irénée* (Louvain, 1950).

Meier, J. P., *Law and History in Matthew's Gospel* (Rome, 1976).

Merkel, H., 'Markus 7, 15 – Das Jesuswort über die innere Verunreinigung', *Z.R.G.G.* 20 (1968), 340–63.

'Das Gleichnis von den "Ungleichen Söhnen" (Matt. xxi. 28–32)', *N.T.S.* 20 (1974), 254–61.

Die Widersprüche zwischen den Evangelien (Tübingen, 1971).

Metzger, B. M., 'Tatian's Diatessaron and a Persian Harmony of the Gospels', *J.B.L.* 69 (1950), 261–80.

Mitton, C. L., Review of Farmer, *The Synoptic Problem*, in *E.T.* 77 (1965), 1–3.

Montefiore, C. G., *The Synoptic Gospels* (2 vols, London, 1927).

Morgenthaler, R., *Statistische Synopse* (Zurich, 1971).

Neirynck, F., 'The Argument from Order and St. Luke's Transpositions', *E.T.L.* 49 (1973), 784–815.

Duality in Mark (Louvain, 1972).

'La matière marcienne dans l'évangile de Luc', in F. Neirynck (ed.), *L'Évangile de Luc. Problèmes littéraires et théologiques* (Gembloux, 1973), pp. 157–201.

'Minor Agreements Matthew–Luke in the Transfiguration Story', in P. Hoffmann (ed.), *Orientierung an Jesus*, Festschrift for J. Schmid (Freiburg, 1972), pp. 253–66.

The Minor Agreements of Matthew and Luke against Mark (Louvain, 1974).

'Les accords mineurs et la rédaction des évangiles', *E.T.L.* 50 (1974), 215–30.

'Urmarcus redivivus? Examen critique de l'hypothèse des insertions matthéennes dans Marc', in M. Sabbe (ed.), *L'Évangile selon Marc. Tradition et Rédaction* (Louvain, 1974), pp. 103–45.

Neusner, J., *The Idea of Purity in Ancient Judaism* (Leiden, 1973).

Nineham, D. E., Review of Farmer, *The Synoptic Problem*, in *J.T.S.* 28 (1977), 548–9.

Orchard, B., 'Are all Gospel Synopses Biassed?', *T.Z.* (1978), 149–62.

Matthew, Luke & Mark (Manchester, 1976).

'J. A. T. Robinson and the Synoptic Problem', *N.T.S.* 22 (1976), 346–52.

A translation of Griesbach's *Commentatio*, in B. Orchard and T. R. W. Longstaff (eds.), *J. J. Griesbach: Synoptic and Text-Critical Studies 1776–1976* (Cambridge, 1978), pp. 103–35.

Owen, H., *Observations on the Four Gospels* (London, 1764).

Palmer, N. H., 'Lachmann's Argument', *N.T.S.* 13 (1967), 368–78.

Paschen, W., *Rein und Unrein* (München, 1970).

Perrin, N., *Rediscovering the Teaching of Jesus* (London, 1967).

Pesch, R., *Naherwartungen. Tradition und Redaktion in Mk 13* (Düsseldorf, 1968).

Pryke, E. J., *Redactional Style in the Marcan Gospel* (Cambridge, 1978).

Rehkopf, F., *Die lukanische Sonderquelle. Ihr Umfang und Sprachgebrauch* (Tübingen, 1959).

Reicke, B., 'Griesbach's Answer to the Synoptic Question', in B. Orchard and T. R. W. Longstaff (eds.), *J. J. Griesbach: Synoptic and Text-Critical Studies 1776–1976* (Cambridge, 1978), pp. 50–67.

Rengstorf, K. H., 'Die ΣΤΟΛΑΙ der Schriftgelehrten. Eine Erlauterung zu Mark 12, 38', in O. Betz, M. Hengel, P. Schmidt (eds.), *Abraham unser Vater*, Festschrift for O. Michel (Leiden, 1963), pp. 383–404.

Ritschl, A., 'Ueber den gegenwärtigen Stand der Kritik der synoptischen Evangelien', *T.J.* 10 (1851), 480–538.

Robinson, J. A. T., 'The Parable of the Wicked Husbandmen. A Test of Synoptic Relationships', *N.T.S.* 21 (1975), 443–61.

Robinson, J. M., *The Problem of History in Mark* (London, 1957).

Roloff, J., *Das Kerygma und der irdische Jesus* (Göttingen, 1970).

Roth, C., 'The Cleansing of the Temple and Zechariah xiv. 21', *N.T.* 4 (1960), 174–81.

Sanday, W. (ed.), *Oxford Studies in the Synoptic Problem* (Oxford, 1911).

Supplement to art. 'Gospels', in Sir W. Smith and J. M. Fuller (eds.), *A Dictionary of the Bible* (London, 1893), pp. 1217–43.

Sanders, E. P., 'The Argument from Order and the Relationship between Matthew and Luke', *N.T.S.* 15 (1969), 249–61.

'The Overlaps of Mark and Q and the Synoptic Problem', *N.T.S.* 19 (1973), 453–65.

The Tendencies of the Synoptic Tradition (Cambridge, 1969).

Schiffman, L. H., *The Halakah at Qumran* (Leiden, 1975).

Schmid, J., *Matthäus und Lukas* (Freiburg, 1930).

Schmidt, K. L., *Der Rahmen der Geschichte Jesu* (Berlin, 1919).

Schmithals, W., Review of Farmer, *The Synoptic Problem*, in *T.L.Z.* 92 (1967), 424–5.

Schnackenburg, R., 'Der eschatologische Abschnitt Lk 17, 20–37', in A. Descamps (ed.), *Mélanges Bibliques*, Festschrift for B. Rigaux (Gembloux, 1970), pp. 213–34.

Schneider, G., 'Das Bildwort von der Lampe', *Z.N.W.* 61 (1970), 183–209.

'"Der Menschensohn" in der lukanischen Christologie', in R. Pesch and R. Schnackenburg (eds.), *Jesus und der Menschensohn*, Festschrift

for A. Vögtle (Freiburg, 1975), pp. 267–82.
Parusiegleichnisse im Lukasevangelium (Stuttgart, 1975).
Verleugnung, Verspottung, und Verhör Jesu nach Lukas 22, 54–71 (München, 1969).
Schramm, T., *Der Markus-Stoff bei Lukas* (Cambridge, 1971).
Schrenk, G., 'βιάζομαι κτλ.', *T.D.N.T.* I, 609–14.
'δικαίος κτλ.', *T.D.N.T.* II, 178–225.
Schulz, S., 'Markus und das Alte Testament', *Z.Th.K.* 58 (1961), 184–97.
Q – Die Spruchquelle der Evangelisten (Zürich, 1972).
Schürmann, H., 'Beobachtungen zum Menschensohn-Titel in der Rede-quelle, sein Vorkommen in Abschluss- und Einleitungswendungen', in R. Pesch and R. Schnackenburg (eds.), *Jesus und der Menschen-sohn*, Festschrift for A. Vögtle (Freiburg, 1975), pp. 124–47.
'Die Dubletten im Lukasevangelium', *Z.K.T.* 75 (1953), 338–45.
'Die Dublettenvermeidungen im Lukasevangelium', *Z.K.T.* 76 (1954), 83–93.
Das Lukasevangelium. Erster Teil (Freiburg, 1969).
'"Wer daher eines dieser geringsten Gebote auflöst . .". Wo fand Matthäus das Logion Mt 5,19?', *B.Z.* 4 (1960), 238–50.
'Protolukanische Spracheigentümlichkeiten?', *B.Z.* 5 (1961), 266–86.
'Sprachliche Reminiszenzen an abgeänderte oder ausgelassene Bestand-teile der Spruchsammlung im Lukas- und Matthäus-evangelium', *N.T.S.* 6 (1960), 193–210.
Schwarz, F. J., *Neue Untersuchungen über das Verwandtschaftsverhältniss der synoptischen Evangelien* (Tübingen, 1844).
Schwegler, A., *Das nachapostolische Zeitalter in den Hauptmomenten seiner Entwicklung* (Tübingen, 1846).
Schweizer, E., 'Matth. 5, 17–20 – Anmerkungen zum Gesetzesverständnis des Matthäus', *T.L.Z.* 77 (1952), 479–84.
'Die theologische Leistung des Markus', *Ev.Th.* 24 (1964), 337–55.
The Good News according to Matthew (ET, London, 1976).
The Good News according to Mark (ET, London, 1975).
Sieffert, K. L., *Ueber den Ursprung des ersten kanonischen Evangeliums. Eine kritische Abhandlung* (Königsberg, 1832).
Simpson, R. T., 'The Major Agreements of Matthew and Luke against Mark', *N.T.S.* 12 (1966), 273–84.
Snape, H. C., Review of Farmer, *The Synoptic Problem*, in *Modern Churchman* 9 (1966), 184–91.
Sparks, H. F. D., 'The Semitisms of St. Luke's Gospel', *J.T.S.* 44 (1943), 129–38.
Stanton, V. H., *The Gospels as Historical Documents. Part 2. The Synoptic Gospels* (Cambridge, 1909).
Steck, O. H., *Israel und das gewaltsame Geschick der Propheten* (Neukirchen-Vluyn, 1967).
Stendahl, K., *The School of St. Matthew and its Use of the Old Testament* (Lund, 1954).
Stenton, D. M., 'Roger of Howden and Benedict', *E.H.R.* 68 (1953), 574–82.
Stoldt, H. H., *Geschichte und Kritik der Markushypothese* (Göttingen, 1977).

Storr, G. C., *Ueber den Zweck der evangelischen Geschichte* (Tübingen, 1786).

Strack, H. L., and Billerbeck, P., *Kommentar zum Neuen Testament* (4 vols, München, 1922–8).

Strauss, D. F., *The Life of Jesus Critically Examined*. Edited with an Introduction by P. C. Hodgson (ET, London, 1973).

Strecker, G., *Der Weg der Gerechtigkeit* (Göttingen, 1971).

Streeter, B. H., *The Four Gospels. A Study of Origins* (London, 1924).

'St. Mark's Knowledge and Use of Q', in W. Sanday (ed.), *Oxford Studies in the Synoptic Problem* (Oxford, 1911), pp. 166–83.

Strobel, A., 'In dieser Nacht (Luk 17, 34). Zu einer älteren Form der Erwartung in Luk 17, 20–37', *Z.Th.K.* 58 (1961), 16–29.

Stubbs, W. (ed.), *Gesta Regis Henrici Secundi Benedicti Abbatis* (Rolls Series. London, 1867).

Styler, G., 'The Priority of Mark', Excursus IV in C. F. D. Moule, *The Birth of the New Testament* (London, 1962), pp. 223–32.

Suggs, M. J., *Wisdom, Christology and Law in Matthew's Gospel* (Cambridge, Mass., 1970).

Suhl, A., *Die Funktion der alttestamentlichen Zitate und Anspielungen im Markusevangelium* (Gütersloh, 1965).

Sundberg, A. C., 'Canon Muratori: A Fourth Century List', *H.T.R.* 66 (1973), 1–41.

Swete, H. B., *The Gospel according to St. Mark* (London, 1909).

Talbert, C. H. and McKnight, E. V., 'Can the Griesbach hypothesis be falsified?', *J.B.L.* 91 (1972), 338–68.

Taylor, V., *The Gospel according to St. Mark* (London, 1966).

Behind the Third Gospel (Oxford, 1926).

'The Order of Q', *J.T.S.* 4 (1953), 27–31.

'The Original Order of Q', in A. J. B. Higgins (ed.), *New Testament Essays. Studies in Memory of T. W. Manson* (Manchester, 1959), pp. 246–69.

Thomas, R. L., 'An Investigation of the Agreements between Matthew and Luke against Mark', *J.E.T.S.* 19 (1976), 103–12.

Throckmorton, B. H., 'Did Mark know Q?', *J.B.L.* 67 (1948), 319–29.

'Mark and Roger of Hovedon', *C.B.Q.* 39 (1977), 103–6.

Tödt, H. E., *The Son of Man in the Synoptic Tradition* (ET, London, 1965).

Trilling, W., 'Der Einzug in Jerusalem Mt 21, 1–17', in J. Blinzler, O. Kuss, F. Mussner (eds.), *Neutestamentliche Aufsätze*, Festschrift for J. Schmid (Regensburg, 1963), pp. 303–9.

Das wahre Israel (München, 1964).

'Die Täufertradition bei Matthäus', *B.Z.* 3 (1959), 271–89.

Trocmé, E., 'L'expulsion des marchands du Temple', *N.T.S.* 15 (1968), 1–22.

The Formation of the Gospel according to Mark (ET, London, 1975).

Tuckett, C. M., 'The Argument from Order and the Synoptic Problem', *T.Z.* 36 (1980), 338–54.

'The Griesbach Hypothesis in the 19th Century', *J.S.N.T.* 3 (1979), 29–60.

Turner, H. E. W., *Historicity and the Gospels* (London, 1963).
Turner, N., 'The Minor Verbal Agreements of Mt and Lk against Mk', *St.Ev.* 1 (T.U. 73), 223–34.
Vaganay, L., *Le Problème synoptique. Une hypothèse de travail* (Tournai, 1954).
Vielhauer, Ph., 'Gottesreich und Menschensohn in der Verkündigung Jesu', *Aufsätze zum Neuen Testament* (München, 1965), pp. 55–91.
Volkmar, G., *Die Religion Jesu* (Leipzig, 1857).
Walker, W. O., 'The Quest for the Historical Jesus: A Discussion of Methodology', *A.T.R.* 51 (1969), 38–56.
(ed.), *The Relationships among the Gospels* (San Antonio, 1978).
Weeden, T. J., 'The Heresy that necessitated Mark's Gospel', *Z.N.W.* 59 (1968), 145–58.
Weiser, A., *Die Knechtsgleichnisse der synoptischen Evangelien* (München, 1971).
Weiss, B., 'Zur Entstehungsgeschichte der drei synoptischen Evangelien', *Th.St.u.Kr.* (1861), 29–100, 646–713.
A Manual of Introduction to the New Testament, vol. II (ET, London, 1888).
Weisse, C. H., *Die evangelische Geschichte kritisch und philosophisch bearbeitet* (Leipzig, 1838).
Wenham, D., 'The Synoptic Problem Revisited: Some New Suggestions about the Composition of Mark 4: 1–34', *Tyndale Bulletin* 23 (1972), 3–38.
West, H. P., 'A Primitive Version of Luke in the Composition of Matthew', *N.T.S.* 14 (1967), 75–95.
Wette, W. M. L. de, *Lehrbuch der historisch-kritischen Einleitung in die kanonischen Bücher des Neuen Testaments* (6th ed., Berlin, 1860).
Wilckens, U., *Weisheit und Torheit* (Tübingen, 1959).
'σοφία', *T.D.N.T.* VII, 496–528.
'στολή', *T.D.N.T.* VII, 687–91.
Wilke, C. G., 'Ueber die Parabel von den Arbeitern im Weinberge', *Zeitschrift für wissenschaftliche Theologie* 1 (1826), 71–109.
Der Urevangelist, oder exegetisch kritische Untersuchung über das Verwandtschaftsverhältniss der drei ersten Evangelien (Leipzig, 1838).
Wilson, R. McL., 'Farrer and Streeter on the Minor Agreements of Matthew and Luke against Mark', *St.Ev.* 1 (T.U. 73), 254–7.
Studies in the Gospel of Thomas (London, 1960).
Wilson, S. G., *The Gentiles and the Gentile Mission in Luke–Acts* (Cambridge, 1973).
Wink, W., *John the Baptist in the Gospel Tradition* (Cambridge, 1968).
Woods, F. H., 'The Origin and Mutual Relation of the Synoptic Gospels', in S. R. Driver, T. K. Cheyne and W. Sanday (eds.), *Studia Biblica et Ecclesiastica*, vol. 2 (Oxford, 1890), pp. 59–104.
Wrede, W., *The Messianic Secret* (ET, London, 1971).
Wrege, H.-T., *Die Überlieferungsgeschichte der Bergpredigt* (Tübingen, 1968).

Zeller, E., 'Vergleichende Uebersicht über den Wörtervorrath der sämmtlichen Schriftsteller', *T.J.* 2 (1843), 443–543.

Zmijewski, J., *Die Eschatologiereden des Lukas-Evangeliums* (Bonn, 1972).

INDEX OF AUTHORS

INDEX OF PASSAGES CITED

Tuckett, C   M
      The revival of the Griesbach hypothesis : an
analysis and appraisal / C.M. Tuckett. --
Cambridge : Cambridge University Press, c1983.

      viii, 255 p. ; 22 cm. (Society for New
Testament studies monograph series; 44).
      ISBN 0-521-23803-X

      I. Title.   II. Series.